JN260377

Chunking and Instruction

Hituzi Linguistics in English

No.1 Lexical Borrowing and its Impact on English — Makimi Kimura-Kano
No.2 From a Subordinate Clause to an Independent Clause — Yuko Higashiizumi
No.3 ModalP and Subjunctive Present — Tadao Nomura
No.4 A Historical Study of Referent Honorifics in Japanese — Takashi Nagata
No.5 Communicating Skills of Intention — Tsutomu Sakamoto
No.6 A Pragmatic Approach to the Generation and Gender Gap in Japanese Politeness Strategies — Toshihiko Suzuki
No.7 Japanese Women's Listening Behavior in Face-to-face Conversation — Sachie Miyazaki
No.8 An Enterprise in the Cognitive Science of Language — Tetsuya Sano et al.
No.9 Syntactic Structure and Silence — Hisao Tokisaki
No.10 The Development of the Nominal Plural Forms in Early Middle English — Ryuichi Hotta
No.11 Chunking and Instruction — Takayuki Nakamori
No.12 Detecting and Sharing Perspectives Using Causals in Japanese — Ryoko Uno
No.13 Discourse Representation of Temporal Relations in the So-Called Head-Internal Relatives — Kuniyoshi Ishikawa
No.14 Features and Roles of Filled Pauses in Speech Communication — Michiko Watanabe
No.15 Japanese Loanword Phonology — Masahiko Mutsukawa

Hituzi Linguistics in English No. 11

Chunking and Instruction

The Place of Sounds, Lexis, and Grammar in English Language Teaching

Takayuki Nakamori

Hituzi Syobo Publishing

First published 2009

Author: Takayuki Nakamori

Book Design © Hirokazu Mukai (glyph)

Hituzi Syobo Publishing
Yamato bldg. 2F, 2-1-2 Sengoku Bunkyo-ku Tokyo, Japan
112-0011

phone +81-3-5319-4916 fax +81-3-5319-4917
e-mail: toiawase@hituzi.co.jp
http://www.hituzi.co.jp/
postal transfer 00120-8-142852

ISBN978-4-89476-404-0
Printed in Japan

Preface

Recently, the role of the lexicon and chunks in foreign language learning and teaching has attracted a lot of attention. Researchers who argue the significance of the lexicon and chunks view foreign language learning as sequence learning: Foreign language learners process phonological sequences of their target language, which are stored in phonological short-term memory. In extracting grammar rules from the stored elements, the lexicon and chunks play important roles. The *lexicon* is a stock of established words that speakers can draw on when they speak and access in order to understand what they hear (Clark, 1993: 2). Lexical entries contain pieces of information on the meaning, syntactic form, morphological structure, encyclopaedic properties, and the phonological shape. The lexicon consists of terms for objects, persons, general local references, and relations between objects and location. The lexicon is now universally recognised as the dictionary of grammar: the repository of all idiosyncratic and unpredictable properties of individual lexical items (Stowell & Wehrli, 1992: 1). According to Stowell & Wehrli (1992: 2), most syntacticians have little to say about the phonological side of the lexical entry, but they have much to say about the semantic side, at least to the extent that this determines the syntactic behaviour; the ability or inability of a lexical entry to occur in particular structural positions or in particular types of constructions. The term *chunk* was introduced into the field of psycholinguistics by George Miller in his classic review of short-term memory published in 1956: A chunk is a unit of memory organisation formed by bringing together a set of already formed unanalysed units in memory and welding them together into a larger unit. In the case of language, chunks are sets of unanalysed sequences of words or phrases, memorised as a whole. In other words, a chunk is a group of words that the mind treats as a single lexical item. The component words in a chunk may either be individually analysed or not. In this book, we consider chunking as a communicative, phonological, lexical, and grammatical unit and process. Putting it more precisely, Myles, Hooper, & Mitchell (1998: 325) suggest a range of criteria for chunk identification as follows:

1. at least two morphemes in length;

2. phonologically coherent, that is fluently articulated, non-hesitant;
3. unrelated to productive patterns in the learner's speech;
4. greater complexity in comparison with the learner's other output;
5. used repeatedly and always in the same form;
6. may be inappropriate syntactically, semantically, or pragmatically or otherwise idiosyncratic;
7. situation-dependent; and
8. community-wide in use.

This book takes what Rod Ellis (1997: 31–36) calls 'an applied linguist's perspective' (or, more strictly, 'applied SLA'). Ellis (1997: 31) defines an applied linguist as a person who seeks to apply ideas derived from linguistics, psycholinguistics, sociolinguistics, education, and any other area of potentially relevant enquiry to language pedagogy. This book attempts to examine the relevance of foreign language learning theories in educational terms. Widdowson (1990: chapter 3) proposes that the applied linguist's task is to mediate between disciplinary theory and language pedagogy. Ellis (1997: 33–36) summarises Widdowson's suggestion on the mediation processes as follows: The first process is application, which involves specific techniques based on the conclusions of the conceptual evaluation or teachers' customary practices ('Making SLA accessible' and 'Theory development and its application'). Then, empirical evaluation is undertaken by teachers, and involves monitoring the effects of their actions by examining the relationship between teaching and learning ('Researching the L2 classroom' and 'The teacher as a researcher').

This book is devoted to argue for a lexical approach to foreign language pedagogy, aiming at finding a way to teach future-applicable fundamental knowledge of language and skills to be used in comprehending and producing English. Starting from the investigation of how communication ability develops and how input is processed, it will provide an underlying rationale based on my ten years of inquiry that is to be discussed in the following chapters. In other words, I propose new ways of teaching foreign sounds based on phonetics and grammar points based on the Lexical Approach after I argue for the fundamental theoretical paradigms. This research project aims at finding a way of overcoming the problems in teaching English sounds and grammar points that teachers face when relying on the traditional methods. Teachers have recognised that the standard methods for sound and grammar instructions are problematic and need some revision in practice, but have felt that there is no other way. In the field of grammar instructions, for example, transformational grammarians appeal to Chomskyan transformational generative grammar when promoting the transformational methods. The crucial problem is that transformational grammarians did not test their methods in the classroom nor listen to teachers' dissatisfactions.

In the field of English language teaching, it has been said that teaching English sounds is just as important as grammar and vocabulary teaching. We mainly communicate with each other by means of sounds, and if we cannot process sounds, it is impossible for us to communicate orally. Sound perception and processing are prerequisites for daily oral communication. In order to promote communicative language teaching, it is necessary to investigate what the foreign sound processing mechanism is like, how such a mechanism develops, and what the efficient and effective teaching methodology is in order to help learners develop such a mechanism. Some people claim that we should start to teach English to young learners as soon as possible and that adults cannot master non-native sounds. However, there is little scientific evidence available to support these claims. In the field of speech language pathology, researchers have suggested that wrong methods of instructing language to children are extremely harmful and irreversible. In addition, intensive training of non-native sounds for adults is much more effective than that for children. In this research project, I have investigated the acquisition of foreign sounds by different age groups to gain insight into English language teaching at various levels, and propose an efficient and effective way of instructing foreign sound systems based on linguistics and phonetics.

Let us now look more closely at the overall structure of the book. In part one, the theoretical foundations are discussed. Chapter one investigates how foreign language processing and thought/inference are related. In order to communicate naturally and smoothly, learners must understand what the speakers actually as well as intend to say. Sometimes, speakers employ indirect ways of communication. In such cases, the additional burden to foreign language learners is obvious: even if they can interpret literally, they are often unable to understand the intended meanings. We will first look at what is meant by the term *communication*, second, how communication ability develops according to past research findings, and then, how different Japanese learners of English in various learning stages are in activating foreign language processing and inferential abilities. The empirical study will reveal that inferential ability is autonomous, subconscious, automatic, and universal, but sometimes culture-specific, and that learners need to develop the foreign language processor together with some culture-specific knowledge on the target language use with a large amount of exposure to the target language. Chapter two is intended to discuss how the foreign language processing mechanism develops in a learner's mind. We first look at the language processing system, and then review past research by Bill VanPatten and Manfred Pienemann. Lastly, I test VanPatten's input processing theory and Pienemann's Processability Theory in the Japanese context, and propose a formal model for foreign language development appealing to a structure-building model. Note that as the main focus of this book is on the internal mechanism of learning a foreign language, I shall not include discussions on the socio-cultural or psychological aspects of foreign language learning that may influence the degree of success in learning another language; those pertaining to affect such things as intelligence, motivation, anxiety, personality, attitude, etc.

In part two, we focus on learning and teaching English sounds. Chapter three investigates the ability to unlearn allophonised sounds in a foreign language, mainly focusing on phonemic errors. Speech-language pathologists have hypothesised that new sounds should be taught consciously in speech therapy for bilinguals, paying attention to the differences between sounds in L1 and those in L2. Otherwise, the learner activates similar sounds in L1, and unconsciously analyses the new sounds as the same group of L1 sounds. This phenomenon, the allophonic treatment of L2 sounds, is called *allophonisation*. Past studies have shown that adult foreign language learners allophonise non-native sounds and that instruction would help both learn and unlearn them. However, it is unclear whether all learners of any age can unlearn every allophonised sound. Comprehension and production test results in this chapter reveal that it was extremely difficult (or nearly impossible) for children to unlearn allophonised sounds. The adolescents and adults showed similar results, while it was possible to train them to overcome allophonic treatment of L2 sounds. Speech-language pathologists' claims that new sounds must be paid much attention are true to second language acquisition as well. Based on this research, I propose that in English as a foreign language environment, children can attain native-like proficiency of English if (and only if) allophonisation does not take place, because it is extremely difficult for children to unlearn allophonised sounds. Adults, on the other hand, can unlearn allophonised sounds and relearn new sounds by means of training. Chapter four argues the significance of teaching weak forms in listening and speaking classes. According to current English phonetics and phonology, rhythm and intonation, as well as phoneme, are important in describing actual language use in communication. In order to listen actively and speak fluently, rhythm and intonation, which are realised by weak forms, are crucial. I propose that weak forms should be focused on implicitly and explicitly in English language teaching for Japanese in order to overcome allophonisation and the influence of mora, which enables them to process foreign language as chunks. In this chapter, I report on my classroom research, in which I show how to put theoretical knowledge into practical use effectively in listening and speaking classes. Chapter five focuses on acoustic data obtained from native speakers and Japanese learners of English. Acoustic analyses enable us to clarify the differences in production among them. First, we have a look at some of their performances. Second, we discuss the data by referring to the notion of mora in phonology. Uniform syllable duration and vowels after consonants where inappropriate (termed *epenthesis*) can be seen clearly in the Japanese data. The focus of this chapter is on phonetic and phonotactic errors. In addition, this chapter proposes the effectiveness of applying computerised acoustic programmes in the classroom. I report on my classroom research, in which I show how effective it is to use such programmes in order to help students master weak forms and how to put acoustic programmes into practical use effectively in listening and speaking classes.

In part three, I argue for the Lexical Approach to foreign language teaching. In chapter six, we will have a look at what the Lexical Approach is, and see that it is based on the input processing perspective discussed in chapter two. Chapter seven proposes that the Lexical Approach is applicable to English language teaching in Japan. I report the results of three empirical studies in which three grammar points were introduced by utilising and comparing the Lexical Approach and the standard transformational methods. Three grammar targets - passives, infinitives, and relative clauses - are commonly taught using transformational methodologies, and cause serious problems. Chapter eight discusses the way to deal with verbs in L2. First, we review two approaches to the learning of verb meanings in a second language: the Lexical parameter approach based on a Bootstrapping perspective and the Item-by-item approach based on the Verb Island Hypothesis. Second, we focus on the acquisition of verb forms. We review two approaches to the acquisition of verb forms in L2: the semantic-oriented approach and the form-oriented approach. Third, we discuss the data obtained from my eight-year longitudinal study in detail. The results are to be interpreted as showing that there is a developmental sequence of learning verb meanings and verb forms, which is not influenced by instruction or L1 performance. After looking at some problems in verb learning, we discuss a longitudinal study where three potential teaching methods of verbs to beginners of English are compared: the Lexical Approach, noticing, and English-Japanese comparison. The study shows the advantages and disadvantages of each method. Overall, the Lexical Approach seems to be the most effective methodology.

In part four, Chapter nine discusses the implications for English language teaching curriculum design in Japan. Integrating the previous proposals, I discuss the place of lexis and grammar in English language teaching.

For those who are familiar with Krashen's second language acquisition theory, this book takes the following positions on his hypotheses. Regarding the Acquisition-Learning Hypothesis, I will not distinguish between acquisition and learning, but consider that second language acquisition is one type of learning. For instance, Jacobs & Schumann (1992: 287) claim that a cognitive approach (that I will take in this book) does not consider human language acquisition to be fundamentally different from the learning of any other type of knowledge. Regarding the Natural Order Hypothesis, I will focus on the development of foreign language from words to grammar in detail in chapter two and on the acquisition of verbs in chapter eight. Regarding the Monitor Hypothesis, I propose the two ways of looking at grammar in chapter nine: internalised knowledge of language for processing and the body of taught rules of language for analyses and description. Regarding the Input Hypothesis, I reinterpret his i+1 condition under the development of language processing ability in chapter two. In this book, as I mentioned before, I shall not focus on the Affective Filter Hypothesis, which is about the learner's psychological and socio-cultural state of mind.

Many people have encouraged me, made comments and suggestions, and supported my research project. I express my gratitude to them in alphabetical order: Mr Michael Ashby, Professor Nick Ellis, Professor Rod Ellis, Mrs Jackie Greenwood, Professor Hiroko Hagiwara, Professor Hideo Hayashibe, Professor Yukihito Hirano, Professor Yoshiaki Kohno, Mrs Laura Inoue, Professor Mayumi Kudo, Professor Yuri Kuno, Ms Marilyn Lewis, Professor James Lantolf, Professor Mamoru Morizumi, Professor Nobuo Okada, Professor Yukio Otsu, Professor Masayuki Sano, Professor Neil Smith, Professor Kunitoshi Takahashi, Dr Christopher Tancredi, Professor Kiyotada Tazaki, and Professor Deirdre Wilson. I acknowledge that the following teachers kindly provided me with data from their students, without which this research project could not have been completed: Mr Domon, Mr Leung, Mr Nakagawa, Mr Sato, Ms Ukita, and Mr Wong, and members of staff at the Institute of Language Teaching and Learning. I am really grateful that members of the committee at the Japan Society for the Promotion of Science and the Japanese Ministry of Education chose me as a research fellow and have fully supported me financially for five years in total. This ten-year research project was partially supported by a Grant-in-aid for Scientific Research (11–02600 and 16720129). I have tried hard to meet their expectations. I thank JABAET and Oxford University Press for permission to reprint articles. Lastly, I would like to thank my parents sincerely for their love and support.

July 2008
Takayuki NAKAMORI, Ph.D.

Contents

LIST OF TABLES

LIST OF FIGURES

PART I

Learning and teaching communication

This part of the book discusses the development of communication ability (chapter one) and input processing (chapter two) in foreign language learning. This part considers chunking as a communicative unit and process.

The aim of chapter one is to investigate how second language (L2) processing and thought/inference are related. In order to communicate naturally and smoothly, learners must understand what the speakers actually as well as intend to say. Sometimes, speakers employ indirect ways of communication. In such cases, the additional burden to foreign language learners is obvious: even if they can interpret literally, they are often unable to see the intended meanings. We will first look at what is meant by the term *communication*, second, how communicative competence develops according to past research findings, and then, how different Japanese learners of English in various learning stages are in activating foreign language processing and inferential abilities. The empirical study will reveal that inferential ability is neutral and sometimes culture-specific, and that learners need to develop the foreign language processor together with some culture-specific knowledge on the target language use with a large amount of exposure to the target language.

Chapter two discusses how foreign language learners process input. After Schmidt (1990), many studies have been done by applied linguists, such as Robinson (1995), N. Ellis (1996b), and R. Ellis (1994), amongst others, taking a cognitive psychological position. These researchers have been trying to show that learners learn foreign language by means of an Attention – Noticing – Comparing – Memory process: foreign language learning results from general processes of human inductive reasoning being applied to the specific problem of language. What is crucial to the cognitive approach, then, is to explain *how* learners extract rules from input assisted by a problem-solving mechanism. Little past research, however, has tackled this difficult but important question. In this chapter, appealing to VanPatten's (1996) and Pienemann's (1998a, 1998b) input processing theories, I argue, by analysing and interpreting the data obtained from longitudinal observation in the classroom, that:

1. The process of chunking in perception leads to word boundary information, the acquisition of lexical forms, word sequence information, collocations, and idioms.
2. Sequential analysis of chunks results in word class information, including thematic structures.

3. Sequential analysis of lexical forms leads to the acquisition of morphosyntax.
4. Functional Categories are unacquirable in full.

The aim of this chapter is to review cutting edge research findings in language processing and to discuss the insights they provide into foreign language pedagogy. Foreign language learners must process, i.e., comprehend and produce, a target foreign language, and one of the important roles of foreign language education is to help them obtain such a processing system gradually. I suggest that we need to know what a foreign language processing system is like and how it is acquired in order to identify useful methods of communicative language teaching. This chapter looks at how native speakers of English process English, and native speakers of Japanese process Japanese and English in detail. A learner's foreign language processor that operates under the Meaning-over-Form Principles (VanPatten, 1996), Processing Procedures (Pienemann, 1998a), and pre-existing world knowledge including knowledge of a first language (L1) guides the learner to process his or her target language in a certain order. Learning to understand a foreign language involves parsing the speech stream into chunks which reliably mark meaning. Learners' attention to the target language to which they are exposed demonstrates that there are recurring chunks of language. An essential task for the learner is to discover the patterns within the sequence of the target language, which is explained formally under a structure-building model of language development.

Part one is meant to backup my argument of instructions based on phonetics and the Lexical Approach that follows. The theoretical discussion of this part provides a rationale for the chunking and lexicon-oriented approach to foreign language teaching that is to be discussed in parts two and three.

Chapter 1

The acquisition of communication ability in L2: Focusing on the development of inferential abilities

Introduction

One day, the headmaster of a private school came into the classroom and said in Japanese, 'kono heya wa totemo atsukute kusai ne'. Some students stood up immediately and opened the windows. Mr Sato, Ms Ono, and Mrs Saito, Japanese teachers, said the same thing, and students reacted in the same way, which means that students behaved as they did, not because of any psychological reasons (e.g., they respect the headmaster), but because of their normal reaction to that utterance. On the same day, Australian English teachers, Michael and Pat, said exactly the same thing in English, 'This room is very hot and it smells bad in here'. No students responded to what they said. Both Michael and Pat had to open the windows by themselves, murmuring ironically that students hated them. Everybody at the school knows, however, that students really like Michael and Pat and enjoy their classes very much.

Why did the students react differently to the same underlying concept? To answer this question, Bloom (2000: 19) proposes the principle of relevance based on Sperber & Wilson (1995). According to the principle of relevance, language learning is enhanced when the language a learner hears bears upon and is pertinent to the objects/events of engagement, interest, and feelings that are the learner's contents of mind. Relevance is determined by the things/events learners care about in the real world and provides the direction for language learning, determining what the language learners say and understand. In the situation above, students did not reach the conclusion that Michael or Pat wanted them to cool down the classroom, because both teachers claimed this indirectly in the students' foreign language. Before learners understand what speakers intend to say in a foreign language, they must process the language. Only after they succeed in figuring out what the speakers actually say in a foreign language do they process how relevant the speakers' utterances are. In this chapter, we shall investigate how foreign language learners process the indirect ways of communication in detail. I assume that we should not mix up and confuse language comprehension or production, and language learning or teaching (Brown & Hagoort, 1999; Iwanska & Shapiro, 2000). In this chapter, we mainly focus on comprehension and learning: production and teaching are beyond our scope here.

1.1. What is *communication*?

The term *communication* is used in various contexts to refer to many different things. Frey et al. (1991: 27) claim that defining the term *communication* is like trying to define the purpose of life itself, as there are an enormous number of interpretations and points of view. Many approaches have been proposed to investigate communication. As a result, various kinds of definitions for communication have been put forward. Finnegan (2002: 9–11) lists sixteen statements about communication based on communication theory, psychology, media research, cultural studies, anthropology, socio-biology, cognitivist approach, and ethology. According to Frey et al. (1991: 27), definitions of communication tend to emphasise one of two different concerns. The first definitions originate from the scientific study of how information could be transferred from one place to another, thus representing an information processing view. Because it was derived from a behavioural perspective, communication is seen as a behaviour, the intentional act of conveying information from one person/source to another person/receiver. The other definitions originate from the phenomenological study of how communication produces meaning and leads to developing effective interpersonal relationships, thus representing a meaning-based view. Communication is seen as a process of attributing meaning to people's actions and developing a relationship between people.

The degree to which a speaker is successful in communicating measured by appropriateness and effectiveness is called *communicative competence*. The competent communicator is able to conceive, formulate, modulate, and issue messages and to perceive the degree to which intended meanings are successfully conveyed

(Owens, 1996: 11). Speakers try to abbreviate linguistic expressions as much as they can, and listeners try to make sure that speakers do not go so far in this direction that the message becomes incomprehensible. In this chapter, we take the cognitivist position. In this perspective, communication is presented as essentially something of the mind: it is in the mind that our acts of communication originate and are formulated with action following on from the mind's command. The mind itself and with it human communication is conceived in terms of information processing. Human minds are pictured as computer systems. Sperber & Wilson (1995: 1) state that communication is a process involving two information processing devices. One device modifies the physical environment of the other. As a result, the second device constructs representations similar to those already stored in the first device. Oral communication, for instance, is a modification by the speaker of the hearer's acoustic environment, as a result of which the hearer entertains thoughts similar to the speaker's own. An individual's mental representations get communicated; that is, first transformed by the communicator into common representations, and then re-transformed by the audience into mental representations (cf. Fujisaki's 1997 numerical analyses of information in communication).

Communication is achieved by the communicators providing evidence of their intentions and the audiences inferring their intentions from the evidence. How does one recognise another individual's intentions? According to Sperber & Wilson (1995: chapters 2 & 3), one observes another's behaviour using one's knowledge of people in general and of the individual in particular, and one infers which of the effects of this behaviour he or she could have both predicted and desired. One then assumes that these predictable and desirable effects were also intended. In other words, one infers the intention behind the behaviour from its independently observed or inferred effects. Such effects are called *contextual effects*. There is some contextual effect, in the form of an erasure of some assumptions in the context, a modification of the strength of some assumptions in the context, or the derivation of contextual implications. In the case of language used intentionally, we would suppose that what the speaker says should be at least one indication of what the speaker intends to achieve by speaking. The speaker offers the utterance as evidence for what the speaker wants the listener to understand, assuming that the listener will interpret the utterance in the relevant context. The nature of the performance of the utterance may offer a clue to the speaker's intention in uttering (Brown, 1995: 231). The contextual effects of an assumption in a given context are not the only factors to be taken into account. Contextual effects are brought about by mental processes. Mental processes involve a certain *effort*, a certain expenditure of energy. Human beings automatically aim at the most efficient information processing possible. As information processing involves effort, it will only be undertaken in the expectation of some reward. Humans try to process information as productively as possible, that is, they try to obtain from each new item of information as great a contextual effect as possible for as small as possible a processing effort. If we recognise that someone is saying something to us, then we will assume that it is *relevant* in some way, and off our system goes seeking the first interpretation which has contextual effects worth deriving. Since our system will not put in any more effort than it has to, then we will stop at that first interpretation, unless there is something else leading us on. The hearer is mostly in the position of seeking the most easily accessible interpretation of an utterance that could have been what the communicator intended.

1.2. Cognitive abilities required in understanding utterances

The task of understanding conversation is time-pressured in that information about mental states must be processed fast enough to keep up with the flow of a speaker's language. Thus, an awareness of conversational abilities to interpret messages as intended and to resist misleading information is fundamental in investigations of cognition and development, as it is a prerequisite for appraising what speakers know about each other and about the subject domains of their conversations (Siegal, 1996: 243). It is basic to our everyday human understanding that both we and others have beliefs; we assume that all people have an awareness that other people have minds. We know this in many ways: we know that we have beliefs about the world, that our beliefs change, that they might be wrong, and that what we say and do are based on our beliefs. We can also assume that other people have beliefs: they can tell us those beliefs directly or we can work them out indirectly from the way they behave. This is vital if we are to make sense of what others say and how they act. Having an understanding of other people as people who have desires, beliefs, and their own interpretations of the world is often referred to as having *a theory of mind* (Hirschfeld & Gelman, eds., 1994; Smith et al., 1998: chapter 13). The theory of mind system interprets the behaviour of others by attributing to them such intentional mental states as beliefs, desires, and intentions, and this pragmatic comprehension system interprets communicative behaviour in terms of an intention on the part of the speaker to bring about a certain intentional mental state in the addressee (Carston, 2002: 7). A fully developed theory of mind requires not only that one has the cognitive ability to build complex mental representations of other people's attitudes to propositions, but also that he or she is exposed to sufficient examples of social contexts and behaviours to learn how people react in different situations (Bishop, 1997: chapter 8).

To fully appreciate what happens in the development of communication ability, we must understand that learners are developing the ability to process and produce goal-directed, intentional communication behaviours. Learners are able to do this only to the extent that they take into consideration the persons with whom they are communicating, and only to the extent that they are able to formulate messages for people other than themselves (Hulit & Howard, 1997:124; Warren & McCloskey, 1997; Mercer, 2000). Ninio & Snow (1999: 358) argue that learners move from a holistic to a selective type of mapping between their intents and verbal expressions. At the onset of speech, communicative meaning is packaged into words in a holistic, undifferentiated fashion, either because the concepts underlying learners' early words are themselves holistic and undifferentiated, or because of specific limitations in their inter-mapping capacities. According to this view, the selective mapping of analysed components of communicative intentions onto verbal expressions is a later development. Tomasello (2001: 153) argues that the major cognitive skill that underlies learners' ability is their understanding of the intentional actions of others, especially their understanding that other persons have intentions towards their intentional states. Learners' ability to reproduce these intentional communicative actions via some form of cultural or imitative learning involves a role reversal, i.e., the learner has intentions towards the other person's intentional states, which leads to the creation of linguistic conventions. Hulit & Howard (1997: 144) claim that the functions and intentions can be combined and modified into at least three functions: pragmatic, mathetic, and informative. The pragmatic function of language is the most basic. Learners use language to get things done. They use language to make requests and demands, to satisfy their needs, and to interact with and control the behaviour of other people. The mathetic function of language is manifested in communications concerned with learning. Learners use language to learn about themselves and their world. They comment, question, predict, and remember. They use language to express their developing understanding of how people, things, and events are connected. The informative function emerges when learners use language to give new information to others. They cannot use language to inform until they know something others do not or until they think they know something they assume others do not. Brown (1995) shows examples of apparently fully correct interpretations by listeners as well as a wide range of examples of apparently adequate and inadequate interpretations. Brown distinguishes between occasions when a listener has apparently not heard what the speaker said, has heard but not interpreted what was said, has heard but not interpreted until later on what a speaker said, or has heard but not understood all of what a speaker said. There are many occasions when a listener selects just some part of the speaker's utterance to pay attention to, because only that part was relevant to the listener's current intentions, since, for the listener, understanding what the speaker said is only a means to an end, and for the listener, it is the listener's end which is at issue. According to Pan & Snow (1999: 237–244), in order to be able to communicate, learners need a number of new cognitive and linguistic skills: (1) they must be able to take the listener's perspective into account; (2) they must be able to express their own perspective; (3) they must be able to take and signal alternative stances towards the information being conveyed; and (4) they must master the conventions of different genres of discourse.

1.3. Communication ability in L2

Considerations beyond sentence grammar affect the way speakers choose to express themselves, or the interpretations that hearers impose on utterances. Pragmatic factors determine which out of a range of possible structures allowed by the grammar of a language is actually realised in a particular context, or which out of a range of possible interpretations is assigned to a particular syntactic structure. Pragmatic knowledge presumably draws on many different domains including knowledge and beliefs.

Researchers who adopt a pragmatic approach to the study of second language learning typically start with the ways in which L2 learners set about making meaning and achieving their personal communicative goals. They argue that the great variety of interlanguage forms produced by second language learners cannot be sensibly interpreted unless we pay attention to the functions which learners are seeking to perform. These meaning-making efforts on the part of the learner are the driving force in ongoing second language development (Mitchell & Myles,

1998: 100). On a large scale of this kind, the European Science Foundation project brought a pragmatic perspective to bear on the problem of second language learning (Perdue, 1993). This project was funded by the European Science Foundation over a period of six years. The research teams worked with groups of adult immigrants in the process of learning one of five target languages in Europe. In their general conclusion, they give priority to communicative needs: learning is pushed by the communicative tasks that the learner takes part in.

According to Bardovi-Harlig (2002: 182), the most dominant area of pragmatics in second language research is the study of *speech acts*. Speech acts include five categories: assertives, committing the speaker to the truth of the expressed proposition (*state, suggest, boast, complain, claim, report, warn*); directives, having the intention of eliciting some sort of action on the part of the hearer (*order, command, request, beg, beseech, advise, warn, recommend, ask*); commissives, committing the speaker to some future action (*promise, vow, threaten, offer, contract, undertake*); expressives, making known the speaker's psychological attitude to a presupposed state of affairs (*thank, congratulate, condole, praise, blame, forgive, pardon*); and declaratives, bringing about a change in reality (*resign, dismiss, divorce, declare, bid, christen, name, open, excommunicate, sentence, consecrate*) (Achiba, 2003; Cruse, 2004: 356–357). The effect of learners' utterances and their development would be relevant in second language research (Ellis, 1994: chapter 5).

The least investigated area in second language pragmatics, on the other hand, is conversational implication or implied meaning termed *implicature* (Bardovi-Harlig, 2002: 183; Spencer-Oatey & Zegarac, 2002: 76–77). Conversational implicatures are those aspects of the intended meaning of an utterance which are not encoded in its linguistic structure, but are read between the lines. Implicature plays an important role in the interpretation of indirect speech acts. Let us look briefly at the following well-known illustration: 'A: Where's Bill?' 'B: There's a yellow VW outside Sue's house.' It is unlikely that people listening to B would interpret this remark irrelevant and nonsense. Instead, they would see it as deliberately suggesting that since Bill drives a yellow VW, he might well be at Sue's house. The implicature the listeners arrive at here linking Bill to the yellow VW and Sue's house has arisen only because they have assumed that B was being relevant in answering A's question as he did. The main import of an utterance may in fact easily lie not with the thought expressed by the utterance (i.e., with what is communicated directly) but rather with the thoughts that the hearer assumes the speaker intends to suggest or hint at. For implicature to be effective, the speaker and the listeners must have a common understanding of what constitutes relevant speaker behaviour so that they will agree as to when implicature is necessary to grasp the speaker's message. In addition, the way the two perceive the world must lead them to derive the same implicature from the utterance in question. It might seem reasonable to assume that beginners use language only in literal ways, but they are able to understand sentences that include what are called implicatures, which include irony, sarcasm, metaphor, idiom, or other indirect speech acts. Interpreting implicatures is based on words and phrases with multiple meanings or on sentence structures that can be interpreted in two or more ways. The listener anticipates the most obvious meaning and is caught off guard by a different meaning or by an unexpected twist in the way a word is used. Learners will understand implicatures only to the extent that they know and understand all the possible meanings of the words contained in such a language use, and only to the extent that they understand that a single sentence might have two or more possible underlying meanings.

According to Bardovi-Harlig (2001: 22–30) and Kasper & Rose (2002: 118–124, 195–196, 256–258), Lawrence Bouton has conducted a series of studies on the interpretation of implicature in English by non-native speakers (some of which were unavailable). Bouton (1988) tested 436 international students arriving at the University of Illinois using a multiple choice instrument with thirty-three items, finding that although native and non-native speakers interpreted the same implicature in the same context 75% of the time, that left a full 25% of the time in which different implications were drawn by the non-native speakers. Bouton (1994) retested thirty of the original subjects four-and-a-half years later, and found that the non-native speakers had improved to the point where twenty items showed no significant difference in interpretation between them and the native speakers, whereas only five of the items showed no difference from the previous study. In other words, learners performed noticeably better on implicature whose interpretation is idiosyncratically dependent on the meaning of the utterance in its particular context. In Bouton's study, the experimental group achieved results as high as those observed with previous immersion students who had spent four years living in the United States, but there was no such improvement for the control group. Bouton found that after seventeen months of residing in the United States, learners continued to have difficulty with some implicature types, but after four years of residence, they were able to interpret implicature as well as native speakers, having difficulty only with items that required culture-specific knowledge that they did not have.

1.4. The empirical study

Bouton's conclusions, i.e., foreign language learners acquire implication abilities as time goes by and culture-specific implicatures had better be instructed, only appeal to our common sense. Moreover, his research methodology, relying only on multiple-choice questionnaires administered to non-native speakers in L2, seems to be insufficient, because learners might translate them into their L1 and then answer the questions, spending a long time in pondering what the questions mean. (Reaction time data were not reported.) He did not show their performance in L1, which I assume is important. The study of communication in L2 should involve the collection of three sets of data: (1) samples of the speech act performed in the target language by L2 learners; (2) samples performed by native speakers of the target language; and (3) samples of the same speech act performed by the learners in their L1. In the following study, we discuss *how* L2 learners process implicatures, focusing on the contextual effect, the processing effort, and the influence of L1. In other words, we focus on the *process* of interpreting implicatures rather than the product of interpreting them, as Bouton investigated.

1.4.1. Participants

One hundred and twenty second-year junior high school students (age 14), 120 second-year high school students (age 17), and 120 second-year university students (age 20) were randomly selected. They are all Japanese students at upper-intermediate private boys' schools. Both the junior and senior high schools are annexed to the university, which means that all students are educated under similar conditions. (There are no entrance examinations at the senior high school and university before enrolling.) This study investigates the changes in similar groups of students who are taught English under similar conditions after a period of exposure to English. The junior high school students learn English for five hours a week (total previous exposure to English lessons: about 400 hours), the high school students for five hours a week (total exposure: about 700 hours), and the university students for four hours a week (total exposure: about 1,100 hours). All of them take one-hour compulsory writing and speaking classes every week, in which writing/speaking skills and basic grammar for writing/speaking are taught. Regarding the control group, thirty 18-year-old university students taking a cognitive science course (with no knowledge of linguistics), who grew up in Britain or New Zealand were selected.

1.4.2. Procedure

Let us begin with how implicatures can be measured. Interpreting implicatures involves the process of inference. In common terminology, inference refers to activities on the part of the hearer. In the study of language processing, ideas which were not included in a message but which are captured by the internal representation of that message are called *inference* (or *pragmatic inference*) (Singer, 1994: 480). Bybee (2003: 156) claims that an important feature of the communication process is the ability to make inference. The speaker must be able to judge which details the hearer can supply and formulate his or her utterances accordingly, and the hearer must fill in details not supplied by the speaker. When the same pattern of inferences occurs frequently with a particular grammatical construction, those inferences can become part of the meaning of the construction. Inferences include understanding implicatures on which we will focus in this chapter as well as disambiguation and reference assignment.

Singer (1994: 504–506) claims that the evaluation of inference processes is inherently complicated and subtle. Nonetheless, researchers are in agreement on a number of issues. Evidence that inferences of a certain category accompany comprehension ought to converge from on-line measures of processing. On-line measures, collected while the learner comprehends a discourse, are commonly used to reveal the processes and/or immediate products of comprehension. Reading/response time, the most frequently used on-line measure, is considered to have the potential to reflect the time that learners require to draw inferences. The reading/response time may be collected for different units, such as words, phrases, and sentences, and under different conditions of computer-controlled text display.

For any utterance involving implicature, there is one interpretation that will tend to be dominant among native and non-native speakers of English. That is not to say that there is only one possible implicature that native and non-native speakers can derive from a given utterance in a particular context. If speakers are asked to interpret an utterance, there will be a strong tendency for them to draw the same implicature and to interpret the utterance in essentially the same way. If such an interpretation exists, it can provide a native speaker norm with which to compare non-native speaker responses. In order to determine how native and non-native speakers interpret implicatures, a number of open-ended questions were developed and administered. For each question, participants were asked to read a description of a situation with enough contextual information containing a dialogue in which one of the characters expressed a message at least partially through the use of implicature. Following each situation was a dialogue directing the attention of the participants to the utterance containing the implicature.

For this study, materials for on-line measure were produced based on Bouton's questionnaires (See more examples in Appendix A). The on-line role-play test goes as follows. Participants were asked to respond to the utterance orally. For instance:

<Situation: Two students are talking in a cafeteria during a coffee break.>
A (You): Let's play tennis after coffee.
B (Your friend): It's raining outside.
A: ______________________________.

Just after B's utterance, a time counter started to measure the response time up to the very moment of the first meaningful word that is part of the contextually appropriate response. Note that students' responses were recorded: students were asked to answer them orally, not to write down answers on a piece of paper. Any response was accepted if it was acceptable in the situation/context. Some answered, 'OK. Forget about tennis.' Others said, 'Let's play cards, then.' etc. This is why this kind of test is called 'open-ended'. Since hearers try to understand what the speakers say in relation to the context, and since there are a couple of possible interpretations, I analysed the data based on the appropriateness in the given context. Participants were asked to indicate in their own words what the character may say in that context. Since the meaning of an implicature is central to the message that a speaker intends to convey, someone who understood the message completely would include the meaning of the implicature in his or her paraphrase (Bouton, 1988: 184–185). Participants were asked to answer the 20 role-play dialogues orally as fast as they could. All the participants took the on-line test in a classroom with a modified computerised Sony LLC-2000M system. Their response was recorded through the LL system. Sentences were given visually and orally at the same time. Vocabulary and grammar were controlled so that junior and senior high school students did not face difficulties in understanding what was said. In this test, as a time constraint was put on them, they had little time to exercise their knowledge of grammar and to answer the questions with care.

In addition, free-conversation data were taken in oral communication classes taught by British and Australian teachers. Investigators video-recorded students in the lessons (recordings took place from the beginning to the end of the lesson) and transcribed them, focusing on teacher-student and student-student interactions. L1 data were obtained from students' conversations during breaks and lunch time, as Blum-Kulka & Snow (2002) suggest, meal-time conversation might be one of the best possible situations to record the most natural language use.

1.4.3. Results and discussion

Let us now consider the following data obtained from the empirical study in the language classroom. This study is cross-sectional, that is, I investigated three different groups of students with two sub-groups each (i.e., L1 group: 60 students who took the test in Japanese; and L2 group: 60 students who took the test in English). Note that L1 groups never took the test in L2 and vice versa, just in case students remember L1/L2 tests, which would affect the results.

As Bloom & Tinker (2001: 19) clearly state, language learning is enhanced when events in the context bear upon and are pertinent to what the learner has in mind. This is called the principle of relevance. Relevance is the single property that makes information worth processing and determines the particular assumptions an individual is most likely to construct and process. This principle determines the things that prompt a learner's attention, interest, and emotional investment in the personal and physical world. The relevance of other persons' behaviours is assured, and their language made accessible for learning, when interlocutors either tune in to what a learner is already feeling and thinking or succeed in redirecting the learner's focus of attention to new information in a context that might be worth knowing. If the pragmatics of the comprehension process in L2 learners works in the same way as for native speakers, what differs is only the logical form generated in the case where the linguistic system is unable to generate the logical form that would be generated by a native speaker and the cognitive context that is brought to bear during the derivation of the implicature.

It is important to note that the results (especially the slow response time in

Table 1–1: Summary of overall on-line test results

(Items answered appropriately using a 100-point scale)

	L2 mean	L2 SD	L1 mean	L1 SD
Junior	71.3	4.8	82.2	3.8
Senior	76.8	3.7	80.1	3.1
University	86.6	2.9	84.8	2.7
Native control	—	—	90.3	2.5

Table 1–2: Summary of overall on-line test results

(Average response time in milliseconds)

	L2 mean	L2 SD	L1 mean	L1 SD
Junior	4560	22.8	2240	8.9
Senior	3810	19.4	1740	7.7
University	2690	12.2	1490	6.1
Native control	—	—	1380	5.8

Table 1–3: Frequency of indirect speech acts (that occur per 100 utterances)

	Junior	Senior	University	Natives
Occurrence	0	2	3	11

Table 1–2) show what is called the *foreign language effect* (Takano & Noda, 1995). The foreign language effect refers to a temporary decline in the thinking ability of people who are using a foreign language in which they are less proficient than in their own first language. When two demanding cognitive tasks are performed in parallel, they interfere with each other. Ordinary linguistic activities (conversation/negotiation) consist of both linguistic processing and non-linguistic information processing (thinking/inferring) that usually have to be performed in parallel. Performance of one or both should decline due to interference as a result. As the completion of linguistic processing is a prerequisite for an appropriate response in most cases, thinking is typically sacrificed. While extensive practice reduces the interference, the amount of practice is smaller for a foreign than for a first language. This is why interference with thinking is greater when a foreign language is processed, which results in a much longer processing time, as Table 1–2 shows. In addition to this, Takano & Noda (1995) argue that the foreign language effect is greater for those whose L1 is less similar to the employed foreign

language than for those whose L1 is more similar to it, because L1 transfer is smaller for the former provided that experience in that foreign language is comparable. According to them, Japanese learners of English performed more poorly in their experiments regarding the foreign language effect than German learners of English. This claim is parallel to Bouton's (1988) results that reveal Japanese learners of English had done quite poorly in his study.

In addition, as Keenan (1976) has shown, implicatures may not be interpreted and implemented in the same way across cultures. Sometimes, what one thought was being communicated by a simple sentence would be understood quite differently by another. Communication would have broken down because of cross-cultural differences in what is seen as relevant behaviour on the part of the speaker and in what implicatures it would be appropriate to draw in this particular context. Even when the participants in a conversation share the same understanding of relevance, the exact inference that each person draws from any particular utterance will vary with that person's world view. Individuals with different backgrounds draw different implicatures from the same utterance. In our study, some students reported that they could understand literal meanings but found it difficult to capture implicatures. Let us focus on this aspect in more detail.

As our free conversation data reveals, it is rare to employ indirect ways of communication in Japanese, more precisely, in Tokyo dialect (as Kyoto people like to employ indirect ways). Japanese speakers clearly indicate how they wish the hearer to interpret their utterances. For instance, most likely speakers or hearers put a conclusive sentence as follows: 'Where's Bill?' 'There's a yellow VW outside Sue's house, *so he's perhaps at her house.*' On the other hand, native speakers of English commonly employ indirect communication. This might be associated with politeness: It may be more polite to state conclusions clearly in order not to mislead the hearer rather than to let others infer what the speaker intends to say. In English, it is quite natural to converse with implicatures. Looking closely at the L1 data, we can clearly see that while native speakers of English could interpret utterances containing implicature quickly, native speakers of Japanese take much longer to decipher them.

In addition, as Table 1–4 shows, I found that there were stylistic differences in the way Japanese- and English-speaking people talk in their L1. Some people like to employ indirect communication including irony, metaphor, sarcasm, etc. Among Japanese, such people seem to be considered as humorous, and some-

Table 1–4: Impressions of indirect ways of communication (percentage)

	Junior	Senior	University	Native control
Negative	41	43	39	6
Neutral	31	30	35	78
Positive	28	27	26	16

Negative responses: ridiculous; strange; funny; annoying; misleading; better to avoid; awful; stupid, etc.

Positive responses: natural; humorous; interesting; nice; enjoyable, etc.

times funny, misleading, annoying, or ridiculous (because they seem to go against the culture-specific rule of politeness). Surprisingly, Japanese students might show negative feelings to such people. As such usage is uncommon among students, conversational partners always try to clarify what they wish to convey with some effort, considering what their contextual effect is. For instance, even in a simple dialogue, this tendency can be seen. 'A: Let's play tennis.' 'B: It's raining outside.' Many students reacted, 'A: So what? You mean, you DO NOT want to play tennis, huh.' (DO NOT is strongly emphasised here.) Although I shall not investigate culture-specific language use focusing on politeness profoundly here, in order to fully understand politeness, we should investigate the use of jokes or how people refuse, decline, reject, criticise, blame, or complain, paying special attention to whether they prefer to use direct or indirect ways of communication.

According to Sperber & Wilson (1995: 155–157), to achieve its effect, an act of communication must attract the audience's attention. In that sense, communication is a request for attention. Someone who asks you to behave in a certain way suggests that he or she has good reason to think it might be in your own interests, as well as his or her, to comply with his or her request. An act of communication cannot achieve its effect unless the audience pays attention to the stimulus. People will pay attention to a phenomenon only if it seems relevant to them. A communicator who produces a stimulus must intend it to seem relevant to his or her audience. To achieve his or her communicative intention, the communicator has to choose one of a range of different stimuli to make his or her particular informative intention obvious. The communicator should choose the most relevant stimulus, the one that will call for the least processing effort. This chapter has shown that indirect communication with implicatures is sometimes considered as irrelevant among Japanese learners of English in three ways: (1) it needs a lot of processing effort; (2) it lacks enough contextual effects; and (3) it is sometimes uninterpretable even if it is translated. The stylistic differences between English and Japanese (linguistic barrier), as well as foreign language effect (cognitive or psychological barrier), cause the problem.

The following tables summarise the statistical analyses of the data. Table 1–5 shows that the performance of Japanese students is significantly different from that of native speakers of English in all age-groups. In addition, L1 performance is significantly different until they become university students. Surprisingly, performance in L1 and L2 is not significantly different at senior high school and university level. Table 1–6 shows that students' development in understanding implicatures enhances as time goes by. On the other hand, their understanding of implicatures in L1 is fairly stable as the difference is not significant.

Table 1–5: Significance in performance (t-value)

	L2 vs. native		L1 vs. native		L1 vs. L2	
	Correct response	Response time	Correct response	Response time	Correct response	Response time
Junior	5.73*	10.05*	4.71*	4.69*	1.48*	8.17*
Senior	3.68*	7.89*	2.99*	3.38*	**1.26**	6.64*
University	2.88*	5.24*	**1.21**	**1.23**	**1.06**	4.98*

Table 1–6: Developmental differences (t-value)

	L2 development		L1 development	
	Correct response	Response time	Correct response	Response time
Junior-senior	3.26*	4.38*	**1.14**	**1.27**
Senior-Univ.	5.67*	5.76*	**1.21**	**1.19**
Junior-Univ.	8.21*	10.09*	1.51**	1.66**

For Japanese students, L2 means English and L1 means Japanese.

* means significant at 0.5% level. ** means significant at 5% level.

$t(59)<1.31\ p>0.1$; $1.30<t(59)<1.67\ 0.05<p<0.1$; $1.68<t(59)<2.39\ 0.01<p<0.05$;
$2.40<t(59)<2.66\ 0.005<p<0.01$: $t(59)>2.67\ p<0.005$

In this study, we have found that there is a difference in the way native speakers of English and Japanese interpret indirect ways of communication. The results show that someone's linguistic background is an important influence on the nature of implicatures that he or she draws.

1.5. Teaching implications

Should pragmatics be taught? Most researchers say 'yes', simply because if students do not know something, they have to be taught. I argue, however, that this is too simplistic: even if they are not taught, students gain communicative ability if their basic language proficiency develops by exposing themselves to L2. What is important is their ability to process a foreign language. Pragmatic knowledge comes in when syntax finishes the job (Carston, 2002; Kempson et al., 2001; Turnbull, 2003). There is a clear-cut distinction between grammar formalism and a model of utterance interpretation in context. Grammar-based generative systems do not take it to be part of the responsibility to articulate how hearers actually make choices as the information they process unfolds within a given overall context, on the grounds that this is the concern of pragmatics (Kempson et al., 2001: 263). Approaching this from a different angle, the hearers can interpret utterances properly if and only if they can process the language syntactically and semantically. People first analyse what the speakers have said based on their grammatical and lexical knowledge, then inferential processing (i.e., interpreting implicatures) takes place.

Matsumura (2003) includes both L2 proficiency and exposure to L2 as potential causal factors in pragmatic development, i.e., the effect of proficiency on pragmatic development via exposure and the effect of exposure on pragmatic development via proficiency. The former effect could mean that an increase in L2 proficiency would result in an increase in the amount of exposure to L2, which in turn would cause pragmatic development. The latter effect could mean that the increase in exposure would cause an increase in L2 proficiency, which in turn would result in pragmatic development. It has been widely claimed that advanced learners show a better ability to emulate native English speakers' pragmatic behaviour than intermediate learners, suggesting that pragmatic ability may develop with increasing L2 proficiency (Kasper & Rose, 2002). (Note, Takahashi & Beebe, 1987 found that highly proficient Japanese learners of English transferred more L1 socio-cultural norms to L2, making more pragmatic errors than the low-proficiency group. A high level of L2 proficiency may be correlated with negative pragmatic development.) Matsumura (2003) concludes that the interrelationships of the effects of proficiency and exposure on pragmatic development are as follows: the amount of exposure has a greater potential to account for the development of pragmatic ability than the levels of proficiency, and the amount of exposure is determined in part by levels of proficiency.

We must be aware of the fact that the above studies discuss how L2 learners learn to use their L2 naturally comparing with the native norms. Most past studies use the TOEFL® test and the like to measure their learners' proficiency in L2. However, TOEFL®, TOEIC®, placement tests, etc., in the twentieth century, were not developed to measure learners' communicative performance, but rather their linguistic competence. (Note that the present-day TOEFL® iBT Test is meant to measure some kind of communication ability as well as academic English skills.) Scoring well in these tests did not necessarily mean that such learners could use their target language properly. For instance, Kasper & Rose (2002) report on some articles that claim advanced Japanese learners of English, who scored over TOEFL 600 points, cannot apologize, advise, or refuse properly, which makes their native partners feel quite negatively toward them, i.e., Japanese are impolite and rude, or that even beginners can communicate naturally with native speakers without giving unfavourable impressions. The 'advanced' learners of English do not know how to communicate naturally with respect to native norms. Japanese are not rude or impolite people at all, they just do not know how to use English properly. This is where English language teaching comes in. As I mentioned above, pragmatic knowledge is required if learners are to generate sentences with their linguistic knowledge. This means that not only grammar but also pragmatics need to be learned. What is necessary for learners is to understand the shared attitude and background knowledge related to language use, which associates with different expectations in communication in different cultures. (I must stop here, because much more research is necessary to propose whether we should or should not provide pragmatic instruction.)

As Kasper & Rose (2002: chapter 5) suggest, the relationship between pragmatics and grammar in learners' developing interlanguage is complicated. The research evidence supports two conflicting hypotheses, showing that communicative language ability moves from pragmatics to grammar and from grammar to pragmatics. This is because researchers use the term *pragmatics* to refer to different phenomena: L2 learners face different learning tasks at different developmental stages in their development of L2 pragmatics and grammar. As my longitudinal observation which will be discussed in the next chapter reveals, in the very early phases they build on their available pragmatic knowledge, making do with whatever L2 grammar they have and at the same time acquiring the grammar skills needed to accomplish actions in L2. Words or phrases, often called chunks, are used frequently at this stage in order to communicate. A chunk is a group of words that the mind treats as a single lexical item. Many learners, particularly in the early stages of L2 acquisition, acquire ready-made phrases, like 'I don't know' 'What's the time?' 'What's your name?' and 'Can I have a ___ ?', to communicate somehow. Some researchers call this way of communication 'pragmatic'. In order to understand what others say and what the learner wishes to say, the beginner infers by means of limited vocabulary or chunks. Partial interpretation and expression in this phase are realised by pragmatic knowledge. As learners progress, their learning task increasingly changes to figuring out the various pragmatic, often diverse meanings that specific grammatical forms have beyond their primary meaning. This process will evolve differently for different grammatical forms and their pragmatic meanings, and will depend on the activities learners engage in and on whether grammatical and pragmatic knowledge of other languages helps acquire new L2 pragmatic meanings of grammatical forms. Hence, the accurate use of much more complicated structures including modals and the subjunctive mood needs to be acquired in order to accomplish their needs and speech acts. The appropriate use of L2 to fulfil natural communication must be grounded in grammatical and pragmatic knowledge. Articles in Rose & Kasper eds. (2001) argue for the positive effect of pragmatic instruction in order to perform various speech acts appropriately. We can imagine that subjunctive mood or modals that make utterances polite need to be taught, otherwise learners do not notice such complicated structures. Students need to know when and where they should and should not use a particular form, paying attention to the function of grammar. As grammatical knowledge does not guarantee suitable use (i.e., even if grammatically correct, some utterances are unnatural or inappropriate in actual use), pragmatic knowledge must compensate for such generated sentences in production.

Returning to the data in this study, we can clearly see that: (1) students can process implicatures more and more rapidly and aptly when exposure to L2 increases (supporting Matsumura, 2003); (2) Japanese students do not commonly employ indirect communication as English-speaking people often do; (3) Japanese students sometimes feel negatively about employing indirect communication; (4) even if L1 and L2 language use is different, Japanese learners of English can interpret implicatures; and (5) the foreign language effect results in the slow processing of implicatures in L2. The following figure clarifies the process:

Beginners:

L2 input → Translator → L2 processor → Relevance → Inference → Understand implications

Advanced learners:

L2 input → L2 processor → Relevance → Inference → Understand implications

L1 processing:

L1 input → L1 processor → Relevance → Inference → Understand implications

<Linguistic/Input system> <Central system>

Figure 1–1: The flow of L1 and L2 processing

Linguistic processing and inferential processes are independent if we take Fodor's (1983) modular view. The former locates in the input systems and the latter in the central system. If learners can derive meanings from what the speaker said, the central system starts to operate as it does in L1 processing. What differs, then, is the additional processing load (effort of translating and foreign language effect) when dealing with L2. Students reported that they can see the literal meaning but cannot derive implicatures, which means that there is some trouble in the central system: they do not figure it out even though they try hard to search for the meaning in their central system. This is because of individual, stylistic, or cultural differences, which relate to past exposure to contexts or functions: beyond the operation of the language processor. Mostly, as our data on the reaction time and correct response rate reveal, if exposure to L2 increases, students get to understand implicatures more quickly and accurately. As implicatures are processed in the central system, learners need to develop the foreign language processor. Even if students cannot figure out implicatures, they respond to them somehow (e.g., asking for clarification) and avoid a break-down of communication. A well-developed L2 processing ability supplements the inferential process as we do in L1 communication.

Conclusion

In this chapter, we have discussed whether foreign language learners acquire communication ability focusing on the development of inference abilities. The main task for them is to develop a foreign language processor which enables them to decipher grammatical and semantic aspects of the input. If (and only if) the foreign language processing system works properly, they can interpret the intended meanings of the utterances. We have seen that the term *pragmatics* is used to refer to two things: the very beginning limited use of words or phrases to get things done, and a much more advanced use of the language with complicated structures to make communication natural and smooth with respect to the native norms. The crucial point in communication is to understand the message: if we understand the message in grammatical and semantic terms, we can respond to it somehow even if we cannot figure out implicatures, asking for clarification. However, I am not denying the fact that it is better and time-saving to teach how to use the language aptly (e.g., the way to apologise, advise, complain, request, and perform other speech acts). The argument concerning the teaching of the actual or apposite use (i.e., language production) is beyond our scope in this chapter. We have seen that grammar (syntax) and meaning (semantics) are prerequisites for use (pragmatics) in proper and fluent communication. In my terms, the development of linguistic systems (foreign language processor) is a prerequisite for appropriate operation of the central system (inference) which is commonly comprehensible in L1 and L2. Though grammar and pragmatics do different things at different levels, they develop hand in hand. In the following chapter, we shall look at what a foreign language processing system is like and how the foreign language processor develops in detail.

First published as 'The acquisition of communicative competence in L2: Focusing on the development of inferential abilities' in *JABAET Journal* 8 (2004): 45–62

Chapter 2
Input processing

Introduction

In this chapter, we shall see that psycholinguists who take a cognitive perspective have been concerned primarily with analysing and modelling the inner mental mechanisms available to the individual learner for processing, learning, and storing new linguistic knowledge. Their aim is to document and explain the mechanism and the developmental route along which a learner travels. The route of development is the sequence of linguistic stages through which learners seem to pass.

Recently, researchers have been interested in language processing and language acquisition (e.g., Alcon, 1998; Frazier & Villiers eds., 1990; VanPatten, 1996, 2004; Hillert ed., 1998; Mazuka, 1998; Pienemann, 1998a, 1998b, 2002, 2005; Heredia & Altarriba eds., 2002). They consider that the language learning problem is the language processing problem. For language learners to learn a facet of grammar, they must process the language. While the Parameter Setting Model (Chomskyan Universal Grammar paradigm) can handle whether a particular parameter is set/reset or not, it does not reveal how language learners process input and when setting/resetting takes place. The Parameter Setting Model presupposes that foreign language learners can automatically process input somehow, and it accounts for the final state of the learners. Most of the experiments in past research have used grammaticality judgement tests in order to reveal whether Universal Grammar (UG) is working or not, but little attention has been paid to the mechanisms for language processing and the development of language processing abilities. According to Mitchell & Myles (1998: 69–71), one of the reasons why processing and developmental issues have been left open is that the aim of the studies in linguistic approaches is to test and construct linguistic theories of foreign language learners. Longitudinal developmental issues are out of their scope. If UG is shown to be working properly, what foreign language learners need to do is to expose themselves to the foreign language, letting UG guide them. Bearing foreign language instructions in mind, however, developmental and input processing issues should not be ignored, especially in a monolingual environment like Japan, where foreign languages are taught and mainly used only in the classroom. We need to know the learning processes of foreign language learners. This is a motivation of the input processing perspective to be discussed in this chapter.

While UG-based researchers put emphasis on the linguistic dimension of foreign language learning, input processing or cognitive perspective mainly focuses on the learning component of foreign language learning. This approach views foreign language learning as one instance of learning among many others. One can comprehend the foreign language learning process better by understanding how the human mind processes and learns new information. While UG theorists draw their hypotheses from the study of linguistic systems, the hypotheses that cognitive theorists are investigating come from the field of cognitive psychology or cognitive science in general. The distinction between linguistic and cognitive models is that the former are considered as descriptions of knowledge of rules for linguistic structures and the latter as descriptions of methods of storage and means of accessing these rules (Bialystok, 1991). Traditionally, researchers who take a cognitive position argue against the role of UG in foreign language learning (Cook, 1993: chapter 10). They have tried to construct a theory without appealing to the notion of UG, because foreign language learning is nothing more than one example of general human learning processes. VanPatten's and Pienemann's position that I shall take, however, does not deny the analyses that UG exists in the learner's mind. VanPatten and Pienemann assume that the domain-specific language processing mechanisms with UG do not disappear in the human mind, even if foreign language learners do not have access to every parameter or principle in full. In this chapter, I discuss how foreign language learners process linguistic input.

2.1. Language processing system

2.1.1. Overview

Language is a highly complex human skill. Emphasising one or two of the characteristics of language has led investigators to devise radically different models of language processing. Language facilitates human communication, and so is normally used to convey meaning. Such meaning is accessed through knowledge of the sound structure, semantics, syntax, and pragmatics (Tartter, 1998: 265). In this book, *language processing* refers to a sequence of operations, each of which transforms a mental representation of a linguistic stimulus into a mental representation of a different form.

Nearly two decades ago, Frazier & de Villiers (1990: 1) pointed out that studies of language acquisition had largely ignored processing principles and mechanisms. Questions concerning the analysis of an informative linguistic input have also been ignored. Especially in linguistic approaches to language acquisition, the role of language processing has not been prominent. They suggest that an explicit model of the ways processing routines are applied in acquisition would help solve some central problems of grammar acquisition, since these routines regulate the application of grammatical knowledge to novel inputs. In the absence of a processing theory, the only way input data can influence grammar acquisition is by unanalysed input directly fixing a grammatical parameter or by the acquisition system using compounds of linguistic relations already present in the learner's current grammar. While psycholinguists have been interested in language acquisition and language processing in normal and abnormal settings, these fields have been investigated rather separately (Fodor, Bever, & Garret, 1974; Clark & Clark, 1977; Garman, 1990; Taylor, 1990; Kess, 1992; Gernsbacher ed., 1994; Gleason & Ratner, 1998; Tartter, 1998; Carrol, 2004; Steinberg & Sciarini, 2006; Harley, 2008). The lack of research can be witnessed in the field of second language acquisition as well. Harald Clahsen and Manfred Pienemann have taken this issue seriously, and, in the field of second language teaching, Bill VanPatten seeks to apply processing theories to practice.

Since communicative language teaching came onto the scene, researchers and practitioners have been seeking effective and efficient ways of developing students' ability to communicate. Recently, task- and content-based approaches have attracted their attention. On the other hand, some teachers criticise these approaches, claiming that grammar is ignored, only conversational style is focused on, or speaking cannot be taught by non-native teachers. More importantly, sufficient fundamental research on the development of foreign language processing has not been conducted. A foreign language processing system, which comprehends input and produces utterances, develops step by step, without us knowing what it is and how it develops, and a consistent curriculum, teaching materials, and teaching methods that fit the developmental route, which would fulfil our needs, cannot be proposed.

Investigations on how people comprehend and produce sentences and how they learn to do so have played a central role in the development of cognitive science. In this section, I focus on the following:

1. How native speakers of English process English;
2. How native speakers of Japanese process Japanese; and
3. How Japanese learners of English process English.

As the following sections show, there are two positions as to how Japanese people process languages: the first position claims that there is a universal language processor. This position supports the idea that Japanese and English are processed in a similar way. The second position claims that there are language-specific processing systems. According to this position, Japanese and English are processed differently. In the following sections, we look at each rationale, focusing on their linguistic evidence. Then, we discuss their implications for foreign language pedagogy. In order to comprehend and produce language, the sentence processor must bridge the automatic perceptual task of word recognition and lexical access. The interpretation and production of a sentence are determined by the particular way its words can be combined. In this section, to narrow down the scope, lexical processing is not reviewed; only syntactic (or grammatical) processing is focused on in detail. In addition, this section mainly focuses on comprehension and not on production, because less research has been done in the area of language production: most research argues for or modifies Levelt's (1989) model. Computational approaches, including machine translation, natural language processing, or cognitive architecture, are not discussed (Altmann ed., 1990; Mitkov & Nicolov eds., 1997; Kintsch, 1998; Jackson & Moulinier, 2002).

Let us first look at the mechanism of language processing. Figure 2–1 shows how human beings are expected to process linguistic input. Traditionally, this hypothesis has been widely adopted by researchers such as Ogden & Richards (1923: chapters 1 & 4), Palmer (1924), Merleau-Ponty (1962: Parts 1–6 & 2–1), Ryle (1949: chapters 2 & 10), Fodor, Bever, & Garrett (1974: chapter 7), Miller & Johnson-Laird (1976: chapters 2 & 4), Johnson-Laird (1983), Levelt (1989, 1999), Garman (1990), Kess (1992), Jackendoff (1997), and Tartter (1998: chapter 7). I will follow the line of approach put forward by Jackendoff (1997) for input processing, and Bock & Levelt (1994) for output processing.

Let us consider viewing a tree. The visual system constructs a representation

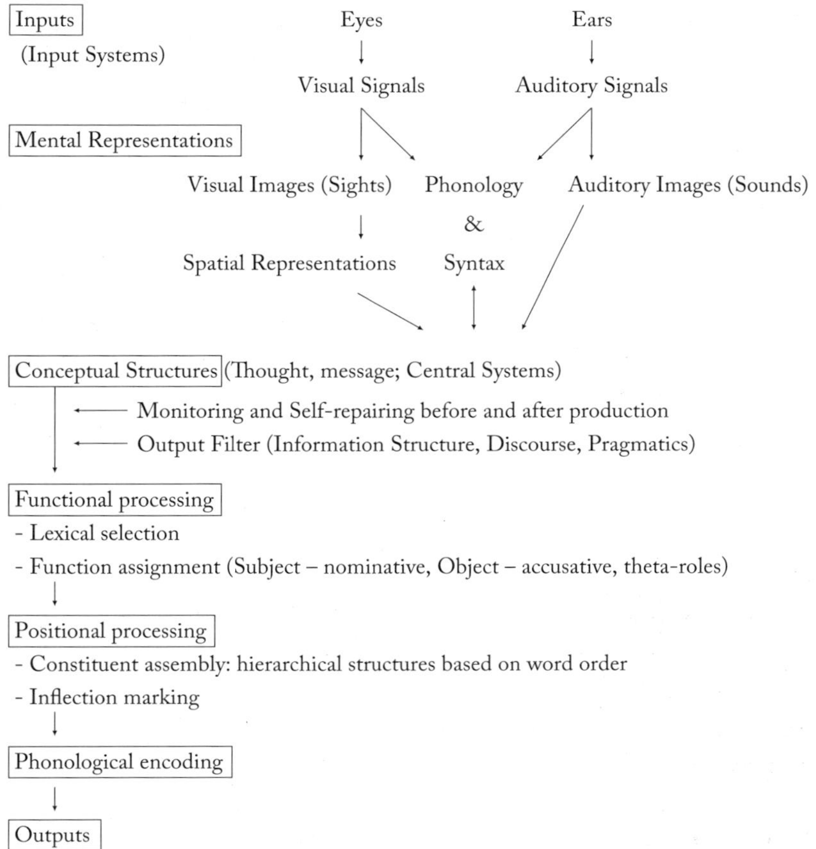

Figure 2–1: Language processing system

This diagram shows how human beings process linguistic and other perceptual inputs. This diagram is a modified version of Jackendoff (1997) and Bock & Levelt (1994).

of the form of the tree, and it also drives the conceptual system to retrieve the concept of a tree. Our understanding of what we see is a consequence not only of visual images but also of the conceptual organisation connected to those images. We have no direct awareness of our understanding of trees: we have only a perceptual awareness of the visual form of what we are seeing. If the visual system drives the conceptual system to develop a conceptual structure for the tree, then, this conceptual structure can drive the linguistic module to create an utterance through its lexical and phrasal interface with syntax and phonology (Jackendoff, 1997: chapter 8).

Conceptual structure is largely independent of linguistic structures of a particular language, while it is dependent on abstract forms of language, called 'Language of Thought' (Fodor, 1975). A Japanese speaker can have essentially the same concepts as an English speaker. If different languages can express the same concepts, then concepts cannot be connected directly with the form of any single language. Translation between languages seeks to preserve a concept behind an expression. They must be neutral with respect to what language they are expressed in. The same concept can be expressed in English (SVO word order) and in Japanese (SOV word order).

According to Bock & Levelt (1994), the processes of language production can be divided into those that create the skeleton of an utterance (grammatical encoding) and those that flesh out the skeleton (phonological encoding). Grammatical encoding comprises both the selection of appropriate lexical concepts and the assembly of a syntactic framework. Phonological encoding comprises the assembly of sound forms and the generation of intonation.

The message (conceptual structure) captures features of the speaker's intended meaning, and provides the lexicon and chunks for the processes of grammatical encoding. These processes are grouped into two sets, functional and positional. The primary components of functional processing are lexical selection, which involves the identification of lexical concepts that are suitable for conveying the speaker's meaning, and functional assignment, which involves grammatical rules or syntactic functions. Positional processing involves the creation of an ordered set of word slots (constituent assembly) and morphological slots (inflection). Finally, phonological encoding spells out the phonological structure of the utterance in terms of the phonological segments of word forms and the prosody of larger units (Levelt, 1989, 1999; Bock & Levelt, 1994, Bock, 1995).

I have no intention of going into the argument of whether this point of view needs further modification. The question I wish to address is the applicability of this model to foreign language learning. De Bot (1992, 1993, 1996, 1997), De Bot et al. (1995), Grosjean (1997), Paradis (1997), Dornyei & Kormos (1998), and Kormos (1999, 2006) have shown that foreign language learners create a new foreign language processor. One controversy among researchers is the way to treat conceptual structures for L1 and L2. De Bot argues that L1 and L2 conceptual structures are independent, i.e., learners create another conceptual structure for L2. De Groot (1993), Kroll (1993), Appel (1996), Kroll & de Groot (1997, 2005), Grosjean (1997), Dufour (1997), Paradis (1997), Gonzalez (1998), Jiang (2000), and Libben (2000), however, hypothesise that the L2 conceptual structure is attached to or stored in parallel with the L1 conceptual structure, i.e., one conceptual structure with L1 and L2. What I will discuss in this chapter is not the issue of the conceptual structure, but how foreign language learners create a foreign language processor as above, that is, the developmental issues of foreign language learning. I will presuppose that the model is acceptable and discuss how to build up the foreign language processor gradually in the rest of this chapter.

2.1.2. English processing by native speakers of English

People can read, listen to a speaker, or hold a conversation, and understand most of what the writer or speaker intends to convey. From the perspective of a person trying to understand a sentence, language is a continuous flow of information distributed over time. Sentence comprehension involves determination of the meaning of a sentence as a whole on the basis of a sequence of words, and is concerned with how people perform a particular syntactic analysis for a string of words and assign an interpretation to that analysis (Pickering, 1999: 123). The challenge facing psycholinguists is to account for how people accomplish this. Osterhout et al. (2004: 271) clearly state that asking the reader or listener for an answer to this question provides little useful information: the relevant processes are not generally available for conscious reflection. The ideal method should provide continuous measurement throughout the process of understanding a sentence, show a temporal resolution exceeding that of the relevant processes, and be differentially sensitive to events occurring at different levels of analysis.

Sentence processing is done with respect to grammar, basically a set of rules that say which combinations of which part of speech generate well-formed phrase and sentence structures. Thus, 'Colourless green ideas sleep furiously.' might be syntactically well-formed, since the adjective-adjective-noun is a valid noun phrase structure, verb-adverb is a valid verb phrase structure, and noun phrase + verb phrase forms a valid sentence. Then, semantic analysis involves identifying different types of words or phrases, e.g., recognising a word as a proper noun, and also identifying the role that they play in the sentence, e.g., whether subject or object. Different semantic types have different features, e.g., a word or noun phrase may refer to something animate or inanimate.

When the structure of a sentence is compatible with only one syntactic analysis, the analysis is computed and interpreted immediately before the next word is encountered. When a structure is compatible with more than one analysis, however, how do people process it? Psycholinguists have taken up such cases, referring to the phenomenon as *syntactic ambiguity resolution*.

Firstly, syntactic ambiguity takes place when a verb can allow either a nominal or sentential complement, i.e., *subcategorisation* (Gorrell, 1995: 45). For instance, let us consider:

(1) Ian knows Thomas is a train.

In (1), the onset of the ambiguity is the verb *know*. This is because *know* allows either a nominal or sentential complement. The ambiguity is resolved by the presence of the verb *is*, which signals a sentential complement. The area between the onset of the ambiguity and its resolution, the noun phrase *Thomas* in (1), is the ambiguous region of the sentence. Tanenhaus et al. (1990) suggests that thematic role information is immediately accessed and used when a verb is encountered. Lexical representations could be used to rapidly coordinate a range of different types of information during language processing. (Developing this line of argument, Frazier (1990) proposes that there must be a thematic role processor distinct from the syntax processor, and Fodor (1990) gives thought to this proposal). Overall, Townsend & Bever (2001: 245) show several kinds of evidence that functional words are rapidly accessed, and they prime their syntactically relevant content words. The syntactic category and subcategorisation information have immediate effects on reading. In addition, semantic information becomes available early on in sentence comprehension. The argument structure of verbs has an early effect on reading. (Frazier (1999) investigates what semantic principles or properties are given in the relation between semantics and the syntactic structures motivated independently or dependently by careful, detailed study of the distribution of the formatives of English.)

The second well-known syntactic ambiguity is the *garden-path effect* of reduced relative clauses. The human sentence processing mechanism is not an error-free device. It sometimes makes wrong decisions. When it does, a garden-path can result. A garden-path occurs when the mechanism selects an incorrect analysis at the ambiguity onset but can continue to proceed with that analysis in assigning structure to the subsequent input word string. The mechanism recognises a garden-path when it later discovers an input word that does not fit into the current analysis (Gorrell, 1995: 46).

(2) While Mary was mending the sock fell.
The horse raced fell.

There is growing consensus that the processing difficulty of sentences such as (2) is strong evidence for structuring input as it is received, i.e., *incrementally*. Stabler (1994: 320) defines incremental processing as follows: Human syntactic analysis is typically incremental, in the sense that people typically incorporate each word into a single, totally connected syntactic structure before any following words. Incremental interpretation is achieved by interpretation of this single connected syntactic structure. The psychological complexity of a structure increases quickly when processing proceeds with more than one independent, completed sub-structure. The work of Frazier (1990) and Fodor (1990) argues for an incremental processing which reanalyses structure when necessary. Their proposal is motivated by the need to structure input quickly and efficiently before it becomes a burden to short-term memory. Their work elegantly unites the various processing strategies put forward by Bever (1970) into two general principles: *Late Closure* and *Minimal Attachment* (Gorrell, 1995: 47):

Late Closure: When possible, attach/incorporate incoming material into the clause or phrase currently being processed.

Minimal Attachment: Attach/Incorporate incoming material into the phrase marker being constructed using the fewest nodes consistent with the well-formed rules of the grammar.

The Late Closure principle focuses on the way in which readers or listeners might determine when they have reached a major clause boundary. In doing this, one might attempt to close a clause boundary either at the earliest point possible or to hold off until the latest possible point. According to this principle, readers and listeners tend to do the latter. The Late Closure principle is a special case of a more general principle referred to as Minimal Attachment. This principle states that readers or listeners attempt to interpret sentences in terms of the simplest syntactic structure that is consistent with the input. This is achieved using the fewest phrase-structure nodes possible. In (1), the ambiguity is caused by the verb *know*, which permits either a nominal or sentential complement. Thus, the post-verbal noun phrase is either an object of the main clause or the subject of a possible subordinate clause. It is Minimal Attachment which causes us to attach the noun phrase *Thomas* as the direct object of the verb as it is the minimal attachment site. In (2), the ambiguity is caused by the fact that *mend* may appear either with or without an object. Late Closure causes us to analyse the noun phrase, *the sock*, as the object of *mend* because the verb phrase is the current phrase. The other grammatical attachments would necessitate attaching the noun phrase as part of a new phrase or clause. Minimal Attachment does not apply here if it is assumed that, at the point that *the sock* is processed, the main-clause node has been processed. Without this assumption, Minimal Attachment would suffice to force the object attachment of the noun phrase because it would be the minimal attachment site. When the final verb is processed, backtracking will be required to return to the start of the clause, and there will be no available subject since Late Closure and Minimal Attachment have provided a main clause rather than a relative noun phrase analysis (Pritchett, 1992: 38). More recently, Merlo & Stevenson (2000) propose a lexical-structural account for the differential difficulty of reduced relative clauses. They make the novel observation that extreme garden-path effects appear to be limited to the manner of motion emission verbs, a subclass of intransitive verbs with peculiar properties.

How do psycholinguists measure these phenomena? Traditionally, there are methods that were first introduced about three decades ago and remain in regular use in current psycholinguistic work. The simplest of these is *self-paced reading*. In this task, the text is segmented into words, word strings, or phrases to be displayed one at a time, typically on a computer screen. The participant starts the process by pressing a key to see the first display. When the participant has read this, a second key-press initiates the second text segment, and so on until the end of the text. The main measure of interest for the researcher is the time between successive key-presses in specified regions of the text (Mitchell, 1994, 2004: 16).

In addition, psycholinguists measure subjects' *eye movement* as they read sentences containing ambiguities (Rayner & Sereno, 1994; Trueswell & Tanenhaus ed., 2005). This technique is a particularly useful tool for investigating on-line sentence processing as there is no need to interrupt the processing of the input string for the presentation of a task (Sekerina, Fernandez, & Clahsen, 2008). A subject's fixation durations and eye movements are recorded as each sentence is read. The total reading time per letter for each sentence is also recorded. During reading, the eyes do not sweep along a line of print, but advance through little jumps. The continuous recording of eye movements enables researchers to identify locations and durations of fixations during reading, allowing them to draw inferences about cognitive operations while reading.

More recently, research employing *event-related potentials* (ERPs), brain-related scientific tools, emphasises that ERPs provide an on-line technique not dependent on button pushing or any other secondary task. It also emphasises the multidimensional nature of the ERP waveforms as well as continuous, real-time nature. ERPs are positive and negative voltage changes in the ongoing electroencephalogram that are time-locked to the onset of a sensory, motor, or cognitive event (Kutas & VanPetten, 1994). The advantages of ERPs as measures of real-time cognition are clear: ERPs provide a continuous on-line record of the brain's electrical activity that occurs during the process under study (Osterhout, 1994: 16).

The peak of one language-sensitive component, the N400, reliably occurs about 400 milliseconds after the presentation of a word. The peak amplitude of N400 is reliably larger for contextually inappropriate words than for contextually appropriate ones. However, the response to the syntactically anomalous case is not the negative-going N400, but is instead a positive-going wave. Because the positivity has a midpoint around 600 milliseconds, this wave is labelled P600. P600 is apparent not only with phrase structure and subcategorisation violations but also empty category principle and subjacency violations (Osterhout, 1994). Number- and gender-agreement violations also exhibit P600s, suggesting that they share a pattern with other syntactic violations. Both N400 and P600 are observed in examples where a syntactic violation results in a ungrammatical and uninterpretable sentence. However, in garden-path sentences, the disambiguating word gives rise to either a P600 for most subjects or N400, but never to both within a single individual (Pickering, Barton, & Shillicock, 1994). According to Clifton et al. (1994), the underlying source of N400 versus P600 remains unclear.

P600 might directly reflect the processes underlying syntactic analysis, responding to syntactic violations, or reanalysis. Brown & Hagoort (2000) clearly state that the brain response to semantic processing is distinct from the response to syntactic processing. In particular, the N400 component has been proven to be an especially sensitive index of meaning integration processes, whereas, within the domain of language processing, P600 is only observed in the context of specifically syntactic processes.

According to Hagoort & Brown (1994: 62), existing electrophysiological studies of sentence processing suggest at least two candidate ERP effects that appear to be related to syntactic analysis: P600, a large, broad, symmetric positive-going shift, and left anterior negativity (LAN), a negative shift that is maximal over left anterior recording sites. LAN was observed in response to words indicating mismatches in number agreement between an adjective and noun, to incorrect tense marking, to violations of phrase-structure constraints, and to filler-gap constructions that involve *wh* movements. Hagoort & Brown (1994: 63) advises caution because the extent to which these various LANs are related is unclear, a unifying account of what leads to their elicitation must await further research.

Interestingly, Townsend & Bever (2001) hypothesise that the sentence templates (i.e., word order) are distinct from grammatical knowledge. According to them, left-hemisphere effects of constructions that violate the strategies appear early in the ERP, and prior to semantic violations. ERP effects of syntactic errors that do not violate the strategies appear only late in the overall ERP. They suggest that word order information is processed first, then, semantic information is processed, and then, other properties of grammar are encoded.

Mitchell (2004: 23–24) picked up certain recurrent themes in sentence processing with different methods (self-paced reading, eye-tracking, and ERP), and illustrated the following interesting pattern:

1. When a reader encounters anomalous material, the processing time increases in self-paced reading, and there are also ERP N400 influences, as well as increases in reading time in eye-tracking studies.
2. Though the immediacy or otherwise of the influence remains contentious, the resolution of syntactic ambiguity can be shown to be influenced by changes in the discourse context. After a preliminary eye-tracking failure to show the effect, this was first demonstrated using self-paced reading, and later cor-

roborated using eye-tracking techniques before eventually being tackled using ERP (P600) methods.

3. End-of-sentence wrap-up effects, the demonstration that there is a processing increment associated with the final word or phrase of a sentence, was first demonstrated using self-paced reading and confirmed a little later using eye-tracking
4. Cross-linguistic differences in processing (reduced) relative clauses were demonstrated initially using self-paced reading and later corroborated using eye-tracking methods.

2.1.3. Japanese processing by native speakers of Japanese

Language processing strategies might be universal or determined separately for individual languages. If they are universal, they must be sufficiently general to hold across languages with radically different syntactic properties. Pickering, Clifton, & Crocker (2000: 20) claim that even though Minimal Attachment was originally proposed for verb-medial constructions in English, it can support predictions on the processing of verb-final constructions. On the other hand, Late Closure cannot hold for all languages. Mazuka & Nagai (1995: 3) suggest that, in order to verify that the language processing mechanism is capable of comprehending and generating both head-initial languages such as English and head-final languages such as Japanese with equal efficiency, it is essential to investigate how Japanese speakers process Japanese sentences and then integrate the Japanese results with the English data accumulated over the years. They claim that everyone agrees that the sentence processing mechanism must be universal to a certain degree, although the grammars of languages may vary systematically from one to another. Inoue & Fodor (1995: 50) state that every constituent ends with its head in Japanese: there is no rightward extendability and no right recursion, so the attachment ambiguities in Japanese are on the left, where uncertainty is created by the optionality of arguments and adjuncts. A phrase is closed when its head is encountered, and late closure is simply inapplicable in Japanese. Minimal Attachment might work in Japanese and in English, while head-final vs. head-initial may predict the opposite. Miyamoto (2006) points out that scrambled orders are harder to process than canonical ones. Moreover, given that slow reading times occur before the predicate of the clause, readers are interpreting noun phrases together before reaching the predicate. ERP results support the claim that the slow-downs of reading speed in scrambled sentences reflect both reanalysis of the initial interpretation as well as difficulty in processing the scrambled constituent. The word immediately following a scrambled sentence elicited a P600 response. In addition, scrambling generated a sustained anterior negativity, which means that the dependency between the scrambled constituent and gap is consuming extra working memory. Kamide et al. (2003) and Kamide (2006) suggest that the Japanese processor not only processes pre-head arguments incrementally, but can also predict plausible subsequent arguments using case-marking information and real-world knowledge.

Mazuka & Itoh (1995) propose that there are few serious garden-path effects in Japanese. In Japanese, the presence or absence of the garden-path effect is tied to the surface properties of the sentence. The garden-path effect disappears when the subject noun phrase is dropped or the object noun phrase is scrambled to the left of the subject. The following examples are at issue (Hirose, 2002):

(3) Yoko-wa kodomo-o tasuketa otoko-ni awaseta.
(4) Yoko-wa kodomo-o tasuketa otoko-ni atta.

Sentence (3) is ambiguous, in that it can be translated into two possible English sentences: 'Yoko let someone meet the man who helped a child.' and 'Yoko let a child meet the man who helped the child'. Sentence (4) has one possibility: 'Yoko met the man who helped a child.'

While Mazuka & Itoh (1995) propose a syntactic account, i.e., different filler gap positions, Hirose (2002) suggests that the differences should be resolved by means of thematic relations of verbs. In (3), the main verb *awaseta* requires a direct object, so it becomes apparent that a null object or *kodomo* is a constituent of the main clause. In (4), however, the main verb *atta* does not take an *o*-marked noun phrase as its object, and it becomes obvious that *kodomo* must be an object of the relative clause verb *tasuketa*. According to Hirose & Inoue (1998), processing relative clauses in Japanese inevitably causes a garden-path effect in many cases. Japanese is a head-final SOV language, so, in processing relative clause constructions, the relative clause is encountered before the head noun that it modifies. It is not always obvious to the processing mechanism whether an initial string of words such as (3) and (4), where the argument structure of the verb is consistent with the NPs that precede it, forms one single clause. Hirose (2006) assumes that relative clauses in Japanese pose a tough challenge because they potentially involve multiple kinds of temporary and global ambiguities as above at different stages of processing. In order to interpret a Japanese relative clause correctly, one needs to know that it is a relative clause construction, which is not evident in the early stages of English processing, to determine at which point of the sentence the clause starts and what grammatical or thematic role the head noun is associated with within the relative clause, and to resolve the identity of the head noun.

Aoshima et al. (2004) argue that it is certainly true that English and Japanese differ in their dominant word orders and the types of morphological and syntactic cues that are available early in the sentence. However, they suggest that this does not translate into fundamental underlying differences in how speakers process language. They show a case where, superficially, Japanese and English seem to differ markedly in how they are processed, but, they in fact reflect the same underlying mechanism. Theoretically speaking, the assumption is that the grammatical knowledge is the same but the processing strategies are different. Many studies on processing English report that verb information plays a significant role in processing, but Japanese follows the form of SOV, i.e., it is a head-final language. The fact that verb information does not become available until the end of a clause leads one to ask whether other types of information may be utilised in processing Japanese. Yamashita (1997) suggests that no effect of word order was observed, while the processor was sensitive to a variety of case-marked arguments. Further, Miyamoto (2002, 2006) provides evidence that the processing of verb final clauses proceeds incrementally based on local information that becomes available with each word. Noun phrases in Japanese are associated within clauses before a verb is processed. Although English speakers may depend more on word order and Japanese speakers can also use case markers, in general, the use they make of the information available seems to be similar, and it is a processing strategy that affects different languages in different ways (Fodor, 1998b, 1998c).

2.1.4. English processing by non-native speakers

As we have seen, sentence processing research seeks to understand the processes responsible for the comprehension of sentences in real time. Processing research differs from research on language structure and function in that it is primarily concerned with understanding the mental processes responsible for language as a dynamic real-time entity (Harrington, 2001).

In the field of second language acquisition, memory-based approaches have attracted researchers' attention (Randall, 2007). Brown & Hulme (1992) point out that short-term memory plays a crucial role in syntactic processing in first and second language acquisition. The reduced short-term memory span observed in a second language can arise because of the lack of strong phonological lexical representations for second language items in long-term memory, which causes slow and sometimes inaccurate processing in a foreign language (N. Ellis, 1992, 1994, 1996a, 1996b, 1999, 2001; Harrington, 1992; Nakano et al., 2002).

Regarding foreign language processing, Kilborn & Ito (1989) (see also Sasaki, 1991, 1994), based on Harrington (1987), reported the following interesting tendencies in processing: Native speakers of English and Japanese learners of English listened to sentences containing two nouns and a verb, orthogonalized along the dimensions of order (NVN, NNV, VNN). The task was to identify the actor/agent, i.e., who did it. The native English speakers exhibited the characteristic pattern of noun choice across the three word order types: In NVN, the first noun was chosen 81% of the time, compared with 35% for NNV and 33% for VNN. In native speakers of Japanese, word order had virtually no effect on noun choice: The first noun was chosen in Japanese NVN 59% of the time, in NNV 56%, and in VNN 54%. In the L2 test group, native Japanese speakers performing the task in English chose the first noun 68% of the time in NVN sentences, 59% in NNV, and 56% in VNN. On the other hand, American learners of Japanese were affected more by the word order cue than native speakers of Japanese. The monolingual Japanese speakers chose the first noun 67% of the time in NVN, 63% in VNN, and 77% in NNV orders. In contrast, American learners of Japanese chose the first noun in NVN as the subject 63% of the time, 44% in VNN, and 89% in NNV. This appears to provide evidence that these learners were able to acquire the use of a cue that is appropriate to processing Japanese. Word order cues had the greatest overall effect on the English interpretation, while word order had less of an effect on the Japanese group. Japanese learners of English were more sensitive to the NVN order than the Japanese subjects. Interestingly, Japanese participants were more strongly affected by animacy cues than English speakers, and inanimate subjects were avoided. McDonald & Heileman (1992) examined how L2 learners gain mastery over appropriate L2 strategies with increasing second language proficiency. The time course of this mastery includes an initial abandonment of L1 word order strategies followed by the later development of appropriate L2 word order strategies, and even later strengthening of an appropriate verb agreement strategy. Frenk-Mestre (2002), based on eye-movement and response time measures, showed that second language syntactic analysis need not be considered as a separate case from first language processing. Proficient bilinguals show immediate sensitivity to structural ambiguities in a manner similar to native speakers, quite independently of reading speed. These proficient bilinguals are also able to take advantage of fine levels of analysis to guide the processing of structurally ambiguous sentences in the second language. In the instance that the bilingual's two languages differ as concerns the processing of a given syntactic structure, changes in processing strategies will occur over time as the bilingual gains experience with the second language.

Researchers often suggest in the bilingual sentence processing literature that bilinguals are not two monolinguals in one head (e.g. Hernandez et al., 2007). Specifically, many studies have shown that bilinguals use sentence processing strategies that are sometimes L1-like, sometimes L2-like, and sometimes in between. This has been shown to be true across semantic and syntactic processing. Altogether, these results support a model in which multiple constraints play a role in determining the nature of bilingual sentence processing. In general, the more dominant language will influence the processing of the less dominant one across semantic and syntactic processing. In addition, there is evidence that a similarity in languages can result in increased transfer and vice versa. Osterhout et al. (2004, 2006) addressed the following question: 'How much experience with a foreign language is needed for the learner's brain to distinguish between well- and ill-formed sentences?' Participants were native French speakers and a group of novice adult French learners. Learners were tested after 1, 4, and 8 months of instruction. Native French speakers showed an N400 response to the semantically anomalous words, and very large P600 responses to syntactic anomalies. French learners showed striking individual differences. During each test session, semantically anomalous words elicited a robust N400 effect, and this effect changed minimally with increasing instruction. The finding of real interest pertained to syntactic conditions. After just 1 month of instruction, the learners' brains discriminated between the syntactically well- and ill-formed sentences. However, rather than eliciting a P600 effect, as seen in native speakers, the syntactically anomalous words had an N400-like effect. By 4 months, the N400 effect had largely disappeared and been replaced by a P600-like positivity. By 8 months, this P600 effect increased in amplitude and the N400 effect was completely absent. One interpretation of these results is that the learners initially learned about words but not rules. After one month of instruction, they recognised that a particular word does not fit well in the context but had yet to grammaticalise this knowledge, and so it elicited an N400 effect. With a bit more exposure, this knowledge become codified as a syntactic rule, and hence it elicited a P600 effect. Mueller (2006) shows that ERP patterns in L2 processing often resemble those observed in L1 processing, as N400 and P600 are typically observed in late L2 learners. This suggests that the processing mechanisms in these domains are functionally equivalent or at least similar to native speakers' at an advanced proficiency stage. However, other processes, specifically those relatively automatic syntactic processes such as agreement (reflected in the LAN component), seem to be very difficult to acquire in late L2 learning. Similarly, Clahsen & Felser (2006) claim that the ability to process linguistic input in real time is crucial for acquiring a language successfully, but little is known about how language learners process language in real time. They report on their experimental studies to show that some striking differences to native speakers were observed in the domain of sentence processing in adult L2 processing. Adult learners are guided by lexical semantic cues during processing in the same way as native speakers, but less so by syntactic information. They suggest that the observed differences can be explained by assuming that the syntactic representations adult L2 learners compute during processing are shallower and less detailed than those of native speakers.

2.1.5. Language processing, language acquisition, and foreign language learning

The principal foundation of a psychologically valid approach must lie with the processes whereby learners acquire language. Basic to this understanding is the relationship of speech comprehension (Steinberg & Sciarini, 2006: chapter 11). Speech comprehension performance is schematically described as follows:

Sound/Orthography → Processing mechanism → Comprehension grammar → Meaning

When we examine the mechanisms of language acquisition, it becomes apparent that the language acquisition problem is a language processing problem (Berwick, 1987; Fodor, 1998a). For learners to acquire grammar knowledge, they must process the language that surrounds them (Mazuka, 1998). Given the way natural languages work, readers or listeners must recover much or all of the intended syntactic structure of an utterance. The structural characteristics of an utterance, when combined with the semantics of verbs and other lexical items, convey the role assignments that are essential to propositional thought: who is doing what to whom. To discover and extract this information, one must look for evidence in the linguistic input about the syntactic operations that gave rise to the utterance. The dynamic sentence processing abilities develop stepwise in first and second language acquisition. From the onset, a language learner is attempting real-time incremental processing of the input speech stream, and the detection from the speech stream of already acquired linguistic elements including syntactic and phrasal elements is achieved via probabilistic pattern recognition and pattern completion processes (Williams, 2006; Trueswell & Gleitman, 2007). Townsend & Bever (2001: chapter 9) claim that, as language is acquired and processed in the brain, it is important to delineate a general perspective on acquisition that is consistent with language processing models. How might a learner gain access to linguistically relevant structures from the linguistic environment? Recent research has been devoted to studying this in two ways. One approach is to examine the learner's ability to extract and generalise language-like patterns from input. The other is to examine the information in input, the kind of language caretakers address to learners. At any stage of language development, the learner builds linguistic representations with the kinds of structures he/she has mastered at that point. The architecture of a language processing system itself may have its basis in more fundamental processes of language acquisition. To process and acquire language, the learner needs the following knowledge:

Lexical categories
1. Knowledge of the distinct syntactic categories.
2. Knowledge that referentially concrete words are syntactically nouns.
3. Knowledge that referentially concrete words should provide the base description for the category.
4. A prediction to carry out distributional analysis on repeated sequential phenomena in its environment.

Phrase structure
1. Knowledge of phrase structure as a hierarchy.
2. Knowledge that each phrase has a head that defines its type.
3. Knowledge of categories of possible heads.
4. A predisposition to isolate utterance boundaries.

The relation between conceptual and syntactic features

1. Knowledge of conceptual roles.
2. Knowledge of verb-agreement positions.
3. Knowledge that conceptual features of verbs can determine the distribution of verb arguments.
4. A predisposition to search for the distributional regularities of arguments.

The data from language acquisition literature are broadly consistent with the following:

1. The learner has an available set of structural representations at several levels to apply to language.
2. The learner uses initial representational systems to process patterns of language that relate to different levels of representation.
3. Frequency information derived from patterns is used to isolate canonical sets that link different levels of representation. The canonical representations extend the scope of the initial systems.
4. The processes in 2 and 3 cycle to develop more elaborate and richer representational systems.

The basic research issue addressed in comparing L1 processing and L2 processing is whether processing in the L2 is accomplished in the same way as that in the L1. The degrees of observed similarity hinges on three principal factors (Birdsong, 2006): the age at which L2 acquisition is begun, the level of L2 proficiency, and the type of task demanded of the learners. Berman (1987) and Kail (1987) clearly show which psycholinguistic procedures are utilised by learners at different stages in their linguistic development and how those procedures reveal the level of integration of the processing systems.

Much generative L2 research has been motivated by efforts to understand and explain L1 and L2 by contrasting them. A large portion of work is framed in terms of UG, which guides first language acquisition, and whether it remains accessible to the L2 learner. However, Fernandez (1998) argues that language-specific processing strategies rather than a lack of UG access can help account for apparent differences between first and second language acquisition. Juffs & Harrington (1995, 1996) similarly argue that processing deficits rather than competence deficiencies may help explain apparent first and second language acquisitions. Learners of English and English native speakers have the same problems with garden-path sentences. In terms of accuracy, both of them are almost indistinguishable. Their garden-path and wh-movement data show an increased reading time in sentences that were incorrectly judged, which indicates that accuracy is not necessarily a function of the time taken to judge the sentence but rather of processing difficulty.

On a more general learnability level, Fodor (1998a) argues that the nature and operating behaviour of the processing mechanism crucially contributes to parameter setting in the development of grammars (Klein, 1998). White (1991) argues that processing deficiencies alone cannot explain the lack of L2 acquisition progress. White strongly objects to the notion that processing could replace UG as a guiding force in second language acquisition: Processing may account for language use but not for acquisition when the language comprehension mechanism takes input and assigns this input a syntactic structure. On the contrary, Clahsen (1987) and Fernandez (1998) argue that processing strategies may indeed affect and even constrain the restructuring of the target language depending on how the speaker analyses the input. Thus, non-native-like processing routines may result in poor achievement levels in second language acquisition.

Recently, Truscott & Sharwood Smith (2004) offered a model of language development from a processing perspective. They propose an approach to language acquisition, in which the development of language occurs as a natural product of processing activity. They focus on the development of content words, derivational morphology, functional category, and thematic roles as well as apparent cross-linguistic variation in processing strategies. This line of argument has been developed by Pienemann. Pienemann (1984, 1989, 1998a, 1998b, 2002, 2005) seeks to treat the relationship between speech processing constraints and stages of L2 syntactic development. The processing constraints serve to determine the different stages of L2 development. The strategy tries to account for both developmental grammatical features that determine different stages of acquisition and grammatical features that vary within a given developmental stage. The developmental features are the rules such as those designed for word order, whose emergence is determined by the processing constraints. Pienemann has extended the earlier work on processing into the Processability Theory. Simply put, this theory states that learners cannot access structural hypotheses which they are unable to process. In other words, given that processing mechanisms are distinct from linguistic knowledge, there may be linguistic structural options that the learner cannot access because he/she does not have the necessary processing resources available. From this perspective, L2 acquisition can be seen as the gradual attainment of those processing mechanisms. Pienemann argues that if one can determine how language processing develops in the learner, one can predict which structural hypothesis the learner can entertain at a given point in development. The availability of these processing procedures serves to determine L2 developmental stages. Testing his model in Japan, curriculum design, teaching materials, and teaching methods compatible with the processing ability of each stage can be put forward for Japanese learners of English.

As previously mentioned, many researchers agree that there must be a universal language processor in the human brain. Even though the processing mechanism may be the same, at least theoretically, it is highly likely that L2 learners need some training in order to fine-tune their processing strategies (VanPatten, 1996, 2004). It is possible that Japanese speakers are able to use word order as a source of information when processing English, but they use it less than an English speaker because they are not used to it. They may need some specific training in order to be able to pick up not only the grammatical knowledge but also how to use that knowledge when processing sentences. This is where the Processing Instruction of VanPatten comes in. He suggests that processing strategies should be taught implicitly and explicitly to help learners process input, which enhances learning.

VanPatten's work mainly focuses on teaching and learning morphosyntax such as tense marking. However, there are common errors that are associated with the processing difficulty, as follows:

(5) I know Bob that he is a good friend.
(6) I ate Soba was really nice.
I stayed at a hotel can see beautiful view.

In (5), the students do not seem to understand the thematic roles of the verb, which might be a similar problem faced by native speakers in (1). In (6), relative clause constructions are processed inappropriately. While these examples were taken from their writing, errors that are associated with thematic roles and relative clauses are very common in students' translations (to be discussed in detail in chapter seven). Actually, relative clauses, including garden-path sentences, are problematic in processing English and Japanese. We can see that English is a really structure-oriented language, which needs different processing strategies for Japanese learners of English. While proficient Japanese learners of English can process English like native speakers do, students in the process of learning English cannot. Investigations of language processing and language acquisition reveal that processing strategies in L1 and L2, supported by phonological short-term memory, chunking processes, thematic roles, base structures, and complex structures, need to be clarified. However, it is still unclear what strategy should be taught when, where, why, and how. Researching students' errors to elucidate reasons, including the background mechanism, would suggest one possible direction to go. Such research is still in its infancy, and much more psycholinguistic and pedagogical research is needed.

2.2. VanPatten's and Pienemann's approaches to input processing

In this book, I assume that Interlanguage grammar, which represents the foreign language learner's current knowledge (Competence) of foreign language, underlies language use (Performance) (See Brown et al., 1996; Klein, 2004). Some researchers including Pienemann and VanPatten hypothesise that this grammar is constrained by UG, especially by its principles. There are processing mechanisms mediating analysis of the input, and production mechanisms mediating output. There is no direct connection between the input processing mechanisms and the production mechanisms (White, 1991; Fodor, 1998a). These assumptions are presented schematically as follows:

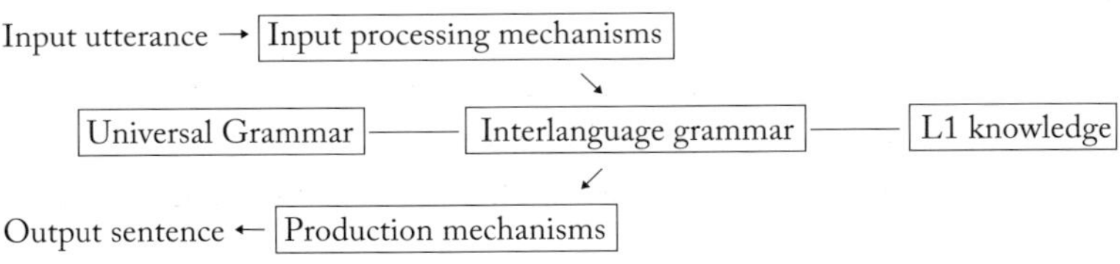

Figure 2–2: Foreign language processing

In order to start building up Interlanguage grammar, the learner must be able to process input. VanPatten (1996, 2004) proposes a number of operating principles to explain the learner's strategies to master a foreign language. The function of operating principles is to help the learner get to grips with the input. The idea presupposes that foreign language learners can process only input that is accessible within the current Interlanguage grammar they hold. When foreign language learners encounter a sentence that cannot be processed, they will judge that their current Interlanguage grammar is incorrect and will modify that grammar so that the sentence can be processed.

An important constraint on input processing is the learner's cognitive capacity for processing information. VanPatten argues that attention is required for learning. Learners first attend to input before they can detect a particular linguistic form. Detection is the process that makes the pieces of information available for further processing. VanPatten claims that one problem is that learners cannot attend to both the content and the grammatical form of the message. This attention to form competes for the processing capacity available to attend to the content. If foreign language learners are seen as limited-capacity processors, they can attend to only so much linguistic information at once, limiting the subset of information that can be detected (VanPatten, 1996: 14). VanPatten (1996: chapter 2) proposes the following input processing principles:

Principle 1 Learners process input for meaning before they process it for form.
(a) They process content words in the input before anything else.
(b) They prefer processing lexical items to grammatical items for semantic information.
(c) They prefer processing more meaningful morphology before less or non-meaningful morphology.

Principle 2 For learners to process form that is not meaningful, they must be able to process informational or communicative content at no (or little) cost to attention.

Principle 3 Learners possess a default strategy that assigns the role of agent to the first noun phrase they encounter in a sentence.
(a) The first noun strategy can be overridden by lexical semantics and event probabilities.
(b) Learners will adopt other processing strategies for grammatical role assignment only after their Interlanguage grammar has incorporated other cues.

Principles 1 and 2 are associated with attention/noticing in foreign language learning. After Schmidt (1990), many studies have been done by applied linguists, such as Robinson (1995, 1996, 1997) and R. Ellis (1999), amongst others, taking a cognitive psychological position. These researchers have been trying to show that learners acquire a foreign language by means of an Attention/Noticing – Comparing – Memory process: foreign language learning results from general processes of human inductive reasoning being applied to the specific problem of language. VanPatten assumes that foreign language learners pay attention to meaning before form when processing input. Principle 3 is derived from well-known psycholinguistic studies on language processing strategies in the 1970's. For instance, C. Chomsky (1969) proposes the Minimum Distance Principle to explain the fact that young children take as the subject the noun phrase that is closest to the verb, irrespective of its grammatical relation to different predicates in the main and embedded clause. Bever (1970) proposes the NVN Strategy, by which children initially interpret such strings as though they mirror the order Actor – Action – Object/Acted-upon. Aitchison (1998) suggests that these strategies should be seen as innate and universal across languages: all human beings are born with these strategies, and when they receive input, the strategies start working unconsciously. Promoting and developing this argument, Pinker (1994), in his evolutionary linguistic perspective, puts forward the idea that human beings have evolved to view the real world as such, which is reflected in language development and linguistic structures.

VanPatten (1996: 147) claims that the acquisition of formal features of language begins with input and input processing. For a learner to be able to eventually access and use a form in output in an unmonitored way, that form must be part of the Interlanguage grammar. We must note that VanPatten's input processing approach is not an account of learning itself. It is an account of what kind of features of Interlanguage grammar are made available for learning. His theory is not meant to be in competition with a theory based on UG, because input processing and UG concern distinct aspects of foreign language learning. VanPatten hypothesises that input processing mechanisms interface with the Interlanguage grammar that is constrained by UG, especially by its principles.

To summarise, attention and detection of grammatical form requires processing capacity. VanPatten proposes that the above principles suggest conditions under which learners can attend to both meaning and form in order to facilitate form-meaning mappings. While recognising that certain kinds of grammatical form present difficulties for foreign language learners, VanPatten advocates grammar instruction that directs learners' attention to form within meaning-bearing input. As the main purpose of VanPatten's research is to propose a theory of new grammar instruction based on the above processing principles, he starts discussing how to teach grammar points, guiding students to learn how to process input in an explicit and implicit way. However, theoretical considerations are still left open: Are the above principles necessary and sufficient to provide a full account for foreign language processing? Exactly when and how do learners gain knowledge of input processing? Isn't it possible to state the developmental stages in formal ways? (VanPatten, 2004, attempts to particularly answer these questions.) A theory that tried to answer these questions was put forward by Pienemann (1998a, 1998b, 2002, 2005). I look briefly at his theory in order to supplement VanPatten's approach.

Pienemann's theory, called *Processability Theory*, aims at formally predicting which structures can be processed by the learner at a given level of development. This capacity to predict which sequence of language is processable at which point in development provides the basis for a unified explanatory framework that can account for a diverse range of phenomena related to language development. Structural options that may be formally possible will be produced by the language learner only if the necessary processing procedures are available that are needed to carry out these computations required for the processing of the structure in question. Describable developmental stages (proposed in Pienemann, 1984, 1989) are caused by the architecture of the language processor. When acquiring a new aspect of language, the processor needs to have the capacity to process it. In other words, a sequence of changes in the learner's processing of the language leads to the gradual attainment of a high-level skill.

The notion of Processability presupposes that linguistic structures that require a high degree of processing capacity are to be acquired later. Under this approach, language processing is seen as the mapping of linguistic structure onto meaning, or how the meaning of an utterance is encoded into a grammatical form. In other words, Processability Theory offers the idea that processing constraints determine the emergence of particular structural rules that are indicators of successive developmental stages of foreign language learning. Given that processing mechanisms are distinct from linguistic knowledge, there may be linguistic structures that learners cannot access because they do not have the necessary processing procedures available. Foreign language learning is seen as the gradual attainment of these computational mechanisms.

In Processability Theory, a set of key grammatical encoding procedures are arranged according to their sequence of activation in the language generation process, and it is demonstrated that this sequence follows an implicational pattern in which each procedure is a necessary prerequisite for the following procedure. The basic assumption of Processability Theory is that the assembly of the component parts will follow the implicational sequence in the acquisition of language processing procedures. Given the ordered route of the procedures, the processing procedures form a hierarchy. Pienemann hypothesises that the processing procedures will be learned in their implicational sequence. The following processing procedure and sequence form the hierarchy that underlies Processability Theory:

1. Lexical procedure
2. Category procedure
3. Phrasal procedure
4. Sentence procedure
5. Subordinate clause procedure

These processing procedures are activated in the above order. The basic assumption of Processability Theory is that the assembly of the component parts will follow the above-mentioned implicational sequence in the acquisition of language processing procedures. The hierarchical nature of the list arises from the fact that the procedure of each lower level is a prerequisite for the functioning of the higher level.

Words (lexical entries) need to be added to the target language lexical base before their grammatical category can be assigned. The grammatical category of a lexical item (such as certain thematic aspects of words) is needed before a category procedure can be applied. Only if the grammatical category of a phrase is assigned can the phrasal procedure be applied. Only if a phrasal procedure has been completed and its value is returned can the function of the phrase (subject, object, etc.) be determined. Only if the function of the phrase has been determined can the sentence be generated. In short, the developmental stages predict which processing procedure is employed at this stage.

It is important to note that Pienemann is dealing not with the origin of the linguistic knowledge but with the learner's ability to process that information in language use. One's notion of linguistic knowledge and its origins is dependent on the theory that is adopted as a theory of UG.

To summarise, when a foreign language learner processes input of his or her target language, he or she is supposed to activate the above cognitive processing strategies and/or procedures. These make it possible to create Interlanguage grammar. VanPatten has suggested that comprehensible meaning-bearing input facilitates foreign language learning. Pienemann proposes that the Processability hierarchy predicts the sequence of production of foreign language learners. The theoretical contributions of processing perspectives are summarised as follows:

(1) Processing influences on L2 comprehension and production.
(2) Processing constraints as determining the subset of input data that becomes available for grammar building.
(3) Definitions of stages of L2 comprehension and production based on speech processing constraints.

2.3. Theory of grammaticalisation: Testing VanPatten and Pienemann in the Japanese context

In this section, we discuss whether VanPatten's proposal and Pienemann's theory are applicable in the Japanese context. One question remains in our mind: originally, VanPatten's approach and Pienemann's theory are based on the naturalistic environments for foreign language learning: both theorists collected data from students learning English or German in English/German-speaking environments. (VanPatten, 2004, and Pienemann, 2005, applied their findings to various ranges of contexts.) It is necessary to test whether their theories are applicable to monolingual environments like Japan, where foreign languages are only taught in the language classroom and are not used at all in the learners' daily lives. In addition, we must note that little attention has been paid to the developmental sequence from words to sentences, but rather people have been more interested in Dulay, Burt, & Krashen's well-known morpheme studies and their applicability in the Japanese context. First, I define what is meant by the term *grammaticalisation*. Second, we discuss the developmental sequence in detail, appealing to the notion of grammaticalisation. Third, I will show some developmental data obtained from English lessons at junior high school, senior high school, and university. The observational data reveal the developmental stages of the learners. Then, the issue in acquiring Functional Categories will be discussed in detail based on an empirical study. Finally, I propose that the learner's development of a foreign language can be explained formally under the structure-building model.

2.3.1. What is *grammaticalisation*?

In this section, we discuss the grammaticalisation processes of foreign language learning. The notion of grammaticalisation is defined as follows:

> The processes whereby lexical items and constructions come in certain linguistic contexts to serve grammatical functions, and once grammaticalised, continue to develop new grammatical functions. (Hopper & Traugott, 1993: 1–2)

According to Newmeyer (1998: chapter 5), grammaticalisation has been a research programme that tries to describe the dynamics of linguistic evolution, change, or acquisition by examining the interaction of grammatical processes. There are striking similarities in the paths of change in language and individual acquisition processes, suggesting that the notion of grammaticalisation provides a suitable basis for examining both the acquisition of grammaticalised semantic relations and historical development in the same area. Along a grammaticalisation scale, the individual learner would start from autonomous lexical elements and step gradually into the grammatical encoding of the target language. Slightly different from the approaches to language evolution, grammaticalisation processes in L2 are considered as having moved items from the lexicon and syntax into grammar (Dittmar, 1992; Ramat, 1992). Case studies by Perdue & Klein (1992), Pfaff (1992), and Skiba & Dittmar (1992) investigate the emergence and development of learners' Interlanguage grammar. What they found in acquisition is the autonomous organisation of subsystems in the developmental sequence that a given learner goes through, where the learner's task is to discover the grammatical structure of the target language and master it.

2.3.2. Developmental stages

This section looks closely at the following six developmental stages based on the grammaticalisation processes in L2 (Skiba & Dittmar, 1992):

Stage 1: No response.
Learners keep silent whatever questions they are asked.

Stage 2: End repetition.
Learners repeat the very end of a word or a phrase that appeared in questions. For instance, when teachers ask 'Where did you go this weekend?', they respond

'weekend'.

Stage 3: Word/chunk communication. (Pienemann's lexical and category procedure)
Learners begin to give responses to the questions with words or set phrases. For instance, when teachers ask 'Where did you go this weekend?', they answer 'Sea', 'To zoo', etc.

Stage 4: Verb island. (Pienemann's phrasal procedure)
Learners produce Subject – Object utterances without verbs, or with a particular verb which is memorised, directly connected to a particular event, such as 'you breakfast', 'I to museum', 'eat eat', 'visit zoo', etc.

Stage 5: Verb acquisition. (Pienemann's sentence procedure)
Learners begin to use verbs structurally in simple sentences, such as SV, SVC, and SVO structures.

Stage 6: Complex structures. (Pienemann's subordinate clause procedure)
Learners start to use subordinate structures.

(1) STAGES 1 and 2
Before learners are able to speak a foreign language, they need to create a processing system to do this job. The first problem learners face is analytic: they must segment the speech stream into units, to which they can ascribe a meaning or function before being able to appropriate such units for their own use. It is important to note that it has been reported that native speakers use a simplified register, called *foreigner talk*, when talking with learners. This helps the learner analyse foreign language (Perdue, 1991). Native speaker's facilitation procedures include clear articulation, stress on important words, topicalisation, use of 'either A or B' and 'yes – no' questions more often than wh-questions, use of short phrases, etc. At this stage, foreigner talk is similar to motherese, that is, the language that is used by caretakers when talking to a small child (Ramat, 1992).

The second problem is a lexical one. Because of the lack of content words, learners cannot identify and understand the message. The identification of items in the flow of speech and their association with context would result in initial noun- and chunk-based learner languages. The learners, recognising a lexical item they can identify in an utterance, repeat it or isolate an item they cannot associate with a meaning and repeat it to get an explanation of it.

(2) STAGE 3

Given a stock of words and phrases, learners are faced with a synthetic problem: how they should use those words. First, the learner acquires the means for essential reference and relations. Nouns for things, calendric expressions, and some phrasal expressions (chunks) begin to appear. This is the initial stage of grammaticalisation: the transformation of communicative formats of expressions such as words and unanalysed chunks into specific productive patterns and toward morphosyntactic norms of the target language. What is crucial at this stage is to extract rules from input assisted by a problem-solving mechanism. According to N. Ellis' (1996a, 1996b, 2001, 2004) sequence learning theory, the following steps are hypothesised to be taken:

1. The process of phonological chunking that leads to phonotactic regularities, word boundary information, the acquisition of lexical forms, word sequence information, collocations, and idioms.
2. Sequential analysis of chunks results in word class information, including thematic structures.
3. Sequential analysis of lexical forms leads to the acquisition of morphological form.(Parts two and three of this book focus on these in depth.)

As we have seen in section 2.2, a learner's input processing mechanism that operates under VanPatten's Principles 1 to 3 (VanPatten, 1996), Pienemann's Processing Procedures (Pienemann, 1998a), and pre-existing world knowledge including knowledge of L1 guides the learner to process his or her target language in a certain order. Learning to understand a foreign language involves parsing the speech stream into chunks which reliably mark meaning. Learners' attention to the target language to which they are exposed demonstrates that there are recurring chunks of language. There are limited sets of sounds and of written symbols, which occur in more or less predictable sequences. An essential task for the learner is to discover the patterns within the sequence of the target language.

(3) STAGE 4

One hypothesis that has gained widespread acceptance in the study of language development is that early language is underlain by some basic categories of sensory-motor cognition. For instance, Brown (1973) proposed that such features as Agent, Possessor, Location, Patient, and so forth were responsible for the fact that the learners, no matter what language they spoke, talked about the same kinds of events in similar ways. In addition to semantic content, these categories are thought to provide some basis for syntax as well. The idea is that the learner has cognitively based formulae for producing syntactic phrases such as 'Agent + Patient', 'Possessor + Possessed', or 'Object + Location'. Tomasello (1992) reports that almost all of the learners' early multi-word utterances revolve around the specific patterns based on the above thematic roles. This is referred to as the Verb Island, since each lexically specific pattern with an invisible (covert) verb in combined speech is evident (Tomasello, 1999). This forms a universal word order of Subject – Object ordering, and a verbless sentence is generated across languages at this stage in first language acquisition and foreign language learning, such as *apples up, you in car, Tom lunch, here my house,* etc. Learners' acquired lexical entries and chunks are combined as above to satisfy the universal ordering patterns (Perdue & Klein, 1992).

(4) STAGES 5 and 6

The relation between grammar and the lexicon is strong in this period of development. Bates & Goodman (1999: 51–53) offer three reasons why grammar and the lexicon are closely related in this phase of development.

(a) Perceptual Bootstrapping

Efficient word perception requires a certain amount of top-down processing, which permits the listener to weed out inappropriate candidates from a large pool of items that overlap with the blurred word tokens often occurring in fluent speech. Grammatical function words and inflections are particularly hard to perceive because of their tendency to be short and weak in stress (see chapter four). In informal and rapid normal speech, speakers tend to exploit the frequency and predictability of function words and inflections. Foreign language learners are unable to acquire grammatical forms until they have sufficient content words that provide enough top-down structure to permit perception and learning of the items.

(b) Logical Bootstrapping

Verbs are acquired later than nouns in first and foreign language learning. Function words tend to appear well after the first verbs appear. Tomasello (1995) suggests that this progression from nouns to predication to grammar is logically necessary. Learners cannot understand relational terms until they understand the things that these words relate to.

(c) Syntactic/Semantic Bootstrapping

The perceptual and logical bootstrapping presuppose that the causal link runs from lexical growth to grammar. Tomasello (1992, 1995, 1999, 2003) and Goldberg (1995, 1999, 2006) show that learners are able to exploit sentential information to learn about the meaning of a new word. It has been shown that learners can use many different aspects of a sentence frame for this purpose, including thematic structures, word order, morphological cues, etc. The lexical elements are projected onto the syntax of the sentence. A syntactic structure is constructed and accepted when a lexicon is found that corresponds with it. The thematic roles and argument structures of the current version of generative grammar offer a useful basis for this. The subject and complement of a verb are called the *arguments* of the verb, and each of the arguments corresponds to precisely one thematic role. Under this view, the meanings of the words indicate which places can or should be filled in what way. Goldberg captures the regularities between the form and meaning of the clause as follows:

Table 2–1: Construction, meaning, and form (Goldberg 1999: 199)

Construction	Meaning	Form
Intransitive motion	X moves to Y	S V Preposition
Transitive	X acts on Y	S V O
Resultative	X causes Y to become Z	S V O Adverb
Double object	X causes Y to receive	S V O O
Caused motion	X causes Y to move Z	S V O Preposition

Although verbs and associated argument structures are initially learned on an item by item basis, increased vocabulary leads to categorisation and generalisation (for more on verb acquisition, see chapter eight). Syntax is considered to facilitate the acquisition of lexical entries and vice versa.

The importance of argument structure in language acquisition is one of the core issues for language acquisition theorists. Bates, Bretherton, & Snyder (1988), Pinker (1984, 1989), Clark (1993, 1995), Bloom (1996), Nelson (1996), Hirsh-Pasek & Golinkoff (1996, 2006), Holzman (1997), Kirby (1999), Bates & Goodman (1999), and Gleitman & Gillette (1999) argue, along with cognitive development including sensory-motor and real-world representations, that children are equipped with an innate ability to process the world as such, which is directly reflected in the sequence of acquisition. Although surface linguistic forms vary across languages, mental representations of the real world are neutral. When children express the events in the real world, they usually need verbs. The above researchers suggest that argument structures of verbs, whether they are innate or not, should play an important role in acquisition. In the field of foreign language learning, Bogaards (1996) and Juffs (1996a, 1996b, 1998, 2000) propose that learning the argument structures of the target language is crucial in grammaticalisation. Bogaards and Juffs argue that foreign language learners implicitly and explicitly focus on the argument structures of their target language while they are learning it.

The interdependence of lexical and grammatical development is compatible with a lexical approach to grammar. However, we must note that a modular dissociation between grammar and the lexicon emerges overtime as the outcome rather than the cause of development (Bates et al., 1988; Karmiloff-Smith, 1992). Grammar and the lexicon are mediated by distinct neural systems in the adult brain. Two kinds of evidence are relevant: neural imaging studies of grammatical and lexical processing, and dissociation between grammar and the lexicon in patients with focal brain injury. The Modularity Hypothesis of Fodor (1983) claims that there is a domain-specific language processor in the human mind, and the grammatical encoder and the lexicon are independent. This hypothesis has been hotly debated among linguists and psychologists (Garfield, 1989; Hirschfeld & Gelman, 1994). Recent development in brain science sheds new light on the argument. Experiments involving fMRI and ERP have revealed which part of the brain is activated during comprehension and production. Regarding the grammatical encoder and lexical storage, it is now widely accepted that the lexicon is processed in the lower part of the temporal lobe, while grammatical encoding and decoding is done by the deeper part of the temporal lobe (e.g., Zurif, 1990). During language development, a lexicon plays an important role in building up the grammatical encoder, which is independent from lexical storage in the final state.

2.3.3. Observational data on foreign language development

Let us now consider the following data obtained from longitudinal observation in the language classroom at junior high school (first-year students), senior high school (first-year students), and university (first-year students). The data were taken in oral communication classes taught by British and Australian teachers. This observational study was cross-sectional, that is, three different groups of students were observed for one year. Students' utterances were recorded in the lessons once a week (recordings took place from the beginning to the end of the lesson), transcribed focussing on teacher-student interactions, a scatter diagram was drawn, and finally the average line of the distributions in the diagram was connected. Fifteen students each took the lessons, and their developmental sequences were observed. Interestingly, the developmental sequences in the classroom are similar among the learners, no matter how long they have been exposed to English. Although senior high school and university students learned English before, their command of speaking had not developed; in other words, automatic processing of their grammatical competence for production lags behind other skills. On the other hand, when they were asked to write something in English, they could produce complicated structures with ease. Their linguistic knowledge of English cannot work automatically in oral communication settings.

At the very beginning of the lesson, all students' proficiency in speaking was tested, and it turned out that most of them were at stage one. (Note that the high school and university students had not taken oral communication classes before. They learned English by means of grammar-translation only.) I assume that sociological factors might be more or less influencing the results. A new environ-

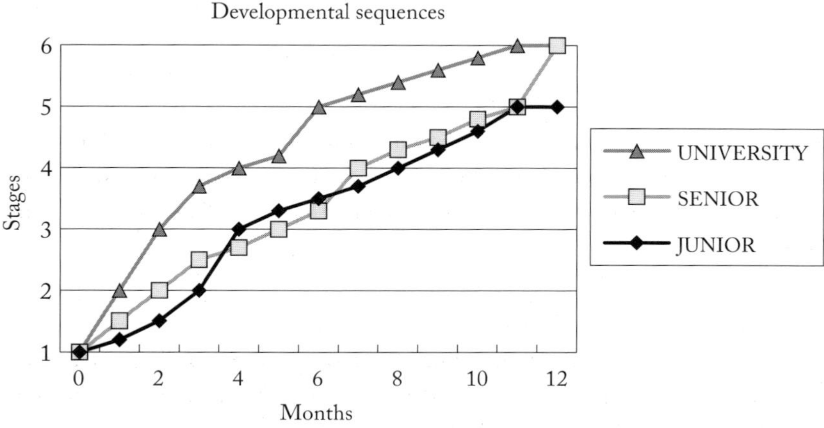

Figure 2–3: Development of foreign language production

ment with new people and a native teacher, students' personality, the amount of previous experiences of speaking English and exposure to spoken English, students' motivation and awareness of English, etc., might affect the results. In addition, the way of talking to the students was different. The native teachers tended to produce short utterances slowly when talking to the junior high school students, but longer sentences with natural speed when talking with the university students. The topics of the lessons were different as well. While junior high school students talked about simple things such as their hobbies, pets, friends, plans, etc., university students discussed more complicated matters like social problems. The mismatch between students' intellectual level and their speaking skill results in the similar developmental sequences shown below. Because senior high school and university students have learned basic English grammar, their speed of development was much faster than the 'genuine' beginners at junior high school even if all of them had proceeded along the same route, but most interestingly, they followed the same developmental routes.

2.3.4. The acquisition of Functional Categories

In this section, I propose that it is difficult for Japanese learners of English to acquire native-like competence of Functional Categories and seek the reasons for this difficulty, appealing to the notion of Maturation in language development. In section 2.2, we have seen that there is a developmental sequence of comprehending and producing English. The developmental stages, however, are characterised by particular phrases and sentence structures of each stage. What I would like to say here is that productions of Japanese learners of English of every stage mainly consist of content words (nouns, verbs, adjectives, adverbs, prepositions, etc.) without obligatory functional elements (determiners and inflections). In this section, first, I define Functional Categories, second, I discuss an empirical study on the acquisitions of Functional Categories, and finally, I seek the reasons for why it is hard for Japanese learners of English to acquire Functional Categories.

2.3.4.1. What are Functional Categories?

In this section, we define what Functional Categories are. According to Chomsky (1988), Functional Categories are 'non-lexical'. Lexical Categories are defined by the features [+/- V (Verbal), +/-N (Nominal)]: [+V +N] = Adverb/Adjective, [+V -N] = Verb, [-V +N] = Noun, [-V -N] = Preposition. Functional Categories are Determiners, Inflections, and Complementizers, all of which lack the above lexical features.

Fukui (1995) claims that Japanese has no Functional Categories. He gives some evidence supporting his claim as follows: As for Determiners, there are no articles such as *a/an* and *the* in Japanese. He assumes that English demonstratives should be considered as Determiners, and Japanese ones as nominal elements. For instance, it is ungrammatical to say '*John's this/that/the book' in English, but in Japanese, it is grammatical to say 'John-no kono/ano/sono hon'. As for Inflections, English has Spec-head relations associated with Agreement and Case-assignment, i.e., feature checking. Japanese, however, has no subject-verb and number Agreement. As for Complementizers, English has I-to-C movement, while Japanese does not. Actually, I-to-C movement presupposes an analysis which itself requires the existence of Functional Categories. Because of these linguistic observations and analyses, Fukui concludes that there are no Functional Categories associated with Agreement, Case-assignment, and Movement in Japanese.

Then, he moves on to claim that Japanese has no Specifiers. He assumes that Specifiers exist only in a language that has Functional Categories. In English, we can witness overt wh-movement, which requires a Spec-CP position. NP in Spec-VP must move to the Spec-IP position to check Case and Agreement features. Japanese, however, has no feature checking of Case, Agreement, and Movement in syntax.

Following these arguments, Fukui finally proposes that structures of Japanese only consist of Lexical Categories. This idea implies that a subject in Japanese stays within a projection of V, and that no Spec-head relations exist in Japanese syntax. (Note that Fukui does not account for Covert syntax in Japanese, nor does he argue whether the existential sentences (*iru, aru*) in Japanese are lexical or functional here. His fairly strong position in his 1995 book has been reanalyzed, weakened, and modified afterwards.) The comparative syntactic approach leads Fukui to propose the existence of a Spec-parameter (Fukui, 1995:141):

The existence of Spec itself could be a parameter, encoded in the X-bar schema, or it might be that the existence of Spec is derived from some other parameter(s), for example, the existence of Functional Categories, the existence of agreement (Spec-head agreement, in particular), etc.

The idea of parameterising Functional Categories is supported by researchers such as Borer (1984), Chomsky (1988, 1992), and Ouhalla (1991). Especially, Chomsky claims that 'If substantive elements (verbs, nouns, etc.) are drawn from an invariant universal vocabulary, then, only functional elements will be parameterised' (Chomsky, 1988: 2). In this approach, parameters are defined in relation to the feature specification of a given Functional Category. Features, as the building blocks of Functional Categories, constitute a universal inventory from which all languages make a selection (Liceras, Zoble, & Goodluck eds. 2008: 8). As the aim of this section is not to construct linguistic theory on parameterisation of Functional Categories, I will not discuss Chomsky's and Ouhalla's proposals in detail. I would rather accept Fukui's proposal which clearly shows how different English and Japanese syntactic structures are under parameterisation. What I hypothesise here is that such structural differences cause learning problems for Japanese learners of English. In the following section, applying Fukui's theoretical linguistic analysis, we will see some data that reveal it is extremely difficult for Japanese learners of English to acquire Functional Categories.

2.3.4.2. Functional Categories are not acquired in full: An experimental study

In this section, we discuss data taken from Japanese learners of English. The aim of this investigation is to show that it is very hard for Japanese learners of English to acquire Functional Categories. If this is the actual case, the result should be that the errors associated with Functional Categories will be made constantly at or above the level of chance by Japanese students regardless of the amount of exposure to English.

(1) Participants

Eighty-two third-year junior high school students (age 15), eighty-two second-year high school students (age 17), and eighty-two second-year university students (age 19) were randomly selected. They are all Japanese male students at upper-intermediate private schools. Both the junior and senior high school are annexed to the university, which means that all students are educated under similar conditions. (There are no entrance examinations at the senior high school and university before enrolling.) This study investigates the changes in similar groups of students who are taught English under similar conditions after a period of exposure to English. The junior high school students learn English for seven hours a week (total previous exposure to English: about 500 hours), the high school students for six hours a week (total exposure: about 900 hours), and the university students for four hours a week (total exposure: about 1,400 hours). All of them take a two-hour compulsory writing class every week, in which writing skills and basic grammar for writing are taught.

Regarding the control group, forty 9-year-old children who grew up in New Zealand and forty 18-year-old university students taking a cognitive science course (with no knowledge of linguistics) who grew up in Britain were selected.

(2) Procedure

All participants were asked to write about a trip in summer as fast as they could in less than 200 words. This free writing test was held in a normal classroom setting. The students were encouraged not to consult a dictionary. Sentential structural patterns of their writing are shown in Appendix B. All students wrote an average of 163 words. As the shortest composition was 150 words in length, investigators stopped counting the errors of all participants' writing at the 150th word. After two British teachers and I read through their writing picking up all the errors associated with Functional Categories, the grammaticality judgement test (shown in Appendix C) was produced based on these errors. All participants took the grammaticality judgement test in a classroom in twenty minutes. In this test, they had time to exercise their knowledge of grammar and to answer the questions with care.

(3) Results and discussion

Figure 2–4 presents the total number of errors associated with Functional Categories in the 150-word writing, and Figure 2–5 shows the percentage of students who made errors. These figures, showing the results of free writing, reveal that errors of Functional Categories exist no matter how long Japanese students are exposed to English. Moreover, errors of subject-verb Agreement (Types 6 and 7) increase in number. (Note that these two figures are insufficient in showing successfully that most of the students made cross-sectional errors, i.e., some students made errors of types 1, 4, and 7 for instance.) However, the situation is slightly different if we analyse the results of the grammaticality judgement test: Figures 2–6 and 2–7 show that students tend to judge grammaticality more correctly as their exposure to English increases, even if the correct response rate is significantly different from native controls ($p<0.01$).

In the writing test, students made many errors of Functional Categories, because they must focus on various aspects of grammar, context, or stylistics, and

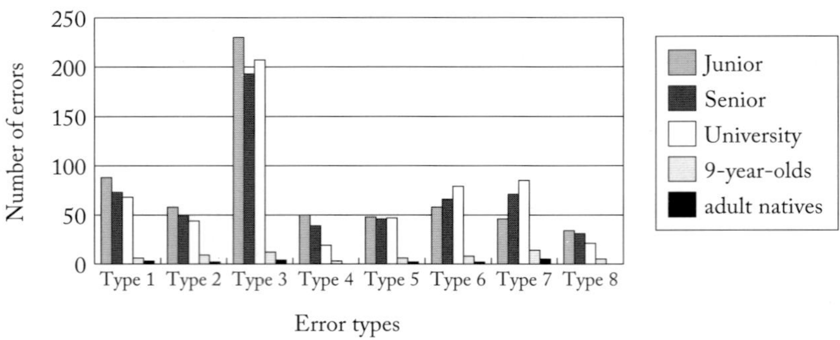

Figure 2–4: Total number of errors in free writing

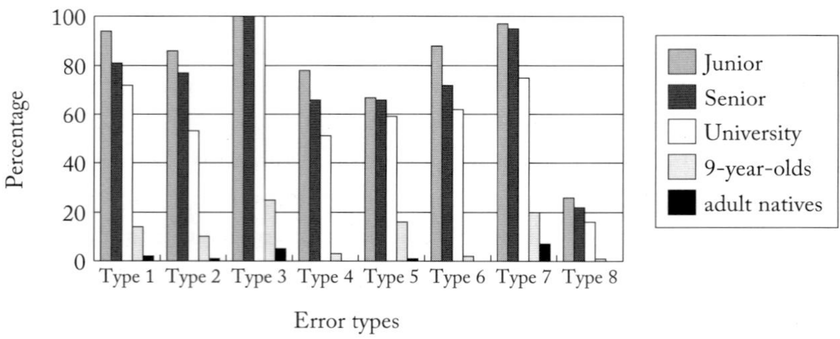

Figure 2–5: Percentage of students who made errors

Type 1: Plural determiner + singular noun (*these book, three car*)

Type 2: Singular determiner + plural noun (*a boys, this pictures*)

Type 3: No determiner where necessary

Type 4: Possessive + determiner (*my a book, his an uncle*)

Type 5: Determiner + possessive (*a his chair, that my room*)

Type 6: Plural noun (subject) + singular verb (*they plays, teachers likes*)

Type 7: Singular noun (subject) + no inflection of verb (third-person-singular)

Type 8: Discourse agreement errors (*Mr Sato taught us English last year, but #they teach math this year.*)

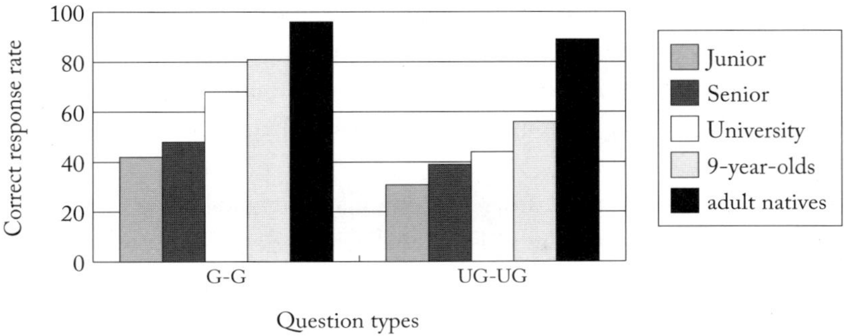

Figure 2–6: Correct responses to grammaticality judgement test

In this grammaticality judgement test, two types of questions were given: grammatical and ungrammatical. The figure above shows the correct response to each type of question.

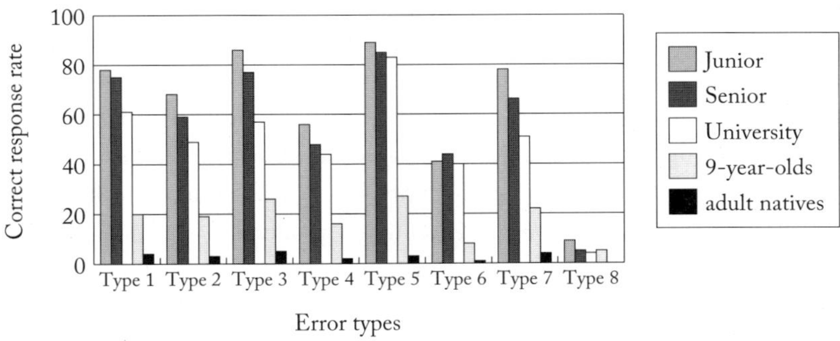

Figure 2–7: Error types in grammaticality judgement test

This figure shows the percentage of students who made each type of error in the grammaticality judgement test.

checking the accuracy of Functional Categories has less priority. Extremely large numbers of Type 3 errors means that Japanese students produce English sentences only with lexical categories. In the grammaticality judgement test where students must use their grammatical knowledge of Functional Categories, fewer errors are made.

The results of the free writing and grammaticality judgement test show that students gain more knowledge of Functional Categories as time goes by, but such knowledge remains as explicit knowledge, which is to be activated consciously. In addition, the grammar rules of Agreement are strictly applied among beginners, but more loosely among older students. Type 6 and 7 errors reveal that although correct responses to grammaticality increase, more and more errors come out in free writing: by consulting the chi-squared tables, we find that, with 2df, the values 6.2 (Type 6) and 8.2 (Type 7) are significant at the 5% and 2% level, respectively. Other errors decrease, because students gain more knowledge of Functional Categories, but errors never disappear.

What I wish to show in this investigation is that Functional Categories are never acquired completely by Japanese students no matter how long these students are exposed to English. While it is very simple to describe the grammar rules for number and subject-verb agreement, such rules do not become automatised knowledge. These results have to do with Krashen's (1988) Monitor Hypothesis: The degrees of using Monitor in production are different among the testing situations, i.e., time given, types of test, psychological factors, etc. In other words, if knowledge of Functional Categories is put to use consciously as Monitor, this means that this knowledge of grammar never becomes acquired (implicit) knowledge, functioning unconsciously and automatically in production. It is intuitively clear for Japanese learners and teachers of English regardless of age that using Functional Categories (especially Determiners and Inflections) correctly is quite difficult. In Figures 2–6 and 2–7, this intuition is identified quantitatively. In the following section, I will try to explain why Functional Categories cannot be acquired fully in foreign language learning.

2.3.4.3. Functional Categories and Maturation

In this section, we seek the reasons why Functional Categories cannot be acquired fully by appealing to the notion of *Maturation* in language development. Maturation refers to the emergence of instinctive behaviour patterns at a particular point in development. The genetic instructions facilitate the expression of particular behaviour patterns when a certain growth point is reached or a specific time period has elapsed (Smith, Cowie, & Blades, 1998: 36).

The notion of Maturation in first language acquisition was originally proposed by generative grammarians such as Kenneth Wexler (in Roeper & Williams, eds., 1987: 123–187) and Andrew Radford (1990). Maturation has to do with the mental development of a language learner: at certain points during language acquisition, certain principles may not be available to the child. UG becomes available in stages as the child develops. This means that the child is unable to make use of a particular type of first language input when not yet mature enough.

The Maturation Hypothesis presupposes that certain constructs of the innately available linguistic information are subject to a predetermined order of emergence. This implies that transitional stages in linguistic development result from intrinsic changes caused by a biological programme. Schachter (1989a) claims that when the programme is completed, no innate mechanisms of acquiring a language unconsciously are available, but different learning mechanisms take over the function. The time of programme completion is considered to be the end of the Critical Period in Lenneberg's (1967) sense.

The Maturation Hypothesis in foreign language learning is similar to Dulay, Burt, & Krashen's morpheme study (1982) and Pienemann's multidimensional model (1984, 1989), because this hypothesis has to do with a sequence of acquisition as well. What is peculiar to the Maturation Hypothesis is that it appeals to biological aspects in language development. While the morpheme studies and multidimensional model show that there is a developmental sequence as such, the Maturation Hypothesis tries to explain in the light of cognitive science why such orders exist, and why adults cannot acquire a foreign language completely.

Psycholinguists have shown that patients suffering from aphasia cannot re-acquire their linguistic competence completely after the Critical Period for language acquisition (Pinker, 1994). The *Critical Period* is a time limit for acquiring the first language. Lenneberg (1967) sets this at around puberty to coincide with the completion of the specialisation of human brain functions. Although some researchers including Sharwood-Smith (1994) challenge this notion, others support this idea as an intuitively clear explanation of phenomena we encounter (Scovel, 1988; Singleton, 1995; Skehan, 1998; Birdsong ed., 1999; Mayo & Lecunberri eds., 2003; Herschensohn, 2007). Researchers who support the Critical Period Hypothesis in foreign language learning consider that foreign language learners are like deaf people who have had no chance to access the language until a certain age (e.g., Smith & Tsimpli, 1995). Brain scientists explain the difficulty of re-acquiring language caused by aphasia as follows: Because of the continuous loss of brain cells after birth and gradual decrease in plasticity that results, it is impossible for patients to develop a new language processor completely again (Elman et al., 1996: chapter 1). This explanation is somewhat wider in scope than Lenneberg's, because while Lenneberg mainly focused on brain lateralisation, the overall decrease of brain cells has been shown to be more crucial. Uemura (1998) explains why adults cannot acquire a foreign language completely under the same logic: Adults do not have enough brain cells and plasticity to develop a new foreign language processor. (Note: although it is true that brain cells are continuously decreasing in number after birth, there are no accurate experimental studies that show this causes any problems within the language faculty.)

Then, why can we learn foreign languages and use Functional Categories no matter how incomplete and imperfect they are? It has been reported in articles by Klein et al. (1994), Gomez-Tortosa et al. (1995), Perani et al. (1996), Dehaene et al. (1997), Kim et al. (1997), Fabbro et al. (1997), Weber-Fox & Neville (1996, 1999), Fabbro (1999), Green (2001), and Paradis (2004) that experiments involving fMRI (functional magnetic resonance imaging) and ERP (event-related brain potentials) have shown that general problem-solving mechanisms are activated when adults deal with a foreign language. According to the experiments with fMRI, when adults process a foreign language, the same location as seen in mathematical exercises is activated, and this location is not activated when dealing with a first language. Consequently, adult foreign language learners build up a unique mechanism to process a foreign language after the Critical Period. Paradis (1997: 332) claims that multiple languages in one brain are neuro-functionally independent, as evidenced by the various nonparallel recovery-patterns of bilingual aphasic patients. This does not imply that the language systems are neuro-anatomically separated, but the well-documented double dissociation between the languages of polyglot aphasics can be interpreted as evidence that each language is represented as an independent neuro-functional system. The articles show that foreign languages are processed by different networks from the first language processor and that the learner's first language plays some role as a problem-solver. For instance, the brain scientists Ojemann et al. (1978), Grosjean (1989), and Gomez-Tortosa et al. (1995) show that early bilinguals tend to develop one language processing system to process their L1 and L2 altogether. On the other hand, medical reports of late bilingual aphasia show that the patients lose only their foreign language or their first language, which means that the first and foreign languages are processed by different networks inside the brain (e.g., Fabbro, 1999). While bilingual brains might deal with two or more languages at the same place with the same mechanisms, adult learners of a foreign language activate different networks from their first language processors. This is an ongoing research paradigm and still hypothetical, but this line of argument can be considered as one possible explanation for adult foreign language processing.

One pioneering study that addresses the question of whether there is a sudden decrease or a gradual decline in access to UG at puberty is by Johnson & Newport (1991). Firstly, they tested Chinese speakers who learned English as adults (over 17 years old). Subjects had resided in the United States for a minimum of five years and used English constantly in their daily lives. Grammaticality judgement tests show that the Chinese subjects perform significantly below native controls, incorrectly accepting many ungrammatical sentences. Secondly, they reported the maturational issue, testing adult Chinese speakers who learned English at various ages (ages 4–7, 8–13, and 14–16). Grammaticality judgement tests show a continuous decline in performance and a correlation between performance and age on arrival in the United States. The 4–7-year-olds were not significantly different from the natives, whereas the other groups were. Johnson & Newport conclude that access to UG is subject to maturational effects.

Schachter (1996b) proposes two ways of viewing the Maturation Hypothesis. One is that there is a period before which a certain principle or parameter is not available to the learner but is available from a specific point onwards. The other is a period after which the principle or parameter is not available to the learner. For certain principles and parameters that depend on interaction with the environment, the principle or parameter will mature. There exists a sensitive period for that principle or parameter, then the sensitive period ends, and that principle or parameter will no longer be available for fixing. Maturation stages are periods bound on both sides by periods of lessened sensitivity. This leads us to conclude that there would be an age range during which a parameter could be reset and ages before and after it when resetting of that parameter could not take place. Schachter (1996b: 186–187) reports that a group of children aged 8–17 (especially aged 11–13) showed strong evidence that they had reset the Subjacency parameter, whereas children aged 6–7 and adults aged 19–25 showed that they had not been able to reset it. The Subjacency parameter has a definite age range before which children cannot set it, and a definite age range after which adults cannot set it. The maturational effects for setting a parameter appear to exist, and those within its frames are able to reset the parameter.

These arguments support the Maturation Hypothesis in foreign language learning: The innate mechanism for language acquisition operates in certain stages of development, but once such mechanisms disappear (or 'melt down' using Uemura's term) as we grow older, developments in cognitive abilities including problem-solving ability take over the function.

Returning to the acquisition of Functional Categories, Radford (1990), Tsimpli (1991), Zobl & Liceras (1994), and Smith & Tsimpli (1995) have shown that Functional Categories are acquired after the lexical-thematic period, in which children produce utterances only consisting of lexical categories without Functional Categories, and if the child's language development stops before the Functional stage that starts around 24 months onwards, a serious language impairment results. Regarding the learning of Functional Categories of a foreign language, the mechanism to acquire Functional Categories in the natural environment is lost after a certain age. Tsimpli & Roussou (1991), Tsimpli & Smith (1991), Tsimpli (1991, 1997), and Smith & Tsimpli (1995) clearly show that such a Functional Module, which is considered to process Functional Categories, is restricted by the maturational constraint in first and second language development. They suggest that the Functional Module is not created after a certain age, whether we call it the Critical Period or not. They propose that parameter resetting associated with Functional Categories is impossible. It was reported by Curtiss (1977) that a well-known child segregated from the world, Genie, had a problem in acquiring Functional Categories as well.

It is widely reported that adult foreign language learning shows the following five properties in common: lack of success, variation in success, fossilisation, positive effects of instruction, and affective factors (Bley-Vroman, 1989, 1990). Cognitive scientific explanation is as follows: It is natural that we should encounter these properties, because foreign language learning after the Critical Period is not totally guided by innate mechanisms with the predetermined biological programme that leads a learner unconsciously to become fully competent in the language, but is mainly guided by general human cognitive problem-solving mechanisms. Although some developmental sequences appear to suggest that adults can acquire a foreign language in similar ways as children, the mechanisms operating in our brain change as time goes by. After Dulay, Burt, & Krashen's morpheme study (1982), quite a number of studies have been done to find a common developmental route among learners of different L1s and age, but Cook (1993: chapter 2) reports that there is no one rigid, consistent developmental sequence. The reason why a learner sometimes uses Functional Categories correctly and sometimes fails to do so may be explained as follows: when we grow older and mature linguistically and cognitively, general problem-solving mechanisms supplement the loss of plasticity. Functional Categories can be assumed to be processed not by the innate Functional Module, but by general (explicit) knowledge gained with general cognitive problem-solving mechanisms. After the Critical Period, there is no brain plasticity to build up a new language processor for a foreign language completely, so it is difficult for Japanese learners of English to attain native-like proficiency in using Functional Categories of the new language. This is the limitation of all of our brains. However, the grammaticality judgement test has shown that the general cognitive problem-solving mechanisms are powerful and reliable enough to gain a sufficient knowledge base to process Functional Categories.

2.3.5. Formal model for foreign language development

This section seeks a unified model for the developmental stages we have seen, appealing to a structure-building model, originally put forward by Radford (1990, 1996). The structure-building model assumes that syntactic structures are projections of the lexical items they contain. The model presupposes that children acquire some types of lexical items before others, for instance, nouns before determiners, verbs before auxiliaries, etc. It follows from the lexical projection view that children will gradually build up syntactic structures one projection at a time, so that acquiring a new type of item will lead to the projection of a new type of phrase (Radford, 1996: 43).

Under the structure-building model, foreign language learning starts with noun phrases (NPs). At this stage, foreign language learners produce nouns or noun phrases as chunks in order to communicate. Then, all learners' clauses at the first stage are verb phrases (VPs) that are a direct projection of the argument structure. Early clauses have no Functional Categories such as determiners, auxiliaries, connectives, etc., and inflictions such as number, tense, gender, case, etc., and thus lack inflectional phrases (IPs). The model assumes that the learner's attempts at constructing grammatical rules bypass the syntactic notions such as nouns, verbs, etc., that are used in the adult grammar. Under this view, UG is in-

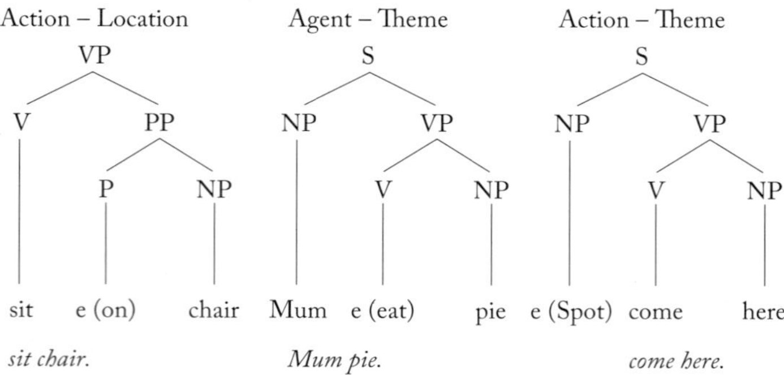

nately designed to make use of syntactic notions from the outset. Utterances in the two-word stage have the following syntactic representations:

The most obvious feature of the representations is that they include positions for unexpressed categories (indicated as 'e') such as the covert preposition, verb, and noun respectively. The positions of unexpressed categories are considered to contribute to a simpler account of a learner's syntactic system. If the unexpressed categories were not present, we would have to assume that intransitive verbs can take a complement NP and that subjects can combine directly with direct objects to form a sentence. Such patterns, however, are not possible in English and do not occur in the speech to which the learners are exposed. The question is why the Interlanguage grammar would permit them. A general explanation put forward by Pinker (1984: 160) is that a type of processing problem occurs between the representation of meaning and the syntactic structure. The idea is that the mechanisms responsible for recognising units of meaning as words in a particular syntactic relation can handle only a very limited number of units per utterance. In the learner's production systems at this stage, a conceptual structure containing long semantic units pass through a filter (sometimes called a 'bottleneck') that generally allows the expression of only two elements or categories.

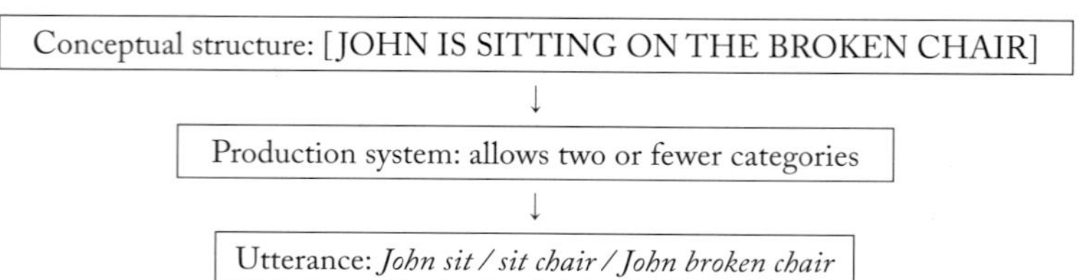

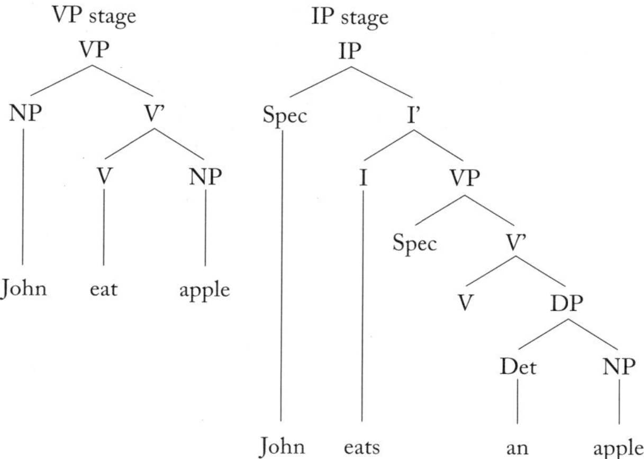

As children mature or the learners develop, this constraint is gradually relaxed, leading to the production of the more complex sentences, and they reach the VP stage.

In a series of studies, Vainikka & Young-Scholten (1994, 1996a, 1996b, 1998a, 1998b) repeatedly show, based on longitudinal observations of various foreign language learners, that learners gradually develop from the VP to IP stage. They propose that if learners arrive at the IP stage, Functional Categories such as determiners and inflections are put to use freely and automatically. As we have seen in the previous section, however, it is dubious that Japanese learners of English can achieve the final IP stage. Putting Eubank's (1994) suggestion into our consideration, features for determiners and inflections are 'optional' for Japanese learners of English, in the sense that these features can be unrealised/covert in their Interlanguage grammar (See *Second Language Research, Volume 16, Number 2, 2000* for further discussion). In their production in a natural environment, few determiners and inflections are used, which means that the IP level is optional in their production systems. They possess a knowledge base for determiners and inflections, which is activated explicitly during production.

Much more recently, Liceras, Zoble, & Goodluck (eds.) (2008) discuss the role of formal features in language acquisition. They claim in the preface and introduction that formal features, which constitute basic components of lexical and Functional Categories and give rise to parametric variation, have played a prominent role in recent generative grammatical theory. Specifically, parameters are defined on the basis of the presence or absence of a feature or a plus or minus value of a feature of a Functional Category in a determiner phrase, an inflectional phrase, or a complementizer phrase. Parametric variation may arise from the fact that languages select different features; a feature may or may not project a Functional Category, which may affect the inventory of Functional Categories that a language possesses. Such variation may spring from the combination of features a language allows for a particular functional projection. It can be suggested that much of the difficulty L2 learners encounter can be traced to the specific constellation of features in the L1 compared with that in the L2. The focus of the researchers now shifts away from a parameter resetting model based on the ability to select features to one where organising features in new combinations becomes the primary task. The question now becomes whether all features remain accessible after a steady state is attained in the L1 or whether features not activated in the L1 are fully available.

Section 2.1 was first published as 'Language processing, language learning, and foreign language education' *JABAET Journal* 12 (2008): 109–129

Section 2.3.4 was first published as 'Parameter resettability' in *Proceedings of the Second International Conference on Cognitive Science* (1998): 400–405

PART II

Learning and teaching English sounds

In this part, we shall discuss how English sounds are acquired and how they should be taught in the classroom. In part one, we concluded that building up a foreign language processing system is crucial, and input processing must be paid much more attention. Input processing includes how learners deal with the stream of sounds, where a lexicon and chunks play an important role. This part considers chunking as a phonological unit and process.

The aim of chapter three is to investigate the ability to unlearn the allophonised sounds in a foreign language. Speech-language pathologists have hypothesised that new sounds should be taught while consciously focusing on the differences between sounds in L1 and those in L2. Otherwise, the learner activates similar sounds in L1, and unconsciously analyses the new sounds as the same group of L1 sounds. This phenomenon is called 'allophonisation'. Past studies have shown that adult foreign language learners allophonise non-native sounds and that instruction would help them unlearn them. However, it is unclear whether all learners of any age can unlearn every allophonised sound. Comprehension and production test results in this chapter reveal that it was extremely difficult (or, nearly impossible) for children to unlearn allophonised sounds. The adolescents and adults showed similar results, while it was possible to train them to distinguish allophonised sounds. Speech-language pathologists' proposal, that is, new sounds must be paid much attention, is true to second language acquisition as well. This chapter shows that in the English as a foreign language environment, children can attain native-like proficiency of English if (and only if) allophonisation does not take place, because it is extremely difficult for children to unlearn allophonised sounds. Adults, on the other hand, can unlearn allophonised sounds by means of training.

Chapter four proposes the significance of teaching weak forms in listening and speaking classes. This chapter shows that weak forms are crucial for English language teaching. This chapter reports on classroom research, in which I show how to put theoretical knowledge into practical use effectively in a systematic way in listening and speaking classes.

Chapter five proposes the effectiveness of applying speech analysing software in listening and speaking classes. According to current English phonetics and phonology, rhythm and intonation, as well as phoneme, are important in describing actual language use in communication. In order to listen actively and speak fluently, rhythm and intonation, which are realised by weak forms, are crucial. In this chapter, I report on classroom research, in which I show how effective it is to use such software in order to help students master weak forms and how to put speech analysing software into practical use effectively in listening and speaking classes.

Chapter 3

Ability to unlearn allophonised sounds

Introduction

When we hear words from an unfamiliar language spoken by a native of that language, we often have difficulty in perceiving the phonetic differences among contrasting consonant or vowel sounds that are not distinct phonemes in our own language. It is commonly believed that attaining native-like proficiency is impossible, which results in foreign accent and fossilisation, and suggested that the earlier you teach/learn a foreign language, the better results you get. However, there are few scientific studies which support such an anecdotal common sense view (cf. Birdsong ed., 1999; Han, 2004; Moyer, 2004). It is unknown how the age factor influences the learnability of non-native sounds. Moreover, inappropriate ways of teaching children L2 might be detrimental. This chapter presents an 'uncommon sense view', discussing age factor involvement in the learnability of non-native sounds and ability to unlearn foreign accent. The focus of this chapter is on segmental rather than suprasegmental contrasts, particularly on consonants rather than vowels and on non-native rather than native contrasts. The successful acquisition of phonological representations requires an accurate perception of phonemic contrasts in the input. It is clear that a comprehensive model of L2 phoneme acquisition must integrate not only a theory of second language acquisition and a theory of phonological acquisition, but also a theory of speech perception (Brown, 2000: 7).

3.1. Allophonisation

The adult learner of a foreign language must learn not only how to produce new sounds (i.e., phones or phonetic segments) in L2, but also how to modify previously established patterns of production. Speech learning requires the ability to establish central perceptual representations for a range of physically different phones which signal differences in meaning, and the development of motoric routines for outputting sounds in speech production (Flege, 1997: 11).

Regarding phonological acquisition in a second language, Major (1987: 109, 2001) and Major & Kim (1996) claim that there will be more interference processes for similar phenomena and more developmental processes for phenomena that are further apart. Thus, L2 phenomena which have similar counterparts in the learner's L1 will be hard to learn because the learner will unconsciously analyse them as identical. On the other hand, the learner will tend to be conscious of L2 phenomena that are very different from the learner's L1. Because of this, the learner will consciously attempt to overcome the L1 interference processes and, in doing so, will produce either developmental substitutions or target language pronunciation. This represents the hypothesis that when an L2 phone is identified with an L1 phone, the L1 phone will be used in place of it. Such interlingual identification appears to depend on the auditory and articulate similarity of L1 and L2 phones. Similarly, Flege & Hillenbrand (1987: 196–197) hypothesise that adult speakers may produce new phones in a foreign language more accurately than L2 phones which have a clear counterpart in the L1, suggesting that new L2 phones may be learned more rapidly than L2 phones which have a clear counterpart in L1.

Flege (1987) examines the ability of adult L2 learners to produce two kinds of sounds: new sounds, which have no direct equivalent in L1, and similar sounds, which differ acoustically from their counterpart in L1. In Flege's view, partial approximation to L2 phonetic norms indicates that an L2 learner has noted an acoustic difference between similar L1 and L2 sounds, and has demonstrated the ability to modify pre-existing patterns of segmental articulation. He hypothesised that learners' incomplete success in producing L2 sounds is due to a cognitive mechanism termed *equivalence classification*: L2 learners develop inaccurate perceptual targets for L2 sounds with a direct counterpart in L1 as the result of equivalence classification. More recently, he elaborates on this as the Speech

Learning Model.

Flege (1995: 263) suggests that the full range of L2 sounds may at first be identified in terms of a positionally defined allophone of the L1, but as L2 learners gain experience in the L2, they may gradually discern the phonetic difference between certain L2 sounds and the closest L1 sound(s). When this happens, a phonetic category representation may be established for the new L2 sound that is independent of representations established previously for L1 sounds. The greater the perceived distance of an L2 sound from the closest L1 sounds, the more likely it is that a separate category will be established for the L2 sound.

Best (1994, 1995) offers one explanation for the difficulty in perceiving non-native phonetic contrasts. Best's *perceptual assimilation model* captures the patterns of influence that a first language has on learning and on perception of another language. According to this model (Best, 1994: 191, 1995: 193–199), difficulty in discriminating a non-native contrast can be predicted according to the relationship between the native and non-native phonologies. If each member of a non-native contrast is similar to a different native phoneme, discrimination of the non-native contrast should be very good. If, instead, both members of the non-native contrast are similar to a single native phoneme, then discrimination abilities depend on the degree of similarity of each member of the non-native contrast and the native phoneme. If members of the non-native contrast are equally similar to the native phoneme, discrimination is hypothesised to be poor. If the characteristics of the non-native contrast are quite different from any native contrast, the non-native items may be easily discriminated as non-speech sounds.

Kuhl & Iverson (1995: 121) claim that, at birth, infants hear differences among all of the sounds of human language, but by the time we reach adulthood, our ability to differentiate the sounds of the world's languages is greatly reduced. Kuhl & Iverson's (1995) study in their laboratory sheds some light on what the mechanism is that underlies the change from a language-general to a language-specific listener. They assume that the crucial developments that lead to phonological transfer depend on changes in the perceptual development of infants during the second half of their first year of life. They suggest a mechanism by which language experience alters phonetic perception. The mechanism is exhibited in a phenomenon called the *perceptual magnet effect*. The perceptual magnet effect shows that exposure to a particular language results in a distortion of the perceived distances between stimuli. In a sense, language experience warps the acoustic space underlying phonetic perception. Language is processed through a distorted lens. The lens acts as a filter through which language passes. Thus, what is perceived as a large difference between two sounds to an individual from one linguistic environment may not be perceived to differ at all by an individual from another. Kuhl & Iverson's theory is that learning a primary language results in alterations of the underlying perceptual mechanisms that affect the processing of language from that time forward.

The perceptual magnet effect shows that a phonetic prototype, good instances of categories, instances that are representative of the category as a whole, and perceptual alternates surrounding a good instance or prototype of the category, exhibits reduced sensitivity and perceptual clustering. The perceptual distance between the prototype and its surrounding stimuli is shrunk, while the region near the phonetic boundary is perceptually stretched. This distortion of the perceptual space underlying phonetic categories is attributed to language experience. This approach holds that nature's initial structuring in the form of natural boundaries combined with the role experience plays in defining language-specific phonetic categories results in the development of first language speech representations that subsequently alter both the perception of speech and its production. The magnet effects exhibited by prototypes of first language categories render certain foreign language contrasts less discriminable, making the acquisition of a foreign language in adulthood more difficult than the acquisition of a primary language. The perceptual magnet effect can illustrate how exposure to language alters perception and may generally reflect a mechanism by which experience can alter the mind of an individual.

Flege (1997: 17) claims that no universally accepted method now exists for differentially classifying L2 sounds as new or similar. To determine this, Flege puts forward three possible criteria for classification. A preliminary step is to consider the IPA symbols used to represent sounds of the L1 and L2. This is followed by acoustic measurements and listeners' perceptual judgements of sounds in L1 and L2. Interlingual identification occurs at a phonetic rather than phonemic level, so the procedures operate on sounds, that is, phonetically relevant phone classes. An identical L2 sound is represented by the same IPA symbol used to represent a sound in the L1. When acoustic analyses are performed for representative native speakers, there is no significant acoustic difference between the L2 sound and its counterpart in L1; listeners cannot detect a difference between the L1 and L2 sounds when a detailed perceptual analysis is performed.

To be classified as either similar or new, some acoustic differences between pairs of L1 and L2 sounds must exist, and there must be evidence that the sounds are auditorily discriminable. An L2 sound that is similar to a sound in L1 is represented by the same IPA symbol as the L1 sound, even though statistical analyses reveal significant and audible differences between the two. An L2 sound that is new differs acoustically and perceptually from the sounds in L1 that most closely resemble it. However, unlike a similar sound, it is represented by an IPA symbol that is not used for any L1 sound.

In the field of foreign language pedagogy, Flege's equivalence classification/ Speech Learning Model (and, roughly speaking, as the explanations for such phenomena, Best's perceptual assimilation model and Kuhl & Iverson's perceptual magnet effect) is termed *allophonisation*. Allophonisation can arise in cases of interlingual identification of phonemes in two languages. A particular sound or allophone that is a manifestation of an L1 phoneme is not always an accepted manifestation of a corresponding target language phoneme (Odlin, 1989: 116).

Let us close this section with an overview of the cognitive mechanism that underlies phonological acquisition. Schmidt (2001: 29–32) claims that the notion of attention in second language acquisition is the function of controlling information processing and behaviour when existing skills and routines are inadequate. Learning in the sense of establishing new or modified knowledge, memory, skills, and routines is a side effect of attended processing. Information that is automatically processed in the L1 without reaching awareness must be suppressed or treated differently in the L2. The learning task is harder in the long run for sounds that are similar in the L1 and L2 than for those that are different. Adult L2 learners are eventually more successful in producing new rather than similar sounds, because they are able to establish phonetic categories for new phones, whereas similar sounds are perceived as equivalent to L1 sounds and therefore escape further attention. It is difficult both to detect and produce the sub phonemic details of L2 categories, because automatic processing is fast and difficult to modify. To do so requires the inhibition of well-established routines so that new ones can be established. In order to acquire phonology, one must attend to the sounds of target language input, especially those that are contrastive in the target language. Attention must be directed to whatever evidence is relevant for a particular learning domain.

Similarly, Pisoni et al. (1994: 155–157) argue that developmental change and associated perceptual recognition in speech perception are primarily due to selective attention rather than any permanent changes in the underlying sensory mechanisms. According to this view, selective attention to linguistically relevant phonetic contrasts operates by warping the underlying psychological space. For speech contrasts that are distinctive in the language-learning environment, the psychological dimensions are stretched so that important phonetic differences become more salient. For speech contrasts that are not distinctive, the psychological dimensions are shrunk so that unattended differences become more similar to each other. This view of the role of selective attention in speech perception can accommodate a wide variety of developmental and cross-linguistic data, and can provide a psychological basis for the mechanisms underlying perceptual change.

In short, the apparent loss of non-native contrasts is due to an active shift in attention away from those acoustic cues that are not phonologically informative. The development of a phonological system is an active process of selecting relevant acoustic properties over the years, learning about the interaction of those properties with the use and meaning of language. The difficulty in relearning the non-native contrast may be a consequence of the difficulty in shifting attention to a set of acoustic properties that have been habitually ignored because they are not linguistically functional in the learner's L1.

3.2. Unlearning

Children acquiring L1 develop accurate perceptual targets for L1 sounds, and eventually acquire the ability to say what they hear. Adult L2 learners have developed perceptual targets for L1 sounds by the time L2 learning commences. If they equate sounds in L1 and L2, the perceptual target they develop for L2 may be based on L1 as well as on the many tokens of L2 sounds they encounter. In order to acquire L2 sounds, adult learners must notice and get rid of (i.e., *unlearn*) allophonised sounds in L2, relearn some muscular habits, and learn to listen in a new way.

Rvachew & Jamieson (1995: 427) argue that adult second language learners have several things in common with people who misarticulate sounds in their first language. First, difficulties in producing sounds are correlated with difficulties in identifying sounds. Second, a structured training programme demonstrably improves perceptual abilities.

The view of some speech-language pathologists is that it is more difficult to remediate patients' production of disordered sounds than to aid them in producing a sound not yet found in their phonetic repertories. If this experience with patients acquiring L1 relates to L2 learning, it may be true that adult L2 learners have more difficulty in producing similar L2 sounds which require the modification of previously established patterns of segmental articulation than new L2 sounds. Gierut (1993: 227) hypothesised that the restructuring of allophones as distinct phonemes is one of the most pervasive and difficult aspects of phonological learning facing second language learners as well as speech-disordered patients. Gierut's study showed that, although it took quite a long time, it was possible to teach adults to restructure allophones as phonemes, but it was extremely difficult for children to restructure allophones. Hardy (1993: 243), based on a longitudinal study with second language learners and speech-disordered people, concludes that learning new sounds not previously in the learner's interlanguage are much easier for them than overcoming allophonised sounds.

It has widely been reported that native speakers of Japanese have considerable difficulty in acquiring /r/ and /l/. One of the reasons why /r/ and /l/ are difficult for Japanese learners to acquire is that there are no phonemes similar to English /r/ and /l/ in the Japanese phonemic system. Native speakers of Japanese perceive the English /r/-/l/ contrast non-categorically, identifying some of the stimuli on the /r/-/l/ continuum as /w/ (Yamada and others, 1992, 1995, 1997; Flege, Takagi, & Mann, 1995). Lively, Pisoni, & Logan (1992) suggest that training adult Japanese listeners to identify /r/ and /l/ appears to be a difficult task but successful. Several factors were shown to be critical to the success of the training programme. A highly variable stimulus set appears to be crucial for the development of robust new phonetic categories. Context sensitivity to both the phonetic environment in which the contrast occurs and to the voice of the talker producing the contrast plays a central role in perceptual learning.

Longitudinal data from Vietnamese learners of English provide insights into interlanguage syllable structure. Sato (1987) argues that L1 transfer emerges as the dominant process influencing syllable structure in interlanguage phonology. Specifically, Sato's study showed that L1 transfer is reflected in Vietnamese English interlanguage as a preference for the L1 syllable in the modification of English syllable final consonant clusters; greater difficulty in the production of final than initial clusters. Broselow (1987a: 272) proposes the syllable structure transfer hypothesis as follows: When the target language permits syllable structures which are not permitted in the first language, learners will make errors which involve altering these structures to those which would be permitted in the first language. Appealing to the notion of *mora*, Archibald (1998: 171) seeks to explain the fact that Korean learners of English sometimes insert an extra vowel in the pronunciation of English words (as Japanese learners of English often do). A mora is a unit of phonological weight that captures the differential behaviour of certain syllable types cross-linguistically. Korean speakers insert epenthetic sounds at the end of the words. Archibald suggests that what the Korean learners are doing is attempting to preserve the mora count of the original English word (which has two morae attached to the vowel). Since this is an illicit structure in Korean, they tend to set up a new syllable which allows the bimoraic structure to be preserved, which is not a difficult task for adults but a very difficult one for children (Young-Scholten & Archibald, 2000).

Regarding teaching phonetic and phonological aspects in a foreign language, Dickerson (1987) reports a study where three groups of participants, Chinese, Japanese, and Korean learners of English, were taught pronunciation formally in a semester-long pronunciation course. They were tested at the beginning and at the end of instruction. Test results showed that the participants were able to use their rules best to improve utterances they had already attempted to say. When they tried to use formal rules before speaking, not only did they fail to progress as much, but they also made more errors than they did before learning the rules. Dickerson (1987: 129) assumes that formal pronunciation rules can facilitate improvement when used for maintaining speech, which are part of learned competence and are of greatest utility when used to identify and correct errors.

Recent studies show that formal instruction of the phonetic and phonological aspects of the target language would be helpful. Pennington (1996, 1998), based on critical analyses of research on the teachability of phonetics and phonology in a second language and an examination of the nature of phonological acquisition, argues that phonetics and phonology can and should be taught to learners of English. Moyer (1999) also suggests that segmental training indicated a performance closer to the native level. Chela-Flores (2001), addressing pedagogical issues on the integration of pronunciation into a language programme, proposes that the learner should be gradually immersed into pronunciation training. According to her, this is better achieved by setting priorities for aural-oral intelligibility in order to better deal with immediate phonological needs, and starting instruction from a beginner level. Instruction is suggested to be effective in meaningful units or tone groups rather than with isolated segments.

3.3. Longitudinal investigation

This section presents data concerned with the acquisition of the /θ/ sound in English, which does not exist in Japanese and causes serious learning problems for Japanese learners of English. Speech-language pathologists' claim, that is, while adults can overcome allophonic treatments of L2 sounds, children cannot, seems to contradict the Critical Period Hypothesis. The Critical Period Hypothesis holds that it is impossible for adults to attain native-like proficiency in L2, and that children can acquire any language(s) before the critical period for language acquisition. If we put the speech-language pathologists' proposal into our consideration, we can predict that it is not difficult for children to acquire non-native sounds if the sounds are not allophonised, but it is hard for children to unlearn allophonised sounds. Adults, on the other hand, can unlearn allophonised sounds with effort. In order to assess these contradictory claims, a detailed longitudinal study was made of 180 Japanese learners of English (children, adolescents, and adults). This study shows the age factor in the ability to unlearn allophonised sounds and in the different distribution of error patterns. The following sections report on this study.

3.3.1. Participants

The participants were Japanese learners of English. Each group consisted of 60 primary school children (age 8), 60 junior high school students (age 12), and 60 senior high school students (age 16). Children and junior high school students had never learned English, while senior high school students had learned English at junior high school for three years. Each of these participants was raised in Japan, and had never been to English-speaking countries. Children and junior high school students had just started to learn English at school. Children learned English for two hours a week, and junior and senior high school students learned it for five hours a week.

3.3.2. Procedure

This longitudinal study took place in the normal classroom. The participants' performance was observed and tested for three years. Three sub-groups were indicated as [+FOCUS], [-FOCUS], and [-FOCUS] → [+FOCUS]. [+FOCUS] means that every time they were taught English, the participants always paid attention to phonological aspects of English in explicit and implicit manners. As suggested by Hardison (1999), visual aids (a picture of a mouth, lip-reading, DVD) were used, and minimal pair exercises were given if necessary. [-FOCUS] means that no explicit instruction of the English sound system was provided at all. [-FOCUS] → [+FOCUS] means that while the participants were not taught phonetic and phonological aspects of English for one year, they received explicit training of English sounds in the second year. The same teaching team (a Japanese teacher of English and a British teacher) taught them for three years.

3.3.3. English sounds investigated

The experimental contrasts were /θ-s/, /θ-t/, and /θ-f/ in an initial, onset, and coda position. In error analysis, /θ-s-t-f/ sound distinction was investigated.

3.3.4. Tasks and materials

An *AX discrimination task* was used to assess the participants' ability to acoustically discriminate English contrasts. In this task, participants hear a sequence of sounds and are asked to indicate whether the words are the same or different. The items used in the test were real and unreal words. The sound contrast in question appears in an initial, coda, and onset position, followed by vowel sounds /a-e-i-o-u/. These tokens were spoken by British teachers in the language laboratory (Sony LLC-2000M system), so that the stimuli were identical for every participant. In order to avoid the *McGurk Effect* (that is, the positive influence of visual or lip-read information on speech perception; see Hardison, 1999: 213), either the British speakers pronounced each stimulus behind a cell or the stimuli were recorded in advance. Note that we did not administer minimal pair exercises. Minimal pair exercise is thought to be effective in the field of speech language pathology (Bernthal & Bankson, 1998: chapter 8). This training enables a learner to notice that differences in sounds lead to differences in meaning. One problem is that some researchers confuse minimal pair with maximal opposition (Yavaş, 2006: 31–36). Minimal pair consists of only one difference in either the manner or place of articulation (e.g., *sun-ton*: manner; *thumb-sum*: place). Maximal opposition, on the other hand, includes more than one difference between the two words (e.g., *chain-main*: manner, place, nasality; *gear-fear*: manner, place, voice). It is difficult to find a 'real' minimal pair. More importantly, minimal pair exercises should be used as a training programme, not as a perceptive testing tool. Learners need to get used to this methodology if researchers adopt it, because sound discrimination without context does not take place in our daily lives (Gierut, 1989, 1990; Logan & Pruitt, 1995). In this investigation, we stuck to AX discrimination tasks.

In addition, participants were given a *picture-verification task*, in which the participant is presented with two pictures and a verbal cue that corresponds to one of the pictures. For instance, the participant would see a picture of a tin cat on the left and a picture of a thin cat on the right side. At the same time, the participant would hear the word 'tin cat'. The participant's task is to indicate which of the pictures the verbal cue names.

Lively et al. (1992) suggest that the presentation of the new contrast that learners developed during training was sensitive both to the phonetic environment in which the contrast occurred and to the voice of the speaker producing the contrast. When listeners are presented with only a single speaker during training, they may become finely tuned to the manner in which that speaker produces the contrast. Retuning perceptual or attentional mechanisms to new speakers may require considerable effort on the part of the listener. Alternatively, participants trained by only a single speaker may lack a strong base of exemplars to compare new inputs against. In this study, the naturally produced tokens used in the training were produced by five different speakers. This presented listeners with a wide range of stimulus variability during learning. In order to dissociate speaker-specific effects, the test items were produced by a different speaker than the ones used to produce the training items. The use of multiple test items produced by several different speakers was motivated by the desire to present the participants with a great deal of stimulus variability during training, which would encourage participants to form robust phonetic representations.

Production tests included a list-reading task and free conversation. Participants read orally from a word list, a list of sentences, and finally a short text. In addition, they were asked to talk about a particular topic freely. Free conversation data were obtained in separate personal interviews (approximately 10 minutes), where the participants met individually with the investigator. Their production was recorded by a Sony LLC-2000M system, and transcribed by British and Japanese phoneticians using IPA symbols. Since I was interested in investigating second language production, the goal was to elicit a variety of sounds in different contrasts. Participants were asked to read a passage. This passage has a wide variety of sounds in different phonological environments. The reading passages were chosen on the basis of the appropriateness of the level for the participants.

Natural texts were altered slightly to increase the occurrence of the target sounds and to reduce excessive repetition of a few specific lexical items. This method was chosen for two reasons: (1) participants would be unable to use avoidance as a strategy; and (2) the pronunciation of words would be elicited within the context of a series of related sentences rather than in isolation. In addition, each participant was interviewed individually and asked to talk about a holiday. Anderson (1987: 284) claims that this topic had proven to be good for eliciting spontaneous speech. Eliciting spontaneous speech rather than administering an articulation test should produce speech samples more akin to performance in a real communicative situation. The participants were allowed several minutes to organise their thoughts before speaking. They were encouraged to speak naturally, and every attempt was made to create a relaxed, supportive environment. Three minutes of spontaneous speech from each participant were recorded, and were transcribed phonetically in narrow transcription using the IPA system of notation. In order to avoid bias, the transcribers, linguists trained in phonetic transcription, were not informed of the objectives of the study.

Students took the above-mentioned tasks twice a year (July and December) for three years. The phonological instructions for [+FOCUS] and [-FOCUS]→[+FOCUS] groups were stopped at the end of the second year, so that the degree of retention could be tested in the third year.

3.3.5. Results

The following tables show the results of comprehension and production tests. In addition, supplementary data, i.e., reaction time of comprehension tests (Appendix D; milliseconds), epenthesis rate of production tests (Appendix E; percentage), and rhythmic impression of production tests judged by native speakers of English (Appendix F; 1: most unnatural to 7: most natural), can be found in the appendices.

3.3.5.1. Children

Tables 3–1 to 3–3 and Figure 3–1 show the performance of children. Differences between Tables 3–1 and 3–2 show that instruction was effective. Looking more closely at Table 3–2, we notice that scores markedly decreased as time went by (average 15% decrease), which means that although children first distinguished new L2 sounds from L1 sounds, this ability was taken over by allophonisation. Interestingly, children confused /θ/ and /f/, which is common among L1 children

Table 3–1: [+FOCUS] (% correct)

		Test 1	Test 2	Test 3	Test 4	Test 5	Test 6
/θ/ - /s/	XV	86	86	87	86	87	87
	CXV	75	77	78	79	78	77
	VXV	83	84	85	85	86	84
	VXC	82	81	83	84	83	81
	VX	93	92	93	94	94	93
/θ/ - /f/	XV	68	70	78	80	83	85
	CXV	55	60	63	69	70	67
	VXV	70	71	70	78	80	78
	VXC	63	68	67	70	68	69
	VX	69	69	71	73	72	71
/θ/ - /t/	XV	83	82	84	88	89	88
	CXV	83	83	82	83	82	80
	VXV	84	84	85	86	85	85
	VXC	83	83	85	86	85	84
	VX	93	95	96	97	97	96

Table 3–2: [-FOCUS] (% correct)

		Test 1	Test 2	Test 3	Test 4	Test 5	Test 6
/θ/ - /s/	XV	71	70	70	68	67	66
	CXV	70	68	67	65	62	63
	VXV	73	75	70	66	68	64
	VXC	68	67	61	62	58	56
	VX	74	69	66	60	62	58
/θ/ - /f/	XV	66	63	58	50	52	48
	CXV	50	51	47	48	43	44
	VXV	49	49	48	43	41	42
	VXC	48	49	44	42	43	44
	VX	50	51	50	48	49	48
/θ/ - /t/	XV	71	70	73	71	74	72
	CXV	73	74	74	70	66	68
	VXV	75	75	73	71	72	72
	VXC	72	73	74	75	72	73
	VX	76	76	75	77	76	75

Table 3–3: [-FOCUS] → [+FOCUS] (% correct)

		Test 1	Test 2	Test 3	Test 4	Test 5	Test 6
/θ/ - /s/	XV	71	70	71	72	70	70
	CXV	70	68	69	71	70	69
	VXV	73	75	76	78	77	75
	VXC	68	67	69	71	70	69
	VX	74	69	71	75	72	70
/θ/ - /f/	XV	66	63	65	68	66	64
	CXV	50	51	54	53	52	50
	VXV	49	49	51	53	52	50
	VXC	48	49	50	54	51	51
	VX	50	51	55	56	53	51
/θ/ - /t/	XV	71	70	72	72	71	69
	CXV	73	74	76	77	74	71
	VXV	75	75	77	78	76	73
	VXC	72	73	74	76	73	73
	VX	76	76	77	77	75	74

(Smith, 1973; Yavaş, 1994: chapters 2 and 3; Gleason, 1997: chapter 3). Table 3–3 shows that instruction was not very helpful if L2 sounds were allophonised. Children could not unlearn allophonised sounds even if instruction was given. Looking at the /θ-f/ distinction, we can see that the children's performance did not improve. Production data in Figure 3–1 show similar results. Although instruction was helpful, the improvement rate was quite low. The /θ-f/ distinction rate was low as well.

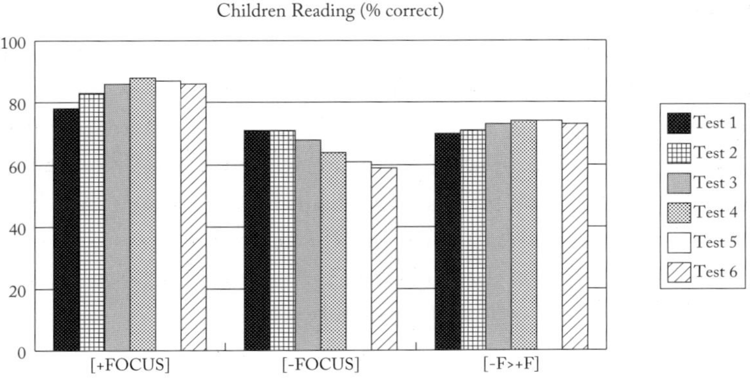

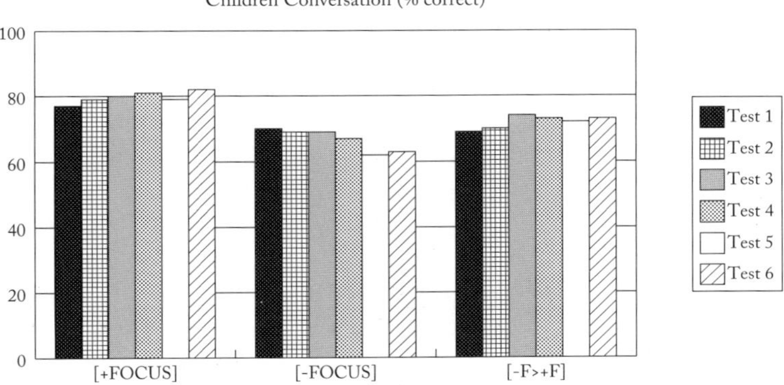

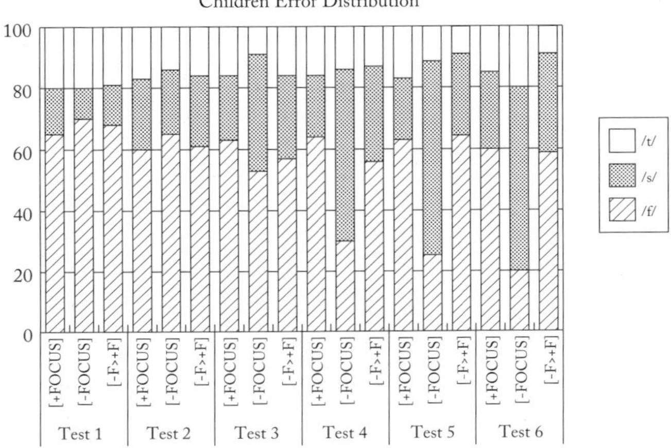

Figure 3–1: Production data

3.3.5.2. Adolescents

Tables 3–4 to 3–6 and Figure 3–2 show the results of the performance of adolescents. Comparing Tables 3–4 with 3–5, we notice that instruction was really helpful for them (average 20 to 30% improvement). /θ-s/ distinction as well as /θ-f/ distinction was difficult, which means that the typical Japanese errors (i.e., confusing /θ/ and /s/) took place among them. Looking closely at Table 3–6, we notice that instruction was helpful even if allophonisation occurred (average 13.5% increase). Production data in Figure 3–2 support this tendency: instruction was helpful and /θ-s/ confusion was noticeable.

Table 3–4: [+FOCUS] (% correct)

		Test 1	Test 2	Test 3	Test 4	Test 5	Test 6
/θ/ - /s/	XV	84	88	90	91	89	87
	CXV	71	77	79	81	80	80
	VXV	80	85	87	89	88	87
	VXC	93	95	97	97	97	95
	VX	96	98	98	98	97	98
/θ/ - /f/	XV	80	80	82	83	82	80
	CXV	78	79	81	83	93	81
	VXV	80	90	89	90	89	88
	VXC	90	90	91	92	90	90
	VX	96	97	98	98	97	97
/θ/ - /t/	XV	83	84	86	88	90	89
	CXV	73	74	75	75	73	72
	VXV	81	84	87	88	88	87
	VXC	80	81	82	83	80	79
	VX	95	95	96	97	95	94

Table 3–5: [-FOCUS] (% correct)

		Test 1	Test 2	Test 3	Test 4	Test 5	Test 6
/θ/ - /s/	XV	66	63	58	59	51	52
	CXV	64	64	61	55	57	54
	VXV	61	60	57	58	53	55
	VXC	59	53	54	50	51	49
	VX	66	68	67	67	63	64
/θ/ - /f/	XV	67	67	65	63	64	63
	CXV	55	56	56	53	54	52
	VXV	53	52	53	51	52	50
	VXC	54	55	55	53	54	53
	VX	53	55	56	55	56	56
/θ/ - /t/	XV	70	71	73	72	71	72
	CXV	68	69	68	70	71	71
	VXV	72	73	72	71	73	72
	VXC	70	71	71	73	72	72
	VX	72	71	70	71	69	70

Table 3–6: [-FOCUS] → [+FOCUS] (% correct)

		Test 1	Test 2	Test 3	Test 4	Test 5	Test 6
/θ/ - /s/	XV	66	63	73	76	74	75
	CXV	64	64	74	77	75	73
	VXV	61	60	69	72	71	69
	VXC	59	53	65	70	68	66
	VX	66	68	73	78	77	76
/θ/ - /f/	XV	67	67	75	77	74	73
	CXV	55	56	69	71	68	67
	VXV	53	52	65	67	64	63
	VXC	54	55	67	69	66	64
	VX	53	55	66	70	69	67
/θ/ - /t/	XV	70	71	77	80	79	78
	CXV	68	69	78	79	73	70
	VXV	72	73	76	80	78	77
	VXC	70	71	76	79	77	75
	VX	72	71	77	79	75	73

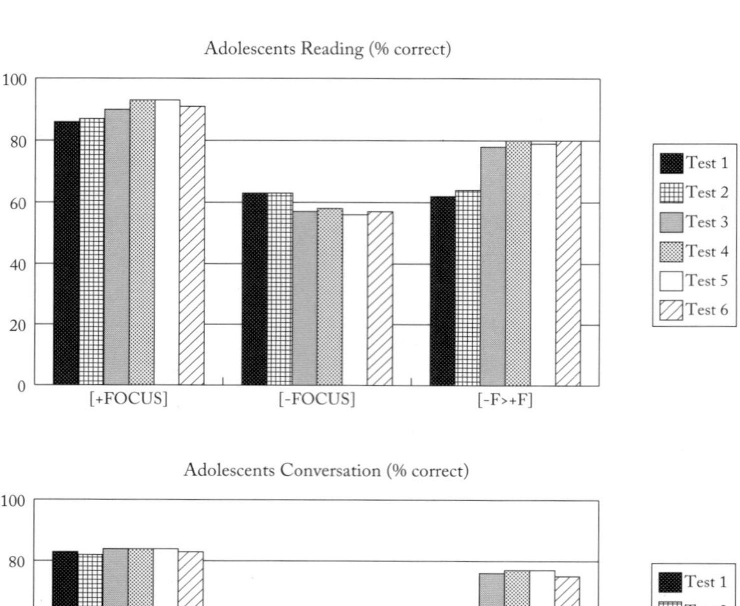

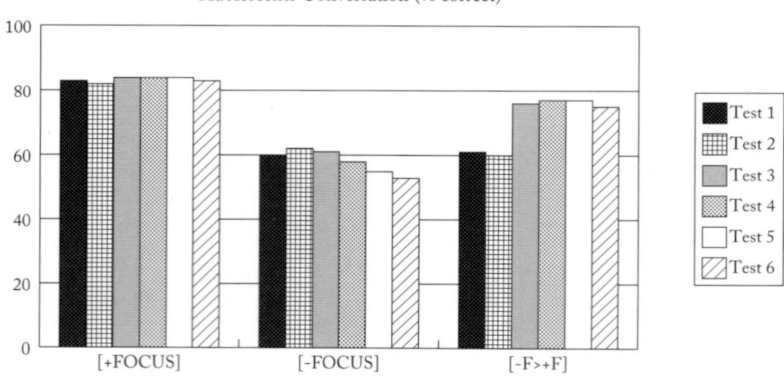

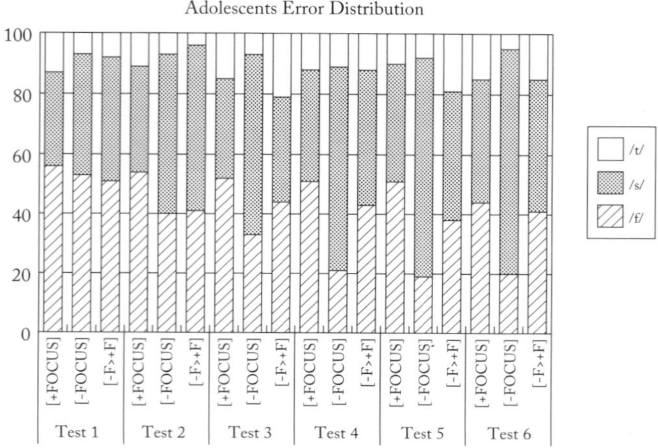

Figure 3–2: Production data

3.3.5.3. Adults

While the overall rate was significantly lower than that of adolescents, adult performance showed a similar distribution. Tables 3–7 to 3–9 and Figure 3–3 show that instruction was helpful (the gap between [+FOCUS] and [-FOCUS] was distinctive), /θ-s/ confusion was noticeable, and the improvement rate was quite high after intensive instruction (average 17.6%).

Table 3–7: [+FOCUS] (% correct)

		Test 1	Test 2	Test 3	Test 4	Test 5	Test 6
/θ/ - /s/	XV	80	81	82	83	81	80
	CXV	68	69	71	73	72	72
	VXV	77	78	77	79	78	77
	VXC	84	84	86	85	85	84
	VX	85	85	85	86	85	86
/θ/ - /f/	XV	71	73	72	74	73	72
	CXV	63	66	69	72	71	70
	VXV	72	74	76	77	75	74
	VXC	80	81	84	84	84	83
	VX	91	90	91	92	91	90
/θ/ - /t/	XV	84	85	86	86	85	84
	CXV	78	82	86	87	87	86
	VXV	83	86	87	87	86	86
	VXC	81	84	84	86	85	84
	VX	91	93	93	94	93	93

Table 3–8: [-FOCUS] (% correct)

		Test 1	Test 2	Test 3	Test 4	Test 5	Test 6
/θ/ - /s/	XV	56	53	48	49	48	47
	CXV	57	55	49	48	48	47
	VXV	58	53	48	47	48	49
	VXC	53	52	49	48	49	48
	VX	63	62	61	62	61	66
/θ/ - /f/	XV	65	63	60	61	62	61
	CXV	53	50	51	49	47	48
	VXV	51	50	51	48	49	48
	VXC	54	51	50	52	48	49
	VX	54	55	53	52	53	51
/θ/ - /t/	XV	71	69	69	70	68	69
	CXV	70	64	66	65	64	65
	VXV	70	67	66	65	64	65
	VXC	71	68	67	69	68	68
	VX	71	69	70	68	69	68

Table 3–9: [-FOCUS] → [+FOCUS] (% correct)

		Test 1	Test 2	Test 3	Test 4	Test 5	Test 6
/θ/ - /s/	XV	56	53	79	81	78	77
	CXV	57	55	69	70	66	67
	VXV	58	53	73	77	75	74
	VXC	53	52	83	84	80	81
	VX	63	62	80	83	81	80
/θ/ - /f/	XV	65	63	71	73	72	71
	CXV	53	50	64	68	66	65
	VXV	51	50	73	76	74	71
	VXC	54	51	76	78	75	75
	VX	54	55	77	79	76	74
/θ/ - /t/	XV	71	69	83	84	82	82
	CXV	70	64	78	80	77	77
	VXV	70	67	79	83	81	82
	VXC	71	68	80	82	80	81
	VX	71	69	84	86	85	83

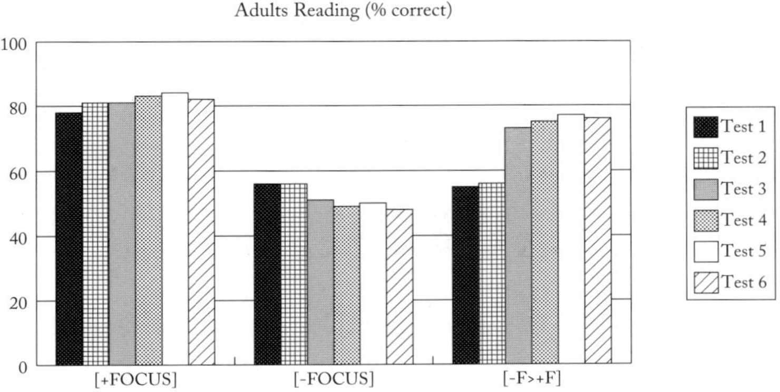

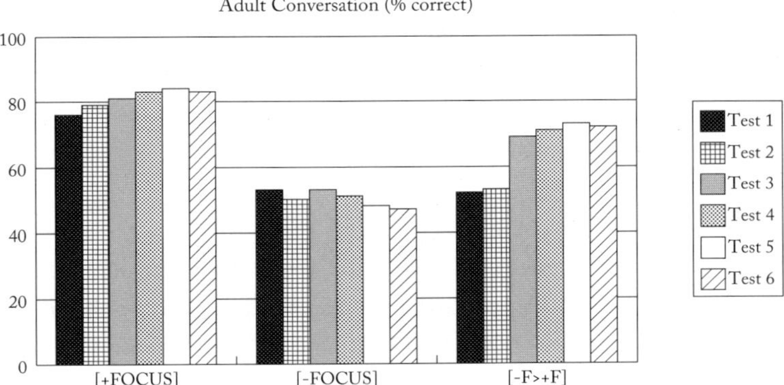

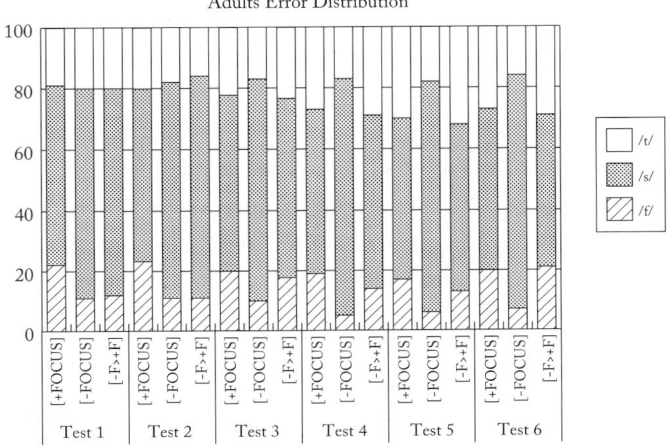

Figure 3–3: Production data

3.3.5.4. [+FOCUS], [-FOCUS], and [-FOCUS] → [+FOCUS]

[+FOCUS] data (Tables 3–1, 3–4, and 3–7) reveal that although developmental errors (i.e., children's /θ-f/ confusion) were inevitable, consistent instruction was helpful in order to avoid allophonisation.

[-FOCUS] data (Tables 3–2, 3–5, and 3–8) reveal that children could discriminate non-native sounds unconsciously at the beginning, but allophonised them as the input increased. Adolescents and adults, on the other hand, allophonised them from the beginning.

[-FOCUS] → [+FOCUS] data (Tables 3–3, 3–6, and 3–9) reveal that while instruction in later stages was effective for adolescents and adults, this was not the case for children. This means that while adolescents and adults could unlearn allophonised sounds, children could not unlearn them. One reason might be that children are resistant to and persistent in the established representations. Even if we emphasised differences explicitly later, they did not recognise them at all.

Production data (Figures 3–1, 3–2, and 3–3) reveal similar results and distributions to comprehension data.

3.3.5.5. Positions

Identification accuracy improved significantly from the average percentage of 57.8% to 79.4%. Correct identification increased from early levels of 66.5%, 63.5%, and 61.3% to levels of 73.1%, 77.8%, and 75.9% (children, adolescents, and adults, respectively) in the later test, demonstrating the effectiveness of the training procedure. As in several of the previous studies (Pisoni et al., 1994; Pisoni & Lively, 1995), large and reliable effects of phonetic environment were observed as well. After instruction, participants were more accurate at identifying /θ/ in word-initial than in word-final positions. Participants were not accurate in intervocalic positions. Targets appearing in final-positions and in final-consonant clusters were identified at a 63.3% level of accuracy. Accuracy in the initial-position, initial clusters, and intervocalic position ranged from 78% correct. Appendix D shows that participants' response times decreased steadily in the environments in which initial preference was good. For environments in which the initial accuracy was low, response times increased at the early stages, but then decreased. This pattern of results suggests that participants required more training trials to determine the appropriate contrastive cues in initial-position, initial-consonant clusters and intervocalic positions.

From the data in Figure 3–1, we can see that children produce a number of interlanguage forms which have /f/ where the corresponding target language forms have /θ/. In addition to this fact, we can also see in Figures 3–2 and 3–3 that some of the interlanguage forms of adolescents and adults manifest alternations between /θ/ and /s/.

The tables show the mean performance scores. As can readily be seen from the tables, the children were significantly poorer than the adolescents and adults at discriminating the /θ-f/ contrast [$t=14.5$, $p<0.001$], and the adolescents and adults were significantly poorer than the children at discriminating the /θ-s/ contrast [$t=-10.8$, $p<0.002$]. (Note that the reason why the t-test rather than the analysis of variance (ANOVA) is used here is that the ANOVA only tells us whether there is a significant difference among the variables but does not necessarily lead us to conclude that one variable is more significant than the others. The t-test, however, makes it possible to suggest that one variable is more significant than the others if it is applied to each variable one by one. In this chapter, statistical support is not reported elsewhere, while ANOVA and ANCOVA were originally applied to raw data. This is because visual inspection of the figures does not lead us to wrong predictions and can minimise statistics, which, I suppose, is important for pedagogical research.)

3.3.5.6. Retention and relearning

Students in the [-FOCUS] group experienced a loss. After this investigation, investigators gave explicit on sound systems (as they did for the [+FOCUS] group) in order to help learners unlearn allophonised sounds. As the [-FOCUS] → [+FOCUS] data clearly show, adolescents and adults could overcome allophonic treatments of sounds, but children could not. Moreover, children could not even notice differences in sound quality even if different sounds were shown with explicit explanations. Their pronunciations were strongly influenced by allophonisation, and explicit correction did not work. L2 phonetic representations of children seem to be firmly grounded and resistant to later treatments. From the very beginning, children need to be exposed to accurate and natural foreign language input which is not influenced by allophonisation because they cannot unlearn allophonic treatments of L2 sounds. (Later investigations reported in chapter five reveal that acoustic programmes, which visualise sound differences, would be helpful for all allophonised learners including allophonised children.)

3.3.6. Discussion

The restructuring of allophones as distinct phonemes has long been cited as one of the most pervasive and difficult aspects of phonological learning facing the foreign language learners as well as phonologically disordered people. Returning to Gierut's (1993: 227) study referred to in section two, it shows that: (1) it is possible to teach second language learners to restructure allophones as phonemes; (2) the training method of minimal pair contrasts is an effective approach to the problem; and (3) the successful acquisition of allophones follows a progressive three-stage course of learning. Prior to treatment, the learner was presented an allophonic problem (stage 1: allophonic rule). Following treatment, the learner's phonology was modified to include an optional neutralisation rule to account for morpho-phonemic alternations (stage 2: neutralisation rule). Then, following more treatment, the learner's phonology was further expanded to no longer include allophonic or neutralising rules (stage 3: phonemic split). Clearly seen in the results above, adolescents and adults follow this developmental route, while children do not if allophonisation occurs.

Regarding Hardy (1993: 243), he claims that the data from phonological restructuring provide the strongest evidence that, for L2 learners, the inventory constraint was easier to overcome than other errored aspects of their system. The inventory constraint was more effective since it resulted in broader changes in the learner's overall phonological system. The Hardy study provides a demonstration that learning new sounds not previously in the inventory will be easier for L2 learners than overcoming other errored aspects of a phonological system. According to Hardy (1993: 244), all trained aspects of the learner's system returned to near 0% baseline levels after only three and a half weeks without training. The learners were not producing any of the treated sounds. In spite of training and demonstrated improvements in performance immediately following training, the phonological changes observed were apparently only temporary. Hardy suggests that the minimal pair method of training actually constrained the more permanent integration of sounds in the phonology. As the data in this chapter show, less intensive, constant, or longer-term training would be effective in order to reach a stable state of phonological processing.

Concerning acquisition of the /θ/ sound in particular, Archibald (1998: 102–103) and Yavaş (2006: 65) claim that it is worth noting that a particular target sound may be realised in different ways depending on the L1. There are non-standard dialects of English which do not have /θ/ sounds: Cockney, L1 children of English: /θ/ → /f/; New York City: /θ/ → /t/. In the realm of second language learning, he asserts that we can see a similar phenomenon when we look at the differing behaviour of speakers:

/θ/ → /t/: Hindi; Hungarian; Portuguese; Russian; Swedish; Turkish.
/θ/ → /s/: Arabic; Chinese; Czech; French; Hebrew; Japanese: Polish.

Weinberger (1997: section 7) discusses the substitution of /s/ for /θ/ and the substitution of /t/ for /θ/ by Russian learners. Articulatorily, Russian /t/ and Japanese /t/ are quite similar, as are Russian and Japanese /s/. Focusing on L1 and L2 phonological rules, he claims that /s/ is to be considered as the default obstruent in Japanese, and /t/ is the default obstruent in Russian, both of which act asymmetrically in relation to their respective obstruents. (Note that spelling th for this sound sometimes triggers the /t/ sound to be produced: for instance, *thing* is pronounced as *ting* among adolescents if they are asked to read out the word, while they pronounced it as *sing* in natural speech.) However, the data in this chapter reveal that it is not possible to make a universal statement as to what sounds will be replaced by what other sounds. Positions of the syllables can affect the pattern of substitution as well: /θ/ → /f/ in initial positions, /θ/ → /s/ in initial and onset positions, and /θ/ → /t/ in onset positions. Our data reveal that non-native children might be sensitive to dental friction just as English children are.

Let us now move on to the age factor in phonological acquisition. The first group of studies of second language acquisition shows marked critical age effects in spontaneity of acquisition and L2 phonology, with progressive deterioration in other L2 areas (Scovel, 1988; Singleton & Lengyel eds., 1995). After the critical period, second language acquisition is no longer involuntary and unconscious. Scovel (1988) claims that phonology acquisition is maturationally determined. On the other hand, Birdsong (1992), Birdsong ed. (1999), Flege & others (1987, 1995, 1999), and Bongaerts & others (1995, 1997, 1999) have tested the nativeness of highly proficient non-native speakers' phonology by asking native speakers to rate the non-nativeness. The results show overwhelmingly that, while native speakers are able to recognise non-native accents even with limited input, advanced learners can attain native-like proficiency, intending to show that no such critical age effects exist. The production accent of L2 learners that appears to shift precipitously to foreign sounding when they are post-pubescent at the age of first exposure is actually susceptible to a more gradual deterioration. In natural settings, child L2 learners initially show L1 influence in their phonology although they ultimately attain a native-sounding accent. Flege (1999) shows that L2 pronunciation accuracy declines linearly with age in natural settings. Flege proposes that non-native-like accents do not result from a loss of ability to pronounce, but rather, they are an indirect consequence of the state of development of the L1 phonetic-phonological system at the time L2 learning is begun. Non native-like pronunciation results from learners' increasing difficulty in establishing new distinct representations of L2 phonetic categories if no training is given. This difficulty is exacerbated when a given target phonetic segment is perceived by the learner to be highly similar to a segment in the L1 repertoire.

Lengyel (1995) and Moyer (1999, 2004) challenge the notion that children are better equipped than adults to acquire native-like sounds in foreign languages. They point to the difficulty of coming to a universally valid conclusion on this matter in the light of the complexity of cross-linguistic phonological relationships. They argue that individual learning strategies will inevitably lead to individual variation in the quality of accent. Their experimental results cast doubt on the claim that foreign accent develops as the critical period ends, and that young children's capacity to speak foreign languages accurately is distinctly unlimited. Bongaerts and others (1995, 1997, 1999) tackle the area of L2 pronunciation, which has been identified as the most vulnerable to critical period effects. Reporting on the results from three experiments, they bring contradictory evidence in the form of late learners who are able to attain native-like accents. The data in this chapter support this position. Adolescents and adults can attain native-like phonological processing in a foreign language.

Finally, let us consider the effects of instruction. Pisoni, Lively, & Logan (1994) report on the results of training experiments demonstrating quite convincingly that adult learners of English can learn to perceive speech contrasts that are not distinctive in their first language. Their findings show that the developmental decline in discriminative capacities is not permanent, and can be relearned in a relatively short period using relatively simple training procedures. Because the underlying sensory abilities are still intact, discrimination training only serves to modify attentive processes that are assumed to be susceptible to realignment. They claim that the previous conclusions about the effects of early linguistic experience on speech perception are unjustified and have been greatly exaggerated in the literature on perceptual development (Pisoni, Lively, & Logan, 1994: 153).

The data in this chapter shed more light on the age-acquisition debate. It has been claimed that before the critical period, children can attain native-like proficiency of L2 while adults cannot. This common sense view needs some modification. In the English as a foreign language environment, children can attain native-like proficiency of English if (and only if) allophonisation does not take place, because it is extremely difficult for children to unlearn allophonised sounds. In other words, if children establish a wrong representation, it becomes poor perceptual ability, and it is difficult for children to remove it later. Adults, on the other hand, can unlearn allophonised sounds by means of training. Training is effective only for adolescents and adults and not for children after allophonisation takes place. Our data clearly show the differences in achievement rates associated with age.

Conclusion

This chapter presented a study which was designed to examine the effects of a number of variables on the acquisition of the English voiceless dental fricative by native Japanese speakers, namely, age of learning (children, adolescents, and adults), explicit instruction (labelled +/-FOCUS), and syllable position. The main issue was age, and whether phonological development could be enhanced by training. Extensive experimental data were reported for both perception and production to show that teaching may help. However, whether it does or does not depends on the age of learners. Children were claimed to be able to develop a native-like accent through training only if allophonisation has not taken place; whereas adolescents and adults could unlearn allophonised sounds and relearn new sounds by training. The key notion was allophonisation. As far as second language acquisition is concerned, the term appears to relate to whether or not there is transfer from the L1 so that L2 target sounds are perceived and/or produced as L1 sounds. Since there is no L2 learner on record who did not show transfer during the initial stages of L2 acquisition, the whole notion of allophonisation occurring or not occurring breaks down. The question that was left to answer was whether there were any restrictions with respect to age and treatment to help learners go beyond transfer and get closer to native-like levels of competence. The empirical data reported in this chapter did appear to provide evidence to support such a claim. Adolescents and adults, who tend to allophonise L2 sounds, noticed and got rid of them through instruction. Children could learn L2 sounds accurately if allophonisation did not take place, but they could not unlearn allophonised sounds. This is where the age factor comes in. This chapter has shown that it is too simplistic to claim that: (1) earlier = better, and (2) adults cannot acquire L2 sounds.

First published as 'Unlearnability of the allophonised sounds' in *JABAET Journal* 7 (2003): 53–87

Chapter 4

Significance of weak forms in listening and speaking classes

Introduction

According to questionnaires on which skills students wish to master, listening and speaking skills are the most desired. Furthermore, from September 2005, the Next Generation TOEFL® iBT Test began to be administered, in which listening and speaking skills are closely focused on. Many overseas students are preparing for it, but seem to struggle with the listening and speaking sections. Every time teachers teach listening or speaking classes, they are often criticised by students who complain that listening/speaking is exhausting, stressful, and boring. Contrary to reading and writing, listening and speaking might be the most difficult skills for students to acquire and for teachers to teach effectively, especially in the English as a foreign language environment. Because sound processing is one of the most difficult facets of language in which to achieve native or near-native competence, we must seek ways of overcoming some of the most challenging aspects of processing a foreign language. In the field of foreign language teaching, although there are numerous publications on how teachers should teach listening/speaking, not all of them are based on firm theoretical foundations. This chapter, following current phonetic and phonological theory, proposes that teaching weak forms is crucial in listening and speaking classes.

4.1. What are listening and speaking?

In this book, based on the communication theory put forward by Sperber &

Wilson (1995) (discussed in detail in chapter one), listening and speaking are defined as the activity to search for, receive, and produce relevant information for the hearer, which is a prerequisite for communication. Listening ability can be considered as the capacity to extract meanings from sequences of sounds, appropriately processing individual differences in pronunciation, wrong-start, hesitation, slips of the tongue, surrounding noise, etc. What is necessary for foreign language learners is the ability to search for words or phrases related to the sounds they hear quite rapidly, to activate encyclopaedic knowledge simultaneously, to process structures based on verbs, to understand pronouns and other referential expressions, and to interpret what the speaker really means.

It is said that there are stages in listening (Brownell, 1996: chapter 1): hearing, understanding, remembering, interpreting, evaluating, and responding. What is most important in teaching any skill is to understand accurately which stage learners are in, and to plan lessons based on this information. There are four types of practice for each stage: phoneme level, word and phrase level, sentence level, and paragraph level. Buck (2001: chapters 1 & 2), Rost (1990, 2002), and Ur (1984: chapters 1 & 2) propose that teachers must be concerned with the following procedures: mastery of the accurate understanding of information given and the fluent processing of sounds to extract meanings. The proposed goals are summarised as follows:

(1) Mastery of sounds and sound sequences that do not exist in the learner's first language
(2) Mastery of intonation including pitch, rhythm, and accent
(3) Mastery of sound change including assimilation and elimination
(4) Accessibility to noise, dialects, and the special habits/properties of individual speakers
(5) Ways of predicting content
(6) Mastery of idioms for conversation
(7) Ways of handling exhaustion of concentration

Concerning speaking as a language skill, learners should be able to produce relevant information for the hearer rapidly in a foreign language, which is quite a difficult task. There are two aspects to be considered (Luoma, 2004: chapter 2):

(1) Linguistic aspects (competence and performance): pronunciation, vocabu-

lary, grammar, pragmatic ability, and processing ability

(2) Psychological aspects: motivation, attitude, willingness, personality, socio-cultural issues, and self-esteem

It is difficult to measure a learner's speaking ability coherently. Let us have a look at the goal of speaking by referring to some speaking tests. In common language tests, speaking ability is evaluated in two ways (Fulcher, 2003: chapter 1; Louma, 2004: chapter 4):

(1) Holistic evaluation (overall measurement of the learner's performance level): ILR rating scale; National Certificate scale; ACTFL OPI; TOEFL iBT evaluation scale

(2) Analytic, diagnostic evaluation (item-based measure): FSI component scales; Test of Spoken English scale; Common European Framework speaking scale

Speaking is evaluated by how fluent and accurate the student's performance is. Some teachers put too much emphasis on either fluency or accuracy, but both fluency and accuracy should be targeted. Traditionally, teachers try hard to teach grammatical accuracy, but recently, pragmatic appropriateness is focused on. On the other hand, regarding fluency, teachers tend to think that pronouncing words accurately leads to fluent speech, and phrase-, clause-, and sentence-level sound changes and intonation have attracted less attention (Hughes, 2002: 39–70). For instance, /l/,//r/,/ð/,/v/ sounds, which do not exist in the learners' L1, have been mainly focused on. In order to teach fluency, however, it is important to teach the rhythm of English as well, which is completely different from the L1 system.

4.2. Relationships between listening (perception) and speaking (production)

It has been said that perception precedes production in language acquisition (Wode, 1997; Pater, 2004). In order to produce language, one must process input, as seen in chapter two. It is reported that children can perceive different sounds that map onto different meanings, but they cannot pronounce these different sounds (Smith, 1973; Kager, Pater, & Zonneveld, 2004). For example, while they can distinguish *fin, sin, tin,* and *thin,* which refer to different matters, they can only pronounce them as *tin*. Smith (2003: 528) suggests that such mispronunciations are not an accurate reflection of the child's perceptual abilities, and that the child's lexical representations are in most respects equivalent to the adult surface forms.

In the field of foreign language learning, if learners cannot pronounce a particular sound, it is highly likely that they cannot perceive it (Rochet, 1995). Leather (1997) argues that while foreign sounds are acquired gradually, students should always be exposed to native sounds, and perceptual training is more important than production exercises. Bohn & Flege (1997) also claim that perceiving new sounds is more difficult than producing them. In the field of frequency research, Sedlmeier & Betsch (2002) and Valdman ed. (2002) argue that in order to achieve fluent and accurate processing, frequency plays a crucial role; learners need to be exposed to the target language frequently in order to create language-processing systems. On the other hand, Goldstein & Fowler (2003) reveal that perception is enhanced by the explicit practice of new sounds. Students learn tongue positions and shapes of the mouth explicitly, and practise producing these new sounds, which enables them to perceive them. Perception and production should be taught simultaneously to help the students become good listeners and speakers.

4.3. Classroom research

In this section, we shall look closely at my practice in the classroom. In this investigation, I did not accept an experimental approach, where the students in the control group experience a loss. I adopted a longitudinal pre-test – teach – post-test research framework instead, which means that effective-ineffective differences would not be shown by calculating significant differences between experimental and control groups. Since listening and speaking are related to each other, both skills were jointly instructed. The goal of this practice was that students could understand and produce English smoothly according to English rhythm.

Investigators taught 100 second-year junior high school students (age 14), 100 second-year high school students (age 17), and 100 second-year university students (age 20). This investigation took place from April to July 2004 (i.e., the first term). They were all Japanese students at upper-intermediate private schools. Both the junior and senior high schools were annexed to the university, which means that all students were educated under similar conditions. (There are no entrance examinations at the senior high school and the university before enrolling.) This study investigated the changes in similar groups of students who were taught English under similar conditions after a period of exposure to English. The junior high school students learned English for five hours a week (total previous exposure to English lessons: about 400 hours), the high school students for five hours a week (total exposure: about 700 hours), and the university students for four hours a week (total exposure: about 1,100 hours). All of them took one-hour compulsory writing and speaking classes every week, in which writing/speaking skills and basic grammar for writing/speaking were taught. Textbooks for them were: the junior high and senior high school textbook series authorised by the Japanese Ministry of Education (*New Crown English Series*); Donald, H. & Kiggell, T. (1993), *Listening Tactics*, Tokyo: Macmillan Language House; Dellar, H. & Hucking, D. (2000), *Innovations*, Hove: Language Teaching Publications; JACET Kansai (2001), *English Listening Strategy*, Tokyo: Kinseido and supplementary materials from phonetics and phonology books.

Pre-test (Listening and speaking)

Let us begin with explanations of how I measured each student's proficiency in listening and speaking. To investigate the development of listening ability, investigators prepared sound discrimination tasks, fill-in-the-blanks, dictations, and content-understanding tasks based on Buck (2001: chapter 5) and Ur (1984: chapter 3). Evaluation of speaking tends to be subjective. While researchers use ACTFL OPI very frequently, lots of training and experience are necessary, without which no valid and reliable results can be expected (Young & He, 1998; Fulcher, 2003: chapter 6). In addition, judgement of fluency depends on how the tester feels: the tester's judgement sometimes differs according to situations, or judgement of non-nativeness differs among testers (Guillot, 1999: chapter 2; Hughes, 2002: 112). In this investigation, in order to avoid inconsistent judgements by teachers, I used a computerised acoustic analytic programme called the *Speech Filing System* (*SFS*) with permission from the distributor. Differences between model pronunciations by native speakers and those of Japanese learners of English were plotted and calculated. A score of 100 means that the model's and learner's performances overlap completely, and 0 means that they do not overlap at all. In order to accept individual differences in pronunciation, some different patterns were programmed (Ashby & Maidment, 2005; Coleman, 2005; Kent & Read, 1992; Yavaş, 2006: chapter 5). Students had chances to use this programme freely in exercises in order to visualise their performances (as Chun, 2002 did). 'Controlled speech' means that students repeat sentences. 'Free speech' means that students speak freely on some topics. Test types shown as numbers are as follows: Sound discrimination task; Fill-in-the-blanks; Dictation; Content understanding; Controlled speech; Free speech. The graphs in Appendix H show the changes in the average score (total score: 100), and the tables in Appendix I show the distribution of the number of students who marked the ranges of the scores.

In order to measure which stage the students were in, investigators administered a pre-test. After the pre-test, the majority of students commented that the recorded speech was too fast to catch, or the audio-system was so old that the sound was unclear. If this is the case, they could score well if provided with recorded speech of a slow speed using crystal-clear CD sounds. The level of the students was the hearing level, that is, the sequences of sounds were meaningless, just sequences of noise. Note that the materials used were not above or below their language levels.

Step 1: Slow speed with clear sound quality (Listening)

Students were taught using materials with crystal-clear sounds guaranteed by CDs at slow speed. As the graphs in Appendix H reveal, however, there were few improvements. This lesson enabled them to recognise that their learning problems could not be overcome by controlling any external factors such as sound quality or speed.

Step 2: Noticing English rhythm (Listening and speaking)

In words, phrases, and sentences, stress and speed change according to whether they are accented, and non-stressed elements tend to be pronounced weakly and quickly, which causes serious problems. Stress is instrumental in the maintenance of rhythm in connected speech. It is said that English is a stress-timed language: stresses occur at roughly equal timing intervals, unlike in Japanese, where the syllable is the most important timing unit of connected speech. In English, the stresses occur rhythmically so that it is possible to tap rhythmic beats coinciding with stressed syllables. This equality in time holds regardless of the fact that the number of unstressed syllables between stresses varies from none to two. Stress equality in time is maintained by variations in the delivery rate of individual syllables (Giegerich, 1992: 181). Students were taught to notice how such sound changes take place. At the same time, rhythmic patterns in English were focused on. Nursery rhymes, poems, rock & pop, TV news, etc., were used to show this. Students listened to and repeated these, focusing on strong-weak sequences of sounds in sentences. The results show, however, that it takes some time to gain higher scores, as students need to automatically recognise such patterns.

Step 3: Teaching weakening processes explicitly (Listening and speaking)
It is not always the case that native speakers of English pronounce each sound/word clearly. Some sounds may be pronounced weakly, even disappear, or are connected and change their quality. Investigators taught the following phonetic properties based on Roach (2001) and Lecumberri & Maidment (2000).

① Elision: disappearance of /t/, /d/, and /h/
last night, bold man, locked door, exactly, send them, etc.
tell him, Does he…?, come here, etc.

② Assimilation: sound-change
・/t/→/p/, /d/→/b/, /n/→/m/, /t/→/k/, /d/→/g/, /n/→/ŋ/
that/p/ man, that/k/ car, bad/b/ boy, bad/g/ girl, ten/m/ pens, ten/ŋ/ keys, front garden /frʌŋk ga:dn/, couldn't be /kubm(p) bi:/, cold cream /kəul(g) kri:m/, won't go /wəuŋk gəu/, red/b/ book, one/m/ by one, shouldn't come /ʃugŋk kʌm/.
・/t/→/tʃ/, /d/→/dʒ/
did you, won't you, would you, etc.
・/s/→/ʃ/, /z/→/ʒ/
Is she…?, dress shop, this year, does she, etc.

③ Linking /r/
China and Japan, draw it, saw it, idea of, Linda and Bob.
In British English, where /r/ is normally unpronounced: bare it, bar and pub, never imagined, where I, before I, care about, our own, there/here is, etc.

④ Vowel shortening: eia → ea, aia → aa, aua → aa/a:
tyre, tower, hour, wire, shower, grower, etc.

⑤ Voiceless
have/f/ to, has/s/ to, of /f/ course, news/s/paper, etc.

Using exercises in Roach (2001) and Lecumberri & Maidment (2000), students had chances to understand the above sound changes concretely. Students were guided to focus on such changes every time they faced them. Exercises included pointing at the sounds that change the quality, filling in the blanks where sound changes take place, and sounding out such sound changes. The results show that accuracy in dictation was improved. They could score well in other tasks as well.

Step 4: Applying knowledge of weak forms to larger units (Listening and speaking)
When processing clauses and sentences, students cannot remember them, and they cannot understand everything at the end. This is called a 'word segmentation problem'. In the field of language acquisition, it is very difficult for children to overcome this stage (Harley, 2008: chapter 8; Tomasello & Bates, 2001: chapters 1 & 4; Echols & Marti, 2004). It is necessary to gain the ability to accurately put the phrasal sequences into chunks so they are easier to remember.

In natural utterances, in order to follow rhythm, functional elements (articles, prepositions, pronouns, axillaries, complementisers, and copulas) tend to be pronounced weakly. Investigators explained the weak forms (see Appendix G), and students practised how to process noun phrases, prepositional phrases, and adverb phrases as single chunks. In the field of first and second language acquisition research, it has been reported that while learners acquire English using stress, rhythm, and intonation as cues, it takes some time to notice weak forms because of their weakness in sounds, which causes a delay in learning (Echols & Marti, 2004).

Fluent speech satisfying rhythms of the language increases accuracy (Pechmann & Habel, 2004). This is because the native speaker's sound processor works smoothly, and processes the speech naturally, correcting any errors automatically. On the other hand, a strong foreign accent inhibits this mechanism, and a conscious correction mechanism starts to operate, which sometimes causes negative feelings. Japanese learners of English are bad at inflections (articles and agreement markers), as seen in section 2.3.4. If they speak with an accurate English rhythm, these elements are weakened. Even if they drop them, native speakers do not care. In the sound spectrogram of natural speech of native speakers, they do not appear clearly as audible sounds (see Appendix J). Investigators explained the list of weak forms, showed them by SFS, and encouraged students to use SFS in order to compare their pronunciations with those of native speakers. As the results show, their scores markedly improved.

Step 5: Processing a verb as the core of a sentence
Paying attention to information structure (Listening and speaking)

English is a structural language, and verbs play an important role in interpreting sentences. In order to process English rapidly, learners need to process agents and patients automatically. Word order functions to show who does what to whom in structural languages. Investigators taught such argument structures together with chunking procedures. In a structural language, one can narrow down the possibilities of what elements (or parts of speech) come before and after a verb, which is helpful in processing such a language.

One of the functions of phrasal stress is to manifest focus. Phrasal stress is a phonological term concerning acoustic prominence, whereas focus is a pragmatic term that has to do with highlighting salient information in the discourse. English has the option of highlighting information via either phonological or syntactic means, i.e., stress or overt movement (Steedman, 2000: chapter 5; Breul, 2004: chapters 6 & 10; Casielles, 2004). Stress is assigned to the new information in a sentence. Archibald (1997) argues that the first language influences the production of phrasal stress in a second language. L2 learners exhibit different patterns of stress placement and completely different rhythm patterns. Experimental studies of intonation and information structure reveal that when a speaker introduces brand new information, it is typically marked with a high pitch. It is only the information which derives saliently from the context or specifically from previous mention in the discourse that the speaker treats as old information of a low pitch.

Japanese learners of English tend to pronounce pronouns too strongly. In addition, modal verbs are strongly accented. These elements are normally weak forms, and if they are pronounced strongly, some intended meanings might be communicated implicitly (Dimroth & Starren, 2003; Breul, 2004). This is related to pragmatics, but advanced learners should master this step. Investigators explained this explicitly, and suggested that students should pronounce weak forms strongly only if they need to be emphasised. Students were shown that stress shifts depending on what the speaker intends to convey, demonstrating the following sentence: *Fred bought a new Japanese car yesterday.* The piece of information a speaker wishes to communicate changes depending on which word is stressed. Strong forms were not taught explicitly, because if a particular form has any informative value it is pronounced strongly carrying emphatic stress, which naturally turns it into a strong form.

Step 6: Understanding contents in detail (Listening)
After students gained knowledge of processing sound sequences, they were taught how to listen to specific details. The prerequisite for this skill is to process the flow of speech with ease. This skill is based on step 5. Students learned to listen to specific details such as key words, time, place, price or events, to capture the situation, theme, as well as main and overall ideas.

Step 7: Retention check (After six months)
In any classroom research on teaching methods, it is important to check whether proficiency is well-grounded after practice. Just after the treatment, good results should be expected, but retention must be checked before researchers propose that any practice is efficient and effective. Six months later, the same method of testing was administered to the students.

Investigators stuck to 'natural English' (i.e., native and native-like English) in their classes. This is because all test results were improved. As Flege (1987) and Valdman ed. (2002) show, frequent exposure to native sounds helps learners learn foreign sounds. It was a pleasant surprise that students did quite well after six months, as sometimes their results decline over time after a period of experimental investigations (see Appendix H).

4.4. General discussion

Much time, energy, and effort are required to master listening and speaking. Creating a new foreign language processing system in the brains needs continuous effort and perseverance. As we discussed in chapter one, using a foreign language imposes a severe burden on one's brain, because thought processing and foreign language processing must be activated at the same time.

Another reason why some foreign language learners do not master listening and speaking is due to psychological barriers. Personality, anxiety, or self-esteem can all affect language performance, which causes differences in motivation, leading to individual differences in finally attainable language skills (Bayley & Preston, 1996; Granger, 2004). As seen in chapter three, in a series of experiments, Bongaerts and his colleagues (Bongaerts et al., 1995, 1997, 1999) demonstrated that the pronunciation of the late starters in their experiments could not be distinguished from that of the native speakers in their tests. Studies by Bongaerts were meant to provide evidence for or against the Critical Period Hypothesis, but one of the side benefits of his studies has been to reveal that certain learners are capable of attaining native-like pronunciation. Probably, only certain learners may be able to achieve this. These learners had the following in common: they were native speakers of Dutch, a language very closely related to English. Moreover, they were English majors at university, being obviously intelligent and highly motivated, and had a great language aptitude as well as positive attitude to English (de Bot, Lowie, & Verspoor, 2005: 192). In my research, those who wished to speak fluently could enhance proficiency, but those who accepted their Japanese accent did not attain either speaking or listening skills very well, which might indicate that production practice influences perception. This is where a child's first language acquisition and adult foreign language learning are different in nature: while children do not care about accent and acquire a native accent unconsciously, adult foreign language learning is influenced by the psychological aspects of learning. More interestingly, production and perception are related to each other, but such psychological aspects hinder foreign language learners in mastering listening and speaking. This tendency becomes more and more obvious when learners grow older, although I have not shown this quantitatively. Some people accept English strongly influenced by L1 (e.g., Japanese-English), and try to establish such a kind of English. However, x-English is like pidgin or Creole. Teaching Creole in the foreign language classroom under the supervision of the Government is somewhat dubious. Native use should be the model learners aspire to, but it is inevitable that non-native use occurs as a result.

Regarding age, there were no significant differences among the junior, senior, and university levels in the results. Looking more closely at the data, junior high school students acquired sound discrimination and fluent speech production faster and more solidly, which might support the view that adolescents attain more native-like fluency, as Snow & Hoefnagel-Höhle (1978) clearly put it. From the very early stage of foreign language teaching and learning, English rhythm should be paid attention to. (More recent debates on the age factor can be found in Mayo & Lecumberri eds., 2003, and Moyer, 2004).

Regarding linguistic aspects, different languages vary in the extent to which they rely on morphology and syntax to signal who does what to whom (Gorrell, 1995; Mazuka, 1998). English tends to rely on word order (syntax: a structural language) to indicate this. In contrast, Japanese permits more variation in word order because it relies instead on special word endings (morphology: an agglutinative language) to indicate this. These differences present foreign language learners with a problem. Japanese learners of English tend to pause between subjects and verbs, and to stress subject pronouns that are not focused (given information in discourse). In addition, they tend to stress every word equally, i.e., pronounce each word quite clearly with the same timing. As we will see in chapter five, this is due to the differences in phonological systems (mora and syllable systems). Under generative hierarchical analyses of phrase structures, the subject noun phase and the predicate verb phrase are located in different positions in a tree diagram. However, studies in language processing reveal that the subject noun phrase and the verb form one chunk (Brazil, 1995, 1997; Levelt, 1989; Vasishth, 2003; Willis, 2003). It is often said that the noun phrase, prepositional phrase, and verb phrase form one chunk. Yavaş (2006: 108) claims that it is important to note that a tone group is a unit of information rather than a syntactically definable unit. Thus, the way speakers shape their utterances depend on what they consider to be the important points in the sentences. From a language processing perspective, the subject noun phrase and verb form one chunk, which leads to smoother and more natural production.

Beginners try hard to follow the strict word order requirement in English, but the results are long pauses between the subject and verb positions and strong stresses on the given-information subject pronouns. Advanced learners produce subjects and verbs as one chunk without any pauses between them and without any stress on the subject pronouns. Native speakers of English feel it more unnatural (and sometimes bothersome) concerning the strongly pronounced subject pronouns and the pauses between subjects and verbs than between verbs and objects. Levelt (1989: 373) found that English speakers tend to store lexical items according to stress patterns, so that if an incorrect pattern is perceived, listeners' comprehension may be hindered because they spend time searching for stored words in the wrong category. Since Japanese is an agglutinative language with overt case marking, the word order is fairly free. On the other hand, English is a structural language with strict word order. In addition, verb inflections must be marked overtly in English. The above problems occur because Japanese learners of English consciously process inflection and strict word order requirements simultaneously.

Conclusion

In this chapter, following English phonetics and phonology, we sought an effective and efficient teaching method for listening and speaking. The results suggest that the following areas should be focused on:

(1) Significance of English rhythm
(2) Significance of stress and accent at the word-, phrase-, clause-, and sentence-level
(3) Significance of weak forms based on rhythm and intonation
(4) Significance of shifting from word level pronunciation instruction to sequences of sounds as chunks

Traditionally, acquiring non-native sounds has been given priority over intonation. For instance, /l//r/, /f//v/, and /θ//ð/ sounds have taken precedence over others. In order to acquire these sounds, new mouth shapes and tongue/muscle movements are crucial. On the other hand, the sound sequence in a sentence has not been focused on. As a result, the Japanese-English accent is flat, and each word is equally stressed through being influenced by the Japanese intonation system. It has been reported that English children are imprinted on by rhythms (Tomasello & Bates, 2001: chapters 1 and 4; McQueen & Cutler, 2001). It is said that native speakers of English can understand what the input means even if nonsense words are given as long as they satisfy English rhythm. In daily communication, rhythm is the most important element in English (Brazil, 1995, 1997). Inflections, including agreement or number, are weak forms, and even if Japanese learners of English drop them, they are amended automatically in the native speaker's brain. Listening and speaking classes should focus on English rhythm consistently from the very beginning to the advanced levels (Pennington, 1996).

English rhythm and intonation are realised by weak forms and sound change. Weak forms, elision, and assimilation need to be focused on from the very beginning. These natural phenomena make the sound sequence smooth, and can be found in any dialect or variation of English. Pennington (1998) and Chela-Flores

(2001) claim that learners of English should become used to English rhythm and learn to produce it in a natural way, otherwise a breakdown in communication might result. No doubt, there is a need for change in the teaching methodology in this context, improving learners' listening and speaking skills. The importance of teaching intonation as opposed to individual sounds and training students to hear as a step towards improving their own speaking have long been accepted among researchers in the field of foreign language pedagogy. However, it is necessary to conduct the rather complex research to show the significance of and an efficient and effective way of teaching it, and convince teachers and textbook writers of its significance in practice in normal classrooms, because weak forms have not been emphasised in English lessons in Japan so far.

Chapter 5

Acoustic analyses of Japanese learners of English

Introduction

In this chapter, we focus on concrete data obtained from native speakers and Japanese learners of English. Acoustic analyses enable us to clarify the differences in production among them. First, we have a look at some of their performances. Second, we discuss the data referring to the notion of mora in phonology. The data to be discussed in this chapter were obtained in the classroom when an efficient and effective teaching methodology discussed in detail in chapter four was investigated. Then, we show the effectiveness of applying acoustic programmes to the language classroom, accepting the instruction put forward in the previous chapter.

5.1. Comparison of British and Japanese speakers

In this section, let us look closely at the acoustic data in Appendix J. The data are based on native and non-native performances. I used a computerised acoustic analytic programme called the *Speech Filing System* (*SFS*) with permission from the distributor (SFS Release 4.5 Windows, SFS Version 1.4 30–01–2004, Free Software distributed by the Department of Phonetics and Linguistics, University College London, http://www.phon.ucl.ac.uk/resource/sfs/).

(1) *Do you ?*

Native speakers produced these two words as one syllable, while Japanese learners produced them as two syllables. Native speakers pronounced the sequence of sound as /ʤú:/, but a vowel sound /u/ was produced after /d/ among Japanese learners. The quality of sound remains the same in Japanese data. The production time of Japanese is twice as long as that of native speakers, because Japanese learners pronounced this as /du:ju:/. In addition, a marked rising tone can be seen in Japanese data, which means that *you* is strongly accented, but pronounced very weakly among native speakers.

(2) *Check it out.*
The native and Japanese pitch curve is similar, but the division of each syllable is obvious in Japanese production. Each word, *check*, *it*, and *out*, were pronounced clearly by Japanese, while *it* was pronounced weakly and changed its quality by linking with *check* and *out* among native speakers. In addition, word final vibration in Japanese data shows that a vowel sound /u/ or /o/ is pronounced at the end of each word. This is one of the commonest errors, i.e., vowel insertion after consonants where inappropriate, called *epenthesis*.

(3) *Tell him about it.*
Native speakers did not pronounce the /h/ sound clearly, pronounced like /telm/, and the /t/ sound in *about* changed its quality to the /r/ sound. Japanese learners pronounced /h/ quite strongly, and the final plosive was strong and clear and vowels were unclear in *about*. The overall syllable duration is different between native and Japanese data. Japanese learners pronounced each word clearly and separately without any sound change.

(4) *Do you play tennis?*
The voice onset time of /p/ and /t/ was long in native speakers, while very short in Japanese. As we saw in (1), *do you* was pronounced differently among them. In addition, lip rounding at the end of *tennis* reveals that this word was pronounced as /tenisu/ or /teniʃu/ among Japanese speakers. This is another typical error that relates to *aspiration*. Although it does not involve a contrast between phonemes, the presence or absence of aspiration in voiceless stops is a source of perceived foreign accent.

(5) *He came to our party last night.*
The pronoun *he* was pronounced clearly among Japanese, while disappearing

among native speakers. The duration of time for pronouncing *he* was nearly three times longer in Japanese, and the vowel sound /i/ was strongly produced. The sequence *to our* was clearly pronounced in Japanese, while it was pronounced weakly in native speakers. Word final /t/ sounds in *last night* were omitted among native speakers, while produced clearly among Japanese. The overall duration and production speed were very different, because Japanese learners pronounced each word clearly with the same timing.

5.2. Mora, epenthesis, and aspiration

Languages are traditionally classified into three basic rhythmic types: syllable-timing, stress-timing, and mora-timing. The fundamental difference between mora-timed and syllable-timed languages lies in the durational difference between C(onsonant)V(owel)s and CVCs or CVVs and its function in the phonological system. In mora-timed languages, the two types of syllable form distinct classes where CVCs and CVVs take twice as long as CVs. In syllable-timed languages, on the other hand, the presence or absence of post-nuclear elements makes virtually no difference and the two types of syllable play essentially the same role in the temporal organisation of speech. In addition, a syllable-timed language like Spanish or French has syllables of roughly equal length regardless of stress. A stress-timed language including English has stressed syllables much longer than unstressed syllables and has equal beats between major stress groups. The durations between the major stresses are roughly equal in length even though the number of intervening syllables varies. In order to accomplish this, English lengthens stressed syllables and shortens or reduces unstressed syllables. In a mora-timed language, the unit of timing is the mora. The mora is a unit of quantity referring to the number of segments in the rhyme but not the onset (Bernhardt, 1994; Major, 2001: 14). Morae are of equal length, so a syllable with two morae is twice as long as a syllable with one. In Japanese, both vowel and consonant length is contrastive and can result in morae of different lengths. It can be assumed that native speakers of mora-timed languages will become sensitive to the distinction between CVs and CVCs or CVVs and come to employ a CV-based segmentation strategy when producing and perceiving speech (Kubozono, 1996). Japanese learners of English have a tendency to lengthen heavy syllables in English, whereas, for a native speaker of English, the syllables are approximately equal in length. The mora functions as a phonological position.

In languages with contrastive vowel length, a short vowel has one mora and a long vowel has two morae. In addition, the mora is a unit of weight. Syllables can be divided into two classes that differ in their degree of prominence in prosodic phenomena. The difference is represented by the number of morae dominated by the syllable: a syllable with one mora is light and a syllable with two is heavy. (For phonological evidence for the existence of mora in Japanese, see Haraguchi, 1996; Lehiste, 1997; Ota, 2003: 17–19). Kubozono (1996: 78) argues that the roles of the mora in Japanese fall into four types: a unit by which to measure phonological weight or distance, a timing unit or a unit of temporal regulation of natural connected speech, a unit by which to segment speech in production, and a unit by which to segment speech in perception. Such phonological differences in languages cause learning problems. One of the commonest errors is vowel insertion after consonants where inappropriate, called *epenthesis*.

Carlisle (1999) investigated the frequency of epenthesis. Epenthesis occurred least after vowels before CC onsets, second most after vowels before CCC onsets, and third after consonants before CCC onsets. In other words, the least occurrences followed vowels and the 2 highest followed consonants. The proportions of epenthesis after word-final vowels were lower than those after word-final consonants. Hammarberg (1997) and Weinberger (1997) reveal that production data of German learners seldom show epenthesis and that this is due to the property of the learner's first language. When these L2 learners encounter consonant clusters in English, they simply apply the general strategy of vowel epenthesis to restructure the syllables. Archibald (1998: 171–174) reports an interesting finding regarding the occurrence of epenthesis. Korean learners of English sometimes insert an extra vowel in the pronunciation of English words, but sometimes do not. He suggests that it is the quality of the vowel in the English root that determines whether epenthesis takes place. The epenthetic vowel is added to words that have long vowels and not to words that have short vowels. In Japanese, however, we could not find this regularity. Tarone (1987) shows that the syllable structure of L2 is often different from that of the target language and that epenthesis is used as a strategy for syllable simplification with the first language background of the learner related to a preference. Epenthesis can be directly attributed to the use by language learners of a phonological rule in the production of second language forms (Broselow, 1987b). On the other hand, Weinberger (1994) claims that vowel epenthesis is not employed regularly among children. Young L1 learners of English rarely utilise epenthesis, which means that epenthesis is a property peculiar to second language learning.

Another typical error can be found in aspiration. Although it does not involve a contrast between phonemes, the presence or absence of aspiration in voiceless stops is a source of perceived foreign accent. Nathan, Anderson, & Budsayamongkon (1987) investigated the way adults acquire aspirated voiceless stops when their first language lacks them. Voiced stops, voiceless unaspirated stops, and voiceless aspirated stops can be arranged along a continuum called the voice onset time (VOT). VOT refers to the interval between the release of the articulators and the beginning of regular vocal cord pulses (Yavaş, 2006: 9–11). Aspiration is acquired gradually by stretching their VOT, learning to produce greater delays in the onset of voicing relative to the release of the consonant.

Our data in section 5.1 show the above phenomenon. If this is the case, what we need to develop is an efficient and effective way of learning target sound systems to overcome such errors. Although past empirical research pointed out typical L2 errors two or three decades ago, few methodologies based on phonetics and phonology can be found. This is why Japanese learners of English in the twenty-first century still cannot overcome the predicted errors. In the next section, we shall move on to identify more efficient and effective ways of instruction based on phonetics and phonology with recent technological developments.

5.3. Effectiveness of acoustic programmes in the classroom

This section proposes the effectiveness of using speech analysis software in listening and speaking classes. The use of such software is a rather new, still-to-be-proven approach in the second language classroom. Furthermore, there is little empirical research on its effects in the speech of second language learners. In this section, I report on classroom research which shows how effective it is to use such software in order to help students master segmental and suprasegmental features, and how to put speech analysis software into practical use effectively in listening and speaking classes. Applying insights from current acoustic phonetics to the English language teaching classroom, I propose that using speech analysis software is quite effective in listening and speaking classes. This section shows that speech analysis software, if used within a precise method that is grounded in existing pedagogical theories, can lead to higher learning gains in foreign language speech perception and production for second language learners.

Speech analysis software, including Kay Visi-Pitch, Kay CSL Speech Laboratory, IBM Speech Viewer, Mac Speech Lab, NEC Kawai, etc. (See Chun, 2002: chapter 5, p. 133, Notes 15 and 16 for a variety of speech analysis software), is helpful for teachers of English in their assessment and planning of lessons/remediation (Ashby & Maidment, 2005; Johnson, 1997). The function of speech analysis software is very appealing and effective as a learning and teaching tool in pronunciation since it allows students to visualise their pronunciation as they learn to associate the patterns on the display with the sounds. Speech analysis software is also very motivating to students because it provides them with a deeper sense of their own articulation by allowing them to compare their own pronunciation visually with that of their teacher. Students visualise their pronunciation and learn to interpret the different patterns of sound segmentals and suprasegmentals by associating the patterns on the screen with the sounds they are producing (Anderson-Hsieh, 1992, 1994; Lambacher, 1996, 1999; Pennington, 1996, 1998, 1999). As Yavaş (2006: chapter 5) clearly argues, it is expected that the speech analysis software currently available makes such procedures a real possibility in classrooms. Since speech that requires remediation reveals patterns that are different from the average native speaker norms, teachers can compare the speech of the student with the norm to determine the amount of deviation. Speech analysis software is a very convenient means of displaying the acoustic characteristics of speech in a compact form. Learning to interpret them is also relatively easy with practice. The spectrographic and pitch curve data can also be utilised to monitor changes in remediation and can guide the practitioner in adjusting the remediation plan. The utility of speech analysis comes from the fact that it provides quantitative and objective data on a wide range of speech parameters, including nasalisation, vowel quality, segmental duration, place and manner of articulation, and voice onset time, and greatly enhances the scope of auditory-based perceptual judgements of speech. Concerning the complexity of interpreting spectrograms and pitch curves, Ertmer and others (1995, 1996, 2004) show how well children, as well as adults, can recognise spectrographic cues for vowels and consonants. Training activities involved instruction, highlighting of target spectrographic cues, matching of spectrograms by the children and adults, and feedback on correctness. Results showed that a variety of spectrographic cues could be recognised with greater-than-chance articulatory accuracy at each age. Ertmer (2004) reveals that elementary school children identify pertinent visual cues for consonant manner and vowel features despite the complex and abstract nature of spectrograms. He claims that spectrograms can provide salient and reliable cues regarding speech production characteristics.

Speech analysis software enables learners to visualise their own intonation patterns and provide specific feedback to help them perceive the meaningful contrasts between L1 and L2 so that they can improve their speech production. The major benefit of electronic visual feedback for teaching intonation is that it provides the students with an accurate visual representation of intonations in real time paired with normal auditory feedback that occurs during speech. Students can more easily replicate native intonation targets using both the target form and visual feedback from their own speech to guide them. Students can see English rhythm and intonation, including weakening processes, very clearly, and practise them effectively. Lambacher (1996, 1999) shows that a combination of auditory and visual feedback can be effective in teaching segmental, suprasegmental, and other aspects of pronunciation. Speech analysing software can provide the language learner with real-time information about the salient acoustic properties of their pronunciation. By showing exact features that need changing, visual displays can instantly provide an objective measurement by which students and teachers can evaluate student speech production. De Bot (1983) was successful in using visual displays to help learners in L2 intonation as long as students were first briefly exposed to theoretical instruction. The main conclusion drawn from his experiment is that visual feedback is helpful in learning foreign intonation, whereas practice time is not a critical factor. In addition, Molholt (1988) was successful in using computer visual displays of sound and suprasegmental production of Chinese international training assistants to overcome pronunciation problems. The results of experiments by de Bot and Molholt demonstrate the effective pedagogical application of speech analysis software. This training strengthened the association between the prosodic and lexical components of sentences through frequent exposure and practice opportunities involving sentences of familiar content with informative feedback, and the training also resulted in improved production at both the segmental and suprasegmental levels (Hardison, 2004).

To summarise, speech analysis software can be used to (Chun, 2002: 120):

(1) provide learners with visualisations of their speech patterns and specific feedback to help them perceive the meaningful contrasts between L1 and L2 so that they can improve their speech production;
(2) provide learners with authentic and extensive speech and cultural input, and,

in turn, hone learners' perceptual abilities;

(3) facilitate, record, and analyse interactions between and among speakers; and

(4) build tools for research purposes, e.g., data collection tools to record student performance, progress, and steps toward self-correction.

Now, let us have a brief look at what can be done using speech analysis software, exemplifying teaching English to Japanese learners. First, the voice onset time (VOT) is very important in English language teaching. As Yavaş (2006: 118) claims, the difference between English /p,t,k/ and /b,d,g/ is not voiced/ voiceless in its initial position, as /b,d,g/ also may show no voicing before the release of the stop closure. Thus, the aspiration of /p,t,k/ is very important for a segment to be perceived as /p/, /t/, or /k/ rather than /b/, /d/, or /g/. The value of speech analysis software becomes more important during the remediation process. Monitoring changes and helping learners become aware of this progress on the computer screen encourages them, and thus accelerates the remediation process. Second, it has often been said that vowel quality is problematic. Vowels can be accurately described in the frequencies of their first three formants. With the help of spectrographic analysis, the practitioner will be in a position to identify the nature and extent of the mismatches between the target system and the system of the student, and plan remediation.

Speech analysis software can be used to gather raw data about pitch variation, the speaking rate, and pausing. A potential new application for speech analysis software would be as a feedback or evaluative mechanism for speaking instruction (Hincks, 2005). The use of speech visualisation technology has only fairly recently become widely available. The current tendency is to fit this technology into traditional pronunciation pedagogy. Software is now capable of presenting longer stretches of speech, and systematic meanings of pitch movement have been described in ways that are more transparent for the learner (Levis & Pickering, 2004).

In this section, we shall look closely at my practice in the classroom. In this investigation, in order to show how effective applying speech analysis software in the classroom is, an experimental approach was used, which means that any effective-ineffective differences would be shown by significant differences between two groups. One group used speech analysis software, and the other group did not. Since listening and speaking are related to each other, both skills were jointly instructed. Based on the practice discussed in chapter four, the goal of this practice was for students to understand and produce English smoothly according to English rhythm.

5.3.1. Participants

The participants were Japanese learners of English (60 university students; age 20). The students had learned English at junior and senior high school for six years. All participants were raised in Japan, and had never been to English-speaking countries. This investigation took place from April to July 2007. They were all Japanese students at an upper-intermediate private university. This study investigated the changes in similar groups of students who were taught English under similar conditions after a period of exposure to English. The university students learned English for four hours a week in total. All of them took two sets of one-hour compulsory writing and speaking classes every week, in which writing/speaking skills and basic grammar for writing/speaking were taught. The overall structure of one lesson was as follows: Introduction (including greeting, checking attendance, short talks, etc.: about seven minutes) – Review (about eight minutes) – New target sounds (explanation of the new segmental or supra-segmental targets: about fifteen minutes) – Exercises including activities (about thirty minutes) – Conclusion (closing remarks). I used the same target sentences, exercises, and language activities, all of which were produced in advance. Textbooks for students were: Donald, H. & Kiggell, T. (1993), *Listening Tactics*, Tokyo: Macmillan Language House; Dellar, H. & Hucking, D. (2000), *Innovations*, Hove: Language Teaching Publications; JACET Kansai (2001), *English Listening Strategy*, Tokyo: Kinseido), and supplementary materials from phonetics and phonology books. Speech analysis software, run in the Panasonic CALL system, was the *Speech Filing System* (*SFS*) with permission from the distributor (SFS Release 4.5 Windows, SFS Version 1.4 30–01–2004, free software distributed by the Department of Phonetics and Linguistics, University College London, available at: http://www.phon.ucl.ac.uk/resource/sfs/).

5.3.2. Training procedure

This longitudinal study took place in the classroom. The participants' performance was observed and tested for one term. The distributions of students' proficiency were the same according to the paper version of the TOEFL® test. Two groups were indicated as [USE] taught in a CALL room and [NOT USE] taught in a language laboratory (LL) (thirty students each). [USE] means that every time they were taught English, the participants always paid attention to phonological aspects of English in explicit and implicit manners using speech analysis software. [NOT USE] means that although they covered the same material as the [USE] group, no explicit instruction of the English sound system with speech analysis software was provided at all. Students in this group only listened to tapes or CDs and they were asked to repeat after the tape/CD many times. The difference between [USE] and [NOT USE] groups was that the former used speech analysis software while the latter group did not, only using traditional audio systems. As suggested by Hardison (1999), visual aids (a picture of a mouth, lip-reading, DVD) were used, and minimal pair exercises were given if necessary in both groups. In this practice, perception and production were taught simultaneously to help the students become good listeners and speakers, while previous research mainly focused on either perception or production in short-term experimental designs. Listening and speaking practice included the following features:

Topic 1: English rhythm (3 weeks)

Teaching rhythm practice began with the development of listening skills to have learners focus perceptually on the placement of stresses and on the overall rhythm of English. Exercises were carried out to attune learners to listening for and actively perceiving features in the natural speech of native speakers as well as in their own speech. Learners were provided with focused practice in listening, e.g., with opportunities to focus consciously on which syllables are stressed and how the rhythm of English can be described. In general, training typically progressed from perception to production; students first listened to spoken input until they were able to discern particular features, then completed active listening exercises where they were asked to mark or code in writing what they were hearing, and finally practised pronouncing words, phrases, and sentences themselves (Chun, 2002: 150).

Following listening and perception exercises, speaking exercises were implemented in order for students to be able to apply what they had learned to listen for in the L2 to their own L2 speech (Chun, 2002: 150–151).

Imitative speaking practice: The purpose of imitative speaking practice was to focus on the controlled production of selected pronunciation features. It included contextualised practice and self-study by individual students, pairs of students, or small groups outside of class as well as use of the computerised speech analysis software that provides visual displays of user pronunciation and intonation.

Rehearsed speaking practice: Rehearsed speaking practice was an interim stage between imitative and extemporaneous speech, and its purpose was to work toward the stabilisation of newly learned speech patterns so that the learner could manipulate them at will. Practice included oral reading of a wide variety of scripts, pre-planned oral presentations, rehearsed performances for audiotape, and one-to-one sessions with the instructor.

Extemporaneous speech practice: For extemporaneous speech practice, the goal was to provide a wide variety of speaking tasks and activities simulating naturally occurring situations. It included various in-class presentations, e.g., small-group panel discussions and follow-up interaction with the audience.

Topic 2: Weakening processes (4 weeks)

Learners were first presented with word pairs and asked to determine which word of the pair contained the feature to be targeted. As a supplement to the listening exercise, the students in the [USE] group were also shown visual representations of actual measurements in order to be able to graphically confirm the differences. Speech analysis software shows graphs of the waveform and amplitude curve for the pairs; the waveform graph is a representation of the vibration of the vocal cords over time during speech, and the amplitude curves represent the intensity or loudness of speech. In addition, the duration of any segment of speech can be measured in milliseconds. Typically, vowel types (long and tense vs. short and lax) and syllable structure (closed syllable ending in voiceless consonants; closed syllable ending in voiced consonants; vs. open syllable) can be shown clearly and convincingly (Chun, 2002: 153).

The focus of this phase was on segmentals, specifically problematic sounds such as the oral stop consonants, fricatives, and liquids. The programme used the spectrogram feature and a display incorporating the waveform, power, pitch, and spectrogram of the recorded speech signal. Students were shown how to recognise the distinctive spectral characteristics, the formant frequencies and acoustic patterns, of the sounds. Learners then produced the sounds within different contexts, analysed the results, and compared them to the target patterns.

Short conversations between native speakers were taken from the materials, pitch-tracked, and then presented to the [USE] group. Learners first performed very close listening and analysis, i.e., they listened to the conversation or selected part thereof many times as well as viewed the intonation curves. They were told which acoustic informational features to focus on. Following the perception activities, they were asked to practise these utterances by recording themselves and comparing their pitch tracks to those of the native speakers. They would note the direction of pitch changes, the syllable(s) on which pitch changes occurred, the steepness of the pitch falls and rises, and the overall pitch range used (Chun, 2002: 127).

Chun (2002: 186–188) suggests that, as a way of introducing the concept of sound reduction in the classroom, one could start with short utterances that are frequent in English taken from real discourse, or utterances that are likely to occur in natural conversation, e.g., greetings and chunks. In listen-and-repeat exercises, students first heard a function word alone spoken in its stressed form and then unstressed in a sentence. A follow-up exercise showed how meaning changes when function words are stressed. Speech analysis software was incorporated into intonation practice and was very useful in helping provide learners with visualisations of their pitch patterns as well as to reflect on the phonetic effects of various degrees of reduction and elision. Various scenarios were presented to learners, e.g., ranging from formal to informal, and learners then compared how such exchanges might be spoken depending on the speed and formality of speech appropriate to the situation. For the [USE] group, they showed them using speech analysis software, and encouraged students to use it in order to compare their pronunciations with those of native speakers. The [NOT USE] group listened and repeated after a tape.

In this phase, speech analysis software was used in teaching not only segmentals but also suprasegmentals, including stress, rhythm, linking, and intonation. Students learned to correct their mistakes by raising their awareness of English phonological characteristics. Students first spoke a sentence into a microphone, their utterance was then digitised and pitch-tracked, and they saw a display of their pitch curve directly under a native speaker's pitch curve of the same sentence. Using the information from the intensity and pitch displays, students learned to shorten the length and intensity of the stressed syllables, thereby approximating more closely to the English sentence stress pattern. By comparing a stretch of speech in the first language with that in the target language on the pitch and intensity displays, learners could clearly see the differences between languages.

Topic 3: The verb as the core of a sentence, paying attention to information structure (3 weeks)

As the next step, the focus was moved to longer phrases and sentences, and the same procedure was followed, whereby students listened to the entire sentence and determined the targeted feature. At this level, the fundamental frequency or pitch curve of the utterance is important. The fundamental frequency curve shows how pitch is used to signal stress in individual words as well as in sentences. For the [USE] group, using computer generated visual displays of pitch curves, the same sentence could be spoken several times in various contexts, with different intonations expressing different pragmatic meanings. Learners first compared native speakers' renditions with each other and then practised producing the different curves themselves. For the [NOT USE] group, students were encouraged to listen and repeat them after a tape.

For perceptual exercises to practise listening for discourse stress and rhythm, I used recorded conversations that, as realistically as possible, represent language in use and illustrate the rhythmic features. Students were asked to listen closely to the conversation, perform a perceptual analysis of it, and identify the heavy beats in each sentence, particularly those that do not occur at the end of an utterance. The students then discussed reasons for the placement of stress and accent by examining the surrounding discourse. Speech analysis software enables learners to visualise how such chunking takes place and try to imitate and practise until they can produce target sequences. For speaking practice, discourse intonation was incorporated into communicative activities that involved such functions as negotiating, repeating, quoting, asking for clarification, and self-correcting (Chun, 2002: 154, 195).

The speech analysis software enabled users to perform an acoustic analysis of their speech with functions for measuring amplitude, intonation, pitch, duration, and frequency, the results of which could be shown on a spectrographic display of voice patterns and pitches. Students' recorded or analysed voice data were retrieved, reproduced, and analysed by the teacher. The teacher also sent their voice data to the students who could compare their results with the teacher's.

Overall, one of the main objectives of the sound analysis software was to assist both teachers and students in obtaining an accurate description of students' speech production at both the segmental and suprasegmental levels. The system was expected to achieve this goal by allowing students to record, analyse, and visualise their speech on their computer screen. Students were first taught how to interpret the basic spectral patterns of sound segmental and suprasegmental properties of pitch, intonation, and loudness. Native speaker recordings of words and sentences were provided for students to practise recording and analysing through sound files that were copied and stored in the computer network system (Lambacher, 1996).

5.3.3. Testing procedure

I adopted exactly the same testing procedure as in chapter three, so I will not explain about it again in this section. An AX sound discrimination task and a picture-verification task were used to assess the participants' perceptual and receptive ability. Production tests include a list-reading task and free conversation, as explained in detail in chapter three. Three minutes of spontaneous speech from each participant were recorded, and were transcribed phonetically in narrow transcription using the IPA system of notation. In order to avoid bias, the transcribers, linguists trained in phonetic transcription, were not informed of the objectives of the study.

As discussed in chapter four, it is important to note that evaluation of speaking tends to be subjective. The tester's judgement sometimes varies according to situations, or judgement of non-nativeness differs among testers. In this investigation, in order to avoid inconsistent judgements, I used computerised automatic speech recognition technology first. However, Neri et al. (2002) suggests caution regarding the possible acceptable range of articulatory variations. Any linguistic community allows for a particular range of variation for any phoneme. Researchers and teachers should evaluate students' pronunciation in terms of intelligibility to a native speaker, although in some evaluations based on sound recognition systems, there is a pressure for students to mimic the model articulation perfectly. It turned out that current speech recognition technology still had a long way to go to measure speech accurately. In order to accept individual differences in pronunciation, data on the epenthesis rate and rhythmic impression by native speakers were collected instead.

Students performed the above-mentioned tasks four times a term, every three weeks. Note that the topics covered were cumulative, in that the topic or topics learned before were learned as well as the current target topic. Two British and Japanese phoneticians, who were not involved in teaching and did not know the purpose of this research, scored the tests. In order to randomise data, students' performances in each group were shuffled.

5.3.4. Results

The following tables show the results of perception and production tests. The visual impression of the results suggests that using speech analysis software (labelled as [USE]) would be beneficial in perception and production. All differences in test results between [USE] and [NOT USE] groups were significant by the t-test. All *t* values showed $p < .002$ or less. Let us look closely at the tables.

Tables 5–1 and 5–3 show the mean scores and standard deviations of each test, and Tables 5–2 and 5–4 summarise the *t* value, effect size (*d*), and significance (*p*). Perception tests (sound discrimination and picture verification tasks) and production tests (list reading and free conversation) reveal that the [USE] group scored significantly better than the [NOT USE] group in all tests ($p < .002$ or less). Looking more closely at the standard deviations, the [NOT USE] group showed much greater variability than the [USE] group [$t(29) = 2.8$, $p = .002$, on test 1; $t(29) = 3.0$, $p = .001$, on test 2].

Table 5–3 shows the impression of production tests judged by native speakers of English (1: most unnatural, to 7: most natural). The [USE] group showed a significant difference from the [NOT USE] group ($p < .001$). In the [USE] group, impression improved, while, in the [NOT USE] group, it remained unchanged or worsened [$F(1,29)=9.33$, $p<.0004$]. This tendency becomes obvious when the target sound stream gets longer, i.e., from word to sentence levels. The epenthesis rate and rhythmic impression might be related, because students' performances are influenced by the Japanese phonological system such as mora. Speech analysis software helps learners overcome this.

Inspection of the group means indicates that the average [USE] group score is significantly higher than that for the [NOT USE] group. The effect size *d* is much larger than is typical in this discipline.

Table 5–5 shows the rate of epenthesis taking place per 100 environments where consonant stops were required. Epenthesis was reduced when speech analysis software was used. The [NOT USE] group, however, made more and more epentheses as time went by [$F(1,29)=12.35$, $p<.000$]. This tendency becomes obvious when the target sound stream gets longer, i.e., from word to sentence levels.

Learners who listened to English sentences, imitated them, and were able to view the spectrogram and pitch contours of both the native speaker model and their own imitation showed greater improvements in their own production of English sentences than did learners who only listened to the model sentences and whose imitations did not undergo graphic representation with computers. De Bot (1983) notes that students who used speech analysis software had many more opportunities to listen to the material than the traditional learning group did while they were handling the software in his investigation. A greater amount of input received by the experimental group might lead to better learning gains. However, in the practice reported here, students in the [NOT USE] group listened to and repeated after the tape much more than the [USE] group did, because they had much more time to do so while the other group was learning with speech analysis software. In addition, both groups recorded and listened to their own speech as well as teachers'. Since the only difference between [USE] and [NOT USE] groups was whether students used speech analysis software or not, I conclude that speech analysis software is useful for both perception and production.

Table 5–1: Mean score (per 100 points) and standard deviation of perception tests

	[USE]		[NOT USE]	
	Score	SD	Score	SD
Test 1	61	5.8	50	9.5
Test 2	65	5.1	52	10.1
Test 3	71	5.0	54	10.2
Test 4	76	4.5	61	10.4

Table 5–2: Comparison of [USE] and [NOT USE] in perception tests (n = 30 students)

	t value	*d* (effect size)	*p*
Test 1	2.8	3.2	.002
Test 2	3.0	3.4	.001
Test 3	3.9	4.6	.000
Test 4	4.0	5.0	.000

Table 5–3: Mean score (per 7 points) and standard deviation of production tests

	[USE]		[NOT USE]	
	Score	SD	Score	SD
Test 1	5.4	1.2	3.9	2.1
Test 2	5.8	1.1	4.0	2.2
Test 3	6.1	1.0	3.8	2.3
Test 4	5.9	1.0	3.4	2.3

Table 5–4: Comparison of [USE] and [NOT USE] in production tests (n = 30 students)

	t value	*d* (effect size)	*p*
Test 1	2.9	3.3	.001
Test 2	3.0	3.4	.001
Test 3	3.3	4.1	.001
Test 4	3.6	4.5	.000

Table 5–5: Mean epenthesis rate
(occurrence per 100 consonant stops) and standard deviation in production tests

	[USE]		[NOT USE]	
	Score	SD	Score	SD
Test 1	22	4.8	50	4.9
Test 2	23	3.3	52	5.5
Test 3	20	3.5	58	5.6
Test 4	18	3.1	60	5.7

Table 5–6: Comparison of [USE] and [NOT USE] in epenthesis rate in production tests
(n = 30 students)

	t value	*d* (effect size)	*p*
Test 1	5.8	6.7	.000
Test 2	5.5	5.9	.000
Test 3	5.9	6.8	.000
Test 4	6.8	7.7	.000

5.3.5. General discussion

Learners differ in how they process language. Sometimes, students say that they cannot notice differences although teachers repeatedly point them out. Even if teachers repeat model pronunciations, they feel that the sounds are the same. Wide ranges of standard deviations in the [NOT USE] group might indicate these individual differences. In the field of cognitive psychology, it has commonly been suggested (Coventry & Garrod, 2004; Henderson & Ferreira, 2004: Meier et al., 2002) that some learners depend on auditory information, while others depend primarily on visual information when processing sounds (called *sensory modality preferences*). Visual learners can be assisted by spelling and any visual stimuli. In addition, this research reveals that speech analysis software helps visual learners understand the differences in sounds that they are unable to detect auditorily. Even if they cannot discriminate them with auditory input only, they are able to discriminate similar sounds gradually with speech analysis software. Such software, which enables sounds to be visualised, would be effective for learners with different sensory modality preferences. Especially, speech analysis software is useful in sound discrimination, sound change, intonation, and weak forms. It is sometimes very difficult to notice them only using tapes and CDs, and speech analysis software would supplement this.

One way to enhance the interactive capability of a computer is to add an electric visual feedback system. Research results indicate that the visualisation of segmental and suprasegmental features significantly enhances learning. Some specific advantages attributed to interaction via electric visual feedback are: accelerated language learning; offers students an objective measure to focus on the exact speech feature or mistake; and the instructor is able to show convincingly that there is a difference by displaying it so students can understand even before they are able to produce the actual sounds. Hirata (2004) tested a computer program which provided visual representations of L2 learner production in addition to visual representations of target L2 pronunciation. The results show that audiovisual training significantly improved L2 production compared to the control group.

Neri et al. (2002) outlined pedagogical requirements that computer-assisted pronunciation training should ideally meet, and looked at how those requirements are technologically implemented in available systems. Hansen (2006) recommends caution in that while some applications provide intonation curves and some provide spectrograms, these feedback modes rarely inform the user of what is wrong, instead relying on the users to self-correct through trial and error. This is true for listening and speaking. To overcome this problem, the use of automatic speech recognition creates the possibility to inform learners what to focus on. Neri et al. (2002) and Hansen (2006) examined various reviews on the utility of speech recognition in pronunciation training. Unfortunately, speech recognition systems at present are poor at analysing and evaluating accurately. The limitations of the technology imply that a learner's utterances have to be predictable, and that detecting errors is only possible with a limited degree of detail, which makes it difficult to give the learner corrective feedback (Hincks, 2005). Most recently, ultrasound technology has attracted researchers' attention. Visual input seems to help in circumstances where phonemic differences can be instigated at an external point on the mouth, but not in cases where phonemic differences are generated inside the mouth. There is an obvious limitation regarding visual data provided by video cameras, since the cameras cannot be put inside the mouth. In contrast, ultrasound technology projects sound waves through the skin and into the mouth, making internal areas visible on a monitor (Meadows, 2007). Engwall & Bälter (2007) discus that while automatic speech recognition has the potential to judge the learner's pronunciation based on a statistical comparison with that of native speakers, the student is not provided with any indication of how the pronunciation should be changed. They claim that pronunciation training software should be improved by studying how feedback is distributed in the language classroom, bearing in mind how classroom feedback may be transferred and adapted to computer assisted language learning. For the time being, teachers must show how to interpret electric visual feedback to each student, but, in the future, automatic speech recognition, together with ultrasound technology, will supplement computer-assisted language learning.

To summarise, in this section, I sought an effective and efficient teaching method for listening and speaking using speech analysis software. This section presented two methods to provide perception and production training to Japanese learners of English. I trained and tested learners at four different times and on a battery of tests measuring the perception and production of English speech. The use of speech analysis software could generate higher learning gains than traditional learning classes with tapes and CDs that do not incorporate the use of such software.

Conclusion

In this chapter, following English phonetics, we first saw acoustic data taken from native speakers and Japanese learners of English, secondly, we discussed these data from phonological perspectives, and then we sought an effective and efficient teaching method with acoustic programmes. In order to acquire non-native sounds, new mouth shapes and tongue/muscle movements are crucial, but all teachers can do is just repeat tapes and CDs, hoping that students can recognise the differences and eventually discriminate such sounds. However, some students are unable to distinguish the sounds as different. On the other hand, the sound sequence in a sentence has not been focused on. It has been said that listening and speaking classes should focus on English rhythm consistently from the very beginning to advanced levels (Pennington, 1996). Again, teachers can only show this with tapes and CDs, and let students practise, but some students, especially visual learners, cannot catch up because they are unable to identify the differences.

English rhythm and intonation are realised by weak forms and sound change. It has been said that weak forms, elision, and assimilation need to be focused on from the very beginning. In order to achieve this, implementing acoustic programmes in listening and speaking classes would be one of the effective ways for many students, including children, to overcome individual differences in sound processing. Acoustic programmes allow a quantification of mismatches between the native speakers' performances and the students' productions (See Chun, 2002: chapter 5, and publications by ATR researchers in Japan for a variety of acoustic programmes). In addition to the fact that such quantification is indispensable for the identification of trouble spots, it greatly enhances the ability of the practitioners as well as students.

First published in part as 'Effectiveness of speech analysing software in listening and speaking classes' in *JABAET Journal* 10 (2006): 21–52

PART III

Learning and teaching grammar and lexis

This part of the book discusses the possibility of a Lexical Approach to teaching languages. The Lexical Approach is based on the theoretical assumption discussed in chapter two. First, I look at the rationale of the Lexical Approach in detail. Then, I discuss the potential of the Lexical Approach in the Japanese context. I propose that this approach is applicable to English teaching at junior and senior high schools as well as primary school. I report on three empirical studies on the most difficult grammar targets for Japanese learners of English – passives, infinitives, and relative clauses. I point out some shortcomings of the present-day standard transformational instructions, propose new ways of introducing these grammar targets based on the Lexical Approach, and test their effectiveness in the classroom. Last, the acquisition and instruction of English verbs are discussed in detail. As we have seen in previous chapters, processing verbs is crucial in a structural language like English. We review past studies on verb acquisition, look at verb learning in the classroom closely, overview some teaching methods for verbs, and test the effectiveness of each method.

The previous parts of this book concluded that a lexicon and chunks play important roles in first language acquisition and foreign language learning. Traditionally, however, researchers have mostly focused on grammatical development, which leads people to think that language acquisition and foreign language learning are grammatical in origin. What we have seen so far, including the development of communication ability and processing non-native sounds, makes us reconsider the role of the lexicon and chunks in language pedagogy.

It has been asserted in newspaper articles and magazines that Japanese learners of English cannot attain fluent speaking skills. I propose that one of the reasons can be found in the present heavily grammar-oriented approach to foreign language pedagogy. What we need to note is that foreign language learning and use are much more lexical, and lexical communication (including using words and chunks freely) should be paid more attention. As we have seen in chapter one, human communication is based on human inferential ability: anyone can infer another's message even with limited linguistic clues. To understand not only what is said but also why it is said, one has first to decode the linguistic content of the utterance concerned, and then use that decoded form as a basis for inferring what one's interlocutor intended to communicate (Smith, 1989: 9). This inferential ability enables us to make ourselves understand without fully grammatically accurate sentences (Widdowson, 1978). The strongest point of the Lexical Approach, which we are about to see, is that it emphasises communicative power by means of lexis and chunks, appealing to the human inferential ability in communication.

In the field of second language acquisition research, it has been considered that the system that it draws upon to achieve meaning is syntactic under a UG approach, and that foreign language learning is much more lexical than is usually accepted under an input processing approach. Let us look briefly at the interrelations between the two approaches and implications to teaching.

In a typical UG model, rules have primary importance, and foreign language is produced by filling these rules with a lexicon. The priority is to construct sentences that conform to the grammar rules of the foreign language. The theoretical advantages of this approach are as follows: First, it enables maximum creativity and flexibility in production. A rule-based system is operating anew for the production of each utterance, and constructions can be accomplished freely. Second, fewer and more elegant rules make fewer demands on memory storage (e.g., Culicover & Jackendoff, 2005). Once the lexical elements are represented in the memory, the rule system is consulted whenever necessary to fill in the frames. In short, the assumptions of a rule-based system are that computation is fast and that memory systems should be compact and organised efficiently.

However, lexicalists argue that foreign language learning is much more memory-based than has generally been considered (Skehan, 1998: chapter 2). Skehan suggests that much of language consists of lexical elements and that these may not even be easily described by rules. Sinclair (1991) claims that while grammar enables endless combinational possibilities, most of these possibilities are ignored in practice, and particular combinations of lexical elements occur repeatedly. Sinclair (1991: 109–115), who has conducted extensive research on written texts stored in computerised corpora, proposes that two principles (the open-choice principle and the idiom principle) are required to give an adequate explanation of how texts are constructed. In many descriptions of language, grammars and lexicons especially words are treated as independent items of meaning. Each of them represents a separate choice (open-choice). *The open-choice principle* is essentially the traditional rule-governed view that sentences are produced creatively based on an underlying system of rules. The sentences contain slots that can be filled by a wide range of possible words, depending on the language user's choice. Collocations, idioms, and other exceptions to this principle are given lower status in the descriptions.

On the other hand, Sinclair (1991) points out that the choice of one word affects the choice of others in its vicinity. Corpus research has revealed that, in practice, lexical choices are much more limited than one would expect if only the open-choice principle were operating. Words commonly come together in combinations or collocations that seem to form relatively fixed expressions. Sinclair thus proposes that the open-choice principle needs to be complemented by *the idiom principle*, which is defined as follows: Language users have available to them a large number of chunks that constitute single choices, even though they might appear to be analysable into segments. For instance, very frequent content words like *take, make, do,* or *get* seem to contribute very little specific meaning of their own, but have to be understood in relation to the entire phrases in which they occur. Sinclair believes that, while the open-choice principle was traditionally taken as the basis for linguistic analyses, the idiom principle is at least as important in the construction and interpretation of texts. Although the rule-based nature of language has been emphasised, the use of memorised chunks of foreign language has attracted researchers' attention. Many of the choices that need to be made to achieve acceptability as a native speaker are choices of lexical phrases. Learners need to make the choice from a range of grammatically acceptable utterances that would be used by native speakers. One way of achieving this goal is to extend the range of lexical entries and chunks that they use (Nattinger & DeCarrico, 1992; Fernando, 1996; Wray, 2002; Willis, 2003; Bogaards & Laufer, eds., 2004; Schmitt, ed., 2004; Kormos, 2006). Thanks to the development of corpus, it is now much easier to arrange such set phrases along with grammar. Along with the developmental sequence, which actually shows that the development of language is lexical rather than syntactic, we are persuaded that a lexicon and chunks are worthy of our attention, and foreign language pedagogy must not exclude these elements of language. In this part, we discuss how to realise the importance of lexicons and chunks in a language curriculum, considering chunking as a lexical and grammatical unit and process.

Chapter 6

The Lexical Approach to language teaching

This chapter describes the rationale of the Lexical Approach in detail. Any language teaching methodology must include a theoretical basis (linguistic, psychological, and pedagogical bases), syllabus design, and particular ways of instruction (Richards & Rogers, 1986). We focus on its theoretical basis, types of syllabus and teaching methodology, teacher's roles and the role of L1, teaching context and materials, and types of proficiency, all of which need to be included when proposing a new approach to foreign language teaching. We compare the Lexical Approach with the traditional grammar-oriented structural approach when necessary.

The Lexical Approach and the structural approach hold opposite views of language: The Lexical Approach views language as 'grammaticalised lexis', that is, lexis plays a central role in extracting syntactic and discoursal as well as semantic information. On the other hand, the structural approach views language as 'lexicalised grammar', that is, grammar picks up lexis to satisfy its constraints. These exclusive views of language lead us to completely different language teaching theories.

6.1. Theoretical basis

6.1.1. Language as grammaticalised lexis (Lexicon-oriented)

According to Lewis (1997b: 255), language has traditionally been divided into grammar and lexis. The former consists of elements of the generative system of the language and the latter is the stock of fixed nongenerative words. (Note that this simplistic position cannot explain where productive morphology fits in.) The lexical view of language considers that language learning is lexical in origin. It appeals to the past studies on early first language development, and proposes that language learning involves the learning and analysis of sequences of forms (N. Ellis, 1996a, 1996b). The view of early first language development on which it stands has been widely supported by many linguists and psychologists (Brown, 1973; Bates et al., 1988; Clark, 1993; Tomasello, 2003). Regarding the development of grammar, it considers that lexical items are first represented as ordered phonological strings, then they form collocations and sequential probabilities in word strings, i.e., chunks, and only later, these patterns of occurrence are analysed to allow syntactic and semantic classification. It suggests that both in first language acquisition and foreign language learning, lexical phrases or 'chunks' are basic and fundamental in processing (Nattinger & DeCarrico, 1992; Fernando, 1996; Wray, 2002; Willis, 2003; Bogaards & Laufer eds., 2004; Schmitt ed., 2004; Kormos, 2006: chapter 3). Willis (1990: 39–40) claims that we carry in our mind chunks of language incorporating the word in the grammatical frames. Knowledge of a language includes a vast amount of collocational knowledge, knowledge of which words combine with which other words or categories of word. Under this view, collocations are features of naturalness in language. Lewis (1993: 95) points out that an important part of language learning is the ability to have access to chunks, and that these chunks become the raw data by which the learner begins to perceive patterns. Grammaticalised lexis makes the lexical entries and chunks do most of the grammatical work of mapping the strings of the language to their interpretations. Language learning mainly reduces to the problem of learning the lexicon, chunks, and the language-specific instances of the combinatory rule types involved. As we have seen in chapter two, lexical learning must depend on the learner having access to mental representations of the concepts underlying words in the earliest stages. The semantic type of such concepts defines the syntactic type. As learning progresses, as the lexical categories are learned, and as the language system becomes tuned to foreign language word sequences, so the foreign language lexical 'auto-associative net' begins to form a structure that is largely independent of the first language network (N. Ellis, 1996a: 100). This line of argument follows the notion of Semantic Bootstrapping in Pinker's (1987) sense: The sequence of words is first analysed into thematic roles such as Agent, Patient, Theme, Experiencer, etc. Then, the location of each element in a sentence is learned, for example, Agent comes at the sentence-first position, then Action follows it, and Patient comes after that. Finally, parts of speech are learned (as seen in chapter two). In the case of language learning, the cognitive processing systems automatically seek the patterning in sequences of language, which helps the development and expansion of the network (N. Ellis, 1999; Willis, 2003). Guided by this cognitive system, unaquired aspects of language are paid attention to, then, are analysed by utilising hypothesis formation and testing processes, with the results stored in the memory. Pieces of information stored by this process are activated in further learning processes. This view of first and foreign language learning, that human beings process linguistic input based on attention and memory in general, reflects a cognitive psychological perspective, as discussed in chapter two.

As the Lexical Approach aims at comprehending and producing words and phrases accurately in appropriate contexts, this approach is based on the analyses of a lexicon and chunks. This approach appeals to corpus linguistics and discourse analysis (Aston, 1995). The impetus for the Lexical Approach came from the research that lay behind the COBUILD project at the University of Birmingham. The Lexical Approach assumes that the patterns and meanings associated with the commonest words of English would afford a basis for syllabus specification that would provide learners with good coverage, and would provide that coverage economically. The Lexical Approach would derive from research into a large corpus of natural language and would use that research to highlight significant items within a learner's corpus. I suggest that the origins of the COBUILD project could be traced back at least to Ogden & Richards' (1923, 1968) BASIC, which tried to list the commonest words and phrases for communication based on literature and conversational use of words. BASIC and COBUILD share the same goal of finding the commonest and most frequently used words and phrases for communication. Such words and phrases are described not as individual lexis, but are connected with contexts in which they are used naturally. Discourse analysis plays an important role in finding appropriate register and contexts where each lexis and chunk appears. *Context* is defined as the totality of the events that surrounds the use of a particular piece of language (Lewis, 1997a: 215). Ellis (1994: 698) suggests that the context of an utterance can mean two different things: the situation in which an utterance is produced, and the linguistic environment in which it is produced. Context includes the situation, place, and circumstances in which some language is used, and co-text, the language that surrounds the language under analysis. Both types of context influence the choice of language forms.

Language that is introduced and taught in context, contextualised language instruction that is based on meaningful language use, and real communication and interactions among learners present real situations that encompass all aspects of a conversational exchange: the physical setting, the purpose of the exchange, the roles of the participants, the socially acceptable norms of interaction, in addition to the medium, topic, tone, and register of the exchange. Grammatical structures that might otherwise be devoid of context become an integral part of the communicative acts that occur in contexts (Shrum & Glisan, 1994: 1). The more familiar the context, the easier it is to understand it and function within it. For information to be meaningful, learners must be able to link or relate it to knowledge they already have: their knowledge of the language, their personal experiences in language use, encyclopaedic knowledge, and their understanding of how language is organised (Shrum & Glisan, 1994: 24).

Regarding a theory of learning, Lewis (1996) argues that a grammatical description of language is inadequate as a model for learning. Although well-established grammar structures clearly provide some economising frameworks, this is no more than a very small part of the learning task. Lewis' model of communicative language use emphasises the lexical mode. Natural language use depends on a huge stock of lexical items and fixed phrases. Taking this as a starting point, Lewis sees language learning as involving a constant cycle of observation, hypothesis, and experimentation. Learners observe and assimilate language forms in use, but the forms they assimilate are not abstract grammatical patterns but prefabricated chunks, often much larger than single words. Learners draw conclusions from the language they observe. As they assimilate a range of patterns, they begin to form hypotheses about the system that lies behind the patterning they observe. As they experiment with these hypotheses and compare their own output with authoritative input, they begin to construct and reconstruct their own language system. They become less dependent on processing prefabricated chunks and more able to assemble languages independently. This process feeds on exposure to language. Only wide exposure can provide learners with the information they need about the collocations and fixed phrases that are essential to natural language use. It is the quality and quantity of the input to which the learners are exposed which is the single most important factor in their progress.

6.1.2. Language as lexicalised grammar (Grammar-oriented)

The structural approach emphasises the role of grammar in language development. Some researchers (e.g., Radford, 1990) in this tradition accept that first language development is lexical at a very early stage of development (before 24 months). This approach assumes that UG plays a crucial role in acquiring the language in question. Its assumption stems from various kinds of errors that children make. These developmental errors have their own rules that can be transcribed. Wexler & Manzini (1987), Wexler (1999) and Pinker (1984, 1989) propose that there is an innate structural frame in the child's mind, and the child has to discover which parameters to set and which principles apply to the language he or she is learning. This innate language acquisition device with abstract grammatical rules operates automatically whenever a child receives linguistic input. In foreign language learning, researchers in this tradition argue how such a mechanism works with foreign language input, and their goals of research are to explain and investigate to what degree such mechanisms work. This view of language presupposes that there is a unique domain-specific module that processes language. This language module, independent from other cognitive systems, consists of abstract computational systems including principles and parameters. Lexical information is stored as conceptual structures in a knowledge base, independent from the language module, connected with thematic roles and functions (Jackendoff, 1983, 1990; Goldberg, 1995, 1999, 2006). This view reflects recent brain-scientific reports showing that the lexicon is stored in the lower temporal lobes, independent from a language module that occupies Broca's area.

The structural approach has a long tradition: Prescriptive, traditional, and generative grammar. Starting from accurate descriptions of language in terms of rules in order to interpret texts, this approach seeks to build a firm foundation of structures of language. As experiences in learning languages under this tradition tell, there are many 'exceptions' that cannot be explained using rules, all of which need to be memorised as such. Regarding language learning, this approach emphasises the role of grammar in language development.

6.2. Types of syllabus and teaching methodology

A *syllabus* is a set of headings indicating items that have been selected by a language planner or materials writer to be covered in a particular part of the curriculum or in a course series. Its content is usually identified in terms of language elements, context, language function, and linguistic skills (Sinclair & Renouf, 1988: 140).

The Lexical Approach is based on the natural use of target language. An accurate description of the contexts of words and chunks is required. Its syllabus starts with one-word communication, which develops into multi-word communication. Note that although learners are encouraged to produce shorter utterances at the early stages, input must be authentic, full sentences in order to guarantee rich input. Regarding grammaticalisation, students are guided to notice the patterning of sentences, and thematic roles are implicitly or explicitly taught. The Lexical Approach based on the COBUILD project teaches sentence patterns by means of grammatical labels such as V PP, V NP, etc. A lexicon meets grammar under the thematic roles. This view is influenced by Halliday's (1994) Functional Grammar. This approach emphasises the importance of patterns in which a word occurs, and a lot of attention is focused on discovering the contexts for each word. Contexts include grammatical as well as semantic and discoursal information. Following the first language acquisition and general learning paradigm, the Lexical Approach is based on the Observe – Hypothesis – Experiment paradigm. By means of this paradigm, learners are to discover word collocations or sequences of words, and learn multi-word chunks. This process is considered as expanding from one word to longer sequences of words, building up the foreign language processing network (bottom-up). The approach in grammar exercises in the Lexical Approach is to present learners with the raw material of language (usually language which is already familiar), and to provide prompts of different kinds to encourage learners to analyse and categorise language forms (Willis, 1990: 82). We should try to devise a methodology that is based on using language in the classroom to exchange meanings, and that offers a focus on language form.

Lewis (1997b: 260–263) believes that activities that raise conscious awareness of the lexical nature of language and its component chunks can aid learning. Conscious awareness of what constitutes a possible chunk provides learners with a tool that enables them to process input more effectively. Within the Lexical Approach, less attention will be paid to individual words and substantially less to traditional grammar structures. In contrast, much more time will be devoted to ensuring that students are aware of the lexical items, particularly collocations, which carry much of the meaning. Instead of receiving decontextualised and teacher-controlled presentations, learners can be asked to analyse texts that they have already processed for meaning. What should be aimed at is exposure that is organised in three ways. First, the language that learners are expected to understand and produce should be graded in some way so that they do not face at an early stage such great difficulties and complexities that they are demotivated. Second, the language they are to be exposed to should be carefully selected so that they do not experience random exposure, but exposure to the commonest patterns and meanings in the language (including the commonest patterns in a particular grammar target). These patterns and meanings are those learners are most likely to meet when they begin to use the language for communication. Third, there should be some way of itemising the language syllabus so that it is possible not simply to expose students to language, but also to highlight important features of their language experience and point out what language teachers might reasonably expect them to have learned from their experience (Willis, 1990: iv). Willis (1990: vi-vii) proposes the basic principles as follows:

- The methodology employed would be based entirely on activities involving real language use. Task-based instruction is one possible option to take.
- Learners would be exposed almost entirely to authentic native speaker language. They would not be taught through the medium of a language that is designed to illustrate the workings of a simplified grammatical system and bearing a beguiling but ultimately quite false similarity to real English.
- We would encourage students to analyse for themselves the language to which they were exposed, and thus to learn from their own experience of language.

The methodology has the following six components (Willis, 1990: 72):

Introduction: This gives students initial exposure to target forms within a communicative context.
Task: This provides an opportunity to focus on and realise target meanings. Students may begin to approximate to the target language form or they may use quite different forms.
Planning: The teacher helps students move towards accurate production.
Report: Students have another opportunity to use target forms.
Reading: Students have a chance to read the target forms used in a context that has become familiar to them through their own attempts to perform and report the task. (By means of listening, this stage may come immediately after *Introduction*.)
Analysis: This is an awareness-raising exercise that gives the learners a chance to

formulate generalisations about the language they have heard.

Lewis (1997a: chapter 6) shows basic types of exercise and testing as follows:

Identifying chunks: Learners who identify chunks correctly can make better use of dictionaries, translate more effectively, and avoid certain kinds of mistake. It encourages accurate recording in their lexical networks.
Matching: This exercise type is given a lexical focus by asking learners to match parts of collocations, expressions, lines of stereotypic dialogue, etc.
Completing: The traditional gap-fill is given a lexical focus by ensuring the gaps are partner-words from relatively fixed collocations, or that gapped expressions are relatively fixed.
Categorising: Much of the lexis is patterned, and the perception of patterns is an aid to memory, so it is helpful to ask learners to sort words or expressions.
Sequencing: The human mind automatically seeks a sequence of events. Some events have a natural order, providing some context, something that happens often enough to be an easily recognisable event. Most adult learners can recognise events by accumulating a vast amount of world knowledge, but do not know the specific expressions that express the meanings in L2. The problem of paying too much attention to meaning is that learners understand the event by means of L1 and no equivalent expressions in L2 are learned.
Deleting: Learners often overgeneralise by analogy with L1. Some errors can be prevented by predicting likely problems of this kind and asking learners to delete the odd one out.
Text search and lexical drills: This exercise asks learners to find chunks they can notice in the text. It helps to give them different kinds of chunks to look for, such as completing fixed expressions, adjective + noun collocations, verbal idioms, etc. Lexical drills quickly remind learners of chunks. Many multi-word items need to be noticed and remembered to be available for production as the prefabricated chunks. The usefulness of lexical drills is not that they teach the language of the drill, but that they increase awareness of the real structure of the target language.

Hugh Dellar has just developed a series of course books, called *Innovations,* published by Thomson Learning, in which these ideas are put into practice.

On the other hand, the structural approach is based on abstract rule systems.

Describing the structure of language (sometimes based on the grammarian's intuition) is required. At first glance, the syllabus for the structural approach is well organised and controlled: the grammar targets are listed and the teaching method is clearly shown. The dominant structural approach commonly uses the Present – Practice – Produce paradigm. This means presenting the grammar rules, which are used in producing the target language. Filling the lexicon satisfies structural rules of the language (top-down). (Note that Rutherford's 1987/1988 Consciousness-Raising approach to grammar takes a hypothesis-forming and hypothesis-testing perspective. This approach guides learners to notice a particular grammar point using a text, listening to the text, focusing on the grammar target, and understanding how it works. This approach, utilising material that is carefully designed for students to focus only on the particular grammar target, does not present grammar rules explicitly. This approach can be applicable to the Lexical Approach, but this approach focuses on grammar targets rather than communicative use.)

6.3. Teacher's roles and the role of L1

In the Lexical Approach, teachers are expected to develop students' ability to chunk, by creating appropriate contexts for each word, lexical phrase, and grammar target. Teachers work as a 'context creator', providing appropriate contexts for each element and guiding students to notice patterns of the target language. This approach emphasises the importance of students building up a foreign language network on their own. It recommends teaching words and phrases of the target language directly, appealing to the students' own world and L1 knowledge. The role of the teacher is to create an environment in which learners can operate effectively, helping them manage their own learning. The teacher should help learners discover for themselves the best and most effective way for them to learn (Willis, 1990: 131).

According to Lewis (1997a: chapter 4), in the field of foreign language teaching, people often complain that learners translate word-for-word, but they rarely suggest a better way. Lewis (1997a: 62) suggests that chunk-for-chunk translation should overcome this problem. Such a translation will have some rough grammatical edges, but almost certainly will successfully convey the content. Learners cannot translate chunk-for-chunk until they can successfully identify the chunks. Developing the ability to chunk texts of various kinds, therefore, is central to implementing the Lexical Approach. Correctly identified chunks do have equivalents in other languages, and to ignore this fact is to make the task of learning the L2 unnecessarily burdensome.

In the structural approach, teachers are expected to develop the students' ability to form, inserting a word into the frame. What teachers are expected to do is to present grammar rules and encourage the students to practise how to apply the rules by inserting a word randomly and producing sentences. Teachers work as a 'formulator' in a sense, assisting students to apply rules accurately. Teachers are required to correct learners' errors. This approach admits the interference from the first language, which can be predicted and avoided.

6.4. Teaching context and materials

Willis (1994: 56) suggests that materials should be offered to learners in such a way that they could not only repeat its surface form but also process it for meaning to discover what lies beneath the surface form. Material should also be generalisable in two ways: it should enable learners to generate language for themselves, and it should be informative when applied to other samples of the language encountered by the learners.

The Lexical Approach was originally developed in the English spoken environment for native teachers of English, who can use and create contexts for words accurately. Learners are surrounded by their target language and have many chances to use it. However, if we take a position in which input is highly valued, reading and listening activities provide such contexts, and non-native teachers can handle it (Medgyes, 1994). For this reason, materials should be developed carefully in collaboration with corpus and, preferably, with native speakers.

On the other hand, the structural approach has been developed in not only English spoken but also English-as-a-foreign-language environments. There are a huge number of publications on how to teach grammar for different levels or different L1 learners. We must note, however, that many grammar exercises generate grammatical but unnatural or unacceptable sentences. Not only learners but also teachers do not notice whether sentences they produce are actually natural and usable in communication, because naturalness in production is out of the scope, as the accurate application of rules is mainly targeted.

6.5. Types of proficiency

The goal of current language teaching is to develop the learner's communicative competence in L2. Communication itself is the principal vehicle of learning, as people learn a language best by actually using it to achieve real meanings and real outcomes (Little, 1994: 114). The Lexical Approach and the structural approach seek to facilitate students' communicative use of the target language. The Lexical Approach emphasises that if the learners learn chunks and lexis such as verbs and nouns, they automatically learn basic structures of the target language by means of hypothesis formation and testing processes. These patterns of language are put to use in communication. The goal of the Lexical Approach is to build up a large vocabulary and assist learners in analysing chunks and extracting rules. This can be promoted pedagogically by selecting vocabulary, making task-based activities, and implicitly or explicitly teaching basic patterns of the language for production (Willis, 2003). The Lexical Approach presupposes that word networks serve as a basis for accurate production; if one can use lexis and chunks accurately in a given context, daily communicative use of language with short phrases and simple sentences is achieved. Willis (1994: 63–64) claims that a lexically based approach is likely to be more powerful than a structural approach in two ways. Firstly, it offers generalisations that are more powerful. Once learners are aware of the hypothetical use of the grammar to encode a hypothesis, they are in principle capable of producing further sentences. They are also in a much better position to make sense of further input. Secondly, a lexical description depends on more powerful generalisations that the learner will have more evidence on which to base useful generalisations about the language. Lewis ed. (2000: 17) recognises the fact that advanced learners become frustrated when they are unable to talk or write about ideas they can comfortably express in their L1. He suggests that more complicated, convoluted grammatical structures do not help them at all, but the language that helps them communicate more complex ideas is different kinds of multi-word chunks. For this reason, what advanced learners need is more lexical entries and chunks that enable them to produce more utterances.

The goal of the structural approach is to develop grammatical rules accurately, in other words, to use the rules of the target language by inserting lexical items. The structural approach insists that the correct application of a grammar rule is the basis of accurate production. There is a domain-specific language module to do this job.

6.6. Learner's age

Lewis (1997a) suggests that the Lexical Approach is promising in English language teaching for all learners, from beginners to the advanced. Lewis seems to presuppose adult learners of English. I hypothesise that the Lexical Approach has some potential in teaching children English. This section discusses the relationship between children's cognitive development and the way to teach a foreign language to them.

Let us begin with reviewing Piaget's theory of cognitive development. Using observations, dialogues, and small-scale experiments, Piaget suggested that children progress through a series of stages in their thinking, each of which corresponds to broad changes in the structure or logic of their intelligence. Piaget called the main stages of development the sensory-motor (age 0–2), pre-operational (age 2–7), concrete-operational (age 7–12), and formal-operational (over age 12) stages, and emphasised that they occur in that order. In our discussion of teaching English at primary school, the concrete-operational and formal-operational stages are relevant. Let us look closely at these stages.

From about the age of seven years, children are able to handle immediately present objects. At this stage, there are limitations to thinking, because children are reliant on the immediate environment and have difficulty with abstract or invisible ideas and things. Take the following question (Smith, Cowie, & Blades, 1998: 353): 'Mary is taller than Lily. Mary is shorter than Susan. Who is the tallest?' This is a difficult problem for concrete-operational children to solve, yet, faced with dolls to rank in order, children could solve the problem immediately. What children at this stage cannot do is speculate abstractly. Abstract reasoning is not found until the child has reached the formal-operational stage.

Although children are only able to reason in terms of objects that are present in front of them during the concrete-operational period, they are able to reason hypothetically during the formal-operational period. Young people no longer depend on the concrete existence of things in the real world. Instead, it is possible to reason in terms of verbally stated hypotheses to consider the logical relations among several possibilities or to deduce conclusions from abstract statements. Young people are also better at solving problems by considering all possible answers in a systematic manner. When children achieve formal-operational thinking, they discover how to calculate and comprehend abstract concepts in science (including mathematics, physics, and linguistic analysis). Having discovered the rules or principles governing the phenomena in question, children realise that science can be used with certainty to predict what would and must happen, testing any predicted outcomes (Wood, 1998: 187–189). From his original work carried out in some schools in Geneva, Piaget claimed that formal-operational thinking was a characteristic stage that children reached between the ages of eleven and fifteen years. This claim, however, has been modified by more recent researchers who have found that the achievement of formal-operational thinking is more gradual and haphazard than Piaget assumed (Smith, Cowie, & Blades, 1998: 355). The period from eleven to fifteen years old signals the start of the possibility of formal-operational thought rather than its achievement.

Let us summarise Piaget's contribution to the field of learning (Wood, 1998: Introduction). Firstly, Piaget's theory places action and self-directed problem-solving at the heart of learning and development. Secondly, Piaget's theory offers a detailed and specific account of universal stages in human cognitive development, which provide a possible explanation as to when and how a child is ready to learn or develop specific forms of knowledge and understanding. Children actively construct their knowledge of the world. Thirdly, Piaget's theory leads to the claim that children's ability to understand what is said to them and their ability to use language informatively depends on their stage of intellectual development. The theory also predicts that young children at certain stages of development are theoretically incapable of expressing ideas that involve the ability to understand the world from another person's point of view. What they are able to say is constrained by their stage of development. The idea that children pass through stages of development and the assertion that they cannot learn or be taught how to function at higher levels before they have passed through the lower ones were taken up widely and formed the basis for the notion of *readiness*. Readiness involves not only the state of the child's existing knowledge but also his or her capacity to learn with help.

If Piaget's theory is sound, it follows that young children are incapable of seeing the world as adults do. Any attempt to teach them by demonstrating how things work is bound to fail if children do not possess the necessary mental operations to make sense of what they are shown. Attempts to show, explain, or question things to children before they are mentally ready cannot foster development, though the child may learn some empty procedures. Premature teaching and questioning may frustrate children who cannot begin to understand what they are being taught.

Piaget provided the most comprehensible account of cognitive growth, and it has had considerable implications for education. Piaget argued that children think quite differently from adults and view the world from a qualitatively different perspective. This means that what is appropriate for adult learning is not necessarily right for the child. From the Piagetian standpoint, children learn from actions rather than from passive observations. For instance, telling a child about the properties of materials is less effective than creating an environment, in which the child is free to explore, touch, manipulate, and experiment. Under this view, it is the child rather than the teacher who initiates the activity. A teacher needs to set tasks that are finely adjusted to the needs of the pupils and consequently are intrinsically motivating. Second, a teacher is concerned with process rather than product. A teacher's role is to create the conditions in which learning may best take place. Especially, in mathematics, science, and language lessons at primary school, a teacher should encourage practical and experimental activities before moving on to abstract deductive reasoning and explanations of rules. Lesh (1999) emphasises the importance of controlling the contents of the curriculum at primary schools: abstract rules should be avoided until children reach the formal-operational stage. This means that abstract rules should be introduced to the curriculum in the latter half of junior high school; otherwise, children will face an inevitable barrier in processing and understanding such rules. Rosser (1994: chapter 8) argues that the general problem-solving mechanism, a powerful device whose routines and programmes are applicable in any context to serve the individual's intellectual goals, is under development during primary school. Children eventually acquire strategies for solving problems in particular situations, and the rules are often quite concrete at the beginning. Gradually, the rules transfer across contexts as the child learns to use them more broadly, but transference may be constrained by time, experience, and opportunity. At each stage of development, the child's thinking becomes increasingly symbolic. With the attainment of operational thought, representation becomes truly co-ordinated and systematic. Concrete-operational thought is tied to the concrete, the real and physical facts of experience, in other words, a tight connection to the empirically real. The same level of intellectual prowess does not extend to either hypothesis or premises contrary to empirical fact. Children at this stage cannot reason about the logical validity of the form of the argument independent of the empirical validity of the premise's content. They can only focus on meaning (semantic content) but not form (syntax). The form cannot be analysed to understand other abstract concepts, but the form is recorded as it is, connected directly with the real-world event (Rosser, 1994: 233). Wood (1998: 216) claims that if we were to ask the concrete-operational children to tell us what a verb is, many would not be able to. Their speech is structured in such a way that only words that serve as verbs in the language are used in conjunction with verb-specific rules (O'Grady, 2005; Tomasello, 2003). The formal-operational stage makes individuals able to reason and problem solve with a truly formal abstract system of mental operations applicable to any and all conceivable content. A point of contrast between concrete and formal thinking is the difference between reasoning about what is possible in all possible worlds and reasoning about what is possible in the actual world (Menyuk & Brisk, 2005).

Regarding the educational implications, mathematical notions such as principles or axioms including abstract X, Y, Z operations, or linguistic categories such as grammatical categories, copula, transformational rules, etc., are inaccessible until children reach the formal-operational stage. In other words, hypothetical-deductive thinking and reasoning are possible only when children mature sufficiently (Rosser, 1994: 237–238). Howe (1999: chapter 3) suggests that teaching will be effective for getting children to learn in so far as the teaching encourages learners to engage in the kinds of mental processing activities that result in information being retained in the memory or learned. The important factor to facilitate this is meaningfulness. First, the information is easy to process at the child's current developmental stage. Second, the information must have personal relevance to the child. Learning relevant, easy-to-process information enhances an intention to learn. In short, the meaningfulness of tasks should be paid the most attention.

Teaching children English by the Lexical Approach is appropriate because this approach does not explain grammar rules in an abstract manner and children can understand what is going on. Children can recognise how lexis and chunks work in a natural setting. Human cognitive development requires that explicit grammar instruction should be given if and only if the learner has matured enough to process the abstract rules.

Conclusion

The following table summarises the differences between the two approaches:

Table 6–1: The Lexical and Structural Approaches

	Lexical Approach	Structural Approach
Theoretical basis	Grammaticalised lexis. Corpus linguistics (COBUILD), Discourse Analysis. Early L1 acquisition theories.	Lexicalised grammar. Prescriptive / Traditional / Generative grammar.
Types of syllabus and teaching methodology	Task-based syllabus. Word-level & Multi-word chunks. Observe-Hypothesis-Experiment. Word collocations/phrasal use.	Structuralised syllabus. Structurised rules + lexicon. Present-Practice-Produce. Accurate application of rules.
Teacher's roles and the role of L1	Develop students' ability to chunk. Produce contexts. Context/Discourse creator. Not word-for-word translation but chunk-for-chunk translation.	Develop students' ability to form. No context. Formulator. L1 interference. (Varies depending on position).
Teaching context	All learners. Suitable for English-speaking environment with native speakers of English. Suitable for advanced learners as well as children / beginners. Lexicon-based materials. Natural use of lexis/chunks.	Well-organised/controlled syllabus for all learners. Native and non-native speakers of English can handle. Grammar-based materials. Accurate application of rules.
Types of proficiency	Wider concepts, communicative use of words/chunks: pragmatic communication. Daily communicative use. Short, simple sentences. Various expressions fulfil advanced learners' needs.	Accurate application of rules. High academic level (accurate translation). Risk of producing unnatural, unacceptable sentences.
Learner's age	Both children and adults can be taught by this approach.	Only adults can be taught by this approach.

Chapter 7

The Lexical Approach in the Japanese context: Beyond the transformational method

Introduction

The Lexical Approach emphasises the importance of learning lexis and chunks, and claims that the role of language teaching is to teach useful stock phrases. It considers that speaking naturally is speaking idiomatically using fragments and familiar collocations, and thus learners have to learn these familiar sequences. Lewis (1993, 1997a) claims that a syllabus that only consists of a list of grammar rules does not lead learners to be accurate and fluent speakers of English, and the Lexical Approach should be one possible option to take. Lewis, however, does not deny the fact that grammar is important in language teaching, and proposes that a selection of grammar is necessary. He considers that metalinguistic knowledge as an analytic tool is not very important in language teaching, but that noticing the patterns of language is essential and crucial.

In this chapter, I will discuss the implications of this approach to English language teaching at junior and senior high schools in Japan. I will report on three empirical studies that show the possibilities of the Lexical Approach in the language classroom. We shall discuss new ways of introducing grammar points by means of the Lexical Approach. I point out the problems of the transformational method, and propose a different way of teaching passives, infinitives, and relative clauses, all of which have been taught by means of transformation and caused severe learning difficulties for many students. The empirical studies took place in normal classroom settings with four (or two) English teachers. I shall refer to them, including myself, as 'we' in reporting the studies. At first glance, the Lexical Approach focuses only on learning and teaching lexis. What I propose here is that the Lexical Approach can handle basic grammar points taught at junior high school. In this section, I will mainly focus on the grammar points widely taught by transformation. I shall discuss how to introduce lexical grammar points including tense and aspect in the next chapter (Willis & Willis, 1996: 92–95; Lewis, 1993: 116, 136; Bardovi-Harlig, 1992, 1997, 1999; Bardovi-Harlig & Reynolds, 1995; Blyth, 1997).

7.1. Passives

At a seminar on developing teaching skills, an expert in introducing passives showed up in high spirits, saying 'Hello, everyone. I open the door!' Then, he encouraged his students to passivise the sentence and to repeat it together, 'The door is opened by the teacher.' In this lesson, by pointing at objects and things in the classroom, the following sentences were continuously produced: 'The chalk is used by the teacher.' 'The tape is played by the teacher.' 'The window is moved by Ken.' etc. Although invited teachers and researchers observed his class closely, some of them, including myself, could not help questioning what he had done. What struck me is that we *never* produce such utterances in our daily lives, unless a particular context requires it.

This section seeks a better teaching methodology based on a real use of passives. First, we look briefly at the properties of passives. Second, we see that there are two different types of passives. Third, I discuss advantages and disadvantages of the standard transformational teaching method of passives. Last, appealing to the Lexical Approach, I propose a new method of teaching passives.

7.1.1. Properties of passives

In this section, we will have a brief look at two major properties of passives (Celce-Murcia & Larsen-Freeman, 1999: chapter 18; Dixon, 1991: chapter 9, 2005).

(1) Passives are used to avoid mentioning the subject.

Passives are usually used in a situation where the speaker does not know who the subject is, where the speaker does not wish to reveal the identity of the subject, or where the identity of the subject is obvious to the addressees and does not need to be expressed explicitly. Kennedy (1998: 134), who analysed a corpus totalling 323,000 words from eight registers, reports that among the agentive passives in the corpus which can be systematically related to active forms, 80% occur without an agent. This poses a question to pedagogical tradition, where the passives with an agent are introduced before the passives without an agent. Real uses of passives place the agent in a less prominent light than the one it has in pedagogical tradition.

(2) Passives are used to focus on the transitive object.
Passives are used in order to express that something happened to a person or a thing and that the person or the thing has been affected. The affected person/thing is focused on in a discourse and occurs in the subject position. A discourse is normally arranged around a topic, and there is always a preference for a topic to be the subject. Most of the exercises in the classroom ignore this requirement in a discourse, only transforming actives into passives in a mechanical fashion, which produces a large number of grammatical but unnatural and unacceptable passive sentences, as seen in the introduction.

7.1.2. Two types of passives

Generative grammarians hold that there are two different types of passives, one verbal and the other adjectival (Wasow, 1977; Jaeggli, 1986). Verbal passives are used with verbs that denote actions. For instance, *The ball was kicked. Mary was hit.* Adjectival passives are used with Psycho-verbs which denote emotions, such as *annoy, disgust, frighten, inspire, interest, please, satisfy, surprise, terrify,* etc. Interestingly, Grodzinsky (1991, 2000a, 2000b) hypothesises that the above two passives are processed by different brain mechanisms in the native-speaker's brain. He reports that adjectival passives are processed as adjectives and stored individually in the lexicon, while verbal passives are processed by conscious/unconscious identification of the agent-patient relations of the action denoted by the verb. This means that adjectival passives are processed as words or chunks and that verbal passives are processed under the abstract grammar rules by native-speakers of English.

7.1.3. Standard teaching method for passives

It has been common practice to introduce passives by means of transformation. First, an active sentence such as 'John loves Mary' is produced. Then, moving the object into the subject position, a passive sentence, 'Mary is loved by John', is generated.

The advantage of this method is as follows: Students soon get used to producing passives from actives by moving the object into the subject position. This mechanical rule application seems to be simple, and students attain high scores in this kind of exercise, which gives them great satisfaction.

However, teachers face the following problems: Students always try to produce actives first, which are then transformed into passives. It takes quite a long time to produce passives in speaking and writing, or students tend to avoid passives because of the operational load. This gives students the impression that passives play a secondary role and are unimportant. In their writing, few passives are used. Even if passives are used in speaking, they are quite awkward, because students have to go through the above transformational steps. Students tend to attach by-phrases every time as well, because they are taught that the subjects in active sentences must appear as by-phrases in passives. Students seem to feel that passives without by-phrases are wrong and so try hard to attach such by-phrases. As we have seen before, the real use of passives is far from the simple application of mechanical transformational rules. While negative aspects of the standard method are obvious, few past studies have been done in the field of grammar teaching to overcome this weakness.

7.1.4. How to introduce passives: Adoption of the Lexical Approach

This section discusses a new teaching methodology for passives taking the Lexical Approach. The Lexical Approach introduces new aspects of foreign language not by means of grammar-rule explanation but by means of words and phrases as a whole.

Regarding passive introduction, Lewis (1993: 136) suggests that passives should be introduced as adjectives:

Many supposed passives are indistinguishable from adjectives: *The road was closed (by the police).* Most supposed passive sentences do not contain the agent, and are best analysed as adjectives.

Lewis (1986: 133) and Willis (1990: 16–18, 1994: 56–59) propose that passives should be introduced as adjectives as well, comparing them with 'real' adjectives as follows:

I would be happy to hear the story.
I would be interested to hear the story.
I would be moved to hear the story.

By introducing passives in this way, students are expected to notice that passivisation is an adjectivalisation process of verbs.

With respect to the standard teaching method, Lewis (1993: 156) severely criticises it as follows:

Only rarely are active and passive alternatives equally suitable in context. Transformation practice based on single decontextualised sentences is fundamentally unsound.

Lewis (1986: chapter 15, 1993: chapter 8) claims that passives should be taught directly without appealing to any transformational rules. According to Lewis, passives are generated without any transformation in our mind. (Notice that he did not show any evidence supporting this claim.) Grodzinsky (1991, 2000a, 2000b), on the other hand, suggests that verbal passives are hypothesised to be comprehended by transformation in the native-speakers' mind. Although the final state of processing passives might include transformations, this section focuses on the process of arriving at such a final state by the learner of English as a foreign language. The empirical study will show that the standard transformational teaching method, which can be considered as the direct application of the processing of passives, needs some thought. The final state of processing passives and the process of reaching such a state guided by teaching do not overlap.

When we tried to teach passives under Willis' and Lewis' Lexical Approach, we faced the following problem. Although their proposals are convincing and inspiring, they did not show sufficiently how to implement their approach in the classroom. It sounds optimistic just to point out that transformation is unrealistic and unsound. We wish to know what the alternative is and how effective it is. I will report what we have done below, accepting the implications of the Lexical Approach.

From the very beginning of introducing passives, we stuck to the real use of passives. Our oral introduction went as follows: (Note that we are not suggesting that this is the best way of introducing passives nor recommending that all teachers accept it. We suppose that while we have taught all words and past tense forms used here, vocabulary used in the passage is too difficult for students at other schools. The important point is that we should stick to the natural use of passives.) Wearing a bandage around our legs, we went into our classes showing a picture of Spot and pointing at him in the photo when necessary to clarify what the pronoun *he/his/him* refers to, saying:

'Yesterday, Tom's dog, Spot, was in a very bad mood. He kept barking at me. Tom got so angry. The noisy dog was beaten. Spot was kicked, and was locked up in his house. After a while, when Tom unlocked his house, I was attacked by Spot. I was bitten by him. I was so shocked.'

Then, we set a language activity session using pictures, objects, and actions. We showed the following simple short dialogue. The pair-work exercise aims at helping students understand when to use passives:

Table 7–1: Dialogue to practise passives

Student A:	Student B:
What happened to X? **What's the matter with X?** X = -person/animal: *you, Jim, Spot, Pochi…* -place: *Iraq, Korea, New York, Quebec, Hiroshima, the library/park…* -things: *the camera, the tulip, the pen, the car…*	**X was __ed (by Y).** _ed = exhausted, arrested, patted, destroyed, conquered, bombed, closed, used, picked…

Finally, creative and communicative activities were introduced. We lent out the pictures and objects if necessary. We encouraged our students to create a story under different situations. We used role-play activities as Table 7–2.

In addition, we have recognised that focusing on passives in the context of spoken language is insufficient, because passives are much more tied up in the needs of formal written communication to have abstract or non-human reference nouns in the subject position. We set reading sessions using our textbook to encourage students to observe real uses of passives in formal texts.

Table 7–2: Role-playing to practise passives

Situation	Role	Target use
Hospital	doctor/nurse & patient	eye – transplanted leg/arm – broken decayed teeth – pulled out…
Airport	passenger & assistant /policeman	seat – reserved bag – stolen passport – issued
Restaurant	waiter/waitress & customer	ice cream – served VAT/GST – included vegetarian food – provided
Hotel	receptionist/porter & guest	suitcase – carried twin room – booked telephone – used

7.1.5. Empirical study

(1) Background

This study was done in a normal classroom setting. Passives are introduced to students in the second term of the second year at junior high school (age 14). Students were previously taught SV, SVC, and SVO structures, present-past-progressive tenses, *when*-clauses, and simple short greetings.

(2) Participants

Two Japanese teachers of English (aged 36 and 41) joined the empirical study. One teaches at a private junior high school and the other at a public junior high school. At the two schools, we set up two groups: class 1&2/A&B for the transformational method (Group A: 160 students) and class 3&4/C&D for the new method (Group B: 160 students). The proportions of the students' proficiency of English had previously been controlled by exam results. Each class was arranged to be well-balanced regarding the students' command of English: 20% of the students received an A (marked over 80% in the mid-term and end-term examinations), 30% received a B (between 79–60 %), 30% received a C (between 59–40%), and 20% received a D (below 39%). As we could not re-arrange classes only for the empirical study and as we wished to investigate the overall differences between the two methods, we pursued our study with the classes as they were.

(3) Procedure

While we had to use a textbook authorised by the Ministry of Education (*New Total English* Book 2: Lessons 10 & 11), exercises could be produced freely. We prepared the teaching plans together. We stuck to using the texts in the textbook, exactly the same passives (amount and content) in exercises, and the same timing of the language activity sessions. This means that students were exposed to exactly the same quality and quantity of passives with two different methods. We spent five lessons teaching passives (45 minutes each) in December 1998 and December 1999.

(4) Testing

We tested the students by means of an English to Japanese translation test and a Japanese to English translation test, as shown in Appendix L. In addition, we tested the students by the picture verification test. In this test (ten questions), students were asked to explain what happened to the person or the animal in the picture. For example, by showing a picture where Jim is attacking Spot, students were asked what happened to Spot. We timed their responses between just after the end of questioning and the completion of answering the question.

(5) Results and discussion

The results of teaching passives by the standard method and by the new method are as follows: At first glance, there were no large differences between the two groups, which seemed to suggest that we should abandon the new method and return to the standard one.

It turned out, however, that the degrees of fluency, accuracy, and preservation were significantly different. (We conducted the empirical study twice and similar results were obtained.) As for fluency, it took an average of 8.625 seconds (SD 2.055) in Group A, but only 4.422 seconds (SD 1.301) in Group B ($p<0.01$) to produce passives in the picture verification test. Students in Group A tended to generate actives first and passivise them, or to ponder just after saying the subjects, which meant that the students spent a long time answering one question. Their typical response went as follows:

__Jim __ Oh, no ___ Spot __ er _ is _ was _ hit _ hitted __ e ___ hittin ___Jim ___ a __ by _ Jim.

As for accuracy, although the two groups reached more or less correct passives with larger standard deviation in Group A, which shows larger differences among students, in the picture verification test (83.1 points SD 8.6 in Group A, and 85.6 points SD 3.4 in Group B; $p<0.05$), the production by the students in Group A was awkward, correcting themselves while generating passives.

As for preservation, we tested the same groups of students after six months. We did not teach passives explicitly during these six months. We used the same testing procedures. Group A took 9.331 seconds on average (SD 3.120) to produce a response, with 77.3 points (SD 7.5), while Group B took 4.315 seconds (SD 1.605) to produce a response ($p<0.01$), with 94.3 points (SD 3.3) ($p<0.05$).

Table 7–3: Differences between standard and new methods

	Standard method (Group A)	New method (Group B)
Fluency	8.625 seconds (SD 2.055)	4.422 seconds (SD 1.301)
Accuracy	83.1 points (SD 8.6)	85.6 points (SD 3.4)
Preservation	9.331 seconds (SD 3.120) 77.3 points (SD 7.5)	4.315 seconds (SD 1.605) 94.3 points (SD 3.3)

The translation test shows similar results. The accuracy ($p<0.05$) and preservation rates ($p<0.01$) were significantly different.

	Standard method (Group A)	New method (Group B)
Accuracy	81.7 (SD 9.2)	88.4 (SD 2.7)
Preservation	74.8 (SD 9.1)	93.1 (SD 2.9)

The first problem regarding the new method was the way to handle past participles. We accepted the generative grammar explanation for this. We explained that past participles are adjectivalised verb forms ([+V –N] → [+V +N]). We showed students a list of the adjectivalised verbs on the blackboard, which helped them access the past participles they wished to use. Some teachers wondered how to handle the present perfect (*have* + *past participles*). The philosophy of language (Reichenbach, 1958; Poidevin & MacBeath, 1993) proposes that the present perfect form reflects the human unconscious processing of time: A state denoted by the verb is 'owned' at the time of speaking in the present perfect, which is embodied by the auxiliary verb 'have'. By appealing to this idea, past participles can be considered as adjectivalised verbs, denoting the state of affairs.

The second problem was that students tend to overgeneralise passives to some verbs. They passivise the following unaccusative verbs (cf. Balcom, 1997; Oshita, 2000): *consist (*The group is consisted of ten members.), happen (*The accident was happened in December 1985.), fall (*Ken was fallen in love with Kim.), arrive (*Bill was arrived in Tokyo more than ten hours ago.), lead (*The economical recession was led Korean students to escape from their country.), remain (*Joe was remained silent.),* etc. (The asterisk * shows that the sentence is ungrammatical.) These errors are generated by students taught by the standard method as well, which means that this is not a problem particular to the new method. I hypothesise, according to their self-analysis, that they process these verbs either by considering consciously or unconsciously that the subject of the sentence is affected, which makes them produce the above passivised sentences, or by directly translating Japanese forms into English. I suggest that teachers should point out the meaning and usage of the verbs before they fossilise, while these overgeneralised errors are interpretable: the hearer does not face serious difficulties in figuring out what happened to whom.

Conclusion

This section argues that the standard transformational teaching method leads learners to become unnatural users of passives, and that teaching passives without any transformation, producing passive sentences directly in the appropriate contexts, is more effective in terms of fluency, accuracy, and preservation.

7.2. Infinitives

This section focuses on the teaching of infinitives to Japanese learners of English. First, we have a brief look at three types of infinitives: nominal, adjectival, and adverbial infinitives. Second, we investigate the reasons why infinitives are difficult for Japanese learners of English to master. Third, I discuss the introduction of infinitives to beginners by means of three potential methods: chunking based on the Lexical Approach, noticing, and transformational instruction. I will show that a modified way of chunking has an advantage over the others when introducing infinitives.

7.2.1. Types of infinitives

Three types of infinitives are required to be taught at junior high school under the current Course of Study regulated by the Japanese Ministry of Education.

(1) Nominal infinitives

Nominal infinitives function as nouns in a sentence. They work as the subject, object, or complement in a sentence.

To climb Mt. Fuji is boring. (Subject)
I want to visit Okinawa. (Object)
Her wish is to study art in France. (Complement)

(2) Adjectival infinitives

Adjectival infinitives modify nouns or pronouns that precede the infinitival clauses.

This is the way to get to the station.
There are many places to visit in Kyoto.
I want something to drink.

(3) Adverbial infinitives

Adverbial infinitives modify verbs, adverbs, adjectives, or sentences as a whole.

We must wait for a few weeks to enjoy beautiful cherry trees.
She went to Paris to study painting.
He was excited to hear the news.

7.2.2. Difficulties in mastering infinitives

There are two major reasons why infinitives are difficult for Japanese learners of English to master.

(1) Two verbs/events in one sentence

Under the Course of Study, infinitives constitute the first grammar point that includes two verbs. Before infinitives are introduced, students are mostly taught simple sentences such as SV, SVC, and SVO structures. Infinitives are introduced as expressions that describe two events at once. Let us consider:

John went to the library to find Jim's book.

In this sentence, two events, i.e., John's going to the library and John's finding Jim's book, are addressed. The problem faced by learners is how to process these two events. Learners find it difficult to process the sentence when the infinitival clause shows up. They tend to be stuck when another verb suddenly appears in one sentence. This processing problem is related to the difficulty caused by the structural differences between English and Japanese: Students tend to interpret the sentence as 'John went to the library, and found Jim's book'. (A similar phenomenon is reported in Flynn, 1987 and Pienemann, 1986).

(2) Opposite modification directions

As was well-researched by Flynn (1987), the structures of English and Japanese are markedly different. As for word order, English is SVO and Japanese is SOV. Regarding modification directions, English modifies from right to left and Japanese from left to right in longer phrases and clauses. Returning to infinitival clauses, let us compare:

Table 7–4: Structural differences between English and Japanese infinitives

	English: main - modifier	Japanese: modifier - main
Adjectival infinitives	N [to V] places [to visit]	[V to] N [tazuneru tameno] basho (visit) (to) (place)
Adverbial infinitives	S V (O) [to V (O)]. John called Mary [to say good-bye].	S (O) [(O) V to] V. John-wa(John) Mary-ni(Mary) [say-onara-o(good-bye) iu(say) tameni(to)] denwaokaketa(called).

The above structural differences between English and Japanese cause marked problems. In the following section, we discuss three theoretically and empirically driven teaching methods to overcome the problems. I report on our empirical study in which the three methods are compared in the classroom.

7.2.3. Teaching methodologies for infinitives

(1) Chunking, based on the Lexical Approach

This method was proposed by Willis (1990), Nattinger & DeCarrico (1992), and Lewis (1993) under the name of the Lexical Approach. These researchers suggest that new aspects of grammar should be introduced not by means of explicit explanations of rules but by direct teaching as chunks. Regarding infinitive instruction, without employing grammatical jargon such as 'nominal/adjectival/adverbial infinitives, modification', etc., the following expressions are to be taught directly in a sentence: *want/wish/hope to, try to, begin/start to, promise to, something to drink/eat/read, places to visit/go, it is (adjective) for (person) to V.* Providing appropriate contexts in which the above expressions are used, students are encouraged to produce and memorise the patterns as chunks. In addition, dialogue exercises as used in the instruction of passives were introduced, in which students could respond only by infinitival clauses. For instance, 'A: Why did you go to New Zealand? 'B: To study English.' 'A: What do you want to do after class?' 'B: To have lunch.' 'A: What did you find in the museum?' 'B: Something interesting to see.' No explicit analyses of grammar were provided.

(2) Noticing

The notion of noticing in language teaching stems from cognitive psychological investigations of foreign language learning: Learning takes place when learners notice new aspects of language. Referring to Ellis & Gaies (1999), one lesson is organised as follows: Note that the structure of the lesson shown below is quite similar to the one proposed in the Lexical Approach, and can be included in chunking instruction above.

Listening to comprehend: Students are to listen to a short conceptualised passage (text in our textbook) and try to understand the general meaning of the text.
Listening to notice: Students next listen to the same text again in order to focus attention on how infinitives work in the text.
Understanding the grammar point: Students now provide a short analysis of a grammar contrast in the text. Through this analysis task, students are guided to see how the grammar point works and to formulate a grammar rule (inductive learning).
Checking: Students check their understanding of the grammar rule by completing a short exercise with a new set of sentences.
Trying it: Finally, students have an opportunity to try out the grammar rule with sentences of their own.

(3) Transformational method
Students' first language is compared with the target structure thoroughly in explicit manners (deductive learning). Translation is the major procedure of this method. Infinitivalisation processes are taught explicitly. For instance, firstly, we generate two sentences, 'John went to the library' and 'John found Bill's book'. Secondly, infinitivalisation, a kind of transformation, generates an infinitival clause, 'to find Bill's book'. Lastly, connecting the two sentences, we can generate 'John went to the library to find Bill's book'.

7.2.4. Empirical study

(1) Background
This study was done in a normal classroom setting. Infinitives are introduced to students in the first term of the second year at junior high school (age 14). Students were previously taught SV, SVC, and SVO structures, present-past-progressive tenses, and simple short greetings. Infinitives are the first clauses that make sentences more complicated.

(2) Participants
Two Japanese teachers of English (aged 36 and 41) joined the empirical study. One teaches at a private junior high school and the other at a public junior high school. At the two schools, we set three groups: class 1&2/A&B for chunking (160 students), class 3&4/C&D for noticing (160 students), and class 5&6/E&F for the transformational method (160 students). The proportions of the students' proficiency of English had previously been controlled by exam results. Each class was arranged to be well-balanced regarding students' command of English: 20% of the students received an A (marked over 80% in the mid-term and end-term exams), 30% received a B (between 79–60 %), 30% received a C (between 59–40%), and 20% received a D (below 39%). As we could not re-arrange classes only for the empirical study and as we wished to investigate the overall differences among three methods, we pursued our study with the classes as they were.

(3) Procedure
While we had to use a textbook authorised by the Ministry of Education (*New Total English* Book 2: Lessons 3 & 4), exercises could be produced freely. We prepared the teaching plans together. We stuck to using the texts in the textbook, exactly the same infinitives (amount and content) in exercises, and the same tim-

ing of the language activity sessions. This means that students were exposed to exactly the same quality and quantity of infinitival clauses with three different methods. We spent four lessons to teach infinitives (45 minutes each). We set the empirical study twice (May 1999 and May 2000).
Chunking: Students were encouraged to practice the infinitival clauses in the textbook, substituting subject and object:

Student A: What do you / does John/Mary/Ken… want to be in the future?
Student B: I/He/She want/wants to be a doctor/teacher/computer programmer…

This kind of practice was done in a natural context.
Noticing: We first played the texts from the textbook, and asked some questions in order to make sure that students understood the content. Second, we gave out blanked texts, and asked the students to fill in the gaps while listening to the same text. For instance:

I want ____ an apple pie. I went ____ her. You wanted cloth ____.

Third, students were encouraged to figure out the grammatical rules (to + verb). Fourth, we gave them some practice. We referred to Ellis & Gaies (1999: Lesson 35) in preparing for our lessons.
Transformational method: First, we read the texts together. Second, we explained each sentence, focusing on the structural differences, doing transformational exercises, and translating into Japanese. Last, we gave them some exercises.
Let us now look at the average timing of our lessons based on the recording in the classroom. ○ means that the activity in the column took an average of more than 15 minutes per lesson. △ means 6–14 minutes per lesson. × means less than 5 minutes per lesson. – means zero minutes. 'Patterns' means that students did pattern practice. 'Translation' means that teachers/students put the texts into Japanese. 'Structure' means that teachers explained the structural differences explicitly. 'Listening' means that students had chances to listen to the texts by CD.

Table 7–5: Overall timing of the three methods

	Patterns	Translation	Structure	Listening	Use of L1	Production
Chunking	○	×	—	△	△	○
Noticing	△	△	△	○	△	○
Transformation	—	○	○	×	○	△

'Use of L1' means that the teachers used Japanese to explain grammar points. 'Production' means that students had a chance to produce infinitives freely.

(4) Testing

After the four lessons, we tested the students using a comprehension and a production test. The comprehension test consisted of listening (choosing a sentence that has a similar meaning to the orally given sentence: 10 questions), and English to Japanese translation (15 questions). The production test included controlled-writing (including Japanese to English translation: 15 questions) and storytelling (including picture verification tasks). Translation tests are shown in Appendix M. Students were told that the results of these tests would be included on considering their final evaluation. The same tests were done after six months to investigate the rate of preservation. We had no opportunities to teach infinitives explicitly after this, because we had to continue teaching new grammar targets from the textbook.

(5) Result and discussion

The following tables summarise the results of the three different teaching methods. Under the column of 'Immediately', the results just after the lessons are shown, and under the column of '6 months', the scores achieved six months later are shown. Note that the results obtained in the two empirical studies are similar.

Table 7–6: Results of comprehension test (% correct)

	Chunking		Noticing		Transformation	
	Immediately	6 months	Immediately	6 months	Immediately	6 months
Nominal	66.5	70.1	65.1	75.4	69.8	74.3
Adjectival	65.9	72.1	66.3	74.4	68.7	75.0
Adverbial	42.7	63.4	51.7	70.6	66.8	73.9

Table 7–7: Results of production test (% correct)

	Chunking		Noticing		Transformation	
	Immediately	6 months	Immediately	6 months	Immediately	6 months
Nominal	71.8	73.4	67.3	75.5	63.4	71.3
Adjectival	73.4	74.8	68.6	76.8	66.5	73.4
Adverbial	60.9	66.7	63.7	67.2	69.4	71.4

By means of the t-test among the three teaching methods, the following conclusions can be drawn. (The reason why I used the t-test rather than analysis of variance (ANOVA) is that ANOVA only tells us whether there is a significant difference among the three methods but does not necessarily lead us to conclude that one method is better than the others. The t-test, however, makes it possible to suggest that one method is superior to the others. See Hoel, 1981.) The average scores of the 160 students taught by each method above reveal that chunking and noticing are better methods than the transformational method when teaching nominal and adjectival infinitives ($p<0.05$), while transformation is superior to the others in adverbial infinitives ($p<0.01$). Focusing on the difference between comprehension and production tests, chunking is strong in production ($p<0.01$), while transformation shows an advantage over the others in comprehension ($p<0.01$). Regarding preservation, noticing is slightly better than the others ($p<0.05$). Interestingly, the students' average scores got better after six months. This is because infinitives continuously appeared in the textbook, and students had chances to review them. The above results can be summarised as follows:

- Chunking is suitable for nominal and adjectival infinitives, because I assume that these infinitives are processable as chunks in natural use. Nominal infinitives can be considered as nominalised verbs like gerunds, and it is natural that we treat them as nouns (Celce-Murcia & Larsen-Freeman, 1999: chapter 31). While adjectival infinitives include structural differences, the combinations of noun + infinitival clause can be processed as a whole with ease.
- Noticing is suitable for nominal and adjectival infinitives as well.
- Regarding adverbial infinitives, chunking and noticing need some modification. Students had trouble figuring out the meaning of the sentences because they were too long to process structurally, unless they knew how to process the different modification directions. The transformational method gives an advantage over others, because structural differences between English and Japanese are explicitly explained in detail and students have ample opportunities to practise them. (However, later practice revealed that this infinitive is often used as chunks to respond to questions in daily communication. For example, 'A: Why did you go to Kyoto?' 'B: To visit temples' or 'C: To see my grandmother'. In writing, a phrase, *in order to,* is commonly used, and this can be introduced as a chunk.)

- Although noticing uses listening most frequently, this method had no visible effect on students' general listening ability. I suppose that this is because listening is used to let students notice new aspects of grammar, rather than to enhance general listening skills. (This point is consistent with Hulstijn & Hulstijn's (1984) empirical results.)

Overall, I propose a lesson design as follows: A framework of a lesson accepts noticing (or the Lexical Approach shown in chapter six), and the way to explain and practise the new grammar target should be slightly modified with respect to the types of infinitives.

Nominal infinitives should be taught as chunks without explicit grammar explanations. One possibility is to treat them as set phrases and not as members of infinitives, because they do not function in the same way as the other infinitives do: Although other infinitives modify sentential elements, nominal infinitives do not, purely working as nouns.

Adjectival infinitives should be taught as chunks as well. However, different modification directions should be explained, as students will be taught relative clauses in the near future. It is essential for students to understand the structural differences.

Adverbial infinitives should include explicit grammar explanations. Even if some adverbial infinitives like 'I'm glad to see you' can be taught as chunks, others such as 'John went to the library to find Bill's book' need some explanation on how to interpret the sentence. At first, this can be introduced as follows: 'A: Why did John go to the library?' 'B: To find Bill's book.' 'A: So, John went to the library to find Bill's book, right?' Students' opportunities to practise them in order to understand them should be assured.

The following table summarises the ideal combinations of teaching each type of infinitive.

Table 7–8: Types of infinitives and teaching methods

Type of infinitives	Combinations of teaching methods
Nominal infinitives	Noticing & Chunking
Adjectival infinitives	Noticing & Chunking with structural explanations
Adverbial infinitives	Noticing & structural explanations

The following year, we tested the above combinations of teaching methods with new students who were arranged in exactly the same way as in the previous year. The results of teaching each type of infinitive are as follows:

Table 7–9: Combinations of teaching methods and results

	Comprehension		Production	
	Immediately	6 months	Immediately	6 months
Nominal	78.3	79.8	77.1	78.6
Adjectival	79.7	80.2	78.9	81.2
Adverbial	77.3	79.5	76.8	78.5

I conclude that chunking and noticing are effective. I propose the following structure of each lesson:

1. Listening to comprehend: students listen to the passage of the lesson.
2. Understanding the grammar point: students try to find the grammar rules.
3. Checking: when teaching adjectival and adverbial infinitives, explicit grammar explanation for the different modification directions is necessary.
4. Trying it: chunking activities for nominal and adjectival infinitives are necessary.

Conclusion

This section searches for a way to introduce English infinitives to Japanese learners which are very difficult for them to master. The empirical study has shown that nominal and adjectival infinitives should be taught by chunking, while adverbial infinitives need some explicit grammar instruction. Ellis & Gaies' proposal on teaching grammar, that is, noticing, which is similar to the Lexical Approach, is worth our attention. Their overall framework of one lesson was shown to be effective, and, if necessary, especially if the learner's first language and his/her target language are extremely different, explicit grammar explanations should be of great help.

7.3. Relative clauses

Relative clauses are one of the most difficult grammar targets for Japanese learners of English to master and for Japanese teachers of English to teach. Restrictive relative clauses are introduced in English classes in the second term of the final year at junior high school (age 15). We have recognised that every time we start teaching these, students struggle with the grammar target. Moreover, I have been informed that Japanese university students at the Language Centres of the University of London and the University of Edinburgh still have difficulty in producing relative clauses accurately despite some years of studying English. In this section, we investigate the reasons why relative clauses are difficult for Japanese learners of English from an applied linguistic point of view, and, then, propose a better way of teaching relative clauses based on the theoretical investigations. Firstly, I discuss the proposed approaches to the learning problems of relative clauses in order to clarify what the problems are. I focus on the Noun Phrase Accessibility Hierarchy Hypothesis put forward by Keenan & Comrie (1977) and Comrie & Keenan (1979a, 1979b), the Head-direction Parameter Hypothesis of Flynn (1984, 1989a, 1989b), the Perceptual Difficulty Hypothesis of Bever & Langendoen (1970), and Functional Category acquisitions discussed in section 2.3.4. In this subsection, I discuss issues of linguistic competence, which are supposed to be faced by all Japanese learners of English. Secondly, I propose a teaching methodology based on the above linguistic investigations. I compare the standard transformational teaching method, that is, the two-sentence connection, with the hierarchical teaching method based on the Lexical Approach, and an empirical study shows how effective the latter teaching methodology is.

7.3.1. The difficulties in learning relative clauses

In this section, I examine past studies on why relative clauses are difficult for Japanese learners of English to master. I look at the Noun Phrase Accessibility Hierarchy Hypothesis and the Head-direction Parameter Hypothesis, which complement rather than compete with each other. These two hypotheses account for the learning problems inside relative clauses. Then, I discuss the Perceptual Difficulty Hypothesis, which tries to explain the problem outside relative clauses. Last, I discuss Functional Category acquisitions, which try to explain problems associated with Agreement.

(1) Noun Phrase Accessibility Hierarchy Hypothesis:
Object relative clauses are more difficult than subject relative clauses.

Keenan & Comrie (1977) and Comrie & Keenan (1979a, 1979b) attempt to determine the universal typological properties of relative clauses by comparing their syntactic forms in about fifty languages worldwide. On the basis of data from these fifty languages, they argue that languages vary with respect to which NP patterns can be relativised and that the variation is not random, but rather the relativisability of certain positions is dependent on that of others and these dependencies are universal. The Accessibility Hierarchy below expresses the relative accessibility to relativisation of NP positions in simplex main clauses:

Accessibility Hierarchy:
SUBJECT > DIRECT OBJECT > INDIRECT OBJECT > MAJOR OBLIQUE CASE NP > GENITIVE > OBJECT OF COMPARISON

- A > B: A is more accessible than B.

Accessibility Hierarchy Constraint:
If a language can relativise any position on the Accessibility Hierarchy, then it can relativise all higher positions.

Many applied linguists set up experimental studies to find out whether this hierarchy can be seen in foreign language learning, and they all support this hierarchy (Gass, 1979; Pavesi, 1986; Hawkins, 1989; Doughty, 1991; and Hamilton, 1994). They all show that L2 learners have less difficulty with the relative clause types higher up the Accessibility Hierarchy and more difficulty with those lower down the hierarchy. We can interpret their results as follows: Both English and Japanese have relative clauses which are structurally parallel except for the head-direction (which is to be discussed below), so it is not necessary for Japanese learners of English to learn any new types of relative clauses. Following the Accessibility Hierarchy shown above, subject relativisation is easier than object relativisation in English and Japanese, which leads us to conclude that it is easier for Japanese learners of English to master the former compared to the latter. This analogy is predicted in the free writing data obtained from Japanese students.

(2) Head-direction Parameter Hypothesis:
It is difficult to master relative clauses because of the opposite head-directions.

Hawkins (1989), in discussing the difficulties in acquiring relative clauses that learners may face, suggests that both relational aspects among languages and structural aspects within a language play an important role. His suggestion about language acquisition can be understood as follows: if we wish to discuss the reasons why a particular grammar target causes a problem, we should look at both relativised universality and structural differences among the languages in question. In our present discussion, the Noun Phrase Accessibility Hierarchy Hypothesis, which tells us the relational universal, and the Head-direction Parameter Hypothesis, which is about structures of languages, complement each other.

In the Chomskyan tradition, it is proposed that the parameter-setting model of language acquisition plays an important role in accounting for both the diversity of languages and the rapid and uniform development of language among children on the basis of a fixed set of principles. As such, it is both a theory of the principles of grammar and a theory of the biological endowment for language with which all individuals are uniformly and uniquely endowed. In X-bar theory, there are two possible parameters proposed regarding the head and branching directions; head-initial (right branching) and head-final (left branching). English is a head-initial language and Japanese is a head-final language. This structural difference reflected in relative clauses is expected to cause difficulties for Japanese learners of English.

Flynn (1984, 1989a, 1989b), as well as Hawkins (1989), focuses on this matter and reports that it is extremely difficult to master relative clauses of a target language which has the opposite head-direction from one's first language. Flynn's experimental design is as follows: An experimenter gives orally, one at a time, sentences from a set of sentence batteries to 53 Japanese ESL students, who are then asked to repeat each sentence as presented. By means of this sentence imitation test, Flynn found that Japanese students had serious difficulty in building up correct relative clauses: they tend to get stuck whenever a relative clause comes up and fail to repeat the sentences accurately. She reports this phenomenon as follows:

Stimulus: The policeman questioned the man who carried the baby.
Response: The policeman questioned a man… *or:* Who carried the baby?

In our free writing and translation tests, I found some common errors associated with the Head-direction parameter as follows:

Errors in writing (indicated by an asterisk*):

a. a girl who is standing over there (English)
mukou-ni tatteiru syoujo (Japanese)
over there standing girl
*over there standing girl
*who is standing over there girl
*who is standing girl over there

b. The picture which I took is beautiful. (English)
watashi-ga totta syashin-wa utsukushii. (Japanese)
I Nom took picture Nom beautiful (Nom = Nominative Particle)
*I took a picture is beautiful.

The common errors above show that students tend to put Japanese structure into English directly, transferring the rightward modification in a Japanese way. (N.B. Pinker (1994) reports that these structures are actually found in the Creole English spoken by Hawaiian Japanese. This fossilisation of Japanese structure in English is worth our attention.)

(3) Perceptual Difficulty Hypothesis:
Centre-embedded relative clauses are more difficult than right-branching ones.

Let us discuss matrix clauses as a whole, showing the perceptual problems involved in understanding a relativised sentence, investigating why the centre-embedded types of relative clauses always cause a problem for Japanese learners of English.

Dating back to the 1970s, Bever & Langendoen (1970) set up some psycholinguistic experiments on sentence processing, and proposed the following 'Perceptual Strategy':

A: NP V → [NP V]
B: NP V NP → [NP V NP]

- The application of strategy A precedes that of B.

They propose that human cognitive systems parse (group up) English sentences as above when processing the flow of a sentence. A is applied to a sequence of NP and V and this is parsed as [NP V], and B, the sequence of NP V and NP is parsed as [NP V NP]. The application of Strategy A must precede that of B.

It is possible to omit the object relative pronouns but not the subject ones. This can be explained by the perceptual differences between them. Consider a subject relative clause without 'who':

[I know] → [I know a boy] → [I know][a boy likes math].
Similar errors: *We stayed at a hotel was very nice.
*I had a lunch named *Soba* was delicious.

Perceptually, this parsing process has two possibilities: 'a boy' can be interpreted as either the internal argument of 'know' or the external argument of 'like'. Usually, consistent with the requirement in grammar that a sentence must have only one subject-and-verb pairing, and the thematic relations of a verb (know: [NP_ NP/CP], like: [NP_NP]), this sentence is interpreted as 'I know that a boy likes math', which is not the expected reading. The grammar makes it obligatory to add a subject relative pronoun to a sentence that begins with the shared noun and a finite verb, and that modifies a noun that precedes the verb in its own clause.

The cognitive aspect of sentence perception is developed in Kuno (1974). He looks closely at the typological differences in relative clauses among languages, inspired by Greenberg's (1963) famous language universals and Chomsky's (1965) cognitive approach to linguistics. Kuno puts forward the idea that centre-embedded clauses always cause perceptual difficulty in human cognition (For similar proposals in the SLA tradition, see Pienemann, 1984, 1989). Kuno states:

> I conjecture that the fact that centre-embedding (but not right- or left-embedding) reduces comprehensibility is related to a limitation on the human capacity of temporary memory. (Kuno, 1974: 120, the claim comes directly from Chomsky, 1965.)

Kuno's idea that centre-embedding causes more perceptual difficulty can be understood as 'discontinuity' in psycholinguistics. The notion of discontinuity applies as follows: Centre-embedding of the relative clause sets up a discontinuity in the main clause, and embedded object wh-traces created by relativisation set up two phrasal discontinuities within the relative clause, i.e., a discontinuous VP and a discontinuous IP, whereas embedded subject wh-traces set up only a single discontinuous IP.

Translation from English into Japanese;

The girl who is standing over there is Mary.
'mukou-ni tatteiru syoujo-wa meari-desu'
*syoujo-ga tatteite, mukou-ni meari-ga iru.
girl Nom standing over there Mary be
(= A girl is standing, and Mary is over there.)

The students who made this error are supposed to parse the English sentence as follows:

[The girl (who) is standing]
→ [The girl (who) is standing][over there is Mary]

They read the sentence as if there were no relative pronoun and two separate sentences were given; their Japanese translation is identical to an English sentence, 'The girl is standing, and over there is Mary'. They fail to recognise that the relative clause 'who is standing over there' which modifies the head noun, interferes with a sentential stream of 'The girl is Mary'.

The tendency of beginners to interpret relative clauses as if two sentences were connected with *and* is observed by L1 acquisition researchers. For example, O'Grady (1997: chapter 9) reports that children in the process of acquiring English relative clauses produce such a co-ordinate structure. He calls this 'the Conjoined Clause Strategy':

The Conjoined Clause Strategy:

Interpret a string of the type NP V…V… as a co-ordinate structure of the type NP V…and…V… (O'Grady, 1997: 182)

Hayashibe et al. (1976, 1977) investigated a sequence of acquisitions of Japanese relative clauses by Japanese children under Bever's framework, and report that the above strategy is used by Japanese children as well. The discontinuity in sentence perception is problematic for all language learners from a human cognitive point of view.

The notion of discontinuity can be applied to the universally accepted conclusion from the Noun Phrase Accessibility Hierarchy Hypothesis that object relativisation is less accessible than subject relativisation. The relative pronouns move across IPs and VPs when we relativise from the object position, but only across IPs from the subject position. These structural differences can be interpreted as showing that discontinuity in the structures causes different degrees of learning problems.

The discontinuity problem reveals the importance of analysing both linear and hierarchical structures. Linear order gives us the sequence 'NP RP (NP) VP VP' and hierarchical structure tells us that the sequence 'RP (NP) VP' is adjoined to NP, that is, the constituent structure of a relative clause, which causes the discontinuity.

(4) Functional Category acquisitions

Apart from the different branching directions and the human cognitive factors, there are a lot of differences between Japanese and English relative clauses, which are associated with Case, Agreement, and wh-movement.

In English, there are two different relative pronouns used, depending on the positions of the relativised nouns: 'who' and 'whom'. In addition, there is a distinction in the choice of relative pronouns; [+/-HUMAN]. In Japanese, there are no relative pronouns at all, so we cannot find such differences. Regarding wh-movement, when we relativise and connect two English sentences, we first find an overlapping noun in the second sentence, which we replace with a relative pronoun, then we move the relative pronoun to the beginning of the Spec-CP position of the second sentence, leaving a trace in the relativised position. In understanding a sentence containing a relative pronoun, we unconsciously pay attention to the original position (O'Grady, 1997: chapter 9; Wolfe-Quintero, 1992). The linear orders of subject and object relative clauses are as follows:

Subject relative clause: HN RP t Verb
Object relative clause: HN (RP) Subject Verb t
(HN = head noun, RP = relative pronoun, t = original position of RP)

In Japanese, there is no overt wh-movement, so we cannot expect any overt movement in a relative clause as well.

It has been repeatedly shown that these differences between Japanese and English cause serious problems for Japanese learners of English in mastering relative clauses. Many grammar books published in Japan focus on them, and try hard to explain how they work, but they offer only descriptions of each distinct situation, as if they involved different kinds of properties in each grammar target without any further associations with more general features of the grammar. I hypothesise, however, that these problems in mastering English are rooted in more fundamental linguistic differences between these two languages. In this section, I would like to focus on the more general syntactic differences between them.

If we accept Fukui's (1995) arguments discussed in section 2.3.4, his basic ideas on Japanese syntax can be employed in order to explain the difficulties of Japanese learners of English in mastering relative clauses. Japanese learners are extremely bad at using Determiners and giving correct Inflections (Agreements). Applying Fukui's proposal to error analysis, we can explain uniformly the Japanese learners' difficulties: As Japanese syntax has no Functional Categories and Specifiers at all, it is natural that students face difficulties in mastering them. All Lexical Categories are assumed to be dominated by Functional Categories in English, but before getting to know this rule, Japanese students try to form a sentence using only Lexical Categories, exercising a Japanese way of producing a language.

Returning to our discussion of relative clauses, we can uniformly explain the learning problems under Fukui's paradigm as follows: Because of the lack of Functional Categories, Spec-CP and Spec-IP, Japanese students find it difficult to master:

- Case assignment under the Spec-head relation: who-whom
- Agreement of the head noun and relative pronoun: [+/- HUMAN]
- Wh-movement of relative pronouns to the Spec-CP position
- Agreement in the numbers of head nouns, relative pronouns, and verbs that follow in subject relativisation.

Common errors associated with Functional Categories are quite numerous: incorrect use of relative pronouns including the wrong choice of *who-whom-which*, no deletion of the relativised noun, mistakes in wh-movement, no Agreement in head nouns and verbs, and so on. Differences in Functional Categories in English and Japanese cause general problems in mastering the structure of English. In order to overcome the barriers illustrated above, Japanese students must generate relative clauses consciously with caution, checking each Agreement feature.

Table 7–10: Common errors and explanatory theories

Common Errors	Explanatory Theories
Object relative clauses < Subject ones	Noun Phrase Accessibility Hierarchy
Rightward modification (Japanese way)	Head-direction parameter
Mistakes in Centre-embedded clauses	Perceptual Difficulty
Delete subject relative pronouns	Perceptual Difficulty
[+/- HUMAN] [who/whom/which]	Functional Category Acquisitions
No deletion of relativised nouns	Functional Category Acquisitions
HEAD NOUN [RELATIVE CLAUSE] V(agreement)	Functional Category Acquisitions
HEAD NOUN [RELATIVE PRONOUN V(agreement)]	Functional Category Acquisitions

The adove Table summarises the common errors and explanatory theories for them discussed in this section.

7.3.2. Standard teaching method: The linear teaching method

In this section, we seek to find a better teaching methodology for relative clauses based on previous linguistic investigations. First, I discuss the advantages and disadvantages of the standard teaching method, that is, the two-sentence connection, what I call 'the linear teaching method'. Then, overcoming the disadvantages of the two-sentence connection approach, I propose 'the hierarchical teaching method'. Last, I show an empirical study, where the standard and new teaching methods are compared in English lessons.

In discussing the teaching aspects, I would like to start by looking at the effects of the instructions in a classroom, known as the Teachability Hypothesis put forward by Pienemann (1984, 1989). His proposal can be summarised as follows: An L2 structure can be learned from instruction only when the learner's Interlanguage is close to the point where this structure is learned in the natural setting. As far as the developmental sequence is concerned, learners have to be ready for the new rule, that is to say, at a stage when all the necessary rules are already in place. (This proposal is quite similar to Krashen's Input Hypothesis.) Teaching may affect or speed up the learner's progress through developmental stages but does not change the developmental sequence.

Regarding relative clauses, the following sequence of acquisition is reported from the observations of L1 children and L2 learners of English:

The developmental stages of relative clause constructions:

S V O… the canonical word order strategy

S V O + relative clause… the finalisation strategy

Centre-embedded relative clause… the subordinate clause strategy

(Cook, 1993: 101)

Not only Pienemann (1989) but also Doughty (1991) and Hamilton (1994) suggest that teaching that follows the above developmental sequences would be of great help for learners of English. In this section, I accept their suggestions to: 'Teach the subject relative clauses, then, teach the object relative clauses', and 'Teach right-branching relative clauses, then, teach centre-embedded ones'.

It has been very common to introduce relative clauses by means of the two-sentence connection. For example, our authorised textbook for junior high schools published in Japan, '*New Total English* 3', accepts this method. In the first section where the relative clause is introduced (Lesson 6: Part 1), the following instruction is given: First, there are two sentences: 'I have a friend.' and 'She doesn't speak English.' Then, using the relative pronoun *who*, we can connect these sentences into one: 'I have a friend who doesn't speak English.'

The advantages of this method are as follows: gradually, students get used to finding antecedents, that is, the expected head noun and the noun to be relativised. We find that these mechanical exercises seem to be popular with many students and teachers. The application of this procedure in a step by step fashion leads the students to the production of relative clauses, which gives them great satisfaction.

However, we have recognised (as have many English teachers at junior and senior high schools) that this method needs some revision. Although many applied linguists including Gass (1979), Eckman (1988), Hawkins (1989), Doughty (1991), and Hamilton (1994) accept the two-sentence connection when evaluating a learner's linguistic competence, the teaching method outlined above is nothing but a mechanical approach that is far from the real use of relative clauses. Even if this is a convincing and interesting way of explaining relative clauses, nobody normally produces two separate sentences first, which are then connected together with a relative pronoun. The function of a relative clause is not to *connect* two different sentences like glue, but to *modify* the head noun, giving more information to it. In this methodology, no clausal relations (i.e., hierarchical relations) are considered, only focusing on what to connect together. This is why I call this method 'the linear teaching method'. Many students taught by this method have trouble in understanding that the function of relative clauses is to modify a head noun. They think that there are two different sentences which are simply connected with *and*. The translation exercises shown below clearly demonstrate this misunderstanding. I argue that the negative aspect of the two-sentence connection is obvious.

Moreover, finding correct antecedents sometimes causes problems. Let us consider the following exercises:

Connect two sentences:
The student is my best friend. He lost his mother the other day.
The boy is my classmate. You can see him at the door.

In these exercises, students find it difficult to choose appropriate antecedents: whether 'the student' or 'my best friend' in the first case, and whether 'the boy' or 'my classmate' in the second case. (According to native-speakers of English, both nouns can be taken as antecedents.) In these kinds of two-sentence connection exercises, no context is given; just two distinct sentences are displayed. In order to teach which noun to choose as an antecedent, some teachers teach 'Information Structure' (sometimes called the 'Given-New Principle'). Teaching Information Structure to beginners in the context of relative clauses is extremely confusing, preventing students from focusing their attention on the important grammar target. The aim of using the two-sentence connection is to let students understand what relative clauses are, but not other properties of grammar.

7.3.3. Hierarchical teaching method

In this section, I would like to propose the following teaching method based on the Lexical Approach: Starting with relativisation, we should illustrate relative clause constructions not as two-sentence connections, but as noun phrases as a whole, emphasising their hierarchical structure. For instance, showing a picture of three dogs, we guide our students to restrict the meaning: in other words, we set a situation or a context where relative clauses are necessary to pick out a specific dog. Then, students are expected to understand the different modification direction in Japanese and English: 'head noun + relative clause (English)' vis-à-vis 'relative clause + head noun (Japanese)', that is, the structure of a noun phrase that contains a relative clause. Let us compare:

English: the dog [which is running over there]
Japanese: [mukoude hashitteiru] inu
over there running dog

In our daily communication, the above relative clause structure is often used: 'A: Which dog is yours?' 'B: The dog (which is) running over there.' This noun phrase structure, i.e., head noun + relative clause, is very useful in communication in order to restrict information. When students master the relativisation process as chunks in English compared with Japanese, this noun phrase as a whole is inserted into a matrix clause at a subject or object position. This process produces right branching relative clauses (OS and OO types) or centre-embedded relative clauses (SS and SO types). For instance, if we put the above noun phrase into a subject position, we can generate the sentence, '*The dog which is running over there* is called Spot' (SS), and in an object position, 'John wants *the dog which is running over there*' (OS). As relative clauses have many unfamiliar properties for Japanese learners of English, it is necessary to introduce them step by step, ensuring the understanding of our students.

The teaching methodology based on transformation can be traced back to the 1970's. Roberts (1971) proposes the Relative Clause Transformation. This transformation generates a relative clause, 'the man who bought the snowmobile', by transforming a simple sentence, 'The man bought the snowmobile'. Under this view, relative clauses should be taught by means of Adjectivalization. Converting the sentence 'Grandpa is making a kennel' into an adjective clause 'that Grandpa is making t (trace)', we can produce a relative clause, then, connecting this clause with a noun 'a kennel', we finally arrive at a noun phrase, 'a kennel that Grandpa is making'. When we sought a better teaching method in the light of transformational grammar, we adopted these transformational methods. However, neither students nor teachers could fully understand what motivates such transformations. The transformational grammarians suggested that their methods should be much better than the two-sentence connection which lacks psychological reality. I argue, however, that their transformations lack the psychological basis as well; because, just as nobody normally connects two separate sentences with relative pronouns, nobody consciously transforms or converts a simple sentence into an adjective phrase (Bever & Langendoen, 1970). Although the transformational approach might explain linguistic competence, direct applications of such theories to a classroom need some thought. What we need to teach is how to communicate and use English. Moreover, these grammarians did not show how effective their proposed methods were in the normal classroom setting. Regrettably, their proposal did not improve the quality of our lessons, nor lead our students to better results.

What I am proposing here is to set a context in which we need relative clauses and then to generate a noun phrase with a relative clause directly as chunks without moving and transforming anything. Although the transformational approach enables us to explain what operation might happen under slow motion, such operations (if they exist) are not accessible to consciousness anyway (Brown et al., 1996). Learning transformations is quite confusing for students. In addition, I suggest that learners' first language (in our case, Japanese) should be compared thoroughly with English in parallel in order to clarify the similarities and differences in the structures of these languages. Some teachers and researchers think that relative clauses should not be taught if they can vaguely understand the meaning. However, students cannot use relative clauses when they are asked to translate such a vague Japanese translation. Their attitude, grammar should not be taught if learners can understand sentences somehow, picking up meanings of nouns and verbs, is negligent.

In the following section, we will discuss the results of our teaching, where we taught relative clauses by utilising both methods.

7.3.4. An empirical study

(1) Participants

Four Japanese teachers of English joined this empirical study:

Mr A: age 39, teaching at a public junior high school
Mr B: age 41, teaching at a private junior high school
Mr C: age 43, teaching at a public high school
Mr D: age 40, teaching at a private high school annexed to the junior high school where Mr B is teaching.

All of them teach one whole grade, so we assigned Classes 1 and 2 for the linear teaching method (160 students in total) and Classes 3 and 4 for the hierarchical teaching method (160 students in total). At junior high schools, we arranged classes guaranteeing similar academic performance (third graders: age 15). At high schools, the arrangement was the same, but just in case their previous learning of relative clauses at junior high school should influence the results, we set a pre-test session to check their levels of performance (second graders: age 17).

(2) Materials

Both the public and private junior high school use '*New Total English* 3: Lessons 6 & 7', a textbook authorised by the Japanese Ministry of Education. However, at the public and private high school, different grammar books were used, so all of us gathered and produced one set of materials based on *Collins COBUILD English Grammar* sections 1: 145–149 and 8: 83–116. To satisfy the theoretical suggestions, we arranged a sequence of introducing relative clauses as follows: OS type (right-branching subject relative clause), OO type (right-branching object relative clause), SS type (centre-embedded subject relative clause), and then, SO type (centre-embedded object relative clause). We wrote teaching plans together and tried hard to follow them. We used exactly the same number of target sentences and exercises including language activities and homework, guaranteeing the same treatment except for the teaching methods. We set the empirical study twice (October 1998 and October 1999).

(3) Procedure

Using the authorised textbook, Mr A and Mr B spent 8 lessons (45 minutes each), and using *Collins COBUILD English Grammar*, Mr C and Mr D spent 8 lessons (50 minutes each) teaching each type of relative clause. The overall structure of our lessons was as follows: Introduction (including greeting, checking attendance, short talks, etc.: about seven minutes) – Review (about eight minutes) – New target grammar (explanation of the new type of relative clauses either by means of the linear or hierarchical method: about fifteen minutes) – Exercises including activities (about fifteen minutes) – Conclusion (closing remarks). We used the same target sentences, exercises, and language activities, all of which were produced in advance by ourselves. We met four times during the period of teaching to ensure that we were all following the same plan and to check whether the teaching plan needed any change. At the end of this series of teaching, we assigned the fill-in-the-blanks test (20 minutes), English-to-Japanese translation test (40 minutes), and Japanese-to-English translation test (40 minutes) shown in Appendix N, and a free writing test (30 minutes). These tests were held in the normal classroom setting, but we put pressure on our students by saying that these tests would be counted in their evaluation.

(4) Results

The results of our teaching show that the hierarchical teaching method was more effective than the linear one (t-test $p<0.001$). Note that the results obtained in the two empirical studies were similar. Let us look closely at each result.

(a) Fill-in-the-blanks test

The figures below present the correct response rate (percentage) of each type of relative clause. All figures show that the hierarchical is more effective than the linear teaching method ($t = -3.65$, $p < 0.001$). In Figure 7–2, the results of the pre- and post-test are shown. Note that although it is more common to use *that* as a relative pronoun, we asked our students to choose wh-type relative pronouns.

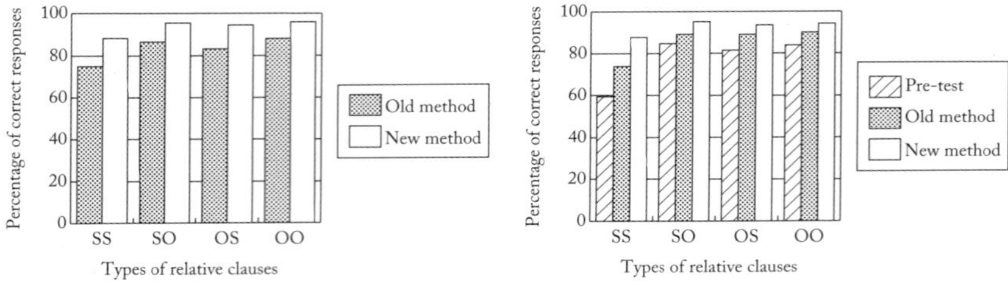

Figure 7–1: Results of junior high school

Figure 7–2: Results of senior high school

(b) English-to-Japanese translation test

The figures show the correct response rate of the test as well as error typologies. Figures 7–3 and 7–4 show clearly that the hierarchical teaching method is more effective than the linear one. Regarding the error typology, '&' means that students translated the relativised sentences as if there were two distinct sentences that were connected with *and.* 'MD' means that students transferred the rightward modification directions of Japanese (direct transfer of Japanese modification). 'WM' means that students translated as if the relative clause modifies the Subject, then, Verb and Head Noun follows it in the right branching relative clauses (i.e., relative clauses do not modify the head nouns but other nouns in the sentence). The relative clause modifies the Object, and Verbs follow it in the centre-embedded relative clauses. To make our discussion concrete, let us see some examples:

Question: I know the man who is dancing over there.
Answer: watashi-wa (I-Nominative Case) mukoude (over there) odotteiru (dancing) otoko-o (man-Accusative) shitteiru (know).
Error '&': watashi-wa otoko-o shitteite, sonohito-wa mukoude odotteiru.
(= I know the man, and he is dancing over there.)
'MD': watashi-ga shitteiru otoko-wa mukoude odotteiru.
(= The man I know is dancing over there.)
'WM': watashi-wa sonootoko-ga mukoude odotteirukoto-o shitteiru.
(= I know that the man is dancing over there.)

Question: The boy who wrote this letter is Mike.
Answer: kono (this) tegami-o (letter-Accusative) kaita (wrote) shounen-wa (boy-Subject) maikudesu (Mike be).
Error '&': shounen-ga tegami-o kaita, sorewa maikudesu.
(A boy wrote a letter, and he is Mike.)
'MD': maiku-wa kono tegami-o kaita shounen-no namaedesu.
(Mike is the name of a boy who wrote this letter.)
'WM': maikutoiu shounen-ga kono tegami-o kaita.
(A boy named Mike wrote this letter.)

We should note that because the total numbers of errors are limited in the hierarchical method, the figures of error typology just show the tendency of errors. What attracts our attention is that students taught by the linear method tend to make many '&' errors, and that students taught by the hierarchical method tend to make 'WM' errors. This means that the former students are poor at determining that the function of relative clauses is to modify the head noun, and the latter students tend to try hard to modify any noun in the sentence even if the noun is

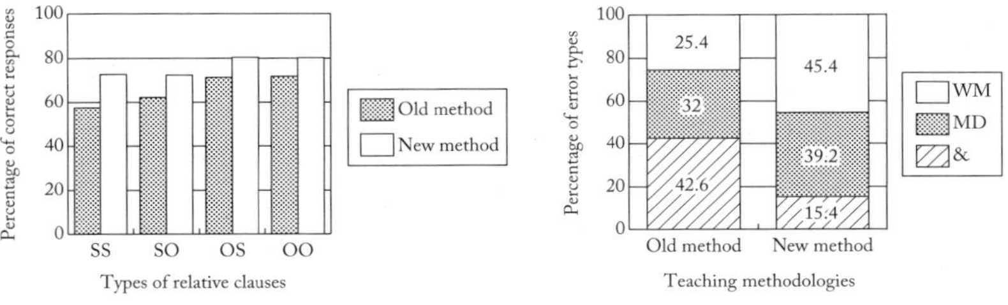

Figure 7–3: Results of junior high school and error types

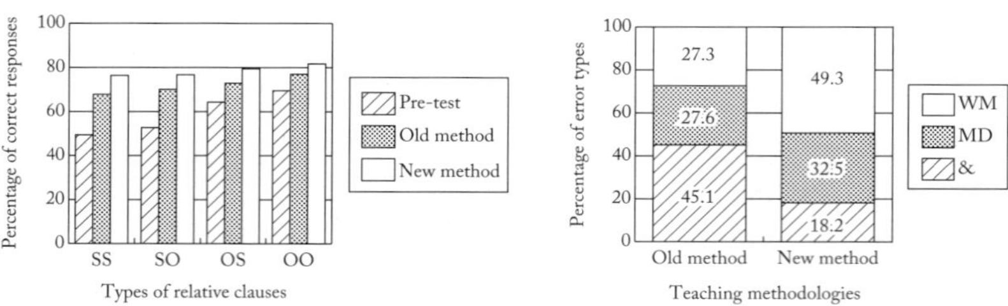

Figure 7–4: Results of senior high school and error types

not the antecedent of the relative clause. Although the total numbers of errors are limited, students taught by the hierarchical method tend to transfer Japanese modification directions. These students need more practice at the noun phrase building exercises.

(c) Japanese-to-English translation

This test should be the most difficult one, because students are expected to integrate all their knowledge of relative clauses when tackling the questions. Consequently, overall scores turned out to be quite low. Figures 7–5 and 7–6 show that the hierarchical teaching method is more effective than the linear one. Regarding the error typology, 'MD' means the rightward modification direction (as seen in (b)). 'ND' means 'no deletion of the relativised noun'. 'NR' means 'No relative pronoun where necessary', in other words, students omit the subject relative pronouns. 'CH' means that students chose incorrect relative pronouns, that is, a wrong choice of who-whom-which (we did not count the common relative pronoun, *that,* as an error). For instance:

'MD' error: *Who is singing a song boy suddenly fell down.

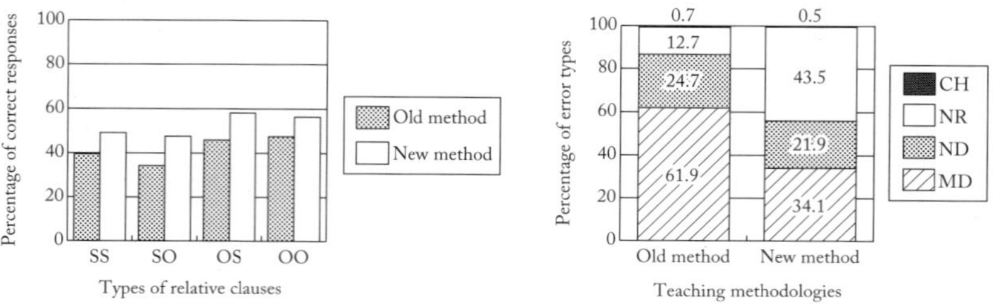

Figure 7–5: Results of junior high school and error types

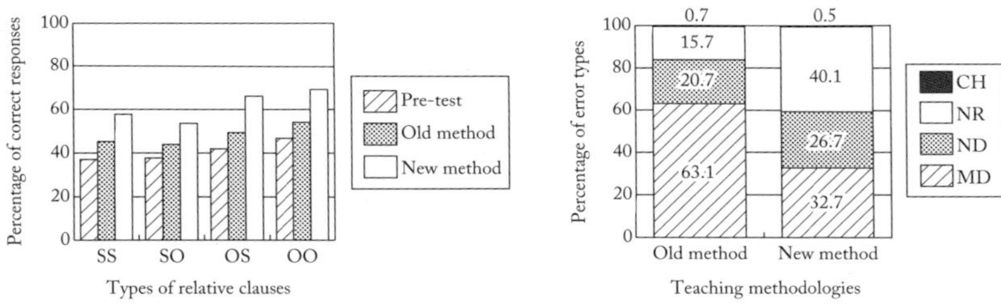

Figure 7–6: Results of senior high school and error types

'ND' error: *This is the difficult question which nobody could answer it / the question.
'NR' error: *I know the man wrote this novel.
'CH' error: *My friend is the student whom/which can speak English well.

Error typologies show that students taught by the linear method tend to make wrong modifications, and students taught by the hierarchical method tend to omit subject relative pronouns.

(d) Free writing test

Although students were asked to use as many relative clauses as possible, they used limited numbers of relative clauses. In addition, they produced more or less accurate relative clauses (Schachter, 1974). The following tables show the total number of relative clauses used and the errors students made.

Table 7–11: Total number of relative clauses

	Old method (Junior)	Old method (Senior)	New method (Junior)	New method (Senior)
SS	36	31	39	47
SO	29	30	27	38
OS	76	70	74	77
OO	26	28	27	36

Table 7–12: Total number of errors

	Old method (Junior)	Old method (Senior)	New method (Junior)	New method (Senior)
MD	21	17	1	0
WM	3	12	1	7
ND	11	12	0	0
CH	3	5	0	2

Important information in the above tables is not the total number of relative clauses, but the accuracy of the relative clauses used. As the number of errors show, the hierarchical teaching method is more effective than the linear one.

(5) Discussion and conclusion

Our empirical study reveals that the hierarchical teaching method for relative clauses is more effective than the linear method overall, irrespective of whether students learn them for the first time at junior high school or the second time at high school. In addition, there were no significant differences among the different schools. Especially, centre-embedded relative clauses were understood. Looking more closely at the results, error patterns were different: when we taught relative clauses by the linear teaching method, students made numerous errors of modification directions or *and* connections. On the other hand, students tried to modify nouns somehow when they were taught by the hierarchical method.

In this section, we have discussed the reasons why relative clauses are very difficult for Japanese learners of English to master. Linguistically, the problem is that English and Japanese have opposite settings of the Head-direction parameter, and, under Fukui's (1995) analysis, Japanese does not have Functional Categories of English type. This means that students must simultaneously process the opposite head-direction and Functional Categories. In addition, the perceptual complexity seen in the centre-embedded types of relative clauses causes a problem with matrix sentences. One possible way to teach this difficult grammar target is by the hierarchical teaching method. I propose that this method is effective in overcoming linguistic barriers. In conclusion, this grammatical target will be demanding for all future Japanese learners of English, as the difficulties stem from the fundamental structural differences between the two languages and human cognition in general. We need to focus on the Noun Phrase Accessibility Hierarchy, the Head-direction parameter, Functional Categories, and discontinuity. We should bear all these in mind in looking for effective ways of teaching relative clauses.

Conclusion

In this chapter, we discussed three empirical studies on three difficult grammar targets taught by the standard method and the new method based on the Lexical Approach. We looked at the advantages and disadvantages of the transformational method, proposed how to introduce passives, infinitives, and relative clauses, and discussed three cross-sectional studies on three difficult grammar targets taught by the standard and new methods based on the Lexical Approach. The Lexical Approach seems to be promising when teaching not only lexis but also basic grammar points. According to the questionnaire, 68% of the students found the new method helpful (28% of them wrote *I don't know* and 4% of them gave no response). Some negative responses were as follows: 'In my mind, I always undergo transformational steps (6 students).' 'It is very difficult to produce passives directly (5 students).' 'I need some explanation on Japanese structures that correspond to English infinitives and relative clauses (11 students).' 'I need more time to master noun phrase level communication (8 students).'

Finally, I should like to reflect on the research briefly, referring to some well-known problems that the classroom research demonstrated. When discussing the effect of a new teaching methodology, we should consider what is called 'the Pygmalion Effect'. If a teacher believes that the new method is effective, this emotion is transmitted unconsciously in his or her words, attitude, facial expression, behaviour, etc. I consider our results also reflect on the teachers' unconscious expectations. What is clear is that our results are consistent across the different teachers involved in this empirical study: there are no significant differences among the results obtained from the different teachers ($p<0.001$). As there is a possibility that all of them consistently show the Pygmalion Effect, I shall observe the effect of instruction longitudinally by means of Action Research with more colleagues. The next question is whether the treatment is really the same. It is true that we prepared the teaching plans including target sentences and exercises together and tried hard to follow them. Although, as all teachers can imagine, we face unexpected reactions by students or happenings, the results are consistent among the four teachers. Regarding other variables, it has been pointed out that there are too many variables when conducting classroom research: how about learning outside a classroom; the time allowed to answer one question in the tests; when and where the test is held; the content of the grammar targets (vocabulary, usage); student's and teacher's mental and health condition, etc. (Schachter & Gass eds., 1996). However, controlling for these variables is only necessary if it can be (or has been) shown empirically that they affect the outcome of the test strongly. We realise that these results are obtained from one particular Japanese-based classroom and one study does not prove everything. What is important now is to evaluate our results longitudinally in a wide range of contexts.

First published as 'Beyond transformational methodology: Possibility of the Lexical Approach to grammar instruction' in *JABAET Journal* 5 (2001): 63–85; 'Relative clauses: A bitter lemon for Japanese learners and teachers of English' in *JABAET Journal* 4 (2000): 43–68; and 'Teaching relative clauses: How to handle a bitter lemon for Japanese learners and English teachers' in *ELT Journal* (2002: Vol. 56/1): 29–40. As original articles were written some time ago, the contents have already had an influence: many recent English textbooks adopt the Lexical Approach to passives and infinitives, and heretical teaching method for relative clauses.

Chapter 8

Verb acquisition and verb instruction in a foreign language

Introduction

How are verbs acquired? How are verbs put to use? Each of these questions is one of the most important but difficult ones to be answered in the field of language acquisition. In this chapter, we will investigate how people acquire verbs (their meanings and forms) in a foreign language.

Let us begin with the definition of a verb. Verbs not only encode semantic content but also establish a grammatical and logical relationship between their arguments. A purely syntactic method for defining a verb is that 'any verb can be seen as something that takes a subject and/or object' (Frawley, 1992: 141). From a semantic perspective, 'a verb is a word that encodes events: a cover term for states or conditions of existence, process or unfolding, and actions or executed processes' (Frawley, 1992: 141). Verbs describe events in which there is at least one participant doing something, being affected by the event, being the recipient of some action, and so on. Every verb is accompanied by a number of obligatory participants that express the core meaning of the event. Some of these participants must always be overt; others can be null, but they remain active in the interpretation of the event. The obligatory participants in the event described by a verb (called *arguments*) are distinguished from other non-obligatory participants and descriptions of the time, place, manner, etc. (*adjuncts*). Different verbs can have different numbers of arguments. For instance, the verb *put* has three arguments: a noun phrase denoting a person who put a thing somewhere, a noun phrase denoting a thing put somewhere by someone, and a prepositional phrase denoting the location where someone puts something. One line of research in linguistics has developed the idea that there are a fixed number of participant roles made available by UG which arguments assume, known as *thematic roles* (Hawkins, 2001: 177–178).

In the field of child language development, Bates et al. (1988: 110) show that there is a sharp increase from 13 to 20 months in the proportion of verbs. Their longitudinal study reveals that although the vocabulary burst that takes place during the second year involves a very large increase in common nouns, there is a greater rate of increase in lexical items that express predicative meanings, especially verbs. This shift is associated with the passage into multiword speech. They found very strong evidence for continuity between lexical and grammatical development. Their findings confirm a link between the vocabulary burst in the second year and the subsequent appearance of multiword speech, and a link between the appearance of verbs and the passage from single to multiword speech. They claim that there is a switch in emphasis from nouns to verbs in the second year; this switch is implicated in the passage from first words to grammar (Bates et al., 1988: 263; Bates & Goodman, 1999; Hirsh-Pasek & Golinkoff eds., 2006).

Clark (1993: 201) observes that children begin to use verbs for talking about events that involve only one participant, typically the actor, or two, typically the agent and the patient. Children use the same verb form to talk about both action types, with intransitive to transitive shifts, and transitive to intransitive shifts. In addition, children begin to use *make* and *get* to express causation. Empirical research has shown that verb learning is gradual and quite difficult for learners to complete.

Pinker (1989) points out that children's cognitive development parallels language development. However, the situation is slightly different from children's first language acquisition when it comes to L2 learning: adult L2 learners possess mature cognition. Is it hard for L2 learners to master verbs in L2 as seen in L1? Ellis & Beaton (1995: 152–158) show that verbs are much more difficult to learn than nouns. Their experimental study with second language learners reveals that nouns are far easier and therefore mastered earlier than verbs.

In this chapter, we focus on verb learning and verb teaching in a foreign language in detail. Classifying verbs, we will discuss the results obtained from longitudinal observational and empirical studies. In section one, we review two approaches to learning verb meanings in a second language: Juffs' Lexical Parameter approach, which is based on the Bootstrapping perspectives of Pinker and Gleitman, and the Item-by-item approach proposed by Bogaards and Barshi & Payne, which is based on Tomasello's Verb Island Hypothesis. In section two, we focus on the acquisition of verb forms. We review two approaches to the acquisition of verb forms in L2: the semantic-oriented approach of Klein and the form-oriented approach of Bardovi-Harlig. In section three, we discuss the data obtained from my eight-year longitudinal study in detail. The results are to be interpreted as showing that there is a developmental sequence of learning verb meanings and verb forms, which is not influenced by instruction or L1 performance. Regarding how verb meanings are learned, students did not overgeneralise previously acquired thematic roles of English verbs to similar contexts, but they tend to undergeneralise them. Juffs (1996a, 1996b, 1998, 2000, 2001) argues that learners overgeneralise the previously acquired theta-role assignment to new situations. However, as White (1991) proposed, learners seem to undergeneralise it and learn each verb on an item-by-item basis. Moreover, many Japanese learners of English show 'the missing argument phenomenon', that is, learners omit obligatory elements in L2 (such as, omitting NP or PP in [put NP PP].) One possible explanation for this phenomenon is that a learner's first language transfers in verb learning. If L1 and L2 have different argument structures, learners transfer their L1 subcategorisation frames to L2. Regarding the acquisition of verb forms, change of the correct and incorrect tense marking will be analysed. Japanese learners of English follow the predictable developmental sequence. In addition, the result of the longitudinal study supports Bardovi-Harlig's (2000) claim that learners seem to find it easier to mark past tense when referring to completed events than when referring to states and activities which may last for extended periods without a clear end point.

From section four, we turn our attention to teaching verbs to L2 learners of English. In section four, we will have a brief look at three approaches to teaching verbs. In section five, we discuss the effect of these potential instructions of verbs to beginners: English-Japanese comparison, noticing, and the Lexical Approach. We argue the advantages and disadvantages of the methods.

This chapter reveals that verbs (their meanings and forms) are acquired in particular sequences and that error analysis theoretically predicts that there are some areas that need caution in practice. These pieces of information are quite suggestive to English language teaching, especially material development, curriculum design, and vocabulary and grammar instructions.

8.1. The acquisition of verb meaning

8.1.1. Bootstrapping perspectives

The problem that all language learners face is that there is no direct relation between the types of information in the input and the types of information in the output: syntactic categories (noun, verb, etc.) and grammatical relations (subject, object, etc.) are not perceptually marked as such in input or their contexts. If a learner wants to determine the relative order of nouns and verbs, he or she must find some nouns and a verb in input. Nevertheless, how does one do this if one does not know anything about the language yet? The fundamental problem of getting the learner started in forming the correct types of rules for natural languages is called the *bootstrapping* problem. Weissenborn & Höhle (2001: vii) define the notion of bootstrapping as follows: The child, based on already existing knowledge and information processing capacities, can make use of specific types of information in the linguistic and non-linguistic input in order to determine the particular language regularities, which constitute the grammar and the lexicon of the child's first language. Pinker (1987: 400) asserts that the bootstrapping problem is the first problem one must solve in designing models of language acquisition. One way in which the learner might break into the verb system is through observation. The first verbs are learned from pairing words with actions. The first basic discoveries about their grammar come when learners pair concrete objects with the grammatical category of nouns and actions with the category of verbs.

Pinker (1984) has constructed a theory of language development consistent with what one knows from observation and empirical research regarding the acquisition of English. Most importantly, (1) language develops gradually in the learner, and (2) there is a rapid and error-free development of word order in sentences. Pinker assumes that learners use the mappings between syntax and semantics not to infer the meanings from their syntax, but to infer their syntactic category from their meanings. Pinker proposes a theory in which semantic constraints serve as conditions defining semantic classes of verbs that may or may not occur in particular argument structures. The constraints characterise the pattern of verb selection of each argument structure (termed *Semantic Bootstrapping*: using meaning to predict syntax). Pinker's model is a competence model and his concern is with whether the language that learners hear makes it possible for them to categorise words as nouns, verbs, and other syntactic categories. Because the nouns and verbs used in natural speech to learners refer to objects, people, and actions the learner is observing, he or she can fit them together into appropriate syntactic categories. Pinker assumes that the categories themselves are innately given in UG. The learner innately knows that an agent is a subject, an action-word is a verb, an object-word is a noun, a patient is an object noun phrase, etc. (Holzman, 1997: 124; Jackendoff, 2002: chapter 4).

On the other hand, Gleitman & Landau (1994) have argued that syntactic frames provide a particularly important source of constraint for verb learning. Because verbs have relational meanings, syntactic cues such as the number and arrangement of arguments in a sentence give information about a verb's meaning. Gleitman proposes that syntactic cues in the linguistic context surrounding verbs play the role of constraints. This requires that learners should know some important syntactic distinctions of the language they are learning before they learn verbs. Gleitman assumes that syntactic structure is innate. According to Gleitman & Gillette (1999), children rely only on a verb's syntactic subcategorisation frames to learn its meaning. Gleitman claims that verbs cannot be learned by observing the situations in which they are used, because many verbs refer to overlapping situations and because parents do not invariably use a verb when its perceptional correlations are present. Gleitman suggests that there is enough information in a verb's subcategorisation frame to predict its meaning. Children use precursors of the same links between sentence structure and meaning to understand sentences and acquire the meanings of verbs. If part of the relational meaning of a verb in a sentence is predictable from the sentence structure itself, a child who hears a sentence containing a novel verb could gain some information about the meaning of the sentence from its structure. So, not only do children use the sentence frames in which a verb appears to identify its argument structure, but also, verb meanings would not be learnable otherwise. If a novel word 'gorp' occurs in an NP-V-NP-PP frame, for instance, it can be safely inferred that the term encodes an action that causes an affected entity to move or change in a certain way. Although such structural information does not uniquely specify the verb's meaning, it does increase the likelihood of the child entertaining a correct interpretation of the verb. Gleitman proposes that the innate sentence frames narrow down the possibility of a wide range of interpretations available for a sentence (termed *Syntactic Bootstrapping*: using syntax to predict verb meaning). Children utilise syntactic cues as a means of gathering word meanings. Gleitman proposes that in the structural information provided by the linguistic code, children can find resourceful evidence for constructing semantic representations. Children attend to the regularities in the input from a very young age, and are sensitive to syntactic and semantic correspondences that exist in the linguistic forms. Gleitman & Gleitman (2001) argue that one potential source for the learning of word meaning lies in the child's capacity to match the occurrence of words with the scenes and events that accompany the words in interactions. Furthermore, within the Syntactic Bootstrapping account, a language's internal contextual information provides another source. They show that adult subjects were much better in identifying the meanings of nouns as compared to verbs if only given an extralinguistic context of a word's use via video scenes. Verb identification abilities were better on giving the subjects sentence structures. Gerken (2001) shows that Semantic Bootstrapping and Syntactic Bootstrapping might be related to the initial dominance of nouns in children's production. Recently, Bowerman & Brown eds. (2008) (1) focus on verbs, examining crosslinguistic variation in the relationship between verb meaning and verb syntax, and weighing the significance of this variation for the bootstrapping proposals, (2) investigate the role of arguments, especially learning problems associated with massive argument ellipsis, and (3) examine the construct of transitivity and associated meanings such as causativity, control, and telicity.

In the field of second language acquisition, Juffs (1996a, 1996b, 1998, 2000, 2001) argues that not all parts of a lexicon can be learned from input alone, and that UG-type knowledge must explain some of what has been assigned to the lexicon. He asserts that if adults can be shown to have knowledge of properties of the L2 lexicon which is derivable neither from the L1 nor from surface properties of the L2 input, then this knowledge will constitute evidence that adult second language learning is constrained by principles active in first language acquisition.

Juffs (1996a: 91–99, 1996b) tries to capture different verb meanings among languages under parameterisation. There are certain core properties of lexical structure which are strictly linguistic and which are the universal elements of lexical entries relevant to argument structure, such things as conceptual or ontological categories (e.g., [STATE], [PATH], [GOAL], [MANNER]), and functions (e.g., [GO], [BE], [ACT]) (Jackendoff, 1983, 1990, 2002). Verb classes are formed by a conflation of these basic elements. The [BE] sentences all describe some state of affairs in which some characteristic is ascribed to the subject of the sentence. The [GO] sentences all describe a change involving the subject of the sentence, in which it comes to have the characteristic ascribed by the corresponding [BE] sentence. The subject's characteristic at the beginning of the change is described by the phrase following [FROM], and at the end of the change by the phrase following [TO]. These rules of meaning component combination are part of UG and are innate. Cross-linguistic differences are the result of parametric variation in the conflation patterns allowed. A series of studies by Juffs (1996, 1998, 2000) tries to capture the lexical transfer from L1 to L2 by means of parameterisation. Let us reconsider the following sentences (Ikegami, 1991: chapter 2, 2000):

*/?John persuaded Mary to come but she did not come.
*Mary drowned, but she did not die.
*John helped Mary to solve the problem, but she could not solve it.
*I burned/boiled/thawed/mixed it, but it did not.
*I woke him, but he did not wake.

Taking Juffs' approach, the English verb *boil,* for instance, has the thematic feature of [GOAL], but the Japanese word for *boil* lacks this feature, so it is difficult for Japanese learners of English to judge the sentence 'John boiled the coffee, but it did not boil.' as ungrammatical. Japanese learners of English must add the thematic feature to the English lexicon.

Another example can be found in Inagaki (2001). In English, manner-of-motion verbs (*walk, run*) and directed-motion verbs (*go*) can appear with a goal prepositional phrase. In contrast, Japanese only allows directed-motion verbs to occur with a goal prepositional phrase. Inagaki proposes that L2 acquisition of motion verbs with goal prepositional phrases was not difficult when the L2 (English) was the superset of the L1 (Japanese), but that it was difficult when the L2 (Japanese) was the subset of the L1 (English).

The result of the experimental study by Juffs (1996a: chapter 6, 1996b) shows that L2 learners start their L1 lexical parametric settings, which are gradually reset. L1 parameter settings will be transferred before the L2 setting is acquired. Juffs (1996a: 228–229) proposes that L2 acquisition of lexical conflation patterns or parameters may have the following stages:

Stage 1: Learners start off with certain syntactic patterns which they can apply independently of verb semantics and independently of L1 lexical patterns (derived from Ard & Gass, 1987).

Stage 2: Input from the L2 and L1 conflation patterns affects lexical entries.

Stage 3: Morphological information begins to play a significant role in argument structure (e.g., Sorace, 1995) along with a reorganisation of the lexical entries to reflect L2 patterns.

Stage 4: Morphological properties of the L2 are acquired, and non-attested forms are expunged from lexical entries.

8.1.2. Item-by-item perspectives

The *Verb Island Hypothesis* proposed by Tomasello assumes that children's early verbs and relational terms are individual islands of organisation in an otherwise unorganised grammatical system (e.g., Tomasello, 2003). In the early stages, the child learns about arguments and syntactic marking on a verb-by-verb basis, and ordering patterns (argument structures) and morphological markers learned for one verb do not immediately generalise to other verbs. Children do not have any adult-like syntactic categories or rules, nor do they have any kind of word class of verbs that would support generalisations across verbs. What children have at this stage is knowledge of specific kinds of events and words to indicate them, and knowledge of the roles played by various entities in these specific events (Tomasello, 1992: 23–24). The lexically specific pattern of this phase is that some verbs are used in only one type of sentence frame and that frame is quite specific to the verb. In a previous report, a child was exposed to and attended to rich discourse and pragmatic functions for the verb, while for other activities, the child was not exposed to or did not talk about events (Tomasello, 1999: 170). The syntactic categories with which the child is working at this stage are not such verb-general abstract thematic roles as agent, patient, instrument, etc., but rather are verb-specific elements such as hitter, a person/thing hit, a thing hit with, etc. This limited generality, according to Tomasello (1999: 172), is due to the difficulty of categorising entire scenes into a more abstract construction.

Maratsos (1999: 196) calls English a 'relatively transparent agent-patient mapping' language: English verbs all have a simple general schema in basic sentences. In English, the agent is encoded before the action, which is encoded before the patient. English uses constituent order, (agent + action + patient) to encode agent-patient relations. On the other hand, Japanese is a language in which constituent order is not the sole means of expressing agent-patient relations (free constituent order). These relations are expressed by morphological inflection on the noun stem. In other words, Japanese is a nominative-accusative language. Morphological cases are overtly marked by postpositions: *ga* for nominative and *o* for accusative. Unlike English, word order is actually irrelevant to case assignment. In addition, Japanese has grammatically unrestricted zero anaphora. Any and all of the core arguments of a predicate can be omitted in a grammatical sentence. Kecskes & Papp (2000: 92–96) claims that the UG theory explains the dichotomy in the acquisition of phrase structures of the configurationality parameter, which may take either a configurational or non-configurational setting. Configurational (we called 'structural' in chapter four) languages (e.g., English or French) have a bound word order governed by grammatical rules. Phrase structure configurations encode the grammatical functions, and logical relations can only be computed at a virtual level of representation. Non-configurational (we called 'agglutinative' in chapter four) languages (e.g., Russian or Japanese) have a complex morphology and word order governed by pragmatic rather than grammatical rules. Phrase structure expresses logical relations, and grammatical functions are encoded morphologically. Such linguistic differences cause a serious problem in L2 learning (Kecskes & Papp, 2000: 92). Let us compare:

Sakana-ga tabeta. (A fish ate something.)
Fish Nom ate
Sakana-o tabeta. (Somebody/something ate a fish.)
Fish Acc ate

In the above sentences, the word order is the same, but the postpositions (*ga* and *o*) that indicate case are different. Maratsos (1999: 200–205) claims that argument structures, which are crucial for constituent order, are not necessarily important for morphologically-rich languages. Verbs do not determine the structure of the language, but sequences of noun + case-marking play an important role in interpretation. Under this line of proposals, Rispoli (1995: 341–345) argues that Japanese children acquire semantic representations of verbs with the aid of the case system. Rispoli (1995: 345) suggests that Japanese children have at their disposal an avenue for determining agency that does not depend on any bootstrapping mechanisms, but rather connects the predicate to morphology. Inflectional morphology (especially, case marking) provides a source of information for the construction of the semantic representations of predicates in Japanese.

Barshi & Payne (1998) argue that we must be careful when employing UG-based theories as the starting point because linguistic theories that assume that syntactic structure is solely determined by argument structure cannot account for the acquisition of morphologically-rich languages such as Japanese or Turkish. If the learner's L1 is a morphologically-rich language, the acquisition of verbs occurs on a one-by-one basis rather than through bootstrapping. Contrary to Juffs, Barshi & Payne (1998) propose that argument structures do not play a significant role in the acquisition of such languages.

The position taken by Rispoli (1995), Barshi & Payne (1998), and Maratsos (1999), that argument structures do not play an important role when acquiring morphologically-rich languages and therefore verbs are learned on an item-by-item basis, is quite strong and needs firm theoretical and empirical bases. Remember that Tomasello (1992, 1995, 1999, 2003) proposed that even children acquiring English might learn verbs in a one-by-one fashion. Moreover, not many past studies addressing the issues in the acquisition of morphologically-rich languages can be found. At present, the claim that verbs in morphologically-rich languages are acquired on an item-by-item basis is controversial. Let us close this section with proposals put forward by researchers who studied the development of the bilingual lexicon.

Bogaards (1996: 371–379), Libben (2000), and Kroll & Tokowicz (2001) claim that learners who have already learned a first language have a semantic memory at their disposal in which all knowledge that they have acquired in their life is filed. This knowledge can best be conceived of as an extensive network of concepts, most of which are closely related to the content of the L1. Just as with other knowledge, the L2 lexicon can only be understood via that pre-existing knowledge. The meaning of the lexical elements of the other language is interpreted in the light of the corresponding elements in the L1 at the early stages of L2 learning. The above researchers assume that conceptual patterns and linguistic/semantic coding practices in the L1 provide the essential criteria for those in the L2. Appel (1996) develops this idea in the light of transfer. Reviewing past studies on positive and negative transfer, Appel (1996: section 5) concludes that L2 learners appeal to translation when encountering new words in another language, and learn them one-by-one. Regarding verb learning, Libben, Bogaards, Kroll & Tokowicz, and Appel propose that L2 learners directly transfer L1 concepts to L2 and that they store new words on an item-by-item basis.

8.2. The acquisition of verb forms

8.2.1. Meaning-oriented approach

In English, time and reference to that time are marked by both verb tense and aspect. *Tense*, such as past or present, relates the speech time in the present to the event time or the time when the event occurs. *Aspect* concerns the dynamics of the event relative to its completion, repetition, or continuing duration. The development of tense and aspect reflects both cognitive and linguistic development (Behrens, 2001).

A basic tenet of the meaning-oriented approach is that adult L2 learners have access to the full range of semantic concepts from their previous linguistic and cognitive experience (Klein, 1987). The meaning-oriented approach has identified three main stages of development in the acquisition of temporal expression: the pragmatic stage (using chronological order, or building on an interlocutor's discourse that provides a temporal reference), the lexical stage (using temporal adverbs), and the morphological stage.

In the earliest stage of temporal expression, there is no systematic use of tense-aspect morphology. Without tense-aspect morphology, learners establish temporal reference in four ways: by relying on the contribution of their fellow speakers (scaffolded discourse), through reference inferred from a particular context (implicit reference), by contrasting events, and by following chronological order in narration (Klein, 1987; Meisel, 1987; Trevise, 1987).

Lexical means for expressing temporality include temporal adverbs (*in the morning, now, yesterday, tomorrow*), connectives (*and then*), and calendric references (*1 August, Saturday, 10 pm*). At the lexical stage, reference to the past is expressed explicitly with lexical expressions (Trevise, 1987; Veronique, 1987). At this stage, verbs occur in morphologically unmarked forms (Meisel, 1987).

Following the adverb-only stage, verbal morphology appears. At first, it is not used systematically, and learners continue to rely on time adverbs (Meisel, 1987). As the use of tense morphology increases, the functional load of the adverbs decreases, and the actual ratio of time adverbs to finite verbs may also decrease. The stabilisation of past tense verbal morphology opens the way for expressions of other temporal relations in the past. Kaplan (1987) observes the actual pattern of past tense forms during the early phases of acquisition in a formal setting, and reports that past tense forms, being morphologically less complex than perfect forms, were supplied correctly more often. The aspectual meaning of the perfect is not acquired if the learners have not yet acquired the past tense.

The identification of the three main means of temporal expression is supported by research in a number of languages (Perdue, 1993; Dietrich et al., 1995). Importantly, however, characteristic use is not the same as exclusive use, although the characteristic use of pragmatic, lexical, and morphological stages can be associated with stages of development.

8.2.2. Form-oriented approach

Adult L2 learners are able to express temporal expressions long before the emergence of tense-aspect morphology. The pragmatic and lexical stages establish a communicatively viable system. The form-oriented approach focuses on the morphological stage. Form-oriented inquiry has investigated three main areas: acquisition sequences (the order of emergence of tense-aspect morphology), the influence of lexical aspect (the meaning associated with each form), and the influence of discourse structure.

The morphological stage is comprised of many individual stages, which are remarkably similar across languages (Dulay, Burt, & Krashen, 1982). Dulay, Burt, and Krashen claim, based on grammatical morpheme research, that the discovery of a common acquisition sequence for L2 learners is one of the most significant outcomes. Copula and progressive form precede past irregular form, which comes before past regular form and third person singular form.

Sanz & Bever (2001) present a theory of how syntactic operations depend on the semantics, via structures that are represented in the functional component of sentences. Learning L2 involves learning uninterpreted features of L2, those features that do not appear in the L1 overtly, or changing the interpretive level of the features that might vary between L1 and L2. Sanz & Bever (2001: 157) predict that there might be some interference from L1 into L2, because the speaker has already classified the features according to levels of interpretation in their first language. For late learners, it might be impossible to change this level. For instance, as seen in section 2.3.4, Japanese learners of English have difficulty in learning that subjects and verbs or numerals and nouns must agree, since that involves representing the feature [+NUMBER], which is uninterpreted in their first language. According to Sanz and Bever, it might be impossible for Japanese learners of English to change the uninterpreted feature of [NUMBER] into the interpreted feature in learning English.

More recently, Liceras, Zoble, & Goodluck (eds.) (2008: 4–5) consider the notion of feature strength and feature interpretability. Feature strength serves to distinguish overt movement in the syntax from covert movement in a Logical Form. Interpretability has to do with the intrinsic nature of features and bears on whether a feature of a particular lexical item makes a semantic contribution to interpretation. Interpretable features such as Definiteness or Cardinality interface with the semantic conceptual system of the mind. In the derivation of a sentence, such features are checked and never eliminated, whereas uninterpretable features such as Case or Gender, making no semantic contribution, need to be checked and eliminated.

Regarding the acquisition of English tense-aspect forms, the body of research conducted thus far (reviewed thoroughly by Bardovi-Harlig, 2000: chapter 4) shows that lexical aspect influences the patterns of distribution of past verbal morphology in initial and later stages of morphological development. Of course, discourse (narrative structure) is a central influence on the distribution of tense-aspect morphology. The influence of lexical aspect interacts with narrative structure. The aspect hypothesis of Andersen & Shirai (1996) and Li & Shirai (2000) can be summarised as follows (Bardovi-Harlig, 2000: 227; Slabakova, 2001: 22):

(a) Learners first use past marking on achievements (which have an inherent culmination point but in which the process leading up to this point is instantaneous) and accomplishments (which involve a process going on in time and an inherent culmination point after which the event can no longer continue), eventually extending the use to activities (where homogeneous processes going on in time with no inherent goal) and statives (which have no internal structure whatsoever).
(b) Progressive marking begins with activities, and then extends to accomplishments and achievements. Progressive markings are not incorrectly overextended to statives.

8.3. Longitudinal study

The aim of this section is to present my eight-year longitudinal study and to discuss the findings of the observational research.

8.3.1. Participants

Eighty Japanese learners of English were observed for eight years. The study began in 1994 when the students entered junior high school (age 12), and ended in 2001 when they became second-year students at university (age 19). They had never learned English before they entered junior high school and had no opportunity to visit English-speaking countries. The learners attended a private junior high school, which is annexed to the senior high school and university (i.e., once they enter the private junior high school, they can automatically enter senior high school and university, which makes this longitudinal study possible.) They learned English mainly in the classroom. Students learned English for five hours a week in the classroom, and exposure to English outside the classroom was limited.

8.3.2. Data collection

Every year, students were asked to write two essays (approximately 200 words in length each) in September within thirty minutes. The titles of the essays included 'The most impressive moment/thing in my life'; 'The place I visited in summer'; 'My first date'; etc., all of which require past tense and perfect forms. They were not allowed to use dictionaries. In December, they were asked to write essays on the same topics in Japanese (their L1). The purpose of L1 writing is to investigate whether their L1 stylistics and linguistic features affect their performance in English essays. The reason why we did not assign English and Japanese essays at the same time is that we needed to prevent them from translating L1 writing into L2 or vice versa.

The essays were analysed focussing mainly on their verb use. Verbs in the essays were classified based on Levin (1993): psycho verbs; state verbs; interaction verbs; movement verbs; and change-of-state verbs. At the same time, tense-aspect markings were analysed: present; past; progressive; and perfect forms. (While we collected copulas as well, we will not include them.)

8.3.3. Data analysis

Let us first look at the overall sentence patterns of their writing.

Figure 8–1 shows that students used simple sentences at the beginning (mainly copulas and intransitives), and gradually used complex sentences (subordinate clauses, relative clauses, etc.).

Figure 8–2 shows the previously-learned verbs. This figure tells us which

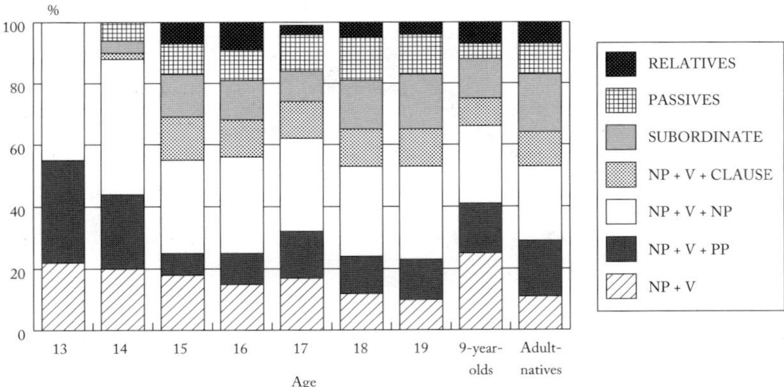

Figure 8–1: Sentential pattern

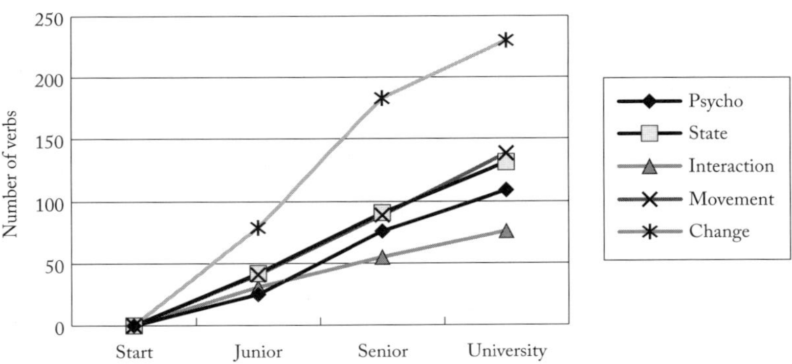

Figure 8–2: Previously-learned verbs

types of verbs were introduced in the textbook and supplementary materials.

8.3.3.1. The acquisition of verb meaning

Figure 8–3 shows the changes of verb use in the essays. It indicates that the proportion of verb use changes as follows: at early stages, psycho verbs 25%; state verbs 14%; interaction verbs 10%; movement verbs 25%; and change-of-the-state verbs 26%, and later stages, psycho verbs 27%; state verbs 14%; interaction verbs 20%; movement verbs 15%; and change-of-the-state verbs 24%.

Figure 8–4 shows the changes of verb use in the L1. It indicates that the proportion of verb use changes as follows: at early stages, psycho verbs 25%; state verbs 9%; interaction verbs 13%; movement verbs 23%; and change-of-the-state

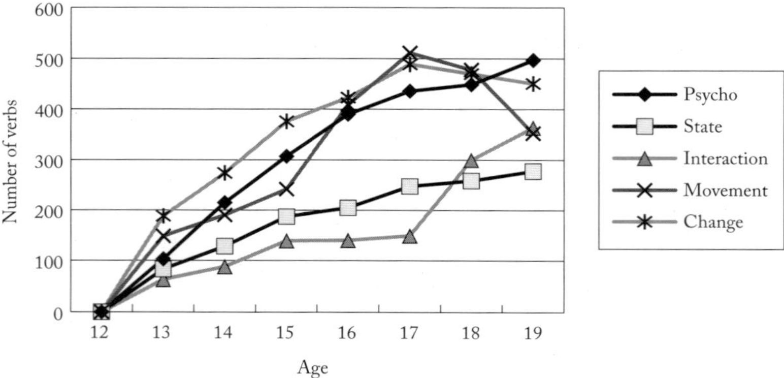

Figure 8–3: Change of verb use in L2

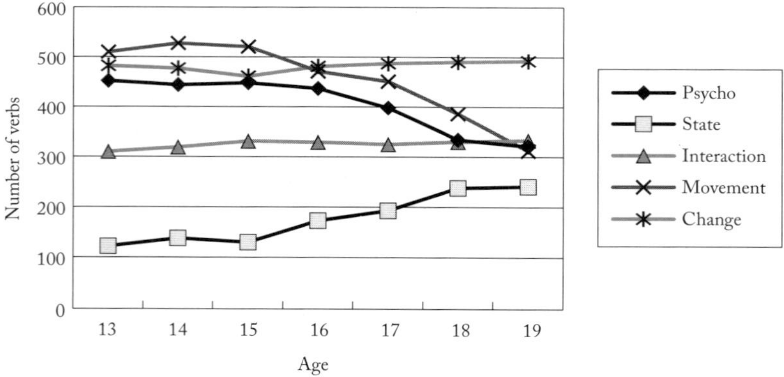

Figure 8–4: Change of verb use in L1

verbs 30%, and later stages, psycho verbs 16%; state verbs 14%; interaction verbs 16%; movement verbs 14%; and change-of-the-state verbs 40%. The change-of-the-state verbs were used the most in L1 and L2. Although the patterns of verb use at the early stages were similar in L1 and L2, those of later stages were different: while students tended to use many psycho verbs in L2, the use of psycho verbs in L1 was decreasing.

Figure 8–5 shows the change of error types. It indicates that while overgeneralisations were quite limited and could only be found at very early stages, missing argument errors were marked.

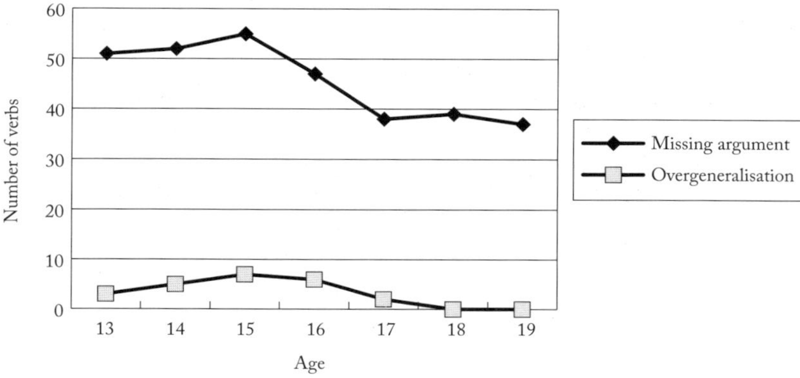

Figure 8–5: Change of error types

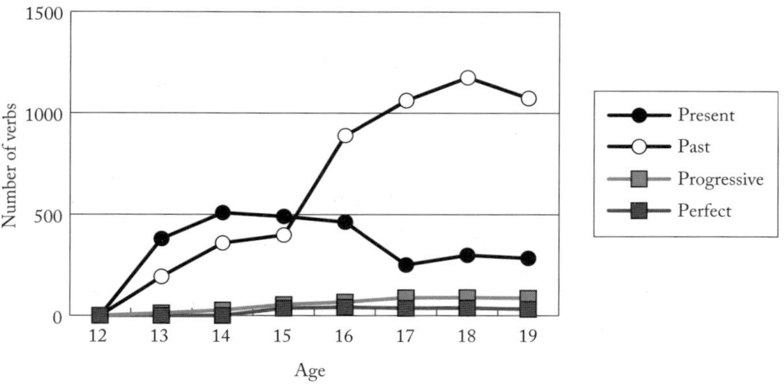

Figure 8–6: Change of verb forms

8.3.3.2. The acquisition of verb forms

Figure 8–6 shows the changes of verb forms. This reveals that students used present tense forms more often during early stages, but past tense forms increased in later stages.

Figures 8–7, 8–8, 8–9, and 8–10 show the use of present, past, progressive, and perfect forms, respectively.

Figure 8–11 shows the changes in errors of tense-aspect marking. Students used present tense forms where past tense forms or perfect forms were appropriate.

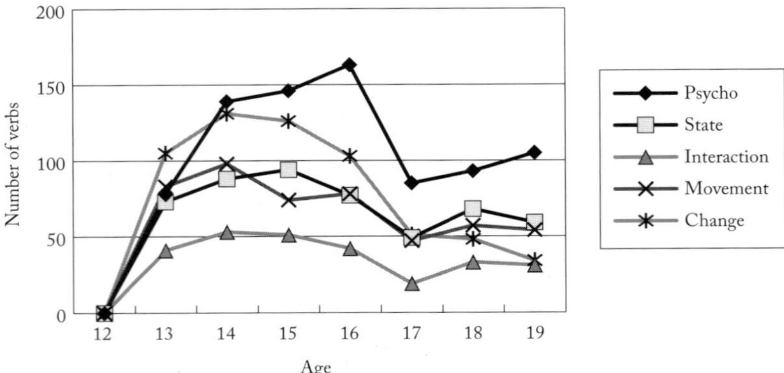

Figure 8–7: Use of present tense forms

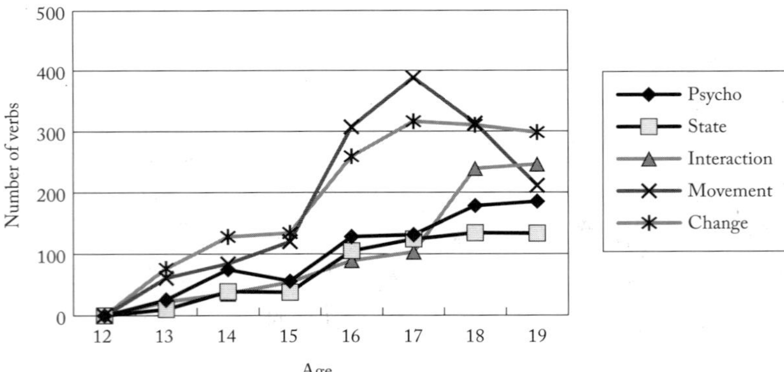

Figure 8-8: Use of past tense forms

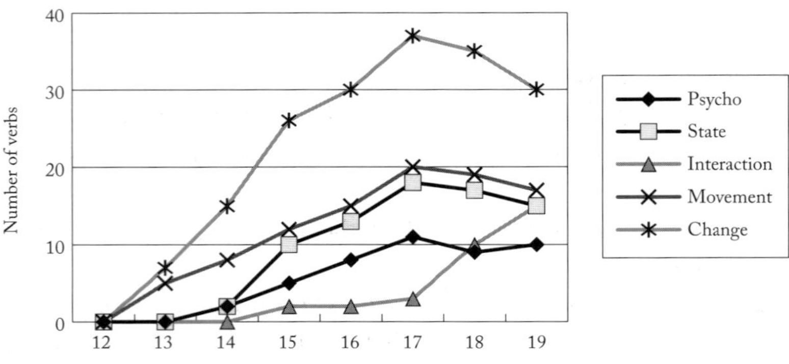

Figure 8-9: Use of progressive forms

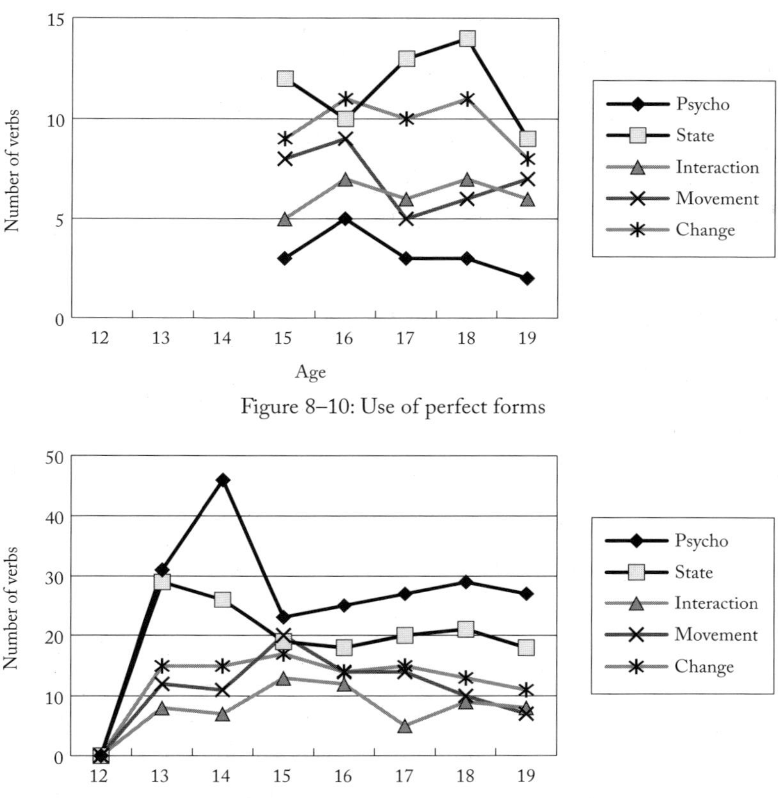

Figure 8–10: Use of perfect forms

Figure 8–11: Change of errors

8.3.4. Discussion

The longitudinal data reveal the frequency of the students' verb use in writing. The point is that the data do not tell us exactly when students started to use a particular verb with a particular form. The data show the changes of verb use over the eight-year period.

Students used verbs that denote concrete events (denoting motions or changes of state, all of which are visible) rather than states. Many psycho verbs were used as well. In parallel with this tendency, students marked tense-aspect morphology with verbs that refer to completed events more often than verbs referring to states.

Figure 8–2 shows that students continuously learned a variety of verbs in the classroom. Students used them freely in accordance with their phase of development.

Comparing Figures 8–3 and 8–4, we notice that verb use in L2 and L1 does not overlap, which suggests that students did not simply translate L1 into L2. Verb use in L2 develops in its own right.

Let us now look more closely at the data, focussing on the issues in verb learning.

8.3.4.1. Overgeneralisation or undergeneralisation

Previous research into L2 acquisition of argument structure has shown that very often overgeneralisation errors occur: L2 learners extend argument structure to other verbs, or overextend other constructions to the wrong class of verbs. L1 influence is not usually obvious, and errors appear to be developmental, linked to default linguistic operations (Montrul, 2001). However, White (1991) argues that L1 influence leads learners to take a conservative approach by which they undergeneralise argument structure in L2. If an argument structure is more restricted in L1 than in L2, L2 learners adopt undergeneralisation, including direct translation. A stronger position taken by Bley-Vroman (1989, 1990) is that aspects of the lexicon that are not represented in the learner's L1 grammar including knowledge of semantic constraints on argument structure cannot be acquired unconsciously by means of positive evidence only. Learners need to learn each verb on an item-by-item basis, referring to L1 knowledge associated with a particular situation or event. Direct translation errors are numerous as a result. Figure 8–5 shows the types of errors that learners made. Few overgeneralisation errors were found, which suggests that Japanese learners of English learned each verb one-by-one. This observation supports Tomasello's Verb Island Hypothesis and the Item-by-item approach to L2 acquisition.

8.3.4.2. Missing argument phenomenon

Rispoli (1995) investigated the acquisition of Japanese. According to his description of Japanese, it has a grammatically unrestricted zero anaphora: any and all of the core arguments of a predicate are omitted in grammatical sentences (missing arguments). Rispoli estimates that only 9% of the action transitive sentences are syntactically determinate and only 1% are fully determinate with overtly case-marked actors and undergoers. In contrast, English word order is strict, and zero anaphora is highly restricted. Rispoli (1995: 345–346) proposes that Japanese are sensitive to discourse-pragmatic information, as this information plays a crucial role in recovering and interpreting missing arguments in Japanese. Figure 8–5 shows that Japanese learners of English transfer missing arguments, a linguistic feature of L1, to English. Especially, in narratives, they tend to omit arguments which are obligatory in English argument structures, but in Japanese it is natural to omit them. Let us have a look at some examples:

Yesterday, I went to library. I borrowed Soseki. I put on the desk for a while. I forgot. Maybe somebody will give it tomorrow… (age 15)
I visited Hokkaido. In there, I bought cute wooden fox. When I get on a boat, I keep in a locker. After I put fox, I ran to boat… (age 16)

One possible explanation for this missing argument phenomenon is that L1 stylistics and linguistic features transfer to L2. Because Japanese is a missing-argument language, in which discourse-pragmatic information aids interpretation, this property is transferred to English narratives.

8.3.4.3. Marked use of psycho verbs

According to Pinker (1994) and Naigles (2000), it is quite difficult for children to master psycho verbs, and hence psycho verbs are acquired very slowly in child language acquisition. The reasons for the difficulties in learning psycho verbs can be summarised as follows:

1. Psycho verbs are abstract and do not follow 'here and now': one cannot act out the meanings of psycho verbs; one cannot see by one's eyes concretely what *think* means.
2. Psycho verbs presuppose the development of a 'theory of mind': in order to use psycho verbs, one can analyse one's and other's states of mind and can express them in words.
3. Psycho verbs require highly sophisticated language processing systems: in order to comprehend and produce psycho verbs, one must parse linguistically complex sentences.

Although it is hard for children to use psycho verbs, Japanese learners of English used many psycho verbs. This is because L2 learners possess mature cognition, and they can express their feelings in L1. Looking closely at Figures 8–3 and 8–4, we notice that Japanese learners of English started to use psycho verbs from the beginning, use them continuously, and employ them most frequently in the later stages. In contrast, they used many psycho verbs in the earlier stages but less in later stages in L1. This suggests that students did not simply translate L1 into L2 when they produced essays in L2. Data associated with native writing shown in Figure 8–1 reveal that while English-speaking children used many psycho verbs, adult English speakers used fewer psycho verbs in narratives. One possible explanation for this phenomenon would be related more to linguistic performance or to psychological factors than to linguistic competence. As psycho verbs are used less in later stages in L1 (both in Japanese and English), we cannot appeal to L1 transfer. In the field of communication strategy research, Kasper & Kellerman (1997) report that adult learners of English use many psycho verbs, such as *I think, I feel, Maybe I know,* etc., in order to express their lack of confidence in L2. They try to avoid affirmative expressions, and tend to add psycho verbs in order to soften their claims. This prevents them from making unexpected strong and sometimes impolite claims in L2, making communication in L2 smoother.

8.3.4.4. Development of tense-aspect marking

Figures 8–6 to 8–10 reveal frequencies of verb forms with respect to different types of verbs. The figures do not tell us about the first appearance of each form: it is unknown when students first used a particular verb form. In a series of research, Bardovi-Harlig (1992, 1997, 1999, 2000) investigated when students first used past tense, progressive, and perfect forms. She took a longitudinal approach together with experimental designs. Bardovi-Harlig (2000: chapter 5) points out that researchers should focus on discourse including narrative structures. In some contexts, the subjects tend to use past tense and perfect forms more often than present tense or progressive forms.

In section 8.3.3, the figures show the total number of each type of verb and total number of errors in tense/aspect marking. However, it is not accurate to just compare total numbers, especially when it comes to the analyses of errors. It is too simplistic to conclude that learners made many errors of tense-aspect marking of a particular type of verb. The situation is different where learners used many verbs and made many errors, or where learners used few verbs and made many errors. In order to illustrate an accurate picture in verb form use, we should calculate the proportion of students' non-target-like use of verb morphology per

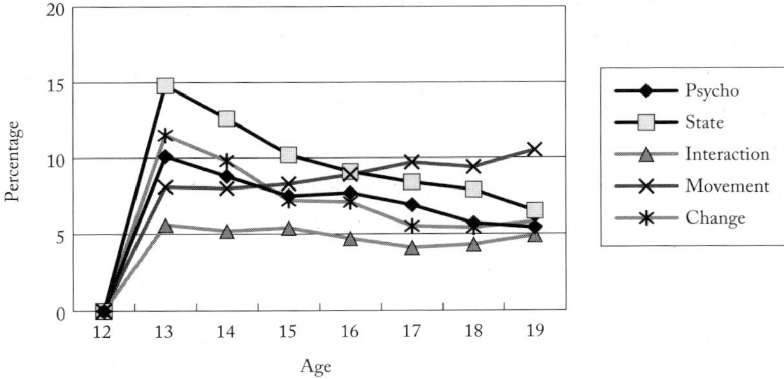

Figure 8–12: Proportion of errors

total number of verbs used. Figure 8–12 shows the changes in the proportion of errors in total use:

The non-target-like use of bare verb forms is high, but this is because they are used as the default verb form in cases where students are not realising regular past tense marking and agreement. What this figure shows is that students made many errors at the early and later stages. This result is interesting (but might be discouraging for English teachers!) because beginners and advanced learners made errors of tense-aspect markings. It is natural that beginners mark tense-aspect wrongly because of the lack of previous exposure to English. Why do advanced learners fail to mark tense-aspect accurately regardless of longer experiences of English learning?

One potential explanation is that intermediate learners who marked tense-aspect most accurately used monitor more frequently than beginners and advanced learners: intermediate learners presumably focused on accuracy, but advanced learners gave way to fluency (Harley et al., 1990; Guillot, 1999). Such a distribution of the proficiency of Japanese learners of English can be found elsewhere: Firstly, section 2.3.4 reports that beginners and advanced learners made many more errors of agreement and determiners than intermediate learners. More research is necessary to conclude that Japanese learners of English shift their attention from accuracy to fluency during the passage of English language learning, or their performance fossilises around the intermediate level. Secondly, DeKeyser (1997) investigates the longitudinal effect of systematic practice on real-time performance in English morphology in comprehension and production, and demonstrates that explicitly learned knowledge could be used automatically, that is, fast, with a low error rate. DeKeyser reports that for both reaction time and error rates, and for both comprehension and production, a clear and gradual drop-off takes place, which slows down overtime (what he calls 'gradual automatisation'), from a marked decrease in the early stages to an almost imperceptible (or somewhat increasing) decline for the later stages, namely, the U-shaped learning curve for morphology (Ellis & Schmidt, 1998).

It is often claimed that Japanese learners of English tend not to use perfect forms, especially the present perfect (as shown in Figure 8–10). Some researchers (Odlin, 1989, 1994) propose that cross-linguistic differences result in the inaccurate use of perfect forms. On the other hand, Bardovi-Harlig (1997) points out that the present perfect is very difficult for any L2 learners to master. As Schachter (1974) points out, difficult features of L2 tend to be avoided, but if they are used, they tend to be more or less correct. This claim is true for our data as well: although the total number of perfect forms used is quite limited, students uapplied them correctly. Students tend to use memorised phrases such as: 'I have been to...' 'Have you ever...?' 'I have never been to...' etc. The avoidance of perfect forms is due to cross-linguistic differences of aspect in English and Japanese and to the universal tendency of L2 learners of English.

8.4. Three approaches to verb teaching

This section discusses the way to deal with L2 verbs in the classroom. In section 8.3.4, some problems in verb learning have been pointed out. In the field of L2 teaching, three possible approaches were proposed. After reviewing them, in order to overcome the problems in verb learning, we discuss a longitudinal study where we compared three potential methods to teach beginners of English, as we did in chapter seven: English-Japanese comparison, noticing, and the Lexical Approach.

The results from the empirical studies on morpho-syntactic marking of temporality (Bardovi-Harlig, 2000; Salaberry, 2000) show that instruction may have a significant effect on language development. The data from most studies on classroom learning show that instruction on verbal morphology is associated with the extended use of verbal morphology. Kaplan (1987) identifies the major role of formal instruction on the development of verbal morphology in the L2 along the lines of frequency, saliency, and sequence of instruction.

8.4.1. English-Japanese comparison

This approach is often called the 'grammar-translation method'. A student's first language is thoroughly compared with the target structure. Translation and explicit analyses of the target language are major procedures of this method.

8.4.2. Noticing

The notion of noticing in language teaching stems from cognitive psychological investigations of language learning: Learning takes place when learners notice new aspects of language. Noticing aims at altering the way in which learners process input. Its purpose is to direct learners' attention to relevant features of grammar in input and to encourage correct form-meaning mappings. Appealing to VanPatten (1995, 1996), Ellis (2002), and Benati (2001), one lesson is organised as follows:

Listening to comprehend: Students are to listen to a short conceptualised passage (text in our textbook) and try to understand the general meaning of the text.
Listening to notice: Students next listen to the same text again in order to focus attention on how verbs work in the text.
Understanding the grammar point: Students now provide a short analysis of a grammar contrast in the text. Through this analysis task, students are guided to see how the grammar point works and to formulate a grammar rule (inductive learning).
Checking: Students check their understanding of the grammar rule by completing a short exercise with a new set of sentences.
Trying it: Finally, students have an opportunity to try out the grammar rule with sentences of their own.

8.4.3. The Lexical Approach

This method was originally proposed by Willis (1990, 1994), Nattinger & DeCarrico (1992), and Lewis (1993, 1996, 1997a/b, 2000). These researchers argue that new aspects of grammar should be introduced not by means of explicit explanations of rules but by direct teaching as chunks. Regarding instruction of verbs, without employing grammatical jargon such as 'tense, aspect', etc., verbs are to be taught directly through their use. Providing appropriate contexts in which verbs are naturally used, students are encouraged to process and get used to a wide range of verb uses with tense marking as chunks. No explicit analyses of grammar are provided. Each new verb is introduced to the students together with many examples with visual aids (Lewis, 1986; Blyth, 1997). The methodology has the following six components (Willis, 1990: 72):

Introduction: This gives students initial exposure to target forms within a communicative context.
Task: This provides an opportunity to focus on and realise target meanings. Students may begin to approximate to the target language form or they may use quite different forms.
Planning: The teacher helps students move towards accurate production.
Report: Students have another opportunity to use target forms.
Reading: Students have a chance to read the target forms used in a context that has become familiar to them through their own attempts to perform and report the task. (By means of listening, this stage may come immediately after *Introduction*.)
Analysis: This is an awareness-raising exercise that gives the learners a chance to formulate generalisations about the language they have heard.

8.5. Comparison of three approaches

8.5.1. Background

This study was conducted in a normal classroom setting. Verbs are first introduced to students in the first term of the first year at junior high school. Students are previously taught SV and SVC structures with copula and simple short greetings.

8.5.2. Participants

Three Japanese teachers of English (aged 36, 38, and 41) joined the investigation. All of them teach English at a private junior high school. The students enrolled in April 1996 were taught English by English-Japanese comparison for three years (1996–1999: 200 students). The students enrolled in April 1997 were taught English by the Lexical Approach for three years (1997–2000: 200 students). The students enrolled in April 1998 were taught English by noticing for three years (1998–2001: 200 students). All the teachers taught the three groups by using the three different methods in order to avoid teacher-related factors. As we could not re-arrange classes only for this study and as we wished to investigate the overall differences among the three methods, we pursued our study with the classes as they were. Note that Japanese learners of English are not supposed to become bilinguals, because the target language community is not present in any way in the L2 environment, and the L2 is rarely the medium of communication outside the classroom. The target language is L2 in a relatively homogeneous language community, where the L2 is learned through instruction in a classroom setting, and students usually do not have direct access to the target language culture.

8.5.3. Procedure

While we have to use a textbook authorised by the Japanese Ministry of Education (*The New Crown English Series*), exercises can be produced freely. We prepared the teaching plans together. We stuck to using the texts in the textbook, exactly the same verbs (amount and content) in exercises, and the same timing of the language activity sessions. This means that students were exposed to the same quality and quantity of verbs but with the three different methods. We stuck to the methods for three years, and observed the performances of the students.
English-Japanese Comparison: First, we read the texts together. Second, we explained each sentence, focusing on the structural differences and translating into Japanese. Last, we gave them some exercises.
Noticing: We first played the texts from the textbook, and asked some questions in order to make sure that students understood the content. Second, we gave out blanked texts, and asked the students to fill in the gaps while listening to the same text. Third, students were encouraged to figure out the grammatical morphemes. Fourth, we gave them some practice. We referred to Ellis & Gaies (1999) in preparing for our lessons.
Lexical Approach: Every new verb was introduced with many examples that show how the verb is used in context. Visual aids (pictures, videos, actions, etc.) were frequently used. Students were encouraged to practice verbs that appear in the textbook on their own in natural contexts.

Let us now look at the average timing of our lessons based on the recording in the classroom. ○ means that the activity in the left column took an average of more than 15 minutes per lesson. △ means 6 to 14 minutes per lesson. × means less than 5 minutes per lesson. – means zero minutes. 'Patterns' means that students did pattern practice. 'Translation' means that teachers/students put the texts into Japanese. 'Structure' means that teachers explained the structural differences explicitly. 'Listening' means that students had chances to listen to the texts by CD. 'Use of L1' means that the teachers used Japanese to explain grammar points. 'Production' means that students had a chance to produce verbs freely.

Table 8–1: Timing of each methodology per one lesson

	Patterns	Translation	Structure	Listening	Use of L1	Production
Comparison	—	○	○	×	○	△
Noticing	△	△	△	○	△	○
Lexical App.	○	×	—	△	△	○

8.5.4. Testing

Twice a year (July and March), we tested the students by a production test. The production test included controlled-writing (including Japanese to English translation), free writing, and story telling (including picture verification tasks). Students were told that the results of the test would be included in considering their final evaluation. We assigned six tests in total. Before test 1, students learned present tense forms (including third person singular). Before test 2, students learned progressive forms and regular and irregular past tense forms. Before test 3, students learned future forms (*will* and *be going to*). Before test 4, students learned the present perfect. Before test 5, students learned the past perfect. Finally, before test 6, students learned all possible English tense-aspect forms.

8.5.5. Results

Test results were analysed by means of error analysis. The percentage of each type of error was calculated: the number of errors was divided by the total number of obligatory contexts.

8.5.5.1. Direct translation

The following figure shows the changes in the proportion of direct translation errors by means of the three different teaching methods.

This figure reveals that students taught by English-Japanese comparison made many errors in the direct translation of L1. Noticing and the Lexical Approach, on the other hand, prevent the students from producing this type of error.

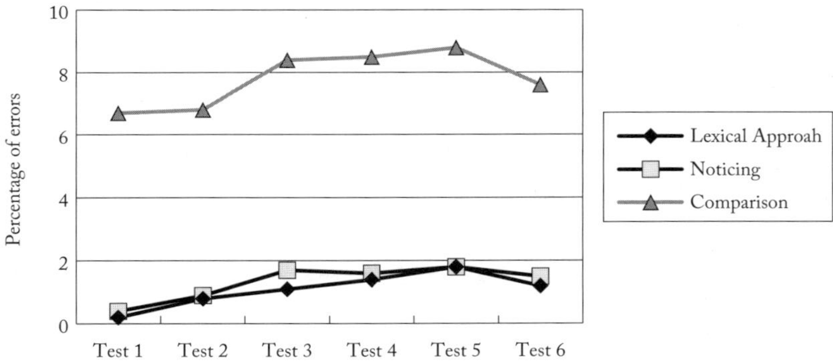

Figure 8–13: Direct translation errors

8.5.5.2. Overgeneralisation

The following figure shows the changes in the proportion of overgeneralisation errors by means of the three different teaching methods.

This figure reveals that students taught by Noticing made many errors of overgeneralisation. English-Japanese comparison and the Lexical Approach, on the other hand, prevent the students from producing this type of error.

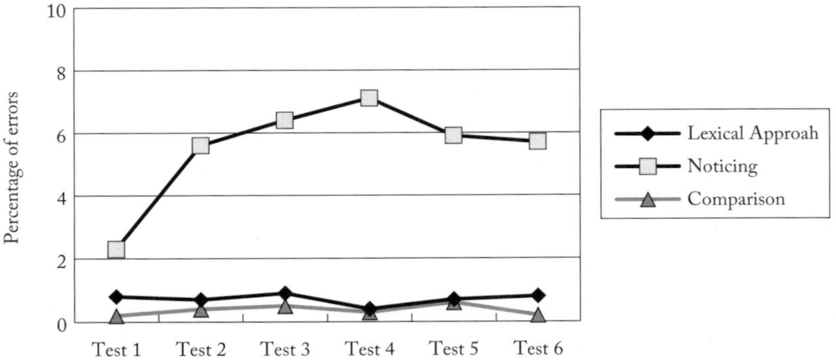

Figure 8–14: Overgeneralisation errors

8.5.5.3. Missing arguments

The following figure shows the changes in the proportion of missing argument errors by means of the three different teaching methods.

This figure reveals that students taught by English-Japanese comparison and

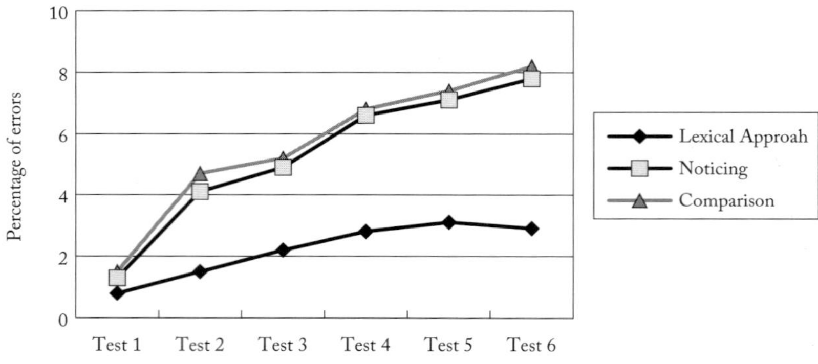

Figure 8–15: Missing argument errors

Noticing made many errors of missing arguments. The Lexical Approach, on the other hand, prevents the students from producing this type of error.

8.5.5.4. Tense-aspect morphology

a) Third person singular

The following figure shows the changes in the proportion of errors associated with the third person singular form by means of the three different teaching methods.

This figure reveals that students taught by Noticing did the best, and the Lexical Approach the second. Students taught by English-Japanese comparison

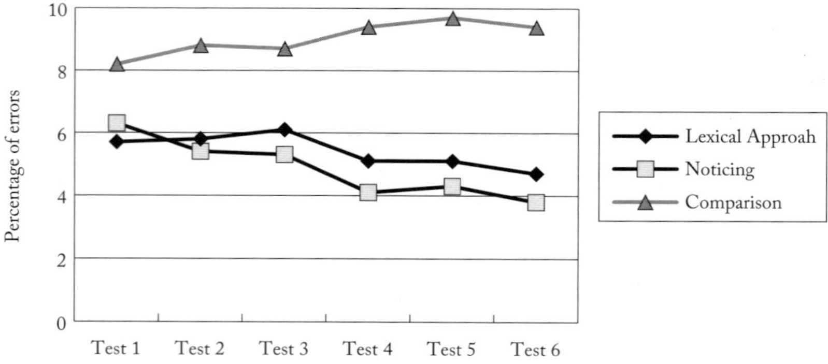

Figure 8–16: Third person singular errors

made many third person singular errors.

b) Progressive

The following figure shows the changes in the proportion of errors associated with the progressive form by means of the three different teaching methods. This figure reveals that students taught by the Lexical Approach did the best, and Noticing the second. Students taught by English-Japanese comparison made many progressive form errors.

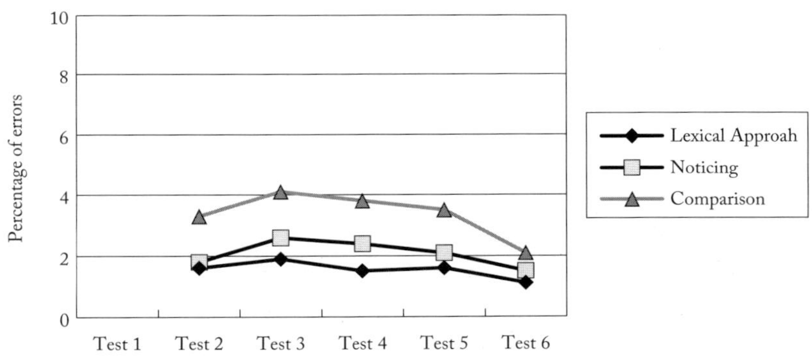

Figure 8–17: Progressive form errors

c) Past tense

The following figure shows the changes in the proportion of errors associated

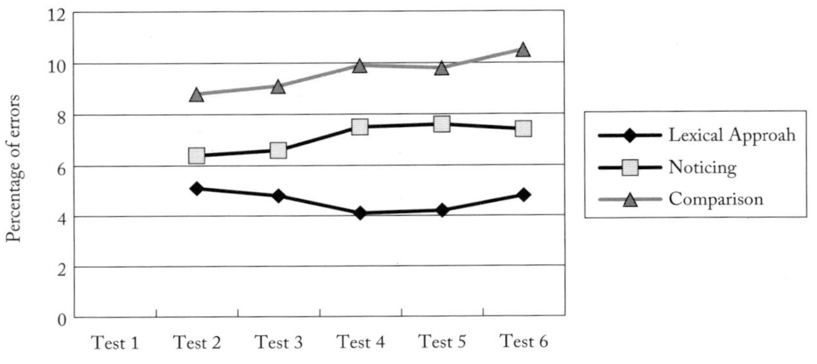

Figure 8–18: Past tense errors

with the past tense form by means of the three different teaching methods.

This figure reveals that students taught by the Lexical Approach did the best, and Noticing the second. Students taught by English-Japanese comparison made many past tense errors.

d) The perfect

The following figure shows the changes in the proportion of errors associated with the perfect form by means of the three different teaching methods.

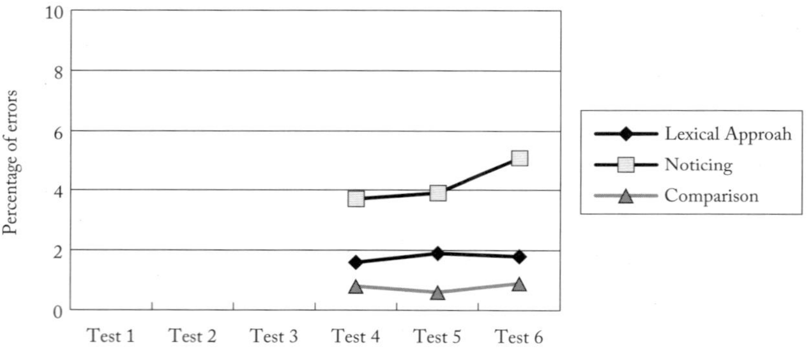

Figure 8–19: Perfect form errors

This figure reveals that students taught by English-Japanese comparison did the best, and the Lexical Approach the second. Students taught by Noticing made many perfect form errors.

8.5.6. Discussion

8.5.6.1. English-Japanese comparison

Figure 8–13 reveals that students taught by English-Japanese comparison made many more errors of direct translation than those taught by Noticing and the Lexical Approach. Table 8–1 shows that teachers used L1 frequently as a major source of instruction. Teachers employed word lists as well: Japanese and English words were directly connected, which led students to search for equivalent expressions in L1 and L2. Teachers taught verbs by means of word-for-word translation, which results in developing students' ability to connect L1 and L2 directly. This might be a reason for students making many direct translation errors.

Figure 8–15 reveals that students taught by this method made many errors of missing arguments as well. Again, this is due to teachers' frequent use of L1. Teachers and students always put English texts into Japanese and vice versa, which causes the students to activate L1 every time they process English. Students often claimed that they wanted to first write a passage in L1, which was then translated into L2. This attitude, that is, a heavy reliance on L1, may result in direct translation and missing arguments, i.e., negative transfer of L1.

Figures 8–16, 8–17, and 8–18 reveal that the results of tense/aspect marking were not so good. This is because these forms were not automatised by utilising this method (Bayley, 1994; Benati, 2001; DeKeyser, 1997; Hinkel, 2002; Robinson, 1995, 1996, 1997; VanPatten, 1996).

Figure 8–19 reveals that students taught by this method did very well in the perfect form. This is because teachers compared English perfect thoroughly with Japanese perfect. Students seemed to understand how the perfect form works in English. If L1 and L2 structures are different, it is more effective to explain it explicitly.

Overall, the problems of English-Japanese comparison can be summarised as follows: students tend to think that L1 and L2 are equivalent, which causes transfer errors. The merit of this method is that students can understand the different aspects of L1 and L2 clearly.

8.5.6.2. Noticing

Figure 8–14 reveals that students taught by Noticing made many overgeneralisation errors. This is because this methodology appeals to the hypothesis formation and hypothesis testing paradigm: students were implicitly and explicitly taught to learn new aspects of L2 by way of consciousness raising. Students tend to overgeneralise rules to a wide range of contexts, just as children in a process of first language acquisition usually do. Overgeneralisation is a natural result of this method. One important thing that needs caution is that we must be careful of students' fossilisation: students sometimes fossilise incorrectly generalised forms, which does not occur in child language acquisition.

Figure 8–15 reveals that students made many missing argument errors. This was unexpected because L1 was not mainly used in the classroom. Presumably, students could not notice rules in discourse: students were only guided to focus on tense/aspect marking in sentences, and not on other features of grammar. Negative transfer of L1 would result.

Regarding third person singular, Noticing is the most effective methodology. Figure 8–16 reveals that student taught by Noticing did very well, because they seem to be able to automatise tense-aspect morphology. This result agrees with Bayley (1994), Benati (2001), DeKeyser (1997), Hinkel (2002), Robinson (1995, 1996, 1997), and VanPatten (1996).

However, the perfect forms were avoided. According to the students, they could not understand how the perfect form works in English. They could not hypothesise how the perfect and past tense forms were different, and decided not to use this unconfident form.

8.5.6.3. The Lexical Approach

Students taught by the Lexical Approach did fairly well in verb learning in general. They did not make many overgeneralisation and missing argument errors. This is because students learned verbs as chunks in natural contexts assisted by visual aids with many examples. At the same time, students could automatise tense/aspect morphology (Figures 8–16, 8–17, and 8–18).

One problem, which did not appear in the figures, is that students tend to produce colloquial writing: their stylistics is not formal. Teachers did not care about stylistics: they taught the communicative use of verbs, putting too much emphasis on oral communication. In addition, creative use of the perfect form could not be found: students only used taught phrases (i.e., memorised chunks). Chunking is an effective way to handle surface forms, but is insufficient when it comes to deeper aspects of language. The perfect forms are closely related to conceptual structure as to how the speakers of a particular language conceptualise time and space (Lewis, 1986; Hornstein, 1990). Such an abstract feature of language needs to be explained explicitly (which should be the strength of English-Japanese comparison).

The above findings are summarised as follows:

Table 8–2: Types of errors and the three methodologies

	Direct translation	Overgeneralisation	Missing arguments
Comparison	Many	Few	Many
Noticing	Few	Many	Many
Lexical Approach	Few	Few	A few

	Third person	Progressive	Past	Perfect
Comparison	Many	Many	Many	Few
Noticing	A few	A few	A few	Many
Lexical Approach	A few	Few	A few	A few

By means of the t-test among the three teaching methods, the following conclusions can be drawn. The distributions of errors of the 200 students taught by each method above reveal that the Lexical Approach and Noticing are better methods than English-Japanese comparison when teaching verb meanings and most of the verb forms ($p<0.01$), while comparison is superior to others for the perfect forms ($p<0.001$). Implications for teaching derived from the above results can be summarised as follows:

1. The Lexical Approach is suitable as an overall introduction of verbs, because we assume that verbs are processable as chunks in natural use ($p<0.05$).
2. Noticing shows an advantage over the others for third person singular ($p<0.01$).
3. Regarding the perfect forms, the Lexical Approach and Noticing are not suitable. Although the Lexical Approach can handle perfect forms as set phrases, students had trouble figuring out the meaning of the sentences because the use of perfect forms in English and Japanese is quite different. English-Japanese comparison gives advantage over others, because structural and semantic differences between English and Japanese are explicitly explained and students have ample opportunities to practise them ($p<0.001$).
4. Although Noticing uses listening most frequently, this method had no visible effect on students' general listening ability. We suppose that this is because listening is used for students to notice new aspects of grammar, rather than to enhance their listening skills. Note that this point is consistent with Hulstijn & Hulstijn's (1984) experimental results.

Conclusion

In this chapter, we first reviewed past studies on the acquisition of verb meaning and verb form. It is now clear that a limited number of studies can be found in the field of verb learning in L2. What we have seen, based on the eight-year longitudinal study, is as follows:

(1) Both verb meaning and verb form are acquired in a certain order.
(2) Learner's errors reveal both L1 influence and universal phenomena among L2 learners.
(3) Verbs in L2 are acquired on an item-by-item basis.
(4) Learners seem to find it easier to mark past tense when referring to completed events than when referring to states and activities that may last for extended periods without a clear end point.

We hypothesised that these pieces of information should be suggestive to English language teaching. The next investigation we conducted was to build up a theory of verb teaching, to develop a teaching methodology, and to test and evaluate it. The latter part of this chapter sought a way to introduce English verbs to Japanese learners of English. There is a developmental sequence of learning L2 verb meanings and verb forms which is characterised by differential error patterns reflecting the type of instruction the learner receives and the emphasis within that instruction given to the L1. It turned out that the Lexical Approach and Noticing were worth our attention. Their overall framework and the ways of introducing verbs were shown to be effective, and, if necessary, especially if the learner's first language and his or her target language are extremely different, explicit grammar explanations should be of great help. We realise that these results were obtained from one particular Japanese-based classroom, and one study does not prove everything. In addition, most teachers will be aware of the fact that no single method works for all students. Most will adopt an eclectic approach, incorporating the most useful aspects from each method for their context and bearing in mind past learning experiences and cultural expectations. What is important now is to evaluate our results longitudinally in a wide range of contexts.

First published as 'Verb acquisition and verb instruction in a foreign language' in *JABAET Journal* 6 (2002): 55–90

PART IV
Implications for curriculum design

This part of the book integrates the overall arguments and discusses the implications for a curriculum design of English language teaching in Japan. First, we review our discussion of why a lexicon and chunks are more important than has been traditionally thought. Then, I argue the significance of grammar instruction in the curriculum. Finally, I propose outlines of curriculum designs for primary school, junior high school, and senior high school that our theoretical arguments predict.

Chapter 9

The place of lexis and grammar in English language teaching

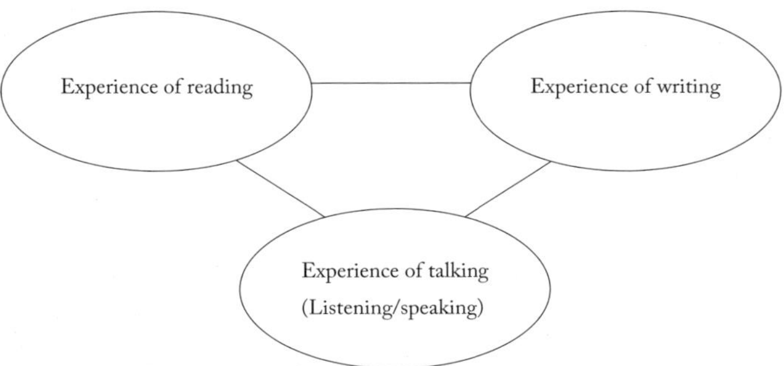

Figure 9–1: Experiences in language

The above figure is intended to show that all persons of normal development possess a store of language knowledge which may be defined as the sum total of their experience to date of language use. This language use is the person's own. The acquisition of this store of knowledge begins at birth and continues throughout life (Wallen, 1994). In order to arrive at possessing such knowledge, the individual must have been engaged in some sort of reflection on language at some level of consciousness (called *metalinguistic awareness*), generalising from many examples of paying specific attention to the facets of the language. Metalinguistic awareness refers to the knowledge that users of a language have about their knowledge of the language. Such metalinguistic awareness reflects the fact that language rules are not only used by the learner but that the learner can reflect on and infer from these rules of language. In the case of grammar, it refers to how the learner becomes able to recognise relevant units of the spoken or written language. Nevertheless, the vast bulk of our stored implicit knowledge about language is never made explicit, which means that the language processing system unconsciously selects and stores only necessary and sufficient linguistic information in the mind. The situation is slightly different in foreign language learning in the classroom. Although the Natural Approach of Krashen & Terrell (1988) promotes the idea that foreign languages should be learned in an implicit way, knowledge of foreign language is taught explicitly in the name of grammar. Before experiencing reading, writing, and talking, all of which construct implicit knowledge of the language, knowledge about foreign language is provided explicitly.

What we have seen so far is that the system to achieve meaning is syntactic under a linguistic approach (the structural syllabus) and that foreign language learning is much more lexical than is usually accepted under a cognitive approach (the lexical syllabus). The following sections discuss the interrelation between the two approaches and implications for teaching.

9.1. Significance of lexis

What we have seen so far claims that a lexicon and chunks need to be paid more attention in foreign language learning and teaching, firstly because foreign language learning is more lexical and secondly because people can communicate by means of lexis and chunks. Processing chunks in the flow of speech is crucial in comprehending and producing a foreign language. This section argues for the lexicalist position and the implications for foreign language pedagogy.

Most linguistic analyses take as the starting point the position that their goal is to provide a powerful, elegant account of language with those qualities being judged by the way in which the rule system proposed generates the correct sentences of the language (Skehan, 1994: 181). The emphasis is on grammar and rules, and lexis is seen as having a subservient fill-the-slot position. This point of view, taken widely by syllabus designers and textbook writers, appears to downgrade the importance of a lexicon and chunks. However, lexicalists argue that rather than being fully governed by a rule system, language is produced on the basis of a capacious and redundantly structured memory system (N. Ellis, 1996a; Skehan, 1994, 1998: chapter 2; Fernando, 1996; Wray, 2002; Schmitt ed., 2004). Skehan suggests that much of language consists of lexical elements and that these may not be easily described by rules. In this view, the language user operates with a more lexical unit of analysis, and achieves communication in real time not by the complexities of producing utterances on the basis of a rule system constructing anew each time, but instead by drawing on ready-made elements and chunks. Larger units are accessed and used as wholes as they have been on previous occasions. People produce utterances by starting with chunks, stitching them together, to communicate the intended meaning (Pawley & Syder, 1983). N. Ellis (2001) argues that learning to understand a language involves parsing the speech stream into chunks which reliably form meaning. This task is made more tractable by the patterns of language. Learners' attention to the evidence to which they are exposed soon demonstrates that there are recurring chunks of language. An essential task for the learner is to discover the patterns within the sequence of language. At some level of analysis, the patterns refer to meaning. Sinclair (1991: 109–115) claims that while grammar enables endless combinational possibilities, most of these possibilities are not preferred and particular combinations of lexical elements occur repeatedly. The choice of one word affects the choice of others in its vicinity. Although the rule-based nature of language has been emphasised, the use of memorised chunks of foreign language has attracted researchers' attention. It is important to survey the ways to investigate the memorised languages in foreign language learning: *native-like fluency* and *native-like selection*.

In a well-known article by Pawley & Syder (1983), they propose that the use of chunks achieves native-like fluency. Pawley & Syder (1983: 205) suggest that the average native speaker knows hundreds of thousands of such lexicalised patterns, and these are available as a repertoire of elements that may be used in ongoing conversation to achieve a degree of fluency. Pawley & Syder argue that the ability to speak fluently is based on knowledge of thousands of memorised chunks and whole sentences that are lexicalised to varying degrees. According to Pawley & Syder (1983: 203), memorised chunks and phrases are the normal building blocks of fluent spoken discourse, and at the same time, they provide models for the creation of many new sequences that are remembered and in turn enter the stock of familiar usage. Fluent performance is made easier if the learner has command of a range of chunks that can be readily accessed as the occasion demands. However, increased chunk usage may not form a satisfactory basis for the quality of the learner's production. Many of the most recognisable chunks are overused expressions or clichés, which may be regarded as inappropriate in the context in which they are used.

The second issue is native-like selection: the capacity to sound idiomatic and to say the sort of things in a foreign language that a native speaker of the language would say. In spoken and written production, one significant aspect of performance is the extent to which the learners have achieved native-like selection. Pawley & Syder claim that foreign language learners might achieve native-like fluency without achieving native-like selection. Such learners can produce the target language at a rate not particularly different from that produced by native speakers, but their choice of language makes it clear that, while grammatical and fluent, they still sound foreign. Many of the choices that need to be made to achieve acceptability as a native speaker are choices of lexical phrases. Learners need to make the choice from a range of grammatically acceptable utterances that would be used by native speakers. One way of achieving this goal is to extend the range of lexical entries and lexical phrases that learners would use (Nattinger & DeCarrico, 1992). Such set phrases, chunks, have traditionally been paid little attention. (For more extensive research on chunks, see Fernando, 1996; Wray, 2002; Schmitt ed., 2004). Thanks to the development of corpus, however, it is now much easier to arrange such set phrases along with grammar.

When we turn to pedagogy, instruction must achieve a balance between syntactic and lexical processing to enable the development of Interlanguage grammar and correctness on the one hand, and natural, fluent language use on the other. What we need to recognise here is that students are reported to have different learning styles. Celce-Murcia & Hilles (1988) suggest two kinds of learners: analytic and holistic learners. Analytic learners form hypotheses and test them. Consciously or unconsciously, they extract paradigms and rules from examples. Analytic learners concentrate on grammatical details and often do not participate well in communicative activities; they would rather find the meanings of words in a dictionary than guess from the context. Holistic learners, on the other hand, learn best by doing little or no analysis, instead, they learn by exposure to large chunks of language. Holistic learners like interactive tasks in which they use main ideas; they have difficulty dealing with grammatical details and are content to use guessing strategies. Learning strategies are affected by age and task type. Children prefer a holistic approach to an analytical one, and even those adults who are generally more comfortable with an analytical style often approach holistically and vice versa. Regarding chunking in language learning, Kormos (2006: 46) claims that holistic learners tend to use chunks at the beginning of the acquisition process and abstract linguistic rules from chunks at later stages, whereas analytic learners tend to construct utterances from single words and attempt to apply simple rules of language already at the start of learning. Individual differences in learning mean that teaching should take account of the way learners may have a predisposition to process language at some point on a syntax-lexis continuum and should offset any undesirable processing predisposition on the part of the learner. Two possible pedagogical approaches can be taken (Shrum & Glisan, 1994: 25–27). The first one is a bottom-up approach. Students learn grammar rules and vocabulary and then later practise using them in communication. Classroom practice activities are sequenced so that meaning increasingly receives more focus. In this approach, activities progress through the following stages: primary focus on form, focus on form + meaning, focus on meaning + form, and primary focus on meaning. The other one is a top-down approach. Students manipulate language to communicate thoughts using higher level skills before attending to discrete language structures with the use of lower level skills. Students attend to the whole language that provides the context or theme when they attempt to construct meaning and deal with the unknown.

9.2. Necessity of grammar

Emphasising the significance of lexis does not necessarily lead us to conclude that we should not teach grammar. On the contrary, lexicalists do not deny the fact that grammar instruction is important and necessary. The question is what sort of grammar is required. In this section, we shall see why grammar is necessary and how grammar instruction would help learners learn a foreign language.

Although one of the most important roles of using language is communication, grammar is often taught in isolated unconnected sentences that give a fragmented unrealistic picture of English, and make it difficult for students to apply what they have learned in actual situations. Realistic and effective contextualisation of an isolated grammar point is not always easy. We need to see grammar not primarily as a unitary object, something whose component parts have to be learned, but as a vehicle to encode our experiences to others in an interpersonally sensitive way, and a device to decode their experiences and beliefs.

The question of how words and chunks can and cannot be combined should be an important part of grammar (Halliday, 1994: chapters 3 & 5). By putting words together in certain ways, we have followed certain syntactic conventions for word order. Batstone (1994: 4) claims that language without grammar would be chaotic: Countless words without the indispensable guidelines for how they can be ordered and modified would be of little use. Stillings et al. (1995: 456) claim that language processing must incorporate a grammar that is in principle fully capable of characterising the set of grammatical sentences in a given language. However possible it may be to understand languages without recourse to grammar, it does not seem possible to constrain language production by meaning or context in ways that would guarantee linguistically well-formed output. A study of grammar reveals a structure and regularity that lies at the basis of language and enables us to talk of a language system. Language is rule-governed, and grammar is a subset of those rules which govern the configurations that the morphology and syntax of a language assume. The recognition of the structure dependency of language as a universal property has been argued by Chomsky (in his major works), Bloomfield (1933: chapter 10), Jespersen (1922: chapter 7), amongst others. As Chomsky (1965) notes, structure dependence is a general constraint on the linguistic principles that language learners hypothesise in grammar formation. Grammar rules are part of what is known automatically by all native speakers of a language.

Let us now turn to the argument of why grammar instruction is necessary. Firstly, grammar instruction helps promote more rapid foreign language learning, and contributes to higher levels of ultimate achievement only if the learners come to the appropriate stage to learn grammar explicitly (Long, 1988; Ellis, 1997, 2002). Long's and Ellis' theoretical implications are schematised as below. Note that the horizontal line means the flow of time and the vertical line means the development of grammatical competence.

The figure shows that students attain much grammatical competence quickly by the structural syllabus and that students taught by the lexical syllabus gradually attain grammatical competence.

Secondly, if students do not become capable analysts, their learning will probably fossilise: that is, their Interlanguage will diverge in more or less perma-

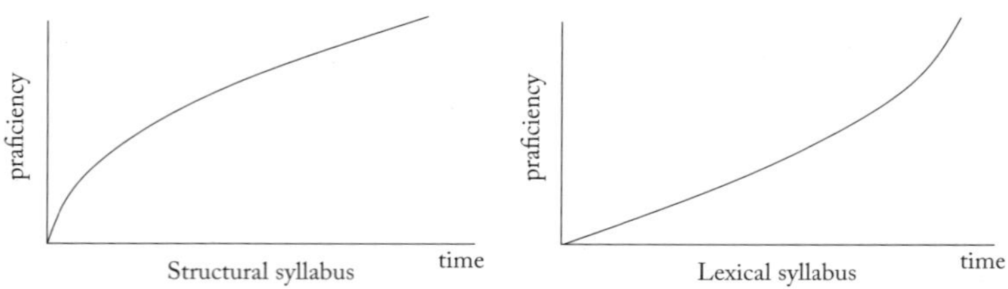

Figure 9–2: Developmental speed of students' grammatical competence

nent ways from the target language grammar (Selinker, 1992). Coppetiers (1987) suggests that most learners who are highly successful require considerable time to master the complexities of grammar and that instructed adult foreign language learning will more often minimise fossilisation in comparison with naturalistic uninstructed acquisition. Even if the naturalistic path can lead to the same or nearly ideal goal, the path appears to be far steeper.

Thirdly, Mitchell (1994: 220–221) clarifies a range of pedagogic purposes for which teachers and learners may require knowledge of grammar: In order to make sense of the advice they are given in syllabus documents or textbooks; in order to diagnose and monitor the learners development and provide feedback, and understand them; and in order to talk about the target language system.

We have seen that grammar instruction is necessary in foreign language teaching. We conclude this section by considering how grammar should be treated in the Lexical Approach as follows:

Grammar as a tool for language processing:
Internalised grammar, i.e., knowledge of grammar in Chomsky's sense, helps learners comprehend and construct messages. In other words, grammar makes it possible to decode what others are saying and to encode what the speaker wishes to say. In a sense, grammar functions as an internal system to analyse a flow of speech, formulate messages, and monitor what has been formulated in language processing. The notion of grammar in this conception should be clearly different from that in language description: 'grammar as a tool for language processing' and 'grammar as a tool for linguistic analyses and description'. In the latter sense, traditionally taught grammar, i.e., an explicit body of rules, helps learners notice and structure by focussing on specific forms and meaning, and gives learners practice in the skills of language use, allowing them to proceduralise their knowledge. In other words, grammar in this sense helps learners analyse and translate the target language.

9.3. Implications for curriculum design

This section discusses the implications for curriculum design that our overall arguments make. What is important is the make-up of the curriculum throughout primary school, junior high school, and senior high school. The other thing is testability: whether the approach I am proposing can be compatible with the present-day English examinations.

9.3.1. Child L2 learning: Implications for teaching English at primary school

As discussed in the previous chapters, the Lexical Approach to teaching children English has an advantage over the grammar-oriented structural approach as follows: Because of the children's rigid cognitive developmental paths, we should avoid teaching grammar, especially abstract operations such as transformations, explicit teaching of word order, negative and question formations, parts of speech, etc. Even if adults wish to teach grammar rules which seem to be simple for them, a child's state of mind cannot handle them (as discussed in section 6.6). The Lexical Approach, on the other hand, introduces foreign languages by means of lexis and chunks. Foreign language learning is lexical, and lexical elements play an important role in the learning processes. Previously, I concluded that it was impossible for children around ten years old to understand and generalise rules abstractly, and they tend to process, memorise, and store words and phrases as a whole. Caution is necessary concerning how to realise this line of teaching: As seen in chapter three, lexis and chunks must be provided by accurate pronunciation and intonation in English, otherwise allophonisation takes place, which cannot be unlearned later. Children are very sensitive to sounds, and subtle differences can be processed unconsciously. For instance, as we saw in chapter three, the /θ/ sound is processed as /f/, because children can sense the friction of lips and teeth unconsciously while adults cannot. If adults correct them by saying /s/ for /f/ where the /θ/ sound is appropriate, for example, saying that they should not say /fə:zdei/ but say /sə:zdei/, children unconsciously group /θ/ in the same group as /s/, the same type as the Japanese sound, which firmly grounds their mind and cannot be gotten rid of afterwards. In addition, very weak sounds of determiners and inflections are processed implicitly, so teachers must pronounce accurately and fluently.

Regarding the teaching methodology, the Lexical Approach encourages the teacher to select words and phrases directly connected with the children's world. Teachers can encourage pupils to collect words on their own (word-search activity: e.g., Kuno, 2000). Starting from one- or two-word expressions, gradually they form patterns. For instance, *a red tulip, a beautiful glass, a big dog* (Determiner – Adjective – Noun patterns: Noun Phrase), *Mr. Kato is angry* (Noun – Adjective Phrase), *Mrs. Sato plays the queen* (Noun –Verb –Noun Phrase). This gradual expansion from a noun to a phrase to a sentence satisfies the structure-building approach discussed in section 2.3.5. Such patterning and set phrases would be stored in the child's mind and be analysed abstractly at the junior high school stage if necessary, when they can be understood and digested in the abstract. What is important here is not to force children to memorise or analyse every sentence, but to let them know implicitly that they can communicate with others by working with words and phrases. Input is to be given in authentic full-length sentences in natural pronunciation and intonation patterns of English.

The other important point to bear in mind is that children around this age tend to judge things from their own point of view: they determine things in physiological ways, that is, like or dislike, good or bad, interesting or boring, pleasant or unpleasant, etc. They are not mature enough to think from another's viewpoint or to express their emotions verbally (Howe, 1999: chapters 3 & 7). This leads us to conclude that we should stick strictly to 'here-and-now', and showing off abstract foreign cultures would not be understood by children. Emotional judgement will motivate or demotivate children, so considerable caution is necessary. The Lexical Approach will make the language classroom more pupil-oriented and communicative than the structural approach. Fulfilling the strict here-and-now requirement, the Lexical Approach helps foreign languages be more accessible to children. Resources that consist of objects, such as pictures, realia, and graphics, will be useful. These can be used for matching structural and semantic factors, since semantic distinctions often need visual reinforcement. For instance, the difference between *in the box* and *on the box* can be illustrated by putting something into and then onto a box, rather than be explained verbally. Utilising the Total Physical Response (TPR) method that is expected to connect sounds, meaning, and actions effectively, teachers can make the classroom active, which Piaget insists it should be. The technique of getting pupils to listen and respond to TPR-style commands facilitates a match between sound, form, and meaning; the technique is best implemented by means of resources such as pictures, realia, and classroom objects, and acting out commands. These techniques promote the learning of a foreign language.

9.3.2. Implications for teaching English at junior and senior high schools

Ellis (1997) claims that an assumption of traditional approaches to grammar is that it should be taught from the very early stages of a language course to avoid the unnecessary labour of having to unlearn wrong habits in order to learn the correct ones later. However, it is now widely accepted that errors are a normal and inevitable consequence of the process of hypothesis formation and testing. Pienemann (1984, 1989, 1998) argues that there are psycholinguistic constraints which govern whether attempts to teach learners specific grammatical rules result in their acquisition. Formal instruction may succeed if the learners have reached a stage in the developmental sequence that enables them to process the target structure. As we have seen in chapter two, there is a natural order of foreign language learning that foreign language learners seem to pass through. If Pienemann were right in saying that learners cannot learn the aspects of foreign language unless they arrive at the appropriate stage, there would be no reason to teach grammar to beginners. According to Pienemann (1998), beginners have received little linguistic input and are able to process lexis and chunks only. Beginners must notice that they can communicate with people by lexis and chunks, appealing to the universal human inferential ability. Nunan (1989: chapter 6) claims that many adult learners try hard to produce full sentences that seem to sound perfect, but this results in low-level fluency, causing difficulty in processing to interlocutors. Nunan suggests that learners must learn to communicate using chunks. The previous section concluded that learners would need grammar to build up lexicons and chunks to satisfy the structural patterns of the language, and grammar should be taught when learners already have a stock of lexis and chunks which they wish to connect in some ways. Grammar instruction facilitates foreign language learning and makes foreign language learning faster if and only if grammar is introduced at the appropriate stage of a learner's development. Depending only on one approach is insufficient, and a combination of approaches should be better theoretically.

As we have seen in chapter six, the open-choice principle is based on grammatical rules and involves generating novel utterances. This rule-based system is required when meanings need to be expressed precisely or creatively. The other mode, the idiom principle, draws on memorised chunks, which can be retrieved quickly as whole units to allow the user to communicate fluently under normal time constraints. Adult native speakers have both modes available to them and can apply them flexibly according to the demands of different situations. This adult capacity has been developing through their experiences in language, as shown in Figure 9–1. As we have seen in chapter two, learners progress through developmental stages, summarised as follows (Skehan, 1998: chapter 4):

Lexicalisation: At the first stage, learners communicate by means of lexis and

chunks that have meaning within their immediate environment.
Syntacticisation: Then, they move into a stage when their linguistic knowledge becomes syntacticised. They are able to separate linguistic structures into individual elements and generate new structures based on grammatical rules.
Relexicalisation: However, effective language use requires the stage whereby language structures that can be analysed grammatically are stored as whole lexical units or chunks.

Read (2000: chapter 8) claims that progress through these stages is not as automatic for adult foreign language learners as it is for children acquiring their first language. Thus, language teachers and course designers need to develop balanced programmes incorporating tasks that allow opportunities for both syntacticisation and relexicalisation to occur.

Shrum & Glisan (1994: 23) claim that elementary school teachers have been combining language and context through techniques such as story-telling, games, role plays, etc. However, at later levels of instruction, teachers have become quite adept at separating linguistic form from content. Bialystok (1991) warns that we should bear in mind that decontextualisation may be the cause of the difficulty experienced by both children and adults in learning a foreign language. Curriculum design for each stage is summarised as follows:

For primary school, children's cognitive development requires the following theoretical implications, which satisfy practitioners' advice on teaching primary children English (e.g., Kuno, 1999):

(1) Abstract rule explanations of grammar should be avoided.
(2) Words and chunks should be used as communicative tools.
(3) Strict 'here-and-now'.
(4) Accurate pronunciation and intonation of English must be provided in order to avoid allophonisation.

For junior high school,

(1) Encourage students to put words and chunks together to form patterns.
(2) Basic forms and patterns (structure of English) should be explained to facilitate their learning.
(3) Grammar should be introduced gradually as skills for enhancing students'

sensitivity to English.

For senior high school and onwards,

(1) Skills to comprehend and produce structures that are more complicated should be taught.
(2) Expressions to satisfy their needs should be expanded. Complicated grammar does not make it possible to express what they wish, but more lexical entries and chunks would help learners speak/write natural English fluently and accurately. Pragmatics should be included in order to communicate appropriately.
(3) To read authentic English written for adults, students need to be taught how to process complicated structures metalinguistically.

The following figure clarifies the proposal:

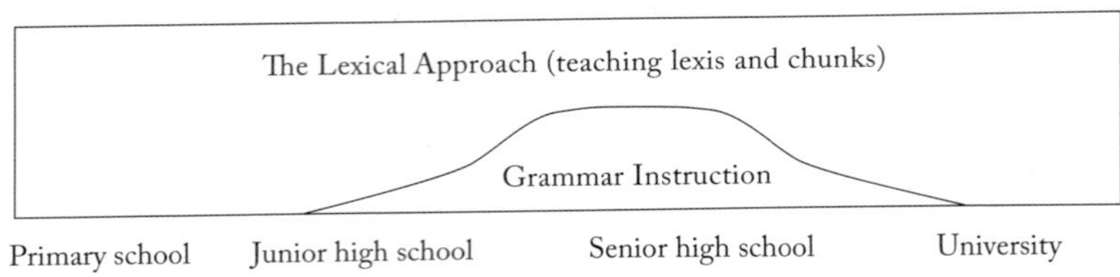

Figure 9–3: Curriculum design

The major difference between the present day curriculum and the proposed one is that the latter one focuses more on the lexical dimension of foreign language learning. If attaining communicative competence in speaking and writing and skills to understand messages accurately in listening and reading is the main goal of English language teaching, the Lexical Approach does not conflict with the present curriculum. Examinations for senior high schools and universities test the above skills. If students were able to capture chunks and structures, they would be more confident tackling questions. Now that the practice of asking students to explain grammar explicitly in technical jargon is disappearing, and as accurate message decoding and encoding is the goal of present communicative language teaching, I conclude the book by proposing that the Lexical Approach is one possible option to be considered in English language teaching in Japan.

Concluding remarks

This book is intended to show how Japanese learners of English learn English sounds, grammar, and lexis and how we should teach them based on the reality of their foreign language learning processes, arguing for the possibility of the Lexical Approach to foreign language teaching.

First, we investigated the place of phonetics in English language teaching. After Communicative Language Teaching came into language classrooms, listening and speaking have been emphasised. Especially, experts suggest that these skills should be strongly focused on at primary schools, because adults cannot learn foreign sounds. Our research should shed some empirical light on these ungrounded claims. Our research findings are as follows:

(1) Students can process implicatures more and more rapidly and aptly when exposure to L2 increases and a foreign language processor is developed.
(2) Japanese students do not commonly employ indirect communication as English-speaking people often do. Japanese students sometimes feel negatively about employing indirect communication. Even if L1 and L2 language use is different, Japanese learners of English can interpret implicatures.
(3) The foreign language effect results in the slow processing of L2.
(4) Teaching foreign sounds explicitly or implicitly may help. However, whether it does or does not depends on the age of the learners. It was claimed that children were able to develop a native-like accent through training only if allophonisation had not taken place; whereas adolescents and adults could unlearn allophonised sounds and relearn new sounds by training.
(5) From the very beginning, English rhythm and intonation should be instruct-

ed, focusing on weak forms.

(6) Phonological differences (mora, syllable, and stress timing) cause learning problems. In addition, as learners grow older, more psychological factors, including motivation and attitude toward foreign language learning, influence the attainment of proficiency.
(7) Acoustic programmes might be one of the best ways to instruct these features effectively. They are suitable for both auditory- and visual-dependent learners. In addition, they assist allophonised learners, including children, to overcome and unlearn allophonic treatments of L2 sounds.

After the introduction of communicative language teaching, teachers have been trying hard to create a communicative language classroom. However, basic methodologies for teaching each facet of grammar have not changed: teachers accept the transformational methods, which are not suitable for communicative language teaching. What many teachers do is to let their students memorise target sentences without any contextualisation. The grammar-oriented approach to English language teaching generates a large number of grammatical but unnatural or unacceptable sentences. I have tried to promote a methodology that helps students and teachers refrain from generating such unnatural utterances. The empirical studies show that the Lexical Approach, which is based on the cognitive perspective of language learning, can handle basic grammar points. What I need to do next is to propose methods to introduce other grammar points that are not discussed in this book, to test them in wider contexts, and to develop course materials in order to put the theoretical and empirical findings into practice. The future direction goes as follows, and I have already started to tackle the issues:

(1) How do auditory and visual systems relate to each other in foreign language processing? The relationships between listening and reading, paying attention to sound processing and letter processing, should be investigated.
(2) Research on mechanisms of language processing and the development of such mechanisms is fairly new. Even L1 processing research has only just begun. We need more extensive research on these matters.
(3) The teaching methodology must be broad, tolerant, flexible, and pliant enough to fit all learners who show individual differences. We touched on the differences in information processing in chapter five (auditory and visual

learners) and on cognitive style (holistic and analytic learners) in chapter nine. Developing a teaching methodology that is suitable for every student with different psychological factors lags behind in mainstream pedagogy.

(4) The way of teaching reading, writing, listening, and speaking under processing perspectives must be developed. There are numerous publications on how to teach these skills independently, but a consistent approach based on language processing has not proposed so far. The four language skills should be integrated to make them closer to natural communication styles. At the same time, we need to know which grammar should be taught how and when. Otherwise, we face the same problem as the Notional-functional and the Task-based approaches did: everything is introduced without any control, which was extremely troublesome for learners and teachers.

Some readers might think that this project is somewhat innovational. Ellis (1997) offers the following categories so that one can evaluate the value of the research in pedagogical terms. Ellis (1997: 31) claims that an innovationist analysis, using the following categories, provides practitioners with an explicit and relatively systematic way of determining whether specific proposals derived from theoretical research are of use to them. The following categories and definitions are attributes of innovation (Ellis, 1997: 29):

Initial dissatisfaction: The level of dissatisfaction that practitioners experience with some aspect of their existing teaching.
Feasiblity: The extent to which the innovation is seen as implementable given the conditions in which practitioners work.
Acceptability: The extent to which the innovation is seen as compatible with practitioners' existing teaching style and ideology.
Relevance: The extent to which the innovation is viewed as matching the needs of the students.
Complexity: The extent to which the innovation is difficult or easy to grasp.
Explicitness: The extent to which the rationale for the innovation is clear and convincing.
Triability: The extent to which the innovation can be easily tried out in stages.
Observability: The extent to which the results of innovation are visible to others.
Originality: The extent to which the practitioners are required to demonstrate a high level of originality in order to implement the innovation.

Ownership: The extent to which practitioners come to feel that they possess the innovation.

Now that you have come to the end of my ten-year project, I should like you to evaluate it by referring to Rod Ellis' categories shown above, and decide whether you were entertained and can share the innovation.

Bibliography

Achiba, M. (2003) *Learning to Request in a Second Language*. Clevedon: Multilingual Matters

Aitchison, J. (1998) *The Articulate Mammal*. London: Routledge

Akmajian, A., Culicover, P. and Wasow, T. (eds.) (1977) *Formal Syntax*. New York: Academic Press

Alcon, E. (1998) 'Input and input processing in second language acquisition' *International Review of Applied Linguistics* 34: 343–362

Altmann, G. (ed.) (1990) *Cognitive Models of Speech Processing: Psycholinguistic and Computational Perspectives*. Cambridge: Cambridge University Press

Andersen, R. and Shirai, Y. (1996) 'The primacy of aspect in first and second language acquisition' in Ritchie & Bhatia (eds.): 527–570

Anderson, J. (1987) 'The Markedness Differential Hypothesis and syllable structure difficulty' in Ioup & Weinberger (eds.): 279–291

Anderson-Hsieh, J. (1992) 'Using electric visual feedback to teach suprasegmentals' *System* 20: 51–62

Anderson-Hsieh, J. (1994) 'Interpreting visual feedback in computer-assisted pronunciation instruction on suprasegmentals' *CALICO Journal* 11: 5–22

Aoshima, S., Phillips, C. and Weinberg, A. (2004) 'Processing filler-gap dependencies in a head-final language' *Journal of Memory and Language* 51: 23–54

Appel, R. (1996) 'The lexicon in second language acquisition' in Jordens & Lalleman (eds.): 381–403

Archibald, J. (1997) 'The acquisition of second language phrasal stress' in Hannahs & Young-Scholten (eds.): 263–289

Archibald, J. (1998) *Second Language Phonology*. Amsterdam: John Benjamins

Archibald, J. (ed.) (2000) *Second Language Acquisition and Linguistic Theory*. London: Blackwell

Ard, J. and Gass, S. (1987) 'Lexical constraints on syntactic acquisition' *Studies in Second Language Acquisition* 9: 233–252

Ashby, M. and Maidment, J. (2005) *Introducing Phonetic Science*. Cambridge: Cambridge University Press

Aston, G. (1995) 'Corpora in language pedagogy: matching theory and practice' in Cook & Seidlhofer (eds.): 257–270

Balcom, P. (1997) 'Why is this happened? Passive morphology and unaccusativity' *Second Language Research* 13: 1–9

Bardovi-Harlig, K. (1992) 'The relationship of form and meaning: A cross-sectional study of tense and aspect in the Interlanguage of learners of English as a second language' *Applied Psycholinguistics* 13: 253–278

Bardovi-Harlig, K. (1997) 'Another piece of the puzzle: the emergence of the present perfect'

Language Learning 47: 375–422

Bardovi-Harlig, K. (1999) 'From morpheme studies to temporal semantics: Tense-Aspect research in SLA' *Studies in Second Language Acquisition* 21: 341–382

Bardovi-Harlig, K. (2000) *Tense and Aspect in Second Language Acquisition: Form, Meaning, and Use.* London: Blackwell

Bardovi-Harlig, K. (2001) 'Evaluating the empirical evidence' in Rose & Kasper (eds.): 13–32

Bardovi-Harlig, K. (2002) 'Pragmatics and second language acquisition' in Kaplan (ed.):182–192

Bardovi-Harlig, K. and Reynolds, D. (1995) 'The role of lexical aspect in the acquisition of tense and aspect' *TESOL Quarterly* 29: 107–131

Barrett, M. (ed.) (1999) *The Development of Language.* Hove: Psychology Press

Barshi, I. and Payne, D. (1998) 'Argument structure and Maasai possessive interpretation' in Healy & Bourne (eds.): 213–230

Bates, E., Bretherton, I. and Goodman, J. (1999) 'On the emergence of grammar from the lexicon' in MacWhinney (ed.): 29–79

Bates, E., Bretherton, I. and Snyder, L. (1988) *From First Words to Grammar.* Cambridge: Cambridge University Press

Batstone, R. (1994) *Grammar.* Oxford: Oxford University Press

Bayley, R. (1994) 'Interlangauge variation and quantitative paradigm: past tense marking in Chinese-English' in Tarone, Gass & Cohen (eds.): 157–181

Bayley, R. and Preston, D. (1996) *Second Language Acquisition and Linguistic Variation.* Amsterdam: John Benjamins

Beebe (ed.) (1988) *Issues in Second Language Acquisition.* Boston: Heinle & Heinle

Behrens, H. (2001) 'Cognitive-conceptual development and the acquisition of grammatical morphemes: the development of time concepts and verb tense' in Bowerman & Levinson (eds.): 450–474

Benati, A. (2001) 'A comparative study of the effects of processing instruction and output-based instruction on the acquisition of the Italian future tense' *Language Teaching Research* 5: 95–127

Berman, R. (1987) 'Cognitive components of language development' in Pfaff (ed.): 3–27

Bernhardt, A. (1994) 'The prosodic tier and phonological disorders' in Yavaş (ed.): 149–172

Bernthal, J. and Bankson, N. (1998) *Articulation and Phonological Disorders.* Boston: Allyn & Bacon

Berwick, R. (1987) 'Parsability and learnability' in MacWhinney (ed.): 345–365

Best, C. (1994) 'The emergence of native-language phonological influences in infants: A perceptual assimilation model' in Goodman & Nusbaum (eds.): 167–224

Best, C. (1995) 'A direct realist view of cross-language speech perception' in Strange (ed.): 171–204

Bever, T. (1970) 'The cognitive basis for linguistic structure' in Hayes (ed.): 279–352

Bever, T. and Langendoen, D. (1970) 'A dynamic model of the evolution of language' *Linguistic Inquiry* 2: 433–462

Bialystok, E. (1991) *Language Processing in Bilingual Children.* Cambridge: Cambridge University Press

Birdsong, D. (1992) 'Ultimate attainment in second language acquisition' *Language* 68: 706–755

Birdsong, D. (ed.) (1999) *Second Language Acquisition and the Critical Period Hypothesis*. Mahwah: Lawrence Erlbaum

Birdsong, D. (2006) 'Age and second language acquisition and processing' in Gullberg & Indefrey (eds.): 9–50

Bishop, D. (1997) *Uncommon Understanding: Development and Disorders of Language Comprehension in Children*. Hove: Psychology Press

Bley-Vroman, R. (1989) 'What is the logical problem of foreign language learning?' in Gass & Schachter (eds.): 41–68

Bley-Vroman, R. (1990) 'The logical problem of foreign language learning' *Linguistic Analysis* 20: 3–49

Bloom, L. (2000) 'The intentionality model of word learning' in Golinkoff et al. (ed.): 19–50

Bloom, L. and Tinker, E. (2001) *The Intentionality Model and Language Acquisition*. Oxford: Blackwell

Bloom, P. (1996) 'Controversies in language acquisition: word learning and the part of speech' in Gelman & Au (eds.): 151–184

Bloomfield, L. (1933) *Language*. New York: Henry Holt

Blum-Kulka, S. and Snow, C. (2002) *Talking to Adults: The Contribution of Multiparty Discourse to Language Acquisition*. Mahwah: Lawrence Erlbaum

Blyth, C. (1997) 'A constructivist approach to grammar: teaching teachers to teach aspect' *The Modern Language Journal* 81: 50–66

Bock, K. (1995) 'Sentence production: from mind to mouth' in Miller & Eimas (eds.): 181–216

Bock, K. and Levelt, W. (1994) 'Language production: grammatical encoding' in Gernsbacher (ed.): 945–982

Bogaards, P. (1996) 'Lexicon and grammar in second language learning' in Jordens & Lalleman (eds.): 357–379

Bogaards, P. and Laufer, B. (eds.) (2004) *Vocabulary in a Second Language: Selection, Acquisition, and Testing*. Amsterdam: John Benjamins

Bohn, O. and Flege, J. (1997) 'Perception and production of a new vowel category by adult second language learners' in James & Leather: 53–73

Bongaerts, T. (1999) 'Ultimate attainment in L2 pronunciation: The case of very advanced late L2 learners' in Birdsong (ed.): 133–159

Bongaerts, T., Planken, B. and Schils, E. (1995) 'Can late starters attain a native accent in a foreign language? A test of the Critical Period Hypothesis' in Singleton & Lengyel (eds.): 30–50

Bongaerts, T., van Summeren, Planken, B. and Schils, E. (1997) 'Age and ultimate attainment in the pronunciation of a foreign language' *Studies in Second Language Acquisition* 19: 447–465

Borer, H. (1984) *Parametric Syntax: Case Studies in Semitic and Romance Languages*. Dordrecht: Foris

Borer, H. and Wexler, K. (1987) 'The maturation of syntax' in Roeper & Williams (eds.): 123–172

Bouton, L. (1988) 'A cross-cultural study of ability to interpret implicatures in English' *World Englishes* 7: 183–196

Bouton, L. (1994) 'Conversational implicature in a second language: learned slowly when not deliberately taught' *Journal of Pragmatics* 22: 157–167

Bowerman, M. and Brown, P. (eds.) (2008) *Crosslinguistic Perspectives on Argument Structure.* New York: Lawrence Erlbaum

Bowerman, M. and Levinson, S. (eds.) (2001) *Language Acquisition and Conceptual Development.* Cambridge: Cambridge University Press

Brazil, D. (1995) *A Grammar of Speech.* Oxford: Oxford University Press

Brazil, D. (1997) *The Communicative Value of Intonation in English.* Cambridge: Cambridge University Press

Breul, C. (2004) *Focus Structure in Generative Grammar: An Integrated Syntactic, Semantic and Intonational Approach.* Amsterdam: John Benjamins

Broselow, E. (1987a) 'An investigation of transfer in second language phonology' in Ioup & Weinberger (eds.): 261–278

Broselow, E. (1987b) 'Non-obvious transfer: on predicting epenthesis errors' in Ioup & Weinberger (eds.): 292–304

Brown, C. (2000) 'The interrelation between speech perception and phonological acquisition from infant to adult' in Archibald (ed.): 4–63

Brown, C. and Hagoort, P. (1999) *The Neurocognition of Language.* Oxford: Oxford University Press

Brown, C. and Hagoort, P. (2000) 'On the electrophysiology of language comprehension: implications for human language system' in Crocker, Pickering & Clifton (eds.): 213–237

Brown, G. (1995) *Speakers, Listeners, and Communication.* Cambridge: Cambridge University Press

Brown, G. and Hulme, C. (1992) 'Cognitive psychology and second language processing: the role of short-term memory' in Harris (ed.): 105–121

Brown, G., Malmkjaer, K. and Williams, J. (eds.) (1996) *Performance and Competence in Second Language Acquisition.* Cambridge: Cambridge University Press

Brown, R. (1973) *A First Language: The Early Stages.* Cambridge: Harvard University Press

Brownell, J. (1996) *Listening: Attitudes, Principles, and Skills.* Boston: Allyn and Bacon

Buck, G. (2001) *Assessing Listening.* Cambridge: Cambridge University Press

Bybee, J. (2003) 'Cognitive processes in grammaticalization' in Tomasello (ed.): 145–167

Bygate, M., Tonkyn, A. and Williams, E. (eds.) (1994) *Grammar and the Language Teacher.* London: Prentice Hall

Carlisle, R. (1999) 'The modification of onsets in a Markedness relationship: Testing the Interlanguage Structural Conformity Hypothesis' *Language Leaning* Volume 49 Supplement 1 edited by Leather: 59–93

Carreiras, M. and Clifton, C. (eds.) (2004) *The On-line Study of Sentence Comprehension: Eye-tracking, ERPs and Beyond.* New York: Psychology Press

Carroll. D. (2004) *Psychology of Language (4th Edition).* Belmont: Wadsworth Thomson Learning

Carston, R. (2002) *Thoughts and Utterances: The Pragmatics of Explicit Communication.* Oxford:

Blackwell

Carter, R. (1987) *Vocabulary: Applied Linguistic Perspectives.* London: Routledge

Carter, R.and McCarthy, M. (eds.) (1988) *Vocabulary and Language Teaching.* London: Longman

Casielles, E. (2004) *The Syntax-Information Structure Interface.* London: Routledge

Celce-Murcia, M. and Hilles, S. (1988) *Techniques and Resources in Teaching Grammar.* Oxford: Oxford University Press

Celce-Murcia, M. and Larsen-Freeman, D. (1999) *The Grammar Book: An ESL/EFL Teacher's Course.* Boston: Heinle & Heinle

Chela-Flores, B. (2001) 'Pronunciation and language learning: an integrative approach' *International Review of Applied Linguistics* 39: 85–101

Chomsky, C. (1969) *The Acquisition of Syntax in Children from 5 to 10.* Cambridge: MIT Press

Chomsky, N. (1965) *Aspects of the Theory of Syntax.* Cambridge: MIT Press

Chomsky, N. (1986) *Barriers.* Cambridge: MIT Press

Chomsky, N. (1988) *Language and Problems of Knowledge.* Cambridge: MIT Press

Chomsky, N. (1992) 'Some notes on economy of derivation and representation' in Freidin (ed.): 417–454

Chun, D. (2002) *Discourse Intonation in L2.* Amsterdam: John Benjamins

Clahsen, H. (1987) 'Connecting theories of language processing and second language acquisition' in Pfaff (ed.): 103–116

Clahsen, H. (ed.) (1996) *Generative Perspectives on Language Acquisition.* Amsterdam: John Benjamins

Clahsen, H. and Felser, C. (2006) 'Grammatical processing in language learners' *Applied Psycholinguistics* 27 (Special issue)

Clark, E. (1993) *The Lexicon in Acquisition.* Cambridge: Cambridge University Press

Clark, E. (1995) 'Language acquisition: the lexicon and syntax' in Miller & Eimas (eds.): 303–337

Clark, H. and Clark, E. (1977) *Psychology and Language.* New York: Harcourt Brace Jovanovich

Clifton, C., Frazier, L. and Rayner, K. (eds.) (1994) *Perspectives on Sentence Processing.* Hillsdale: Lawrence Erlbaum

Coady, J. and Huckin, T. (1997) *Second Language Vocabulary Acquisition.* Cambridge: Cambridge University Press

Coleman, J. (2005) *Introducing Speech and Language Processing.* Cambridge: Cambridge University Press

Comrie, B. and Keenan, E. (1979a) 'Data on the Noun Phrase Accessibility Hierarchy' *Language* 55: 333–350

Comrie, B. and Keenan, E. (1979b) 'Noun Phrase Accessibility revisited' *Language* 55: 549–554

Cook, G. and Seidlhofer, B. (eds.) (1995) *Principle & Practice in Applied Linguistics.* Oxford: Oxford University Press

Cook, V. (1993) *Linguistics and Second Language Acquisition.* London: Macmillan

Coppieters, R. (1987) 'Competence differences between native and near-native speakers' *Language* 63: 544–573

Corder, P. (1981) *Error Analysis and Interlanguage.* Oxford: Oxford University Press

Coventry, K. and Garrod, S. (2004) *Saying, Seeing, and Acting: The Psychological Semantics of Spatial Prepositions*. Hove: Psychology Press

Crocker, M., Pickering, M. and Clifton, C. (eds.) (2000) *Architectures and Mechanisms for Language Processing*. Cambridge: Cambridge University Press

Crookes, G. (1991) 'Second language speech production research' *Studies in Second Language Acquisition* 13: 113–132

Cruse, A. (2004) *Meaning in Language*. Oxford: Oxford University Press

Culicover, P. and Jackendoff, R. (2005) *Simpler Syntax*. Oxford: Oxford University Press

Curtiss, S. (1977) *Genie: Psycholinguistic Study of a Modern Day 'Wild Child'*. San Diego: Academic Press

De Bot, K. (1983) 'Visual feedback of intonation: effectiveness and induced practice behaviour' *Language and Speech* 25: 331–350

De Bot, K. (1992) 'A bilingual production model: Levelt's speaking model adopted' *Applied Linguistics* 13: 1–24

De Bot, K. (1993) 'Word production and bilingual lexicon' in Schreuder & Weltens (eds.): 191–214

De Bot, K. (1996) 'The psycholinguistics of the Output Hypothesis' *Language Learning* 46: 529–555

De Bot, K. (1997) 'Toward a lexical processing model for the study of second language vocabulary acquisition' *Studies in Second Language Acquisition* 19: 309–329

De Bot, K., Cox, A., Ralston, S., Schaufeli, A. and Weltens, B. (1995) 'Lexical processing in bilinguals' *Second Language Research* 11: 1–19

De Bot, K., Lowie, W. and Verspoor, M. (2005) *Second Language Acquisition: An Advanced Resource Book*. London: Routledge

De Groot, A. (1993) 'Word-type effects in bilingual processing tasks: support for a mixed-representational system' in Schreuder & Weltens (eds.): 27–49

De Groot, A. and Kroll, J. (1997) (eds.) *Tutorials in Bilingualism: Psycholinguistic Perspectives.* Mahwah: Lawrence Erlbaum

Dehaene, S. et al. (1997) 'Anatomical variability in the cortical representation of first and second language' *NeuroReport* 8: 3809–3815

DeKeyser, R. (1997) 'Beyond explicit rule learning: automatizing second language morphosyntax' *Studies in Second Language Acquisition* 19: 195–221

Dickerson, W. (1987) 'Explicit rules and the developing interlanguage phonology' in James & Leather (eds.): 121–140

Dietrich, R., Klein, W. and Noyau, C. (1995) *The Acquisition of Temporality in a Second Language.* Amsterdam: John Benjamins

Dimroth, C. and Starren, M. (eds.) (2003) *Information Structure and the Dynamics of Language Acquisition*. Amsterdam: John Benjamins

Dittmar, N. (1992) 'Grammaticalisation in second language acquisition' *Studies in Second Language Acquisition* 14: 249–257

Dixon, R. (1991) *A New Approach to English Grammar on Semantic Principles.* Oxford: Clarendon Press

Dixon, R. (2005) *A Semantic Approach to English Grammar.* Oxford: Oxford University Press

Dornyei, Z. and Kormos, J. (1998) 'Problem-solving mechanisms in L2 communication' *Studies in Second Language Acquisition* 20: 349–385

Doughty, C. (1991) 'Second language instruction does make a difference' *Studies in Second Language Acquisition* 13: 431–469

Dufour, R. (1997) 'Sign language and bilingualism: modality implications for bilingual language representation' in de Groot & Kroll (eds.): 301–330

Dulay, H., Burt, M. and Krashen, S. (1982) *Language Two.* Cambridge: Newbury House

Echols, C. and Marti, N. (2004) 'The identification of words and their meanings: From perceptual biases to language-specific cues' in Hall & Waxman (eds.): 41–78

Eckman, F. (1988) 'On the generalization of relative clause instruction in the acquisition of English as a second language' *Applied Linguistics* 9: 1–20

Eckman, F. (ed.) (1993) *Confluence: Linguistics, L2 Acquisition and Speech Pathology.* Amsterdam: John Benjamins

Eckman, F. (ed.) (1995) *Second Language Acquisition Theory and Pedagogy.* Mahwah: Lawrence Erlbaum

Eckman, F., Bell, L. and Nelson, D. (eds.) (1984) *Universals of Second Language Acquisition.* Rowley: Newbury House

Ellis, N. (1992) 'Linguistic relativity revisited: the bilingual word-length effect in working memory during counting, remembering numbers, and mental calculation' in Harris (ed.): 137–155

Ellis, N. (ed.) (1994) *Implicit and Explicit Learning of Language.* London: Academic Press

Ellis, N. (1996a) 'Sequencing in SLA: phonological memory, chunking, and points of order' *Studies in Second Language Acquisition* 18: 91–127

Ellis, N. (1996b) 'Analyzing language sequence in the sequence of language acquisition' *Studies in Second Language Acquisition* 18: 361–368

Ellis, N. (1997) 'Vocabulary acquisition: word structure, collocation, word-class, and meaning' in Schmitt & McCarthy (eds.): 122–139

Ellis, N. (1999) 'Cognitive approaches to SLA' *Annual Review of Applied Linguistics* 19: 22–42

Ellis, N. (2001) 'Memory for language' in Robinson (ed.): 33–68

Ellis, N. (2004) 'The processes of second Language acquisition' in VanPatten et al. (eds.): 49–76

Ellis, N. and Beaton, A. (1995) 'Psycholinguistic determinants of L2 vocabulary learning' in Harley (ed.): 107–165

Ellis, N. and Schmidt, R. (1998) 'Rules or associations in the acquisition of morphology? The frequency by regularity interaction in human and PDP learning of morphosyntax' *Language and Cognitive Processes* 13: 307–336

Ellis, R. (1994) *The Study of Second Language Acquisition.* Oxford: Oxford University Press

Ellis, R. (1997) *SLA Research and Language Teaching.* Oxford: Oxford University Press

Ellis, R. (1999) *Learning a Second Language through Interaction.* Amsterdam: John Benjamins

Ellis, R. (2002) 'The place of grammar instruction in the second/L2 curriculum' in Hinkel & Fotos (eds.): 17–34

Ellis, R. and Gaies, S. (1999) *Impact Grammar.* Hong Kong: Longman

Elman, J. (1996) *Rethinking Innateness.* Cambridge: MIT Press

Engwall, O. and Bälter, O. (2007) 'Pronunciation feedback from real and virtual language teachers' *Computer Assisted Language Learning* 20: 235–262

Ertmer, D. (2004) 'How well can children recognize speech features in spectrograms? Comparisons by age and hearing status' *Journal of Speech, Language, and Hearing Research* 47: 484–495

Ertmer, D. and Stark, R. (1995) 'Eliciting prespeech vocalizations in a young child with profound hearing loss: Usefulness of real time spectrographic speech displays' *American Journal of Speech Language Pathology* 4: 33–38

Ertmer, D., Stark, R. and Karlan, G. (1996) 'Real time spectrographic displays in vowel production training with children who have profound hearing loss' *American Journal of Speech Language Pathology* 5: 4–16

Eubank, L. (1994) 'Optionality and the initial state in L2 development' in Hoekstra & Schwartz (eds.): 369–388

Eubank, L. (ed.) (1991) *Point Counterpoint: Universal Grammar in the Second Language.* Amsterdam: John Benjamins

Eubank, L., Selinker, L. and Sharwood-Smith, M. (eds.) (1995) *The Current State of Interlanguage* Amsterdam: John Benjamins

Fabbro, F. (1999) *The Neurolinguistics of Bilingualism.* Hove: Psychology Press

Fabbro, F., Peru, A. and Skrap, M. (1997) 'Language disorders in bilingual patients after Thalamic Lesions' *Journal of Neurolinguistics* 10: 347–367

Fernandez, E. (1998). 'Processing strategies in second language acquisition: some preliminary results' in Klein & Martohardjono (eds.): 217–239

Fernando, C. (1996) *Idioms and Idiomaticity.* Oxford: Oxford University Press

Finnegan, R. (2002) *Communicating: The Multiple Modes of Human Interconnection.* London: Routledge

Flege, J. (1987) 'Effects of equivalence classification on the production of foreign language speech' in James & Leather (eds.): 9–39

Flege, J. (1995) 'Second language speech learning: theory, findings, and problems' in Strange (ed.): 233–277

Flege, J. (1997) 'English vowel productions by Dutch talkers: more evidence for the similar vs. new distinction' in James & Leather (eds.): 11–52

Flege, J. (1999) 'Age of learning and second language speech' in Birdsong (ed.): 101–131

Flege, J. and Hillenbrand, J. (1987) 'Limits on phonetic accuracy in foreign language speech production' in Ioup & Weinberger (eds.): 176–203

Flege, J., Takagi, N. and Mann, V. (1995) 'Japanese adults can learn to produce English /ɹ/ and /l/ accurately' *Language and Speech* 38:25–55

Flynn, S. (1984) 'A universal in L2 acquisition based on a PBD typology' in Eckman et al. (eds.): 75–87

Flynn, S. (1987) *A Parameter Setting Model of L2 Acquisition.* Dordrecht: D.Reidel

Flynn, S. (1989a) 'The role of the head-initial/head-final parameter in the acquisition of English relative clauses by adult Spanish and Japanese speakers' in Gass & Schachter (eds.):

89–108

Flynn, S. (1989b) 'Spanish, Japanese, and Chinese speakers' acquisition of English relative clauses: new evidence for the Head-direction parameter' in Hyltenstam & Obler (eds.): 116–131

Flynn, S., Martohardjono, G. and O'Neil, W. (eds.) (1998) *The Generative Study of Second Language Acquisition.* Mahwah: Lawrence Erlbaum

Flynn, S. and O'Neil, W. (eds.) (1988) *Linguistic Theory in Second Language Acquisition.* Dordrecht: Kluwer Academic Publishers

Fodor, J. A. (1975) *The Language of Thought.* New York: Crowell

Fodor, J. A. (1983) *Modularity of Mind.* Cambridge: MIT Press

Fodor, J. A., Bever, T. and Garrett, M. (1974) *The Psychology of Language.* New York: McCraw-Hill

Fodor, J. D. (1990) 'Thematic roles and modularity' in Altmann (ed.): 434–456

Fodor, J. D. (1998a) 'Learnability theory: triggers for parsing with' in Klein & Martohardjono (eds.): 363–406

Fodor, J. D. (1998b) 'Learning to parse' *Journal of Psycholinguistic Research* 27: 285–319

Fodor, J. D. (1998c) 'Parsing to learn' *Journal of Psycholinguistic Research* 27: 339–374

Frawley, W. (1992) *Linguistic Semantics.* Hillsdale: Lawrence Erlbaum

Frazier, L. (1990) 'Exploring the architecture of the language processing system' in Altmann (ed.): 409–433

Frazier, L. (1999) *On Sentence Interpretation.* Dordrecht: Kluwer Academic Publishers

Frazier, L. and de Villiers, J. (eds.) (1990) *Language Processing and Language Acquisition.* Dordrecht: Kluwer Academic Publishers

Freidin, R. (ed.) (1992) *Principles and Parameters in Comparative Grammar.* Cambridge: MIT Press

Frenk-Mestre, C. (2002) 'An on-line look at sentence processing in the second language' in Heredia & Altarriba (eds.): 217–236

Frey, L., Botan, C., Friedman, P. and Kreps, G. (1991) *Investigating Communication.* Englewood Cliffs: Prentice Hall

Fujisaki, H. (1997) 'Sentence production and information' in Kiritani, Hirose & Fujisaki (eds.): 278–296

Fukui, N. (1995) *Theory of Projection in Syntax.* Oxford: CSLI Publishers

Fulcher, G. (2003) *Testing Second Language Speaking.* London: Longman

Garfield, J. (1989) *Modularity in Knowledge Representation and Natural Language Understanding.* Cambridge: MIT Press

Garman, M. (1990) *Psycholinguistics.* Cambridge: Cambridge University Press

Garrod, S. and Pickering, M. (eds.) (1999) *Language Processing.* Hove: Psychology Press

Gaskell, G. (ed.) (2007) *The Oxford Handbook of Psycholinguistics.* Oxford: Oxford University Press

Gass, S. (1979) 'Language transfer and universal grammatical relations' *Language Learning* 29: 327–344

Gass, S. and Schachter, J. (eds.) (1989) *Linguistic Perspectives on Second Language Acquisition.* Cambridge: Cambridge University Press

Gelman, R. and Au, T. (eds.) (1996) *Perceptual and Cognitive Development.* San Diego: Academic Press

Gerken, L. (2001) 'Signal to syntax' in Weissenborn & Höhle: 147–165

Gernsbacher, M. (ed.) (1994) *Handbook of Psycholinguistics.* San Diego: Academic Press

Giacobbe, J. (1992) 'A cognitive view of the role of L1 in the L2 acquisition process' *Second Language Research* 8: 232–250

Giegerich, H. (1992) *English Phonology*. Cambridge: Cambridge University Press

Gierut, J. (1989) 'Maximal opposition approach to phonological treatment' *Journal of Speech and Hearing Disorders* 54: 9–19

Gierut, J. (1990) 'Differential learning of phonological oppositions' *Journal of Speech and Hearing Research* 33: 540–549

Gierut, J. (1993) 'Phonological aspects of emerging grammars' in Eckman (ed.): 213–233

Gleason, J. (ed.) (1997) *The Development of Language.* Boston: Allyn & Bacon

Gleason, J. and Ratner, N. (1998) *Psycholinguistics (2nd Edition)*. Belmont: Thomson Wadsworth

Gleitman, L. and Gillette, J. (1999) 'The role of syntax in verb learning' in Ritchie & Bhatia (eds.): 280–295

Gleitman, L. and Gleitman, H. (2001) 'Bootstrapping on first vocabulary' in Weissenborn & Höhle: 79–96

Gleitman, L. and Landau, B. (eds.) (1994) *The Acquisition of the Lexicon.* Cambridge: MIT Press

Goldberg, A. (1995) *Constructions: A Construction Grammar Approach to Argument Structure.* Chicago: University of Chicago Press

Goldberg, A. (1999) 'The emergence of the semantics of argument structure constructions' in MacWhinney (ed.): 197–212

Goldberg, A. (2006) *Constructions at Work: The Nature of Generalization in Language.* Oxford: Oxford University Press

Goldstein, L. and Fowler, C. (2003) 'Articulatory phonology' in Schiller & Meyer (eds.): 159–207

Golinkoff, R. et al. (ed.) (2000) *Becoming a Word Learner*. Oxford: Oxford University Press

Gomez-Tortosa, E. et al. (1995) 'Selective deficit of one language in a bilingual patient following surgery in the Left Perisylvian Area' *Brain and Language* 48: 320–325

Gonzalez, V. (1998) *Language and Cognitive Development in Second Language Learning.* Boston: Allyn and Bacon

Goodman, J. and Nusbaum, H. (eds.) (1994) *The Development of Speech Perception: The Transition from Speech Sounds to Spoken Words*. Cambridge: MIT Press

Gorrell, P. (1995) *Syntax and Parsing*. Cambridge: Cambridge University Press

Granger, C. (2004) *Silence in Second Language Learning: A Psychoanalytic Reading.* Clevedon: Multilingual Matters

Green, D. (1996) *Cognitive Science: An Introduction.* Oxford: Blackwell

Green, D. (2001) 'The Cognitive Neuroscience of Bilingualism' Special Issue: *Bilingualism: Language and Cognition Volume 4*

Greenberg, J. (1963) *Universals of Language.* Cambridge: MIT Press

Grodzinsky, Y. (1991) 'Neuropsychological reasons for a transformational analysis of verbal passive' *Natural Language and Linguistic Theory* 9: 431–453

Grodzinsky, Y. (2000a) 'The neurology of syntax' *Behavioural and Brain Sciences* 23

Grodzinsky, Y. (2000b) *Language and the Brain: Representation and Processing.* San Diego: Academic Press

Grosjean, F. (1989) 'Neurolinguists, be aware! The bilingual is not two monolinguals in one person' *Brain and Language* 36: 3–15

Grosjean, F. (1997) 'Processing mixed language: issues, findings, and models' in de Groot & Kroll (eds.): 225–254

Guillot, M. (1999) *Fluency and it's Teaching*. Clevedon: Multilingual Matters

Gullberg, M. and Indefrey, P. (eds.) (2006) *The Cognitive Neuroscience of Second Language Acquisition.* Malden: Blackwell

Haastrup, K. (1991) *Lexical Inferencing Procedures or Talking about Words.* Tubingen: Gunter Narr Verlag

Hagoort, P. and Brown, C. (1994) 'Brain responses to lexical ambiguity resolution and parsing' in Clifton, Frazier, & Rayner (eds.): 45–80

Hall, G. and Waxman, S. (eds.) (2004) *Weaving a Lexicon*. Cambridge: MIT Press

Halliday, M. (1994) *An Introduction to Functional Grammar.* London: Arnold

Hamilton, R. (1994) 'Is implicational generalisation unidirectional and maximal? Evidence from relativisation instruction in a second language' *Language Learning* 44: 123–157

Hammarberg, B. (1997) 'Conditions on transfer in phonology' in James & Leather (eds.): 161–180

Han, Z. (2004) *Fossilization in Adult Second Language Acquisition.* Clevedon: Multilingual Matters

Hannahs, S. and Young-Scholten, M. (eds.) (1997) *Focus on Phonological Acquisition* Amsterdam: John Benjamins

Hansen, T. (2006) 'Computer assisted pronunciation training: the four 'K's of feedback' *Current Developments in Technology-Assisted Education 2006*: 342–346

Haraguchi, S. (1996) 'Syllable, mora and accent' in Otake & Cutler (eds.): 45–75

Hardison, D. (1999) 'Bimodal speech perception by native and non-native speakers of English: factors influencing the McGurk Effect' *Language Leaning* Volume 49 Supplement 1 edited by Leather: 213–283

Hardison, D. (2004) 'Generalization of computer-assisted prosody training: quantitative and qualitative findings' *Language Learning and Technology* 8: 34–52

Hardy, J. (1993) 'Phonological learning and retention in second language acquisition' in Eckman (ed.): 235–248

Harley, B. (ed.) (1995) *Lexical Issues in Language Learning.* Amsterdam: John Benjamins

Harley, B., Allen, P., Cummins, J. and Swain, M. (1990) *The Development of Second Language Proficiency*. Cambridge: Cambridge University Press

Harley, T. (2008) *The Psychology of Language (3rd edition)*. Hove: Psychology Press

Harrington, M. (1987) 'Processing transfer: language-specific strategies as a source of interlanguage variation' *Applied Psycholinguistics* 8: 351–377

Harrington, M. (1992) 'Working memory capacity as a constraint on L2 development' in Harris (ed.): 123–135

Harrington, M. (2001) 'Sentence processing' in Robinson (ed.): 91–124

Harris, R. (ed.) (1992) *Cognitive Processing in Bilinguals*. Amsterdam: North Holland

Hatch, E. and Brown, C. (1995) *Vocabulary, Semantics, and Language Education*. Cambridge: Cambridge University Press

Hawkins, R. (1989) 'Do second language learners acquire restrictive relative clause on the basis of relational or configurational information?' *Second Language Research* 5: 156–188

Hawkins, R. (2001) *Second Language Syntax: A Generative Introduction*. Oxford: Blackwell

Hayashibe, H. et al. (1976) 'On the development of perceptual strategies in children: a case study on the Japanese child's comprehension of the relative clause constructions' *Annual Bulletin RILP* 10: 199–224

Hayashibe, H. et al. (1977) 'Comprehension of simple sentences and relative clause constructions in children with hearing disabilities' *Annual Bulletin RILP* 11: 113–130

Hayes, J. (ed.) (1970) *Cognition and the Development of Language*. New York: John Wiley

Healy, A. and Bourne, L. (eds.) (1998) *L2 Learning: Psycholinguistic Studies on Training and Retention*. Mahwah: Lawrence Erlbaum

Henderson, J. and Ferreira, F. (2004) *The Interface of Language, Vision, and Action*. Hove: Psychology Press

Heredia, R. and Altarriba, J. (eds.) (2002) *Bilingual Sentence Processing*. Amsterdam: Elsevier

Hernandez, A., Fernandez, E. and Aznar-Bese, N. (2007) 'Bilingual sentence processing' in Gaskell (ed.): 381–384

Herschensohn, J. (2007) *Language Development and Age*. Cambridge: Cambridge University Press

Hillert, D. (ed.) (1998) *Syntax and Semantics Volume 31: Sentence Processing: A Cross-Linguistic Perspective*. San Diego: Academic Press

Hincks, R. (2005) 'Measures and perceptions of liveliness in student oral presentation speech: a proposal for an automatic feedback mechanism' *System* 33: 575–591

Hinkel, E. (2002) 'Teaching grammar in writing classes: tenses and cohesion' in Hinkel & Fotos (eds.): 181–198

Hinkel, E. and Fotos, S. (eds.) (2002) *New Perspectives on Grammar Teaching in Second Language Classrooms*. Mahwah: Lawrence Erlbaum

Hirata, Y. (2004) 'Computer assisted pronunciation training for native English speakers learning Japanese pitch and durational contrasts' *Computer Assisted Language Learning* 17: 357–376

Hirose, Y. (2002) 'Resolution of reanalysis ambiguity in Japanese relative clauses: early use of thematic compatibility information and incremental processing' in Nakayama (ed.): 31–52

Hirose, Y. (2006) 'Processing relative clauses in Japanese: coping with multiple ambiguities' in Nakayama et al. (eds.): 262–269

Hirose, Y. and Inoue, A. (1998) 'Ambiguity of reanalysis in parsing complex sentences in Japanese' in Hillert (ed.): 71–93

Hirschfeld, L. and Gelman, S. (1994) *Mapping the Mind: Domain Specificity in Cognition and Culture*. Cambridge: Cambridge University Press

Hirsh-Pasek, K. and Golinkoff, R. (1996) *The Origins of Grammar*. Cambridge: MIT Press

Hirsh-Pasek, K. and Golinkoff, R. (eds.) (2006) *Action Meets Word: How Children Learn Verbs*. Oxford: Oxford University Press

Hoekstra, T. and Schwartz, B. (eds.) (1994) *Language Acquisition Studies in Generative Grammar.* Amsterdam: John Benjamins

Hoel, P. (1981) *Elementary Statistics.* New York: John Wiley & Sons

Holzman, M. (1997) *The Language of Children.* London: Blackwell

Hopper, P. and Traugott, E. (1993) *Grammaticalisation.* Cambridge: Cambridge University Press

Hornstein, N. (1990) *As Time Goes By: Tense and Universal Grammar.* Cambridge: MIT Press

Howe, M. (1999) *A Teacher's Guide to the Psychology of Learning.* Oxford: Blackwell

Huebner, T. and Ferguson, C. (eds.) (1991) *Crosscurrents in Second Language Acquisition and Linguistic Theories.* Amsterdam: John Benjamins

Hughes, R. (2002) *Teaching and Researching Speaking.* London: Longman

Hulit, L. and Howard, M. (1997) *Born to Talk.* Boston: Allyn and Bacon

Hulstijn, J. (1990) 'A comparison between the information processing and the analysis/control approaches to language learning' *Applied Linguistics* 11: 30–45

Hulstijn, J. and Hulstijn, W. (1984) 'Grammatical errors as processing constraints and explicit knowledge' *Language Learning* 34: 23–43

Hulstijn, J. and Schmidt, R. (eds.) (1994) *Consciousness in Second Language Learning. AILA Review* 11

Hyltenstam, K. and Obler, L. (eds.) (1989) *Bilingualism across the Lifespan.* Cambridge: Cambridge University Press

Ikegami, Y. (1991) *eibunpou-o kangaeru.* Tokyo: Chikuma

Ikegami, Y. (2000) 'The schemata for motion and action' in Lockwood et al. (eds.) (2000): 185–198

Inagaki, S. (2001) 'Motion verbs with goal PPs in the L2 acquisition of English and Japanese' *Studies in Second Language Acquisition* 23: 153–170

Inoue, A. and Fodor, J. D. (1995) 'Information-paced parsing of Japanese' in Mazuka & Nagai (eds.): 9–63

Ioup, G.. and Weinberger, S. (eds.) (1987) *Interlangauge Phonology: The Acquisition of a Second Language Sound System.* Cambridge: Newbury House

Iwanska, L. and Shapiro, S. (2000) *Natural Language Processing and Knowledge Representation: Language for Knowledge and Knowledge for Language.* Cambridge: MIT Press

Jackendoff, R. (1983) *Semantics and Cognition.* Cambridge: MIT Press

Jackendoff, R. (1990) *Semantic Structures.* Cambridge: MIT Press

Jackendoff, R. (1997) *The Architecture of the Language Faculty.* Cambridge: MIT Press

Jackendoff, R. (2002) *Foundations of Language.* Oxford: Oxford University Press

Jackson, P. and Moulinier, I. (2002) *Natural Language Processing for Online Applications: Text Retrieval, Extraction and Categorization.* Amsterdam: John Benjamins

Jacobs, B. and Schumann, J. (1992) 'Language acquisition and the neurosciences: towards a more integrative perspective' *Applied Linguistics* 13: 282–301

Jaeggli, O. (1986) 'Passive' *Linguistic Inquiry* 17: 587–622

James, A. (1988) *The Acquisition of a Second Language Phonology: A Linguistic Theory of Developing Sound Structures.* Tübingen: Gunter Narr Verlag

James, A. and Leather, J. (eds.) (1987) *Sound Patterns in Second Language Acquisition*. Dordrecht: Foris Publications

James, A. and Leather, J. (eds.) (1997) *Second-Language Speech: Structure and Process*. Berlin: Mouton de Gruyter

Jespersen, O. (1922) *Language: Its Nature, Development, and Origin*. New York: Norton Library

Jiang, N. (2000) 'Lexical representation and development in a second language' *Applied Linguistics* 21: 47–77

Johnson, J. (1992) 'Critical period effects in second language acquisition: the effect of written versus auditory materials on the assessment of grammatical competence' *Language Learning* 42: 217–248

Johnson, J. and Newport, E. (1989) 'Critical period effects in second language learning: the influence of maturational state on the acquisition of English as a second language' *Cognitive Psychology* 21: 60–99

Johnson, J. and Newport, E. (1991) 'Critical period effects on universal properties of language: the status of Subjacency in the acquisition of a second language' *Cognition* 39: 215–258

Johnson, K. (1997) *Acoustic and Auditory Phonetics*. Oxford: Blackwell

Johnson-Laird, P. (1983) *Mental Models*. Cambridge: Cambridge University Press

Jordens, P. and Lallman, J. (eds.) (1996) *Investigating Second Language Acquisition*. Berlin: Mouton de Gruyter

Juffs, A. (1996a) *Learnability and the Lexicon*. Amsterdam: John Benjamins

Juffs, A. (1996b) 'Semantics-syntax correspondences in second language acquisition' *Second Language Research* 12: 177–221

Juffs, A. (1998) 'Some effects of first language argument structure and morphosyntax on second language sentence processing' *Second Language Research* 14: 406–424

Juffs, A. (2000) 'An overview of the second language acquisition of links between verb semantics and morpho-syntax' in Archibald (ed.): 187–227

Juffs, A. (2001) 'Verb classes, event structure, and second language learner's knowledge of semantics-syntax correspondences' *Studies in Second Language Acquisition* 23: 305–313

Juffs, A. and Harrington, M. (1995) 'Parsing effects in second language sentence processing' *Studies in Second Language Acquisition* 17: 483–516

Juffs, A. and Harrington, M. (1996) 'Garden path sentences and error data in second language sentence processing' *Language Learning* 46: 283–326

Kager, R., Pater, J. and Zonneveld, W. (eds.) (2004) *Constraints in Phonological Acquisition*. Cambridge: Cambridge University Press

Kail, M. (1987) 'The development of sentence interpretation strategies from a cross-linguistic perspective' in Pfaff (ed.): 28–54

Kamide, Y. (2006) 'Incrementality in Japanese sentence processing' in Nakayama et al. (eds.): 249–256

Kamide, Y., Altmann, G. and Haywood, S. (2003) 'The time-course of prediction in incremental sentence processing: evidence from anticipatory eye movements' *Journal of Memory and Language* 49: 133–156

Kaplan, M. (1987) 'Developmental patterns of past tense acquisition among L2 learners of

French' in VanPatten (ed.): 52–60

Kaplan, R. (ed.) (2002) *The Oxford Handbook of Applied Linguistics*. Oxford: Oxford University Press

Karmiloff-Smith, A. (1992) *Beyond Modularity: A Developmental Perspective on Cognitive Science*. Cambridge: MIT Press

Kasper, G. and Kellerman, E. (1997) *Communication Strategies: Psycholinguistic and Sociolinguistic Perspectives*. London: Longman

Kasper, G. and Rose, K. (2002) *Pragmatic Development in a Second Language*. Oxford: Blackwell

Kecskes, I. and Papp, T. (2000) *L2 and Mother Tongue*. Mahwah: Lawrence Erlbaum

Keenan, E. (1976) 'The universality of conversational postulates' *Language in Society* 5: 67–79

Keenan, E. and Comrie, B. (1977) 'Noun Phrase Accessibility and Universal Grammar' *Linguistic Inquiry* 8: 63–99

Kempson, R., Meyer-Viol, W. and Gabbay, D. (2001) *Dynamic Syntax: The Flow of Language Understanding*. Oxford: Blackwell

Kennedy, G. (1998) *An Introduction to Corpus Linguistics*. New York: Longman

Kent, R. and Read, C. (1992) *The Acoustic Analysis of Speech*. San Diego: Singular Publishing

Kess, J. (1992) *Psycholinguistics*. Amsterdam: John Benjamins

Kilborn, K. and Ito, T. (1989) 'Sentence processing strategies in adult bilinguals' in MacWhinney & Bates (eds.): 257–291

Kim, K. et al. (1997) 'Distinct cortical areas associated with native and second languages' *Nature* 388: 171–174

Kintsch, W. (1998) *Comprehension: A Paradigm for Cognition*. Cambridge: Cambridge University Press

Kirby, S. (1999) *Function, Selection, and Innateness*. Oxford: Oxford University Press

Kiritani, S., Hirose, H. and Fujisaki, H. (eds.) (1997) *Speech Production and Language*. Berlin: Mouton de Gruyter

Klein, D. et al. (1994) 'Left putaminal activation when speaking a second language: evidence from PET' *NeuroReport* 5: 2295–2297

Klein, E. (1998) 'Just parsing through: notes on the state of L2 processing research today' in Klein & Martohardjono (eds.): 197–216

Klein, E. (2004) 'Beyond syntax: performance factors in L2 behavior' in VanPatten et al. (eds.): 155–177

Klein, E. and Martohardjono, G. (eds.) (1998) *The Development of Second Language Grammars: A Generative Approach*. Amsterdam: John Benjamins

Klein, W. (1987) 'A concept-oriented approach to second language studies' in Pfaff (ed.): 191–205

Kormos, J. (1999) 'Monitoring and self-repair in L2' *Language Learning* 49: 303–342

Kormos, J. (2006) *Speech Production and Second Language Acquisition*. Mahwah: Lawrence Erlbaum

Krashen, S. and Terrell, T. (1988) *The Natural Approach: Language Acquisition in the Classroom*. New York: Prentice Hall

Kroll, J. (1993) 'Accessing conceptual representations for words in a second language' in Schreuder & Weltens (eds.): 53–81

Kroll, J. and de Groot, A. (1997) 'Lexical and conceptual memory in the bilingual: mapping form to meaning in two languages' in de Groot & Kroll (eds.): 169–199

Kroll, J. and de Groot, A. (eds.) (2005) *Handbook of Bilingualism: Psycholinguistic Approaches.* New York: Oxford University Press

Kroll, J. and Tokowicz, N. (2001) 'The development of conceptual representation for words in a second language' in Nicol (ed.): 49–71

Kubozono, H. (1996) 'Speech segmentation and phonological structure' in Otake & Cutler (eds.): 77–94

Kuhl, P. and Iverson, P. (1995) 'Linguistic experience and the perceptual magnet effect' in Strange (ed.): 121–154

Kuno, S. (1974) 'The position of relative clauses and conjunctions' *Linguistic Inquiry* 5: 117–136

Kuno, Y. (1999) *English for Children: A Key to the World.* Tokyo: Sanseido

Kuno, Y. (2000) *Word Book 1 & 2.* Tokyo: Sanseido

Kutas, M. and VanPetten, C. (1994) 'Psycholinguistics electrified: event-related brain potential investigations' in Gernsbacher (ed.): 83–143

Lambacher, S. (1996) 'Using electric visual feedback to teach English segmentals' The *Language Teacher* 20: 22–27

Lambacher, S. (1999) 'A CALL tool for improving second language acquisition of English consonants by Japanese learners' *Computer Assisted Language Learning* 12: 137–156

Landau, B. (ed.) (2000) *Perception, Cognition, and Language.* Cambridge: MIT Press

Leather, J. (1997) 'Interrelation of perceptual and productive learning in the initial acquisition of second language tone' in James & Leather (eds.): 75–101

Leather, J. (ed.) (1999) *Phonological Issues in Language Learning.* London: Blackwell

Lecumberri, G. and Maidment, J. (2000) *English Transcription Course.* London: Arnold

Lehiste, I. (1997) 'The phonetic realization of the Haiku form in Estonian poetry compared to Japanese' in Kiritani, Hirose & Fujisaki (eds.): 241–249

Lengyel, Z. (1995) 'Some critical remarks on the phonological component' in Singleton & Lengyel (eds.): 124–134

Lenneberg, E. (1967) *Biological Foundations of Language.* New York: Wiley

Lesh, R. (1999) 'The development of representational abilities in middle school mathematics' in Sigel (ed.): 323–349

Levelt, W. (1989) *Speaking: From Intention to Articulation.* Cambridge: Cambridge University Press

Levelt, W. (1999) 'A theory of lexical access in speech production' *Behavioural and Brain Sciences* 22: 1–75

Levin, B. (1993) *English Verb Classes and Alternations.* Chicago: University of Chicago Press

Levis, J. and Pickering, L. (2004) 'Teaching intonation in discourse using speech visualisation technology' *System* 32: 505–524

Lewis, M. (1986) *The English Verb.* Hove: Language Teaching Publications

Lewis, M. (1993) *The Lexical Approach.* Hove: Language Teaching Publications

Lewis, M. (1996) 'Implications of a lexical view of language' in Willis & Willis (eds.): 10–16

Lewis, M. (1997a) *Implementing the Lexical Approach.* Hove: Language Teaching Publications

Lewis, M. (1997b) 'Pedagogical implications of the lexical approach' in Coady & Huckin (eds.): 255–270

Lewis, M. (ed.) (2000) *Teaching Collocation: Further Developments in the Lexical Approach.* Hove: Language Teaching Publications

Li, P. and Shirai, Y. (2000) *The Acquisition of Lexical and Grammatical Aspect.* Berlin: Mouton de Gruyter

Libben, G. (2000) 'Representation and processing in the second language lexicon: the Homogeneity Hypothesis' in Archibald (ed.): 228–247

Liceras, J., Zobl, H. and Goodluck, H. (eds.) (2008) *The Role of Formal Features in Second Language Acquisition.* New York: Lawrence Erlbaum

Little, D. (1994) 'Words and their properties: arguments for a lexical approach to pedagogical grammar' in Odlin (ed.): 99–122

Lively, S., Pisoni, D. and Logan, J. (1992) 'Some effects of training Japanese listeners to identify English /r/ and /l/' in Tohkura et al. (eds.): 175–196

Lockwood, D., Fries, P. and Copeland, J. (eds.) (2000) *Functional Approaches to Language Culture, and Cognition.* Amsterdam: John Benjamins

Logan, J. and Pruitt, J. (1995) 'Methodological issues in training listeners to perceive non-native phonemes' in Strange (ed.): 351–377

Long, M. (1988) 'Instructed Interlanguage development' in Beebe (ed.): 115–141

Long, M. (1990) 'Maturational constraints on language development' *Studies in Second Language Acquisition* 12: 251–285

Luoma, S. (2004) *Assessing Speaking.* Cambridge: Cambridge University Press

MacWhinney, B. (ed.) (1987) *Mechanisms of Language Acquisition.* Hillsdale: Lawrence Erlbaum

MacWhinney, B. (ed.) (1999) *The Emergence of Language.* Mahwah: Lawrence Erlbaum

MacWhinney, B. and Bates, E. (eds.) (1989) *The Cross-linguistic Study of Sentence Processing.* Cambridge: Cambridge University Press

Major, R. (1987) 'A model for interlanguage phonology' in Ioup & Weinberger (eds.): 101–124

Major, R. (2001) *Foreign Accent: The Ontogeny and Phylogeny of Second Language Phonology.* Mahwah: Lawrence Erlbaum

Major, R. and Kim, E. (1996) 'The similarity differential rate hypothesis' *Language Learning* 46: 465–496

Maratsos, M. (1999) 'Some aspects of innateness and complexity in grammatical acquisition' in Barrett (ed.): 191–228

Matsumura, S. (2003) 'Modelling the relationships among interlanguage pragmatic development, L2 proficiency, and exposure to L2' *Applied Linguistics* 24: 465–491

Mayo, M. and Lecumberri, M. (eds.) (2003) *Age and the Acquisition of English as a Foreign Language.* Clevedon: Multilingual Matters

Mazuka, R. (1998) *The Development of Language Processing Strategies: A Cross-Linguistic Study between Japanese and English.* Mahwah: Lawrence Erlbaum

Mazuka, R. and Itoh, K. (1995) 'Can Japanese speakers be led down the garden-path?' in Mazuka & Nagai (eds.): 295–329

Mazuka, R. and Nagai, N. (1995) 'Japanese sentence processing: an interdisciplinary approach' in Mazuka & Nagai (eds.): 1–8

Mazuka, R. and Nagai, N. (eds.) (1995) *Japanese Sentence Processing*. Hillsdale: Lawrence Erbaum

McDonald, J. and Heileman, K. (1992) 'Changes in sentence processing as second language proficiency increases' in Harris (ed.): 325–336

McLaughlin, B. (1987) *Theories of Second-Language Learning*. London: Arnold

McLaughlin, B. (1996) 'Information-processing approaches to research on second language acquisition and use' in Ritchie & Bhatia (eds.): 213–228

McQueen, J. and Cutler, A. (2001) *Spoken Word Access Processes*. Hove: Psychology Press

Meadows, B. (2007) 'Implications of ultrasound technology in the L2 classroom' *Arizona Working Papers in SLA* 14: 15–41

Medgyes, P. (1994) *The Non-native Teacher*. London: MacMillan Publishers

Meier, R., Cormier, K. and Quinto-Pozos, D. (eds.) (2002) *Modality and Structure in Signed and Spoken Languages*. Cambridge: Cambridge University Press

Meisel. J. (1987) 'Reference to past events and actions in the development of natural second language acquisition' in Pfaff (ed.): 206–224

Menyuk, P. and Brisk, M. (2005) *Language Development and Education: Children with Varying Language Experiences*. New York: Palgrave MacMillan

Mercer, N. (2000) *Words and Minds: How We Use Language to Think Together*. London: Routledge

Merleau-Ponty, M. (1962) *Phenomenology of Perception*. London: Routledge

Merlo, P. and Stevenson, S. (2000) 'Lexical syntax and parsing architecture' in Crocker, Pickering & Clifton (eds.): 161–188

Miller, G. (1956) 'The magical number seven, plus or minus two: some limits on our capacity for processing information' *Psychological Review* 63: 81–97

Miller, J. and Eimas, P. (eds.) (1995) *Speech, Language, and Communication*. San Diego: Academic Press

Mitchell, D. (1994) 'Sentence parsing' in Gernsbacher (ed.): 375–410

Mitchell, D. (2004) 'On-line methods in language processing: introduction and historical review' in Carreiras & Clifton (eds.): 15–32

Mitchell, D. and Johnson-Laird, P. (1976) *Language and Perception*. Cambridge: Harvard University Press

Mitchell, R. (1994) 'Foreign language teachers and the teaching of grammar' in Bygate et al. (eds.): 215–223

Mitchell, R. and Myles, F. (1998) *Second Language Learning Theories*. London: Arnold

Mitkov, R. and Nicolov, N. (eds.) (1997) *Recent Advances in Natural Language Processing*. Amsterdam: John Benjamins

Miyamoto, E. (2002) 'Case markers as clause boundary inducers in Japanese' *Journal of Psycholinguistic Research* 31: 307–347

Miyamoto, E. (2006) 'Processing alternative word orders' in Nakayama et al. (eds.): 257–263

Molholt, G. (1988) 'Computer assisted instruction for Chinese speakers' *TESOL Quarterly* 22: 91–111

Montrul, S. (2001) 'Agentive verbs of manner of motion in Spanish and English as second languages' *Studies in Second Language Acquisition* 23: 171–206

Moyer, A. (1999) 'Ultimate attainment in L2 phonology' *Studies in Second Language Acquisition* 21: 81–108

Moyer, A. (2004) *Age, Accent and Experience in Second Language Acquisition: An Integrated Approach to Critical Period Inquiry*. Clevedon: Multilingual Matters

Mueller, J. (2006) 'L2 in a nutshell: the investigation of second language processing in the miniature language model' in Gullberg & Indefrey (eds.): 235–270

Myles, F., Hooper, J. and Mitchell, R. (1998) 'Tote or rule? Exploring the role of formulaic language in classroom foreign language learning' *Language Learning* 48: 323–363

Naigles, L. (2000) 'Manipulating the input: studies in mental verb acquisition' in Landau (ed.): 245–274

Nakano, Y., Felser, C. and Clahsen, H. (2002) 'Antecedent priming at trace positions in Japanese long-distance scrambling' *Journal of Psycholinguistic Research* 31: 531–571

Nakayama, M. (ed.) (2002) *Sentence Processing in East Asian Languages*. Stanford: CSLI Publishers

Nakayama, M., Mazuka, R. and Shirai, Y. (eds.) (2006) *The Handbook of East Asian Psycholinguistics: Volume 2 Japanese*. Cambridge: Cambridge University Press

Nathan, G., Anderson, W. and Budsayamongkon, B. (1987) 'On the acquisition of aspiration' in Ioup & Weinberger (eds.): 204–212

Nattinger, J. and DeCarrico, J. (1992) *Lexical Phrases in Language Teaching*. Oxford: Oxford University Press

Nelson, K. (1996) *Language in Cognitive Development*. Cambridge: Cambridge University Press

Neri, A., Cucchiarini, C., Strik, H. and Boves, L. (2002) 'The pedagogy-technology interface in computer assisted pronunciation training' *Computer Assisted Language Learning* 15: 441–467

Newmeyer, F. (1998) *Language Form and Language Function*. Cambridge: MIT Press

Nicol, J. (ed.) (2001) *One Mind, Two Languages: Bilingual Language Processing*. Oxford: Blackwell

Ninio, A. and Snow, C. (1999) 'The development of pragmatics' in Ritchie & Bhatia (eds.): 347–384

Nunan, D. (1989) *Designing Tasks for the Communicative Classroom*. Cambridge: Cambridge University Press

Nyyssonen, H. (1995) 'Grammar and lexis in communicative competence' in Cook & Seidlhofer (eds.): 159–170

Odlin, T. (1989) *Language Transfer: Cross-Linguistic Influence in Language Learning*. Cambridge: Cambridge University Press

Odlin, T. (ed.) (1994) *Perspectives on Pedagogical Grammar*. Cambridge: Cambridge University Press

Ogden, C. (1968) *Basic English; International Second Language*. New York: Harcourt

Ogden, C. and Richards, A. (1923) *The Meaning of Meaning*. London: Routledge

O'Grady, W. (1997) *Syntactic Development*. Chicago: The University of Chicago Press

O'Grady, W. (2005) *How Children Learn Language.* Cambridge: Cambridge University Press

Ojemann, G. (1978) 'The bilingual brain' *Archives of Neurology* 35: 409–412

Osherson, D. and Lasnik, H. (eds.) (1990) *Language: An Invitation to Cognitive Science, Volume 1.* Cambridge: MIT Press

Oshita, H. (2000) 'What is happened may not be what appears to be happening: a corpus study of passive unaccusatives in L2 English' *Second Language Research* 16: 293–324

Osterhout, L. (1994) 'Event-related brain potentials as tools for comprehending language comprehension' in Clifton, Frazier, & Rayner (eds.): 15–44

Osterhout, L., McLaughlin, J., Kim, A. and Inoue, K. (2004) 'Sentences in the brain: event-related potentials as real-time reflections of sentence comprehension and language learning' in Carreiras & Clifton (eds.): 271–308

Osterhout, L., McLaughlin, J., Pitkanen, I, Frenck-Mestre, C. and Molinaro, N. (2006) 'Novice learners, longitudinal designs, and event-related potentials: a means for exploring the neurocognition of second language processing' in Gullberg & Indefrey (eds.): 199–230

Ota, M. (2003) *The Development of Prosodic Structure in Early Words.* Amsterdam: John Benjamins

Otake, T. and Cutler, A. (eds.) (1996) *Phonological Structure and Language Processing: Cross-Linguistic Studies.* Berlin: Mouton de Gruyter

Ouhalla, J. (1991) *Functional Categories and Parametric Variation.* London: Routledge

Owens, R. (1996) *Language Development.* Boston: Allyn and Bacon

Palmer, H. (1924) *Memorandum of Problems of English Teaching in the Light of a New Theory.* Tokyo: Institute for Research in English Teaching

Pan, B. and Snow, C. (1999) 'The development of conversational and discourse skills' in Barrett (ed.): 229–250

Paradis, M. (1997) 'The cognitive neuropsychology of bilingualism' in de Groot & Kroll (eds.): 331–354

Paradis, M. (2004) *A Neurolinguistic Theory of Bilingualism.* Amsterdam: John Benjamins

Pater, J. (2004) 'Bridging the gap between receptive and productive development with minimally violable constraints' in Kager, Pater & Zonneveld (eds.): 219–244

Pavesi, M. (1986) 'Markedness, discoursal modes, and relative clause formation in a formal and an informal context' *Studies in Second Language Acquisition* 8: 38–55

Pawley, A. and Syder, F. (1983) 'Two puzzles for linguistic theory: nativelike selection and nativelike fluency' in Richards & Schmidt (eds.): 191–226

Pechmann, T. and Habel, C. (eds.) (2004) *Multidisciplinary Approaches to Language Production.* Berlin: Mouton de Gruyter

Pennington, M. (1996) *Phonology in English Language Teaching.* London: Longman

Pennington, M. (1998) 'The teachability of phonology in adulthood: a re-examination' *International Review of Applied Linguistics* 36: 323–341

Pennington, M. (1999) 'Computer-aided pronunciation pedagogy: promise, limitations, directions' *Computer Assisted Language Learning* 12: 427–440

Perani, D. et al. (1996) 'Brain processing of native and foreign languages' *NeuroReport* 7: 2439–2444

Perdue, C. (1991) 'Cross-linguistic comparisons: organizational principles in learner languages' in Huebner & Ferguson (eds.): 405–422

Perdue, C. (ed.) (1993) *Adult Language Acquisition: Cross-linguistic Perspectives*. Cambridge: Cambridge University Press

Perdue, C. and Klein, W. (1992) 'Why does the production of some learners not grammaticalise?' *Studies in Second Language Acquisition* 14: 259–272

Pfaff, C. (ed.) (1987) *First and Second Language Acquisition Processes*. Boston: Heinle & Heinle

Pfaff, C. (1992) 'The issue of grammaticalisation in early German second language' *Studies in Second Language Acquisition* 14: 273–296

Pickering, M. (1999) 'Sentence comprehension' in Garrod & Pickering (eds.): 123–153

Pickering, M., Barton, S. and Shillcock, R. (1994) 'Unbounded dependencies, island constraints, and processing complexity' in Clifton, Frazier, & Rayner (eds.): 199–224

Pickering, M., Clifton, C. and Crocker, M. (2000) 'Architectures and mechanisms in sentence comprehension' in Crocker, Pickering & Clifton (eds.): 1–28

Pienemann, M. (1984) 'Psychological constraints on the teachability of languages' *Studies in Second Language Acquisition* 6: 186–214

Pienemann, M. (1989) 'Is language teachable? Psycholinguistic experiments and hypotheses' *Applied Linguistics* 10: 52–79

Pienemann, M. (1998a) *Language Processing and Second Language Development: Processability Theory*. Amsterdam: John Benjamins

Pienemann, M. (1998b) 'Developmental dynamics in L1 and L2 acquisition: Processability Theory and generative entrenchment' *Bilingualism: Language and Cognition* 1 (Special issue)

Pienemann, M. (2002) 'Issues in SLA and language processing' *Second Language Research Volume 18 Special Issue*

Pienemann, M. (2005) *Cross-Linguistic Aspects of Processability Theory*. Amsterdam: John Benjamins

Pinker, S. (1984) *Language Learnability and Language Development*. Cambridge: Harvard University Press

Pinker, S. (1987) 'The bootstrapping problem in language acquisition' in MacWhinney (ed.): 399–441

Pinker, S. (1989) *Learnability and Cognition*. Cambridge: MIT Press

Pinker, S. (1994) *The Language Instinct*. New York: William Morrow & Company

Pisoni, D. and Lively, S. (1995) 'Variability and invariance in speech perception: a new look at some old problems in perceptual learning' in Strange (ed.): 433–459

Pisoni, D., Lively, S. and Logan, J. (1994) 'Perceptual learning of nonnative speech contrasts: Implications for theories of speech perception' in Goodman & Nusbaum (eds.): 121–166

Poidevin, R. and MacBeath, M. (1993) *The Philosophy of Time*. New York: Oxford University Press

Pritchett, B. (1992) *Grammatical Competence and Parsing Performance*. Chicago: University of Chicago Press

Radford, A. (1990) *Syntactic Theory and the Acquisition of English Syntax*. Oxford: Blackwell

Radford, A. (1996) 'Towards a structure-building model of acquisition' in Clahsen (ed.): 43–

89
Ramat, A. (1992) 'Grammaticalisation processes in the area of temporal and modal relations' *Studies in Second Language Acquisition* 14: 297–322

Randall, M. (2007) *Memory, Psychology and Second Language Learning*. Amsterdam: John Benjamins

Rayner, K. and Sereno, S. (1994) 'Eye movements in reading psycholinguistic studies' in Gernsbacher (ed.): 57–81

Read, J. (2000) *Assessing Vocabulary*. Cambridge: Cambridge University Press

Register, N. (1990) 'Influences of typological parameters on L2 learners' judgments of null pronouns in English' *Language Learning* 40: 369–395

Reichenbach, H. (1958) *The Philosophy of Space and Time*. New York: Dover Publications

Richards, J. and Rodgers, T. (1986) *Approaches and Methods in Language Teaching*. Cambridge: Cambridge University Press

Richards, J. and Schmidt, R. (eds.) (1983) *Language and Communication*. London: Longman

Riney, T. and Flege, J. (1998) 'Changes over time in global foreign accent and liquid identifiability and accuracy' *Studies in Second Language Acquisition* 20: 213–243

Rispoli, M. (1995) 'Missing arguments and the acquisition of predicate meanings' in Tomasello (ed.): 331–352

Ritchie, W. and Bhatia, T. (eds.) (1996) *Handbook of Second Language Acquisition*. San Diego: Academic Press

Ritchie, W. and Bhatia, T. (eds.) (1999) *Handbook of Child Language Acquisition*. San Diego: Academic Press

Roach, P. (2001) *English Phonetics and Phonology*. Cambridge: Cambridge University Press

Roberts, P. (1971) *The Robert's English Series*. Harcourt Brace Jovanovich

Robinson, P. (1995) 'Attention, memory, and the 'Noticing' hypothesis' *Language Learning* 45: 283–331

Robinson, P. (1996) 'Learning simple and complex second language rules under implicit, incidental, rule-search, and instructed conditions' *Studies in Second Language Acquisition* 18: 27–67

Robinson, P. (1997) 'Generalizability and automaticity of second language learning under implicit, incidental, enhanced, and instructed conditions' *Studies in Second Language Acquisition* 19: 223–247

Robinson, P. (ed.) (2001) *Cognition and Second Language Instruction*. Cambridge: Cambridge University Press

Rochet, B. (1995) 'Perception and production of second language speech sounds by adults' in Strange (ed.): 379–410

Roeper, T. and Williams, E. (eds.) (1987) *Parameter Setting*. Dordrecht: Reidel

Rose, K. and Kasper, G. (eds.) (2001) *Pragmatics in Language Teaching*. Cambridge: Cambridge University Press

Rosser, R. (1994) *Cognitive Development*. Boston: Allyn & Bacon

Rost, M. (1990) *Listening in Language Learning*. London: Longman

Rost, M. (2002) *Teaching and Researching Listening*. London: Longman

Rutherford, W. (1987) *Second Language Grammar: Learning and Teaching*. London: Longman

Rutherford, W. (1988) *Grammar and Second Language Teaching*. New York: Newbery House

Rutherford, W. (1989) 'Interlanguage and pragmatic word order' in Gass & Schachter (eds.): 163–181

Rutherford, W. (1994) 'SLA: Universal Grammar and language learnability' in Ellis (ed.): 503–522

Rvachew, S. and Jamieson, D. (1995) 'New speech contrasts: evidence from adults learning a second language and children with speech disorders' in Strange (ed.): 411–432

Ryle, G. (1949) *The Concept of Mind.* London: Hutchinson

Salaberry, R. (2000) *The Development of Past Tense Morphology in L2 Spanish.* Amsterdam: John Benjamins

Sanz, M. and Bever, T. (2001) 'A theory of syntactic interface in the bilingual' in Nicol (ed.) 134–158

Sasaki, Y. (1991) 'English and Japanese comprehension strategies: an analysis based on the competition model' *Applied Psycholinguistics* 12: 47–73

Sasaki, Y. (1994) 'Paths of processing strategy transfers in learning Japanese and English as foreign languages: a competition model approach' *Studies in Second Language Acquisition* 16: 43–72

Sato, C. (1987) 'Phonological processes in second language acquisition' in Ioup & Weinberger (eds.): 248–260

Schachter, J. (1974) 'An error in error analysis' *Language Learning* 24: 205–214

Schachter, J. (1989a) 'A new look at an old classic' *Second Language Research* 5: 30–42

Schachter, J. (1989b) 'Testing a proposed universal' in Gass & Schachter (eds.): 73–88

Schachter, J. (1996a) 'Learning and triggering in adult L2 acquisition' in Brown, Malmkjaer & Williams (eds.): 70–88

Schachter, J. (1996b) 'Maturation and the issue of Universal Grammar in second language acquisition' in Ritchie & Bhatia (eds.): 159–193

Schachter, J. and Gass, S. (eds.) (1996) *Second Language Classroom Research.* Mahwah: Lawrence Erlbaum

Schiller, N. & Meyer, A. (eds.) (2003) *Phonetics and Phonology in Language Comprehension and Production.* Berlin: Mouton de Gruyter

Schmidt, R. (1990) 'The role of consciousness in second language learning' *Applied Linguistics* 11: 129–158

Schmidt, R. (2001) 'Attention' in Robinson (ed.): 3–32

Schmitt, N. (ed.) (2002) *An Introduction to Applied Linguistics.* London: Arnold

Schmitt, N. (ed.) (2004) *Formulaic Sequences: Acquisition, Processing and Use.* Amsterdam: John Benjamins

Schmitt, N. and McCarthy, M. (eds.) (1997) *Vocabulary: Description, Acquisition, and Pedagogy.* Cambridge: Cambridge University Press

Schreuder, R. and Weltens, B. (eds.) (1993) *The Bilingual Lexicon.* Amsterdam: John Benjamins

Scovel, T. (1988) *A Time to Speak.* Boston: Newbury House

Sedlmeier, P. and Betsch, T. (2002) *ETC: Frequency Processing and Cognition.* Oxford: Oxford University Press

Sekerina, I., Fernandez, E. and Clahsen, H. (2008) *Developmental Psycholinguistics: On-line*

Methods in Children's Language Processing. Amsterdam: John Benjamins

Selinker, L. (1992) *Rediscovering Interlanguage.* London: Longman

Sharwood-Smith, M. (1994) *Second Language Learning: Theoretical Foundations.* London: Longman

Shrum, J. and Glisan, E. (1994) *Contextualized Language Instruction.* Boston: Heinle and Heinle

Siegal, M. (1996) 'Conversation and cognition' in Gelman & Au (eds.): 244–281

Sigel, I. (ed.) (1999) *Development of Mental Representation.* Mahwah: Lawrence Erlbaum

Sinclair, J. (1991) *Corpus, Concordance, Collocation.* Oxford: Oxford University Press

Sinclair, J. and Renouf, A. (1988) 'A lexical syllabus for language learning' in Carter & McCarthy (eds.): 140–160

Singer, M. (1994) 'Discourse inference processes' in Gernsbacher (ed.): 479–516

Singleton, D. and Lengyel, Z. (eds.) (1995) *The Age Factor in Second Language Acquisition.* Clevedon: Multilingual Matters

Skehan, P. (1994) 'Second language acquisition strategies, interlanguage development and task-based learning' in Bygate et al. (eds.): 175–202

Skehan, P. (1998) *A Cognitive Approach to Language Learning.* Oxford: Oxford University Press

Skiba, R. and Dittmar, N. (1992) 'Pragmatic, semantic, and syntactic constraints and grammaticalisation' *Studies in Second Language Acquisition* 14: 323–349

Slabakova, R. (2001) *Telicity in the Second Language.* Amsterdam: John Benjamins

Slavoff, G. and Johnson, J. (1995) 'The effects of age on the rate of learning a second language' *Studies in Second Language Acquisition* 17: 1–16

Smith, A. (1988) 'Language acquisition: learnability, maturation, and the fixing of parameters' *Cognitive Neuropsychology* 5: 235–265

Smith, M. (1997) 'How do bilinguals access lexical information?' in de Groot & Kroll (eds.): 145–168

Smith, N. (1973) *The Acquisition of Phonology: A Case Study.* Cambridge: Cambridge University Press

Smith, N. (1989) *The Twitter Machine: Reflections on Language.* Oxford: Blackwell

Smith, N. (2003) 'Representations and responsibilities' *Korean Journal of English Language and Linguistics* 3: 527–545

Smith, N. and Tsimpli, I-M. (1995) *The Mind of a Savant.* Oxford: Blackwell

Smith, P., Cowie, H. and Blades, M. (1998) *Understanding Children's Development.* Oxford: Blackwell

Snow, C. and Hoefnagel-Höhle, M. (1978) 'The critical period for language acquisition: evidence from second language learning' *Child Development* 49: 1114–1128

Sorace, A. (1995) 'Acquiring linking rules and argument structures in second language: the unaccusative/unergative distinction' in Eubank, Selinker & Sharwood-Smith (eds.): 153–175

Spencer-Oatey, H. and Zegarac, V. (2002) 'Pragmatics' in Schmitt (ed.): 74–91

Sperber, D. and Wilson, D. (1995) *Relevance: Communication and Cognition (2nd Edition).* Oxford: Blackwell

Stabler, E. (1994) 'The finite connectivity of linguistic structure' in Clifton, Frazier, & Rayner (eds.): 303–336

Steedman, M. (2000) *The Syntactic Processes*. Cambridge: MIT Press

Steinberg, D. and Sciarini, N. (2006) *An Introduction to Psycholinguistics (2nd Edition)*. Harlow: Longman

Stillings, N., Weisler, S., Chase, C., Feinstein, M., Garfield, J. and Rissland, E. (1995) *Cognitive Science*. Cambridge: MIT Press

Stowell, T. and Wehrli, E. (1992) *Syntax and Semantics Vol. 26: Syntax and the Lexicon*. San Diego: Academic Press

Strange, W. (ed.) (1995) *Speech Perception and Linguistic Experience: Issues in Cross-Language Research*. Baltimore: York Press

Stubbs, M. (1995) 'Corpus evidence for norms of lexical collocation' in Cook & Seidlhofer (eds.): 245–256

Swain, M. (1995) 'Three functions of output in second language learning' in Cook & Seidlhofer (eds.): 125–144

Takahashi, T. and Beebe, L. (1987) 'The development of pragmatic ability by Japanese learners of English' *JALT Journal* 8: 131–155

Takano, Y. and Noda, A. (1995) 'Interlanguage dissimilarity enhances the decline of thinking ability during foreign language processing' *Language Learning* 45: 657–681

Tanenhaus, M., Garnsey, S. and Boland, J. (1990) 'Combinatory lexical information and language comprehension' in Altmann (ed.): 383–408

Tarone, E. (1987) 'Some influences on the syllable structure of interlanguage phonology' in Ioup & Weinberger (eds.): 232–247

Tarone, E., Gass, S. and Cohen, A. (eds.) (1994) *Research Methodology in Second-Language Acquisition*. Hillsdale: Lawrence Erlbaum

Tartter, V. (1998) *Language and its Normal Processing*. London: SAGE Publishers

Taylor, I. (1990) *Psycholinguistics*. Eaglewood Cliffs: Prentice-Hall International

Tohkura, Y., Vatikiotis-Bateson, E. and Sagisaka, Y. (eds.) (1992) *Speech Perception, Production, and Linguistic Structure*. Tokyo: Ohmsha

Tomasello, M. (1992) *First Verbs: A Case Study of Early Grammatical Development*. Cambridge: Cambridge University Press

Tomasello, M. (1995) *Beyond Names for Things*. Hillsdale: Lawrence Erlbaum

Tomasello, M. (1999) 'Early syntactic development: a construction grammar approach' in Barrett (ed.): 161–190

Tomasello, M. (2001) 'Perceiving intentions and learning words' in Bowerman & Levinson (eds.): 132–158

Tomasello, M. (2003) *Constructing a Language: A Usage-Based Theory in Language Acquisition*. Cambridge: Harvard University Press

Tomasello, M. (ed.) (2003) *The New Psychology of Language*. Mahwah: Lawrence Erlbaum

Tomasello, M. and Bates, E. (2001) *Language Development*. Oxford: Blackwell

Townsend, D. and Bever, T. (2001) *Sentence Comprehension: The Integration of Habits and Rules*. Cambridge: MIT Press

Trevise, A. (1987) 'Toward an analysis of the interlangauge activity of the referring to time in narratives' in Pfaff (ed.): 225–251

Trueswell, J. and Gleitman, L. (2007) 'Learning to parse and its implications for language acquisition' in Gaskell (ed.): 535–655

Trueswell, J. and Tanenhaus, M. (eds.) (2005) *Approaches to Studying World-Situated-Language Use: Bridging the Language-as-Product and Language-as-Action Traditions*. Cambridge: MIT Press

Truscott, J. and Sharwood-Smith, M. (2004) 'Acquisition by processing: a modular perspective on language development' *Bilingualism: Language and Cognition* 7 (Special issue)

Tsimpli, I-M. (1991) 'Functional categories and maturation: the prefunctional stage of language acquisition' MS. University College London

Tsimpli, I-M. (1997) 'Resumptive pronouns, learnability, and L2A: a minimalist account' MS. University of Cambridge

Tsimpli, I-M. and Roussou, A. (1991) 'Parameter resetting in L2?' *UCL Working Papers in Linguistics* 3: 149–169

Tsimpli, I-M. and Smith, N. (1991) 'Second-language learning: evidence from polyglot savant' *UCL Working Papers in Linguistics* 3: 172–183

Turnbull, W. (2003) *Language in Action: Psychological Models of Conversation*. Hove: Psychology Press

Uemura, K. (1998, June) *The English Teachers' Magazine*. Tokyo: Taishukan Shoten

Ur, P. (1984) *Listening Comprehension*. Cambridge: Cambridge University Press

Vainikka, A. and Young-Scholten, M. (1994) 'Direct access to X'-theory: evidence from Korean and Turkish adults learning German' in Hoekstra & Schwartz (eds.): 265–316

Vainikka, A. and Young-Scholten, M. (1996a) 'Gradual development of L2 phrase structure' *Second Language Research* 12: 7–39

Vainikka, A. and Young-Scholten, M. (1996b) 'The early stages in adult L2 syntax: additional evidence from Romance speakers' *Second Language Research* 12: 140–176

Vainikka, A. and Young-Scholten, M. (1998a) 'Morphosyntactic triggers in adult SLA' in Beck (ed.): 89–113

Vainikka, A. and Young-Scholten, M. (1998b) 'The initial state in the L2 acquisition of phrase structure' in Flynn, Martohardjono & O'Neil (eds.): 17–94

Valdman, A. (ed.) (2002) 'Special issue on frequency and second language acquisition' *Studies in Second Language Acquisition* 24 issue 2

VanPatten, B. (ed.) (1987) *L2 Learning: A Research Perspective*. Cambridge: Newbury House

VanPatten, B. (1995) 'From input to output: processing instruction and communicative tasks' in Eckman (ed.): 169–185

VanPatten, B. (1996) *Input Processing and Grammar Instruction in Second Language Acquisition*. Norwood: Ablex

VanPatten, B. (2004) *Processing Instruction: Theory, Research, and Commentary*. Mahwah: Lawrence Erlbaum

VanPatten, B., Williams, J., Rott, S. and Overstreet, M. (eds.) (2004) *Form-Meaning Connections in Second Language Acquisition*. Mahwah: Lawrence Erlbaum

Vasishth, S. (2003) *Working Memory in Sentence Comprehension*. New York: Routledge

Veronique, D. (1987) 'Reference to past events and actions in narratives in L2' in Pfaff (ed.): 250–272

Wallen, M. (1994) 'What is knowledge about language?' in Wray & Medwell (eds.): 165–176

Warren, A. and McCloskey, L. (1997) 'Language in social context' in Gleason (ed.): 210–258

Wasow, T. (1977) 'Transformations and the lexicon' in Akmajian, Culicover & Wasow (eds.): 327–360

Weber-Fox, C. and Neville, H. (1996) 'Maturational constraints on functional specialisations for language processing: ERP and behavioural evidence in bilingual speakers' *Journal of Cognitive Neuroscience* 8: 231–256

Weber-Fox, C. and Neville, H. (1999) 'Functional neural subsystems are differentially affected by delays in second language immersion: ERP and behavioural evidence in bilinguals' in Birdsong (ed.): 23–38

Weinberger, S. (1994) 'Functional and phonetic constraints on second language phonology' in Yavaş, (ed.): 283–302

Weinberger, S. (1997) 'Minimal segments in second language phonology' in James & Leather (eds.): 263–311

Weissenborn, J. and Höhle, B. (eds.) (2001) *Approaches to Bootstrapping: Vol 1 & 2*. Amsterdam: John Benjamins

Wexler, K. (1987) 'Parameters and learnability in binding theory' in Roeper & Williams (eds.): 41–76

Wexler, K. (1999) 'Maturation and growth of grammar' in Ritchie & Bhatia (eds.): 55–109

White, L. (1989) *Universal Grammar and Second Language Acquisition*. Amsterdam: John Benjamins

White, L. (1991) 'Second language competence versus second language performance: UG or processing strategies?' in Eubank (ed.): 167–189

Widdowson, H. (1978) *Teaching Language as Communication*. Oxford: Oxford University Press

Widdowson, H. (1990) *Aspects of Language Teaching*. Oxford: Oxford University Press

Williams, J. (1999) 'Memory, attention, and inductive learning' *Studies in Second Language Acquisition* 21: 1–48

Williams, J. (2006) 'Incremental interpretation in second language sentence processing' *Bilingualism: Language and Cognition* 9: 71–88

Willis, D. (1990) *The Lexical Syllabus*. London: Collins ELT

Willis, D. (1994) 'A Lexical Approach' in Bygate, Tonkyn & Williams (eds): 56–66

Willis, D. (2003) *Rules, Patterns, and Words*. Cambridge: Cambridge University Press

Willis, D. and Willis, J. (eds.) (1996) *Challenge and Change in Language Teaching*. London: Hieneman

Wode, H. (1997) 'Perception and production in learning to talk' in Hannahs & Young-Scholten (eds.): 17–46

Wolfe-Quintero, K. (1992) 'Learnability and the acquisition of extraction in relative clauses and wh-questions' *Studies in Second Language Acquisition* 14: 39–70

Wood, D. (1998) *How Children Think and Learn*. Oxford: Blackwell

Wray, A. (2002) *Formulaic Language and the Lexicon*. Cambridge: Cambridge University Press

Wray, D. and Medwell, J. (eds.) (1994) *Teaching Primary English*. London: Routledge

Yamada, R. (1995) 'Age and acquisition of second language speech sounds: perception of American English /ɹ/ and /l/ by native speakers of Japanese' in Strange (ed.): 305–320

Yamada, R. and Tohkura, Y. (1992) 'Perception of American English /r/ and /l/ by native speakers of Japanese' in Tohkura et al. (eds.): 155–174

Yamada, R., Tohkura, Y. and Kobayashi, N. (1997) 'Effect of word familiarity on non-native phoneme perception: identification of English /r/, /l/ and /w/ by native speakers of Japanese' in James & Leather (eds.): 103–117

Yamashita, H. (1997) 'The effects of word-order and case marking information on the processing of Japanese' *Journal of Psycholinguistic Research* 26: 163–188

Yavaş, M. (ed.) (1994) *First and Second Language Phonology*. San Diego: Singular Publishing Group

Yavaş, M. (2006) *Applied English Phonology*. Oxford: Blackwell

Young, R. and He, A. (1998) *Talking and Testing: Discourse Approaches to the Assessment of Oral Proficiency*. Amsterdam: John Benjamins

Young-Scholten, M. and Archibald, J. (2000) 'Second language syllable structure' in Archibald (ed.): 64–101

Zobl, H. and Liceras, J. (1994) 'Functional categories and acquisition orders' *Language Learning* 44: 159–180

Zurif, E. (1990) 'Language and the brain' in Osherson & Lasnik (eds.): 177–197

Appendices

Appendix A: Some examples extracted from the test battery (L1 test was produced by translating L2 sentences into L1.)

More than 100 dialogues were prepared. We put them into the computer system. They were randomly presented to each participant. Vocabulary and grammar were controlled with respect to the students' learning stage.

<Normal sentences>

- A: Let's play soccer.
  B: It's raining outside.
- A: Let's go shopping this weekend.
  B: I have exams on Monday.
- A: You must brush your teeth twice a day.
  B: I hate dentists!
- A: Teacher's coming. Run away!
  B: Mr Sato doesn't care about us.
- A: My girl friend ignores me.
  B: Comb your hair!
- (Looking into a terrible exam result.) You did a very good job.

<Do you…?>

- A: Do you like Mr Sato (an English teacher)?
  B: He's my grandfather.
- A: Do you enjoy the Sokeki's book?
  B: I can sleep well with it.
- A: Did you have a good time at the party?
  B: My girl friend did not show up.
- A: Do you play soccer?
  B: Sweating annoys me.

<Wh-questions>

- A: How do you feel about the bullet train?
  B: Japan is at the top of the world.
- A: How did you cook the carrot?
  B: It changed my life.
- A: How was the Fuji-rock festival?
  B: Mt Fuji was exploding!
- A: How old is your sister?
  B: She's getting married.
- A: Where did you go this weekend?
  B: I had a bad cold.
- A: Where is Mr Sato (an English teacher)?
  B: Takeshi (a naughty boy) entered LL again.
- A: Where's my umbrella?
  B: A dog is looking at you.
- A: When is the next test?
  B: Summer is coming!
- A: When did you leave?
  B: You slept well last night.
- A: When is Naoko's birthday?
  B: She is in the USA.
- A: What do you want to be in the future?
  B: I started writing a love story.
- A: What is your favourite subject?
  B: Playing cards would be nice.
- A: What do you think about Akiko?
  B: Daisuke is walking over there.
- A: Who took my bag away?
  B: The building is on fire!
- A: Why didn't you come to skating?
  B: I hate Antarctic.

Appendix B: Typology of sentence patterns in free writing

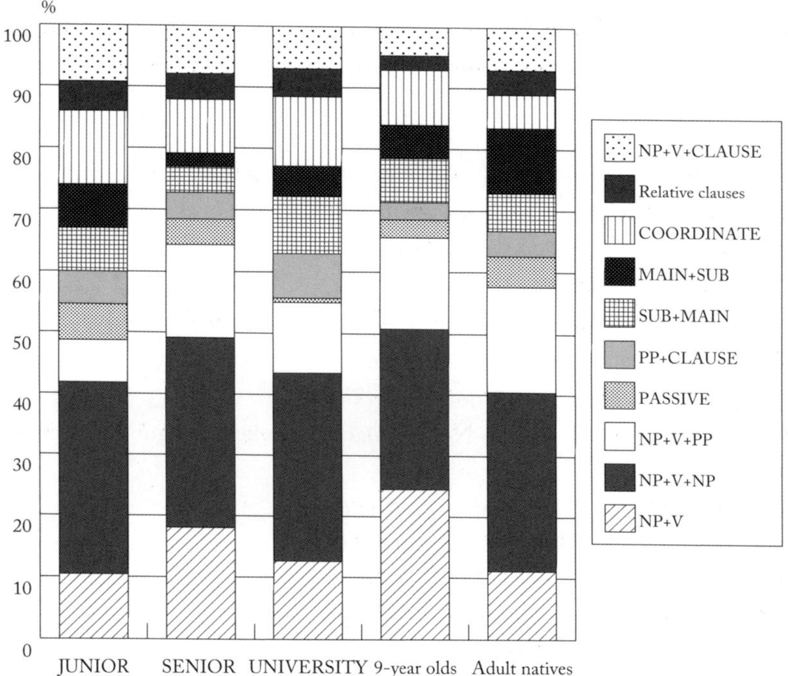

Appendix C: Grammaticality judgment test for Functional Categories

Instruction (translated into English): Please judge whether the following sentences are grammatical or not. If you think the sentence ungrammatical, correct it.

1. All the students in my school joined the school trip to Tohoku.
2. Taro likes to read these book at night.
3. Ken keeps three pretty dog in his house.
4. Those pencils on the desk is mine.
5. Students at this schools study very hard to enter good universities.
6. We stayed at a beautiful hotel in Sendai.
7. This pictures is taken by our homeroom teacher.
8. Japan must sell these cars to New Zealanders to keep Japan's economy going.
9. That house on the hill was built by our uncle.
10. Kumi likes to eat apples when she goes out.
11. My friends and I had to sleep in these car last Saturday.
12. We had a nice party in our classmate's house.
13. Friend likes skiing, but I like skating.
14. Her an uncle lives in Yamagata.
15. The document is on my a desk.
16. His boat is very big and nice. I want to have it/one, too.
17. I know that you went skiing with your friends last weekend.
18. We always visit my grandparents' house in Nara, but this year, I didn't go to their the house.
19. My younger sister likes to go to the zoo.
20. His automobile is very nice.
21. The your pen is on the table.
22. I borrowed his umbrella yesterday.
23. I like to take a trip with those my friends.
24. Jiro put something terrible in her the box.
25. You look pretty in this photo.
26. My friends plays tennis every Sunday.
27. My mother work hard from morning until night.
28. The apples produced in Aomori tastes good, so I often buy and eat them.

29. My teacher give us nice presents at the graduation party.
30. Mr Sato teaches music this year, but they taught English last year.

Grammatical: 1.6.8.9.10.12.16.17.19.20.22.25.

Appendix D: Reaction time (ms)

Children [+FOCUS]

		Test 1	Test 2	Test 3	Test 4	Test 5	Test 6
/θ/ - /s/	XV	1,100	1,050	1,000	980	990	990
	CXV	1,400	1,360	1,310	1,300	1,290	1,300
	VXV	1,380	1,330	1,300	1,200	1,230	1,210
	VXC	1,200	1,150	1,110	1,110	1,130	1,120
	VX	1,110	1,110	1,050	1,030	1,060	1,050
/θ/ - /f/	XV	1,200	1,150	1,160	1,100	1,050	1,090
	CXV	1,210	1,200	1,130	1,100	1,100	1,140
	VXV	1,220	1,220	1,200	1,160	1,170	1,190
	VXC	1,200	1,180	1,180	1,110	1,110	1,140
	VX	1,310	1,300	1,290	1,210	1,220	1,220
/θ/ - /t/	XV	1,140	1,110	1,100	1,000	1,010	1,020
	CXV	1,210	1,160	1,110	1,000	1,030	1,020
	VXV	1,100	1,080	1,080	1,060	1,060	1,080
	VXC	1,200	1,110	1,100	1,100	1,110	1,110
	VX	1,210	1,180	1,170	1,160	1,170	1,170

Adolescents [+FOCUS]

		Test 1	Test 2	Test 3	Test 4	Test 5	Test 6
/θ/ - /s/	XV	1,050	1,180	1,120	1,050	1,010	1,000
	CXV	1,200	1,400	1,300	1,250	1,220	1,200
	VXV	1,250	1,380	1,290	1,210	1,200	1,180
	VXC	1,110	1,050	1,000	990	980	960
	VX	1,050	1,040	930	910	900	890
/θ/ - /f/	XV	950	840	750	740	735	730
	CXV	1,150	1,000	900	890	880	880
	VXV	1,130	950	900	890	900	910
	VXC	1,120	1,000	900	890	890	910
	VX	1,580	1,300	920	900	910	920
/θ/ - /t/	XV	1,100	1,130	1,100	950	940	950
	CXV	1,300	1,250	1,200	1,150	1,180	1,210
	VXV	1,100	1,000	980	950	950	960
	VXC	1,300	1,250	1,100	1,050	1,250	1,300
	VX	1,300	1,200	1,150	1,000	1,000	1,050

Adults [+FOCUS]

		Test 1	Test 2	Test 3	Test 4	Test 5	Test 6
/θ/ - /s/	XV	1,210	1,210	1,200	1,160	1,180	1,200
	CXV	1,380	1,300	1,310	1,280	1,290	1,300
	VXV	1,400	1,380	1,330	1,340	1,350	1,340
	VXC	1,210	1,200	1,200	1,160	1,170	1,180
	VX	1,180	1,140	1,110	1,100	1,100	1,100
/θ/ - /f/	XV	1,180	1,110	1,100	1,100	1,130	1,120
	CXV	1,200	1,210	1,080	1,090	1,100	1,100
	VXV	1,200	1,180	1,140	1,100	1,120	1,120
	VXC	1,190	1,170	1,160	1,100	1,130	1,140
	VX	1,430	1,310	1,300	1,280	1,290	1,280
/θ/ - /t/	XV	1,100	1,080	1,030	1,040	1,030	1,050
	CXV	1,220	1,200	1,130	1,110	1,120	1,120
	VXV	1,040	9,900	980	980	990	990
	VXC	1,310	1,270	1,260	1,200	1,210	1,220
	VX	1,340	1,210	1,140	1,080	1,090	1,100

Children [-FOCUS]

		Test 1	Test 2	Test 3	Test 4	Test 5	Test 6
/θ/ - /s/	XV	1,210	1,240	1,200	1,250	1,240	1,270
	CXV	1,410	1,400	1,430	1,420	1,460	1,480
	VXV	1,430	1,400	1,460	1,500	1,490	1,510
	VXC	1,310	1,300	1,330	1,380	1,440	1,460
	VX	1,190	1,190	1,210	1,260	1,300	1,360
/θ/ - /f/	XV	1,360	1,380	1,390	1,420	1,400	1,410
	CXV	1,300	1,460	1,510	1,500	1,530	1,570
	VXV	1,330	1,350	1,390	1,440	1,510	1,500
	VXC	1,400	1,430	1,470	1,530	1,610	1,620
	VX	1,330	1,310	1,330	1,340	1,320	1,350
/θ/ - /t/	XV	1,200	1,130	1,160	1,150	1,140	1,150
	CXV	1,230	1,200	1,210	1,190	1,220	1,230
	VXV	1,190	1,110	1,160	1,150	1,140	1,160
	VXC	1,280	1,220	1,230	1,210	1,240	1,220
	VX	1,260	1,210	1,220	1,200	1,230	1,250

Adolescents [-FOCUS]

		Test 1	Test 2	Test 3	Test 4	Test 5	Test 6
/θ/ - /s/	XV	1,300	1,310	1,440	1,430	1,510	1,500
	CXV	1,390	1,380	1,410	1,440	1,500	1,430
	VXV	1,400	1,360	1,390	1,440	1,430	1,440
	VXC	1,290	1,280	1,330	1,350	1,350	1,370
	VX	1,200	1,110	1,170	1,240	1,220	1,230
/θ/ - /f/	XV	1,330	1,300	1,320	1,380	1,370	1,400
	CXV	1,310	1,340	1,300	1,320	1,300	1,290
	VXV	1,300	1,270	1,290	1,280	1,290	1,300
	VXC	1,390	1,370	1,360	1,330	1,350	1,370
	VX	1,340	1,300	1,310	1,290	1,280	1,290
/θ/ - /t/	XV	1,310	1,300	1,240	1,210	1,220	1,210
	CXV	1,360	1,300	1,290	1,240	1,260	1,250
	VXV	1,210	1,220	1,200	1,230	1,220	1,200
	VXC	1,360	1,310	1,330	1,340	1,330	1,320
	VX	1,320	1,280	1,240	1,270	1,250	1,240

Adults [-FOCUS]

		Test 1	Test 2	Test 3	Test 4	Test 5	Test 6
/θ/ - /s/	XV	1,430	1,410	1,420	1,440	1,430	1,410
	CXV	1,470	1,460	1,440	1,450	1,440	1,480
	VXV	1,440	1,410	1,420	1,400	1,420	1,410
	VXC	1,310	1,300	1,320	1,310	1,330	1,320
	VX	1,210	1,220	1,200	1,240	1,200	1,210
/θ/ - /f/	XV	1,380	1,360	1,370	1,360	1,380	1,370
	CXV	1,290	1,300	1,280	1,290	1,300	1,290
	VXV	1,310	1,290	1,260	1,270	1,280	1,270
	VXC	1,360	1,330	1,350	1,340	1,360	1,350
	VX	1,300	1,280	1,270	1,290	1,260	1,270
/θ/ - /t/	XV	1,220	1,210	1,170	1,160	1,180	1,170
	CXV	1,270	1,210	1,220	1,230	1,210	1,220
	VXV	1,260	1,230	1,240	1,250	1,230	1,240
	VXC	1,330	1,300	1,310	1,280	1,260	1,270
	VX	1,260	1,210	1,230	1,240	1,250	1,210

Children [-F>+F]

		Test 1	Test 2	Test 3	Test 4	Test 5	Test 6
/θ/ - /s/	XV	1,210	1,240	1,080	1,010	1,050	1,100
	CXV	1,410	1,400	1,300	1,230	1,240	1,250
	VXV	1,430	1,400	1,290	1,210	1,270	1,280
	VXC	1,310	1,300	1,200	1,170	1,210	1,230
	VX	1,190	1,190	1,030	1,010	1,060	1,080
/θ/ - /f/	XV	1,360	1,330	1,200	1,160	1,210	1,290
	CXV	1,300	1,460	1,310	1,290	1,300	1,310
	VXV	1,330	1,350	1,210	1,190	1,230	1,270
	VXC	1,400	1,430	1,300	1,280	1,310	1,330
	VX	1,380	1,310	1,200	1,170	1,210	1,240
/θ/ - /t/	XV	1,200	1,130	1,030	1,010	1,110	1,150
	CXV	1,230	1,200	1,100	1,070	1,140	1,170
	VXV	1,190	1,110	1,070	1,010	1,120	1,120
	VXC	1,280	1,220	1,130	1,120	1,160	1,240
	VX	1,260	1,210	1,100	1,090	1,170	1,190

Adolescents [-F>+F]

		Test 1	Test 2	Test 3	Test 4	Test 5	Test 6
/θ/ - /s/	XV	1,300	1,310	1,200	1,130	1,180	1,190
	CXV	1,390	1,380	1,210	1,160	1,190	1,200
	VXV	1,400	1,360	1,220	1,180	1,190	1,180
	VXC	1,290	1,280	1,130	1,080	1,100	1,140
	VX	1,200	1,110	990	980	1,020	1,040
/θ/ - /f/	XV	1,330	1,300	1,260	1,190	1,210	1,210
	CXV	1,310	1,340	1,210	1,180	1,200	1,210
	VXV	1,300	1,270	1,180	1,110	1,140	1,130
	VXC	1,390	1,370	1,220	1,170	1,190	1,200
	VX	1,340	1,300	1,210	1,160	1,180	1,170
/θ/ - /t/	XV	1,310	1,300	1,190	1,030	1,090	1,110
	CXV	1,360	1,300	1,210	1,130	1,160	1,170
	VXV	1,210	1,220	1,120	1,060	1,140	1,170
	VXC	1,360	1,310	1,180	1,110	1,170	1,220
	VX	1,320	1,280	1,130	1,050	1,090	1,140

Adults [-F>+F]

		Test 1	Test 2	Test 3	Test 4	Test 5	Test 6
/θ/ - /s/	XV	1,430	1,410	1,240	1,220	1,160	1,200
	CXV	1,470	1,460	1,380	1,300	1,310	1,320
	VXV	1,440	1,410	1,370	1,350	1,360	1,370
	VXC	1,310	1,300	1,210	1,200	1,190	1,210
	VX	1,210	1,220	1,160	1,110	1,140	1,150
/θ/ - /f/	XV	1,380	1,360	1,210	1,180	1,200	1,210
	CXV	1,290	1,300	1,190	1,140	1,170	1,160
	VXV	1,310	1,290	1,180	1,140	1,170	1,190
	VXC	1,360	1,330	1,260	1,200	1,230	1,270
	VX	1,300	1,280	1,290	1,270	1,290	1,290
/θ/ - /t/	XV	1,220	1,210	1,150	1,110	1,140	1,150
	CXV	1,270	1,210	1,190	1,120	1,160	1,150
	VXV	1,260	1,230	1,170	1,120	1,170	1,160
	VXC	1,330	1,300	1,220	1,200	1,210	1,210
	VX	1,260	1,280	1,160	1,130	1,130	1,140

Appendix E: Epenthesis in production

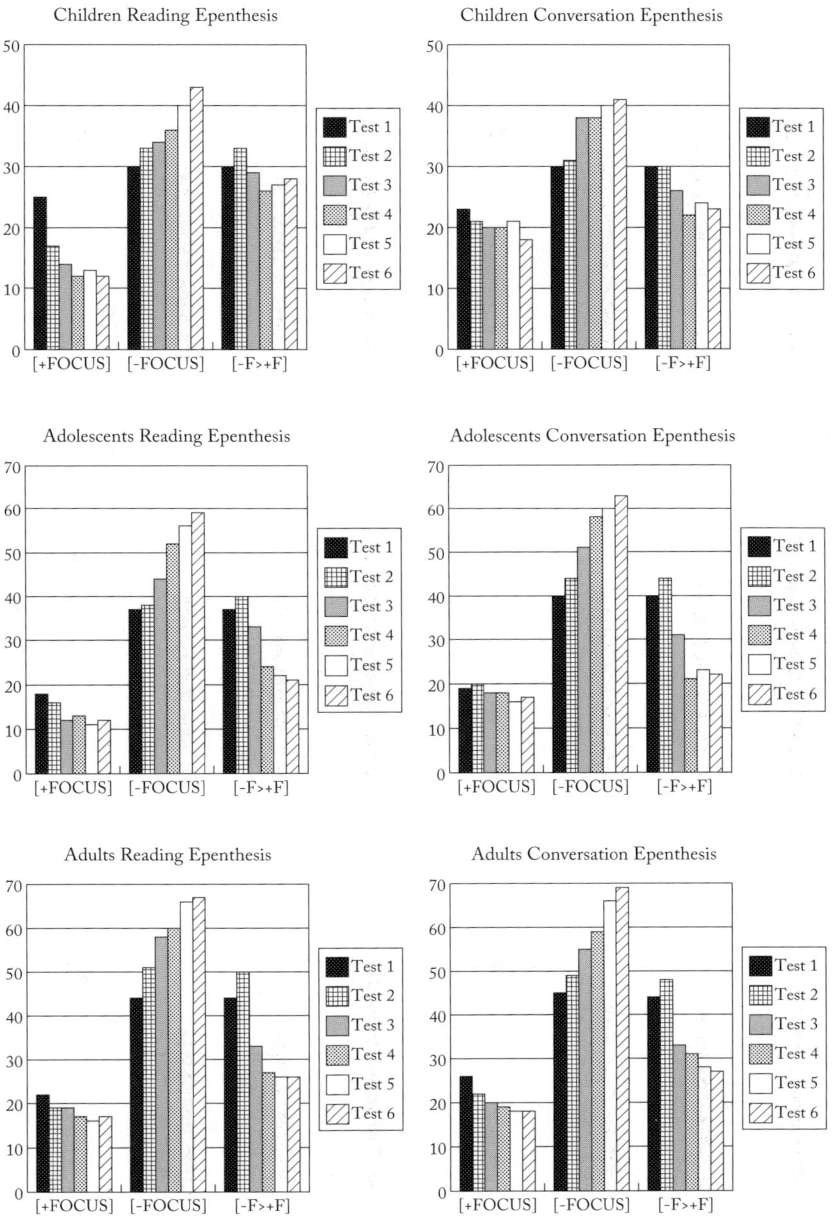

Appendix F: Rhythmic impression in production

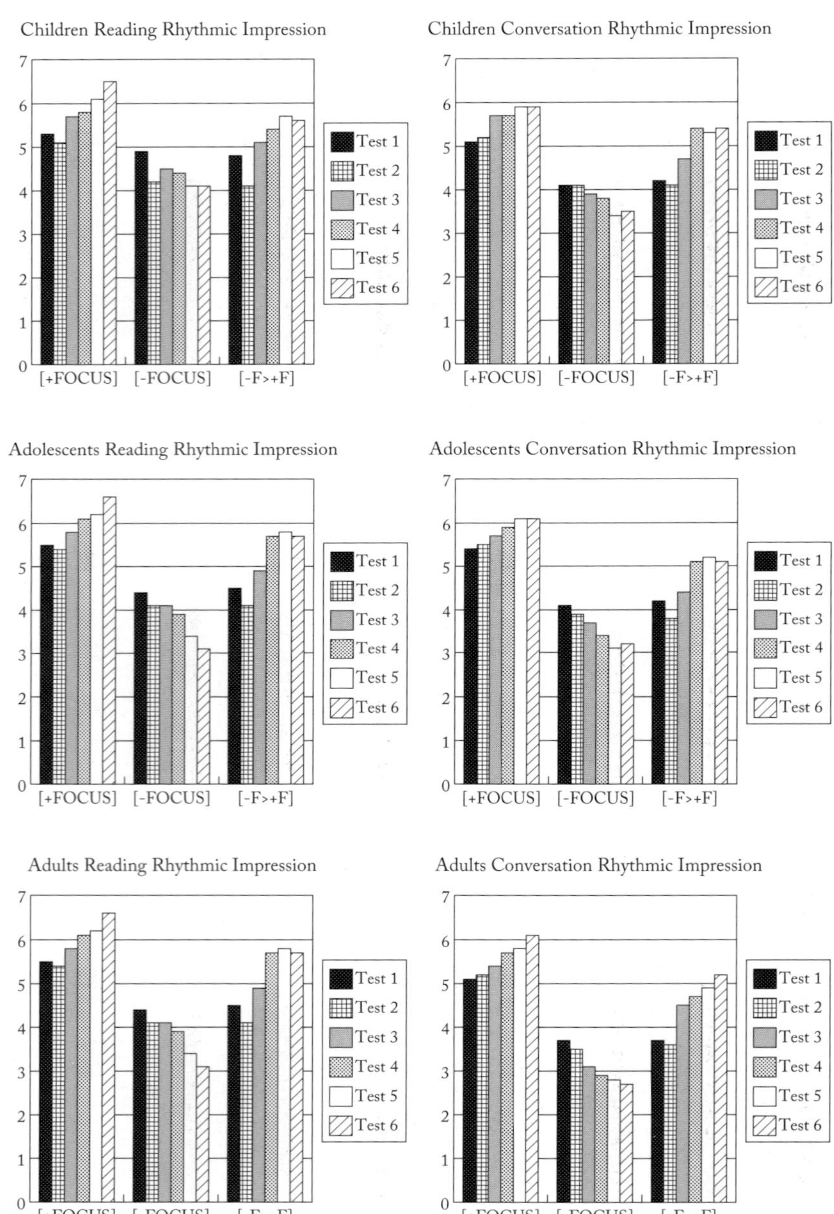

Appendix G: Common words, weak forms, and strong forms

[Copulas]

am /(Weak form) (ə)m; (Strong form) ǽm/

are /(Weak form) ɚ | ə; (Strong form) ɑ̀ɚ, ɑ́ɚ | ɑ̀:, ɑ́:/

be /(Weak form) bi; (Strong form) bí:/

been /(Weak form) bɪn, bən | bɪn; (Strong form) bín | bí:n/

was /(Weak form) wəz; (Strong form) wɑ́z, wʌ́z | wɔ́z/

were /(Weak form) wɚ | wə; (Strong form) wɚ́: | wə́:/

[Auxiliaries]

can /(Weak form) k(ə)n; (Strong form) kæ̀n, kǽn/

could /(Weak form) kəd; (Strong form) kúd/

does /(Weak form) dəz; (Strong form) dʌ́z/

had /(Weak form) həd, əd; (Strong form) hǽd/

has /(Weak form) həz, əz; (Strong form) hǽz/

have /(Weak form) həv, əv; (Strong form) hǽv/

must /(Weak form) məs(t); (Strong form) mʌ́st/

shall /(Weak form) ʃəl; (Strong form) ʃǽl/

should /(Weak form) ʃəd; (Strong form) ʃúd/

would /(Weak form) (w)əd, d; (Strong form) wúd/

[Pronouns]

he /(Weak form) (h)i; (Strong form) hí:/

her /(Weak form) (h)ɚ | (h)ə; (Strong form) hɚ́: | hə́:/

him /(Weak form) (h)ɪm; (Strong form) hím/

his /(Weak form) (h)ɪz; (Strong form) híz/

me /(Weak form) mi; (Strong form) mí:/

she /(Weak form) ʃi; (Strong form) ʃí:/

our /(Weak form) ɑɚ | ɑ:; (Strong form) ɑ́ʊɚ, ɑ́ɚ | ɑ́ʊə, ɑ́:/

their /(Weak form) ðɚ | ðə; (Strong form) ðéɚ | ðéə/

them /(Weak form) (ð)əm; (Strong form) ðém/

us /(Weak form) əs; (Strong form) ʌ́s/

we /(Weak form) wi; (Strong form) wí:/

you /(Weak form) jʊ, jə; (Strong form) jú:/

your /(Weak form) jɚ | jɔ:, jə; (Strong form) júɚ, jɔ́ɚ | jɔ́:, júə/

[Articles]

a /(Weak form) ə; (Strong form) éɪ/

an /(Weak form) ən, (Strong form) æ̀n, ǽn/

the /(Weak form) ðə 《Before consonants》, ði 《Before vowels》; (Strong form) ðí:/

[Prepositions]

at /(Weak form) ət; (Strong form) ǽt/

for /(Weak form) fɚ | fə; (Strong form) fɔ́ɚ | fɔ́:/

from /(Weak form)frəm; (Strong form)frɑ́m, frʌ́m | frɔ́m/

of /(Weak form) (ə)v, ə; (Strong form) ɑ́v, ʌ́v | ɔ́v/

to /(Weak form) (Before consonants) tʊ, tə, (Before vowels) tu, (At the end of clauses or sentences) tu:; (Strong form) tú:/

[Connectives]

and /(Weak form) ən(d), n; (Strong form) ǽnd/

as /(Weak form) əz; (Strong form) ǽz/

but /(Weak form) bət; (Strong form) bʌ́t/

[Other (function) words]

some /(Weak form) s(ə)m; (Strong form) sʌ́m/

than /(Weak form) ðən; (Strong form) ðǽn/

that /(Weak form) ðət; (Strong form) ðǽt/

Appendix H: Overall changes in the classroom

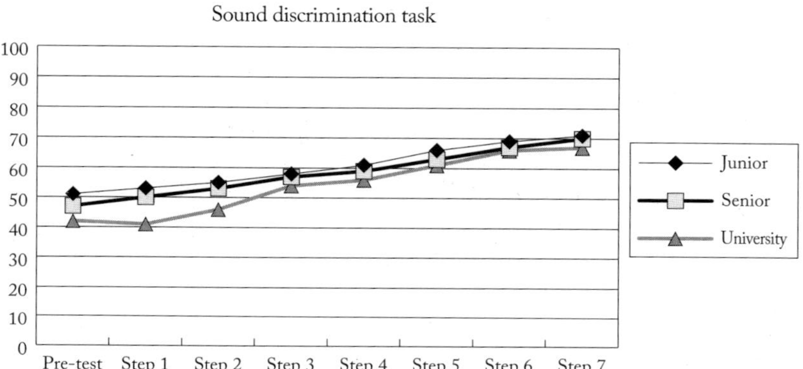

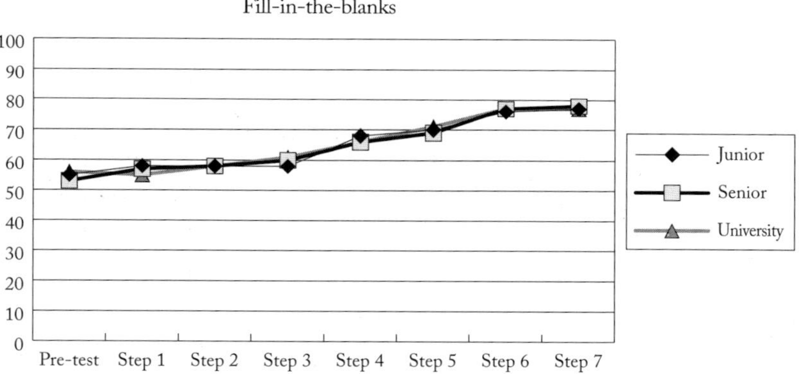

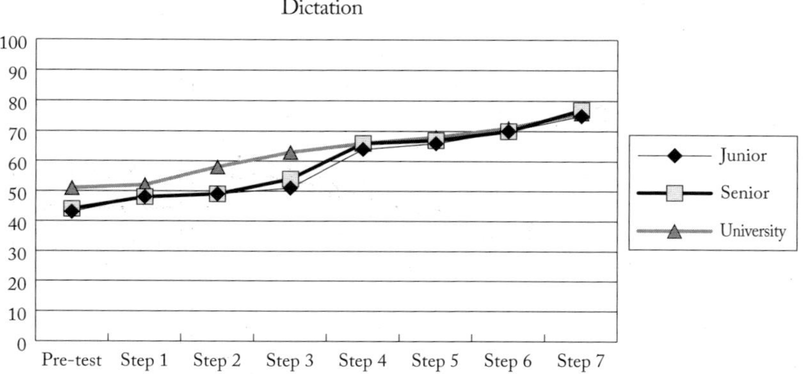

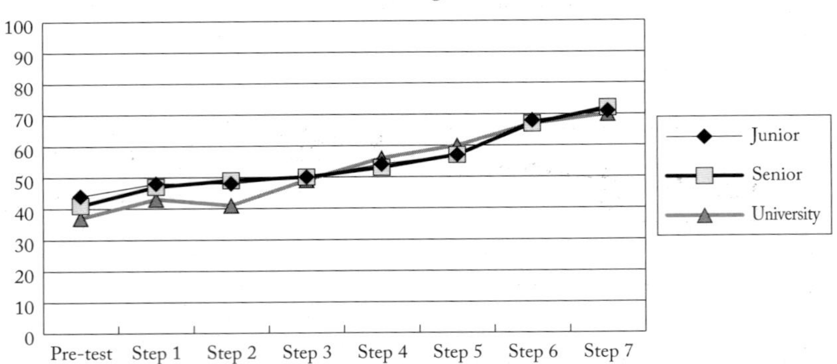

Controlled speech

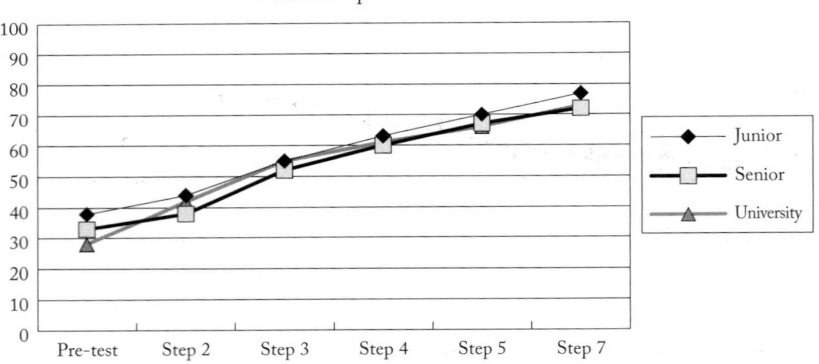

Free speech

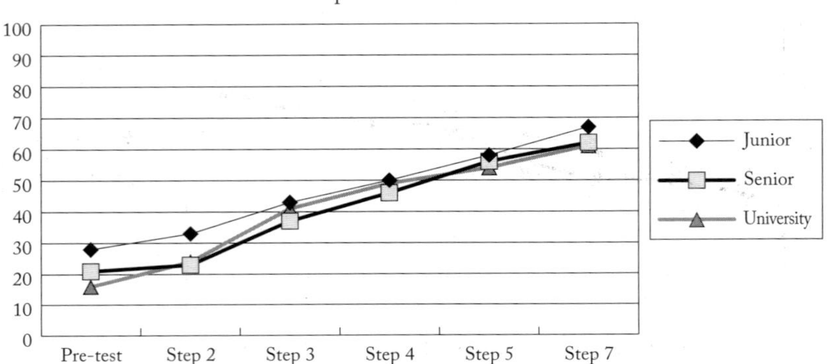

Appendix I: Distribution of the number of students who marked the ranges of the scores

Test types: ① Sound discrimination task; ② Fill-in-the-blanks; ③ Dictation; ④ Content understanding; ⑤ Controlled speech; and ⑥ Free speech
Student types: J: Junior high school students; S: Senior high school students; U: University students

Pre-test

	Over 80 points			79–60 points			59–40 points			39–20 points			Below 19 points		
	J	S	U	J	S	U	J	S	U	J	S	U	J	S	U
①	0	0	0	17	14	13	66	65	62	15	19	21	2	2	4
②	0	0	0	41	40	43	52	52	50	7	8	7	0	0	0
③	0	0	0	12	11	23	65	66	63	13	11	8	10	12	6
④	0	0	0	7	7	1	68	67	41	22	23	56	3	3	2
⑤	0	0	0	6	5	3	45	36	33	48	41	41	13	17	23
⑥	0	0	0	1	0	0	15	10	6	44	38	7	40	52	87

Step 1

	Over 80			79–60			59–40			39–20			Below 19		
	J	S	U	J	S	U	J	S	U	J	S	U	J	S	U
①	0	0	0	16	15	13	71	68	61	13	17	22	0	0	4
②	0	0	0	42	40	42	53	55	50	5	5	8	0	0	0
③	0	0	0	13	13	17	70	67	66	10	11	10	7	9	7
④	0	0	0	8	7	2	71	69	39	19	21	57	2	3	2

Step 2

	Over 80			79–60			59–40			39–20			Below 19		
	J	S	U	J	S	U	J	S	U	J	S	U	J	S	U
①	0	0	0	17	17	12	71	70	68	12	13	18	0	0	2
②	0	0	2	44	41	52	50	52	41	6	7	5	0	0	0
③	0	0	0	16	17	33	62	62	57	13	12	7	9	9	3
④	0	0	0	8	8	3	66	69	43	22	20	52	4	3	2
⑤	0	0	0	7	6	7	46	35	50	37	44	36	10	15	7
⑥	0	0	0	1	1	2	16	11	17	36	40	20	47	48	50

Step 3

	Over 80			79–60			59–40			39–20			Below 19		
	J	S	U	J	S	U	J	S	U	J	S	U	J	S	U
①	0	0	0	20	21	28	70	68	58	10	11	12	0	0	2
②	0	0	6	44	43	53	53	54	38	3	3	3	0	0	0
③	0	0	2	19	19	44	64	64	49	10	11	4	7	6	1
④	0	0	1	10	9	8	67	68	51	20	21	39	3	2	1
⑤	0	0	1	8	8	15	54	47	48	30	34	31	8	11	5
⑥	0	0	0	2	1	5	25	22	50	33	37	21	38	40	24

Step 4

	Over 80			79–60			59–40			39–20			Below 19		
	J	S	U	J	S	U	J	S	U	J	S	U	J	S	U
①	3	2	2	22	23	33	69	69	55	6	6	9	0	0	1
②	9	9	11	43	41	54	48	50	33	0	0	2	0	0	0
③	2	2	5	23	21	51	69	70	41	4	4	3	2	3	0
④	3	2	3	16	17	17	66	68	53	13	11	21	2	2	1
⑤	3	2	4	28	30	21	48	48	44	16	17	18	5	3	3
⑥	2	2	0	5	6	9	50	48	49	17	19	31	26	25	11

Step 5

	Over 80			79–60			59–40			39–20			Below 19		
	J	S	U	J	S	U	J	S	U	J	S	U	J	S	U
①	6	7	2	56	53	39	38	40	51	0	0	8	0	0	0
②	16	14	17	51	56	55	33	30	28	0	0	0	0	0	0
③	9	10	12	56	59	57	35	31	30	0	0	1	0	0	0
④	7	10	8	51	49	23	39	37	54	3	4	15	0	0	0
⑤	19	20	18	40	40	51	37	36	40	4	4	1	0	0	0
⑥	7	8	3	41	44	28	39	37	50	13	11	16	0	0	3

Step 6

	Over 80			79–60			59–40			39–20			Below 19		
	J	S	U	J	S	U	J	S	U	J	S	U	J	S	U
①	10	11	5	68	68	47	22	21	44	0	0	4	0	0	0
②	25	26	22	57	47	59	18	17	19	0	0	0	0	0	0
③	20	21	22	60	63	61	20	16	17	0	0	0	0	0	0
④	18	16	16	60	63	51	22	21	30	0	0	3	0	0	0

Step 7

	Over 80			79–60			59–40			39–20			Below 19		
	J	S	U	J	S	U	J	S	U	J	S	U	J	S	U
①	16	18	7	68	69	51	16	13	40	0	0	0	0	0	0
②	30	31	24	57	59	60	13	10	16	0	0	0	0	0	0
③	23	24	25	64	67	65	13	9	10	0	0	0	0	0	0
④	21	23	19	69	68	54	10	9	27	0	0	0	0	0	0
⑤	21	24	21	57	56	48	20	18	31	2	2	0	0	0	0
⑥	11	13	5	65	70	41	21	15	43	2	3	11	0	0	0

Appendix J: Acoustic data of native and Japanese speakers

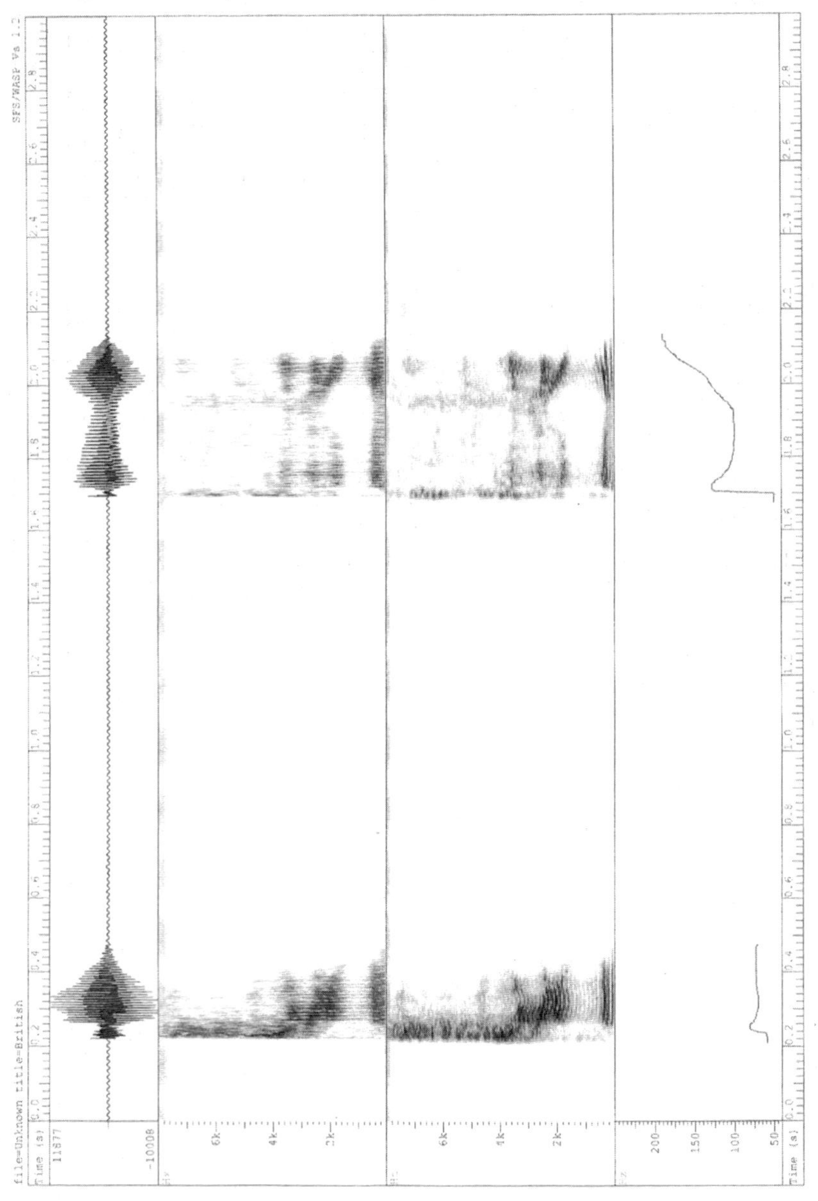

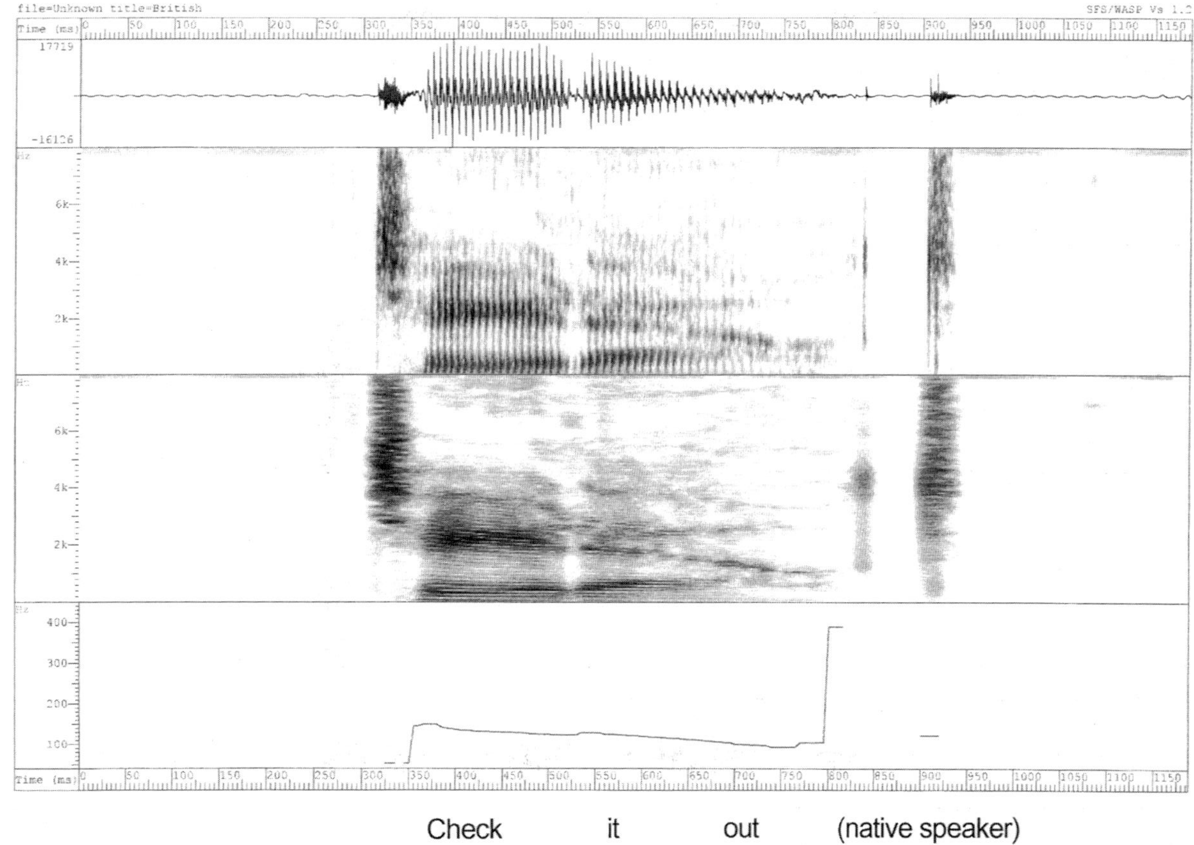
file=Unknown title=British
SFS/WASP Vs 1.2
Time (ms)
17719
-16126
6k
4k
2k
400
300
200
100
Check it out (native speaker)

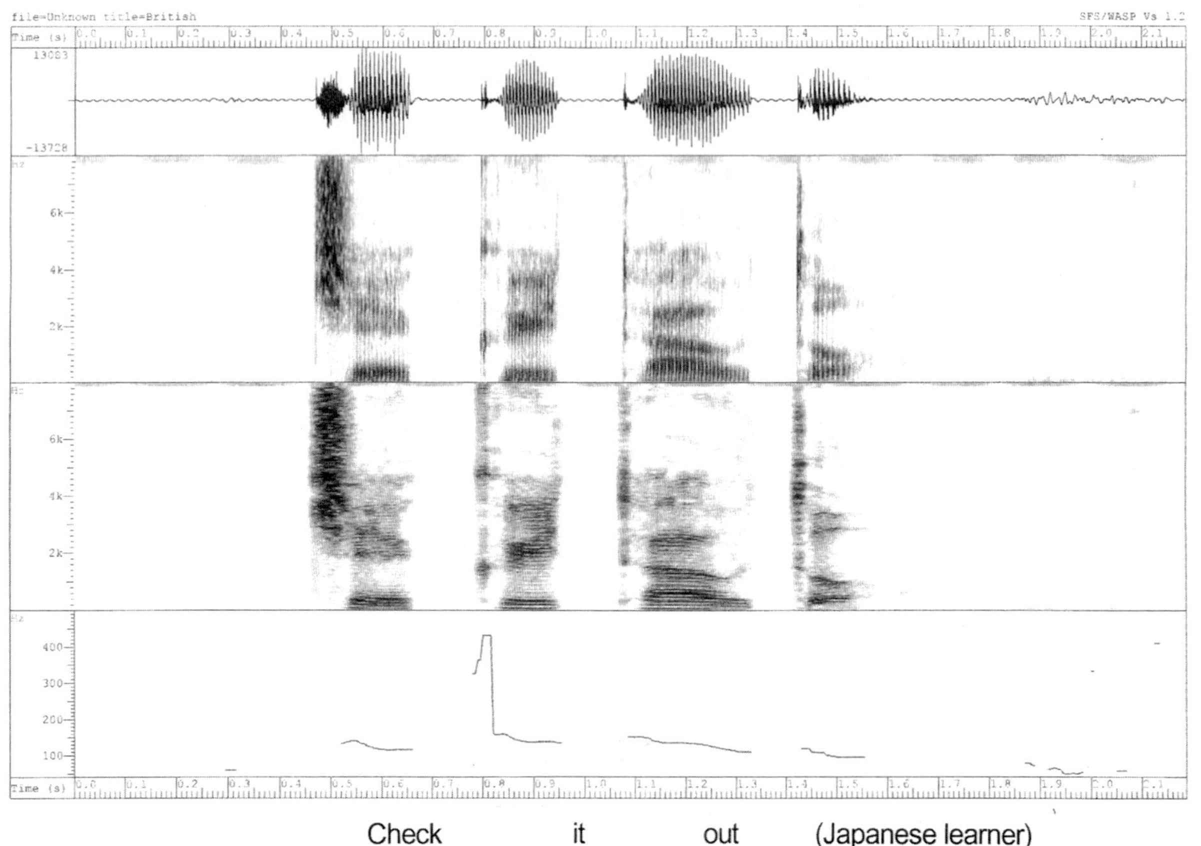
file=Unknown title=British
SFS/WASP Vs 1.2
Time (s)
Check
it
out
(Japanese learner)

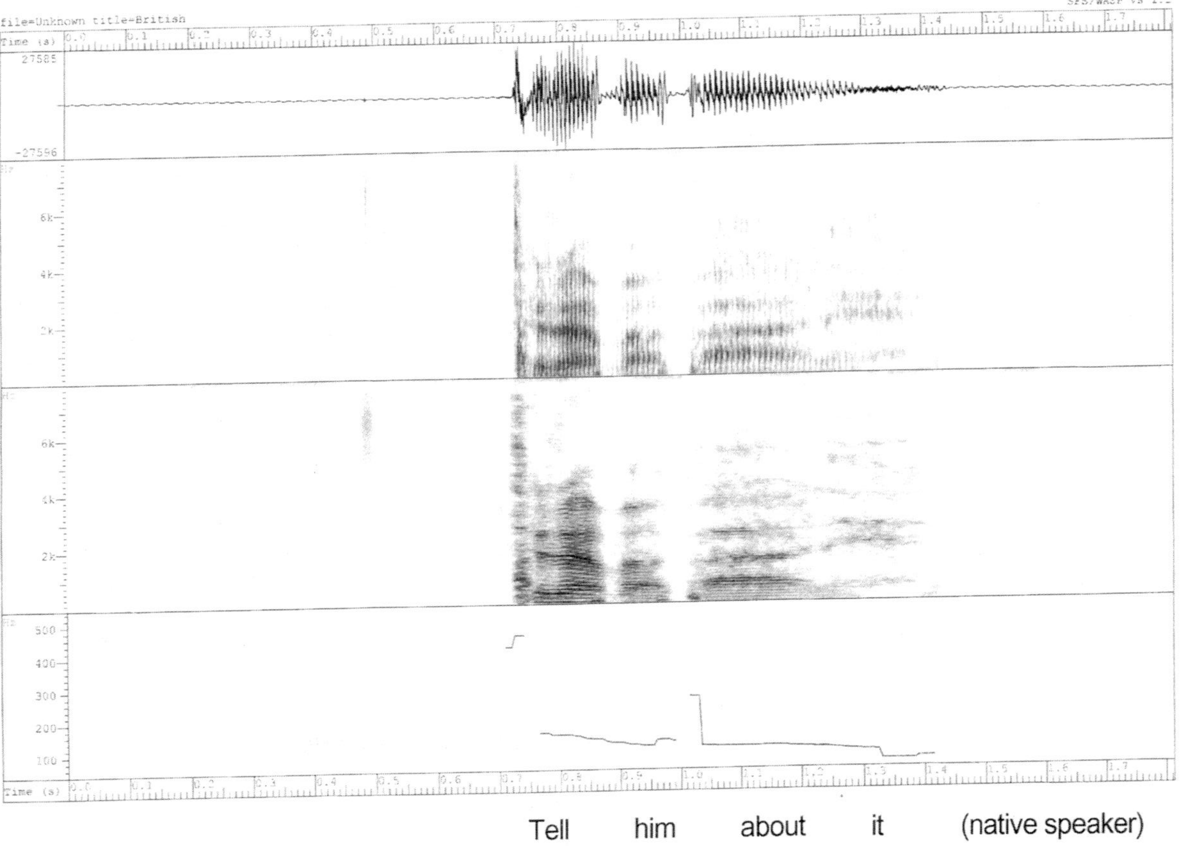
file=Unknown title=British
SFS/WASP Vs 1.2
Time (s)
27585
-27596
6k
4k
2k
500
400
300
200
100
Tell him about it (native speaker)

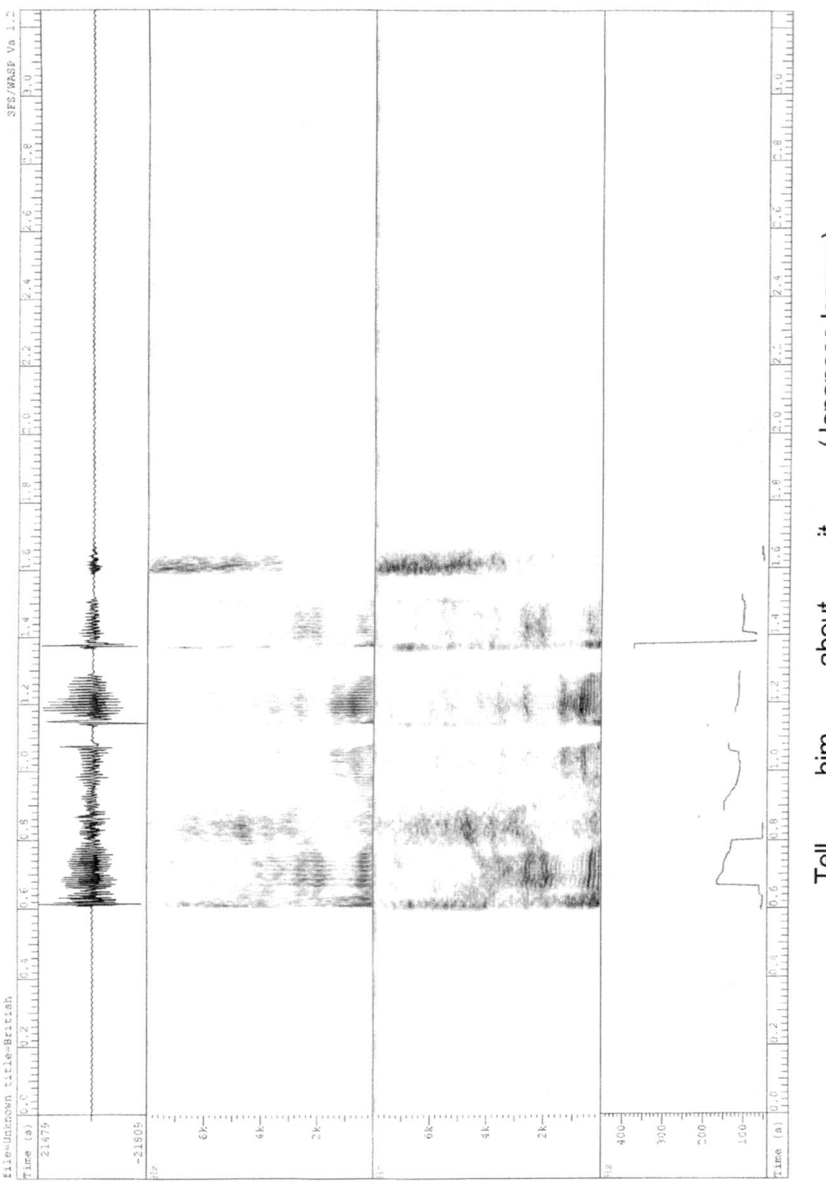
file=Unknown title=British
SFS/WASP Vs 1.2
Tell him about it (Japanese learner)

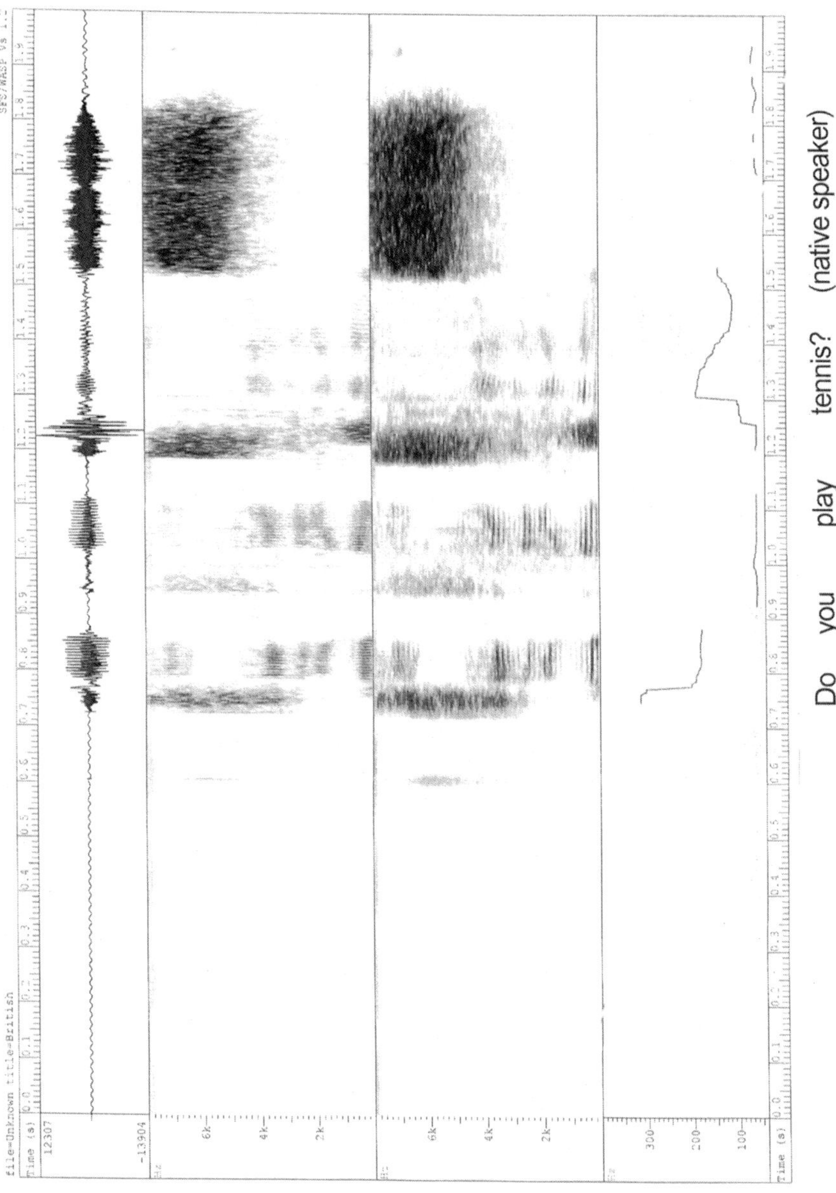
file=Unknown title=British
SFS/WASP Vs 1.2
Time (s)
Do you play tennis? (native speaker)

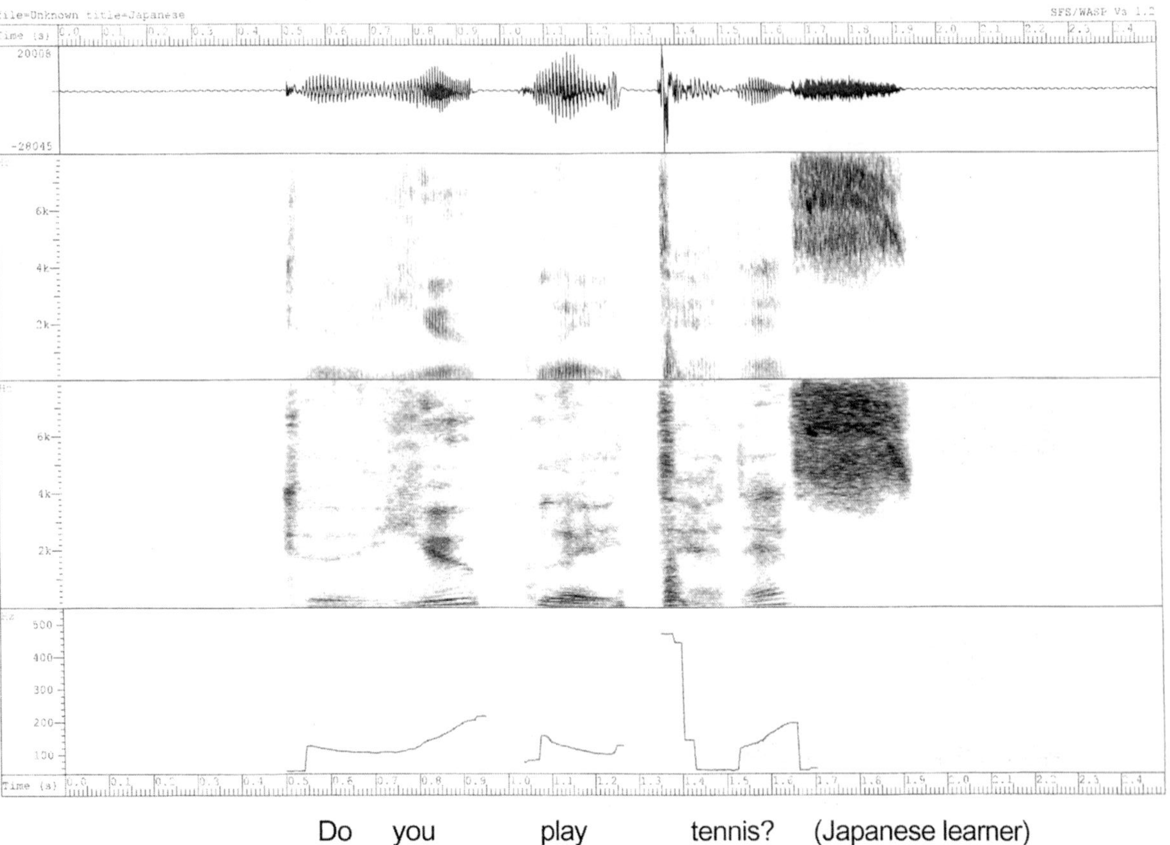

file=Unknown title=Japanese
SFS/WASP Vs 1.2
Do you play tennis? (Japanese learner)

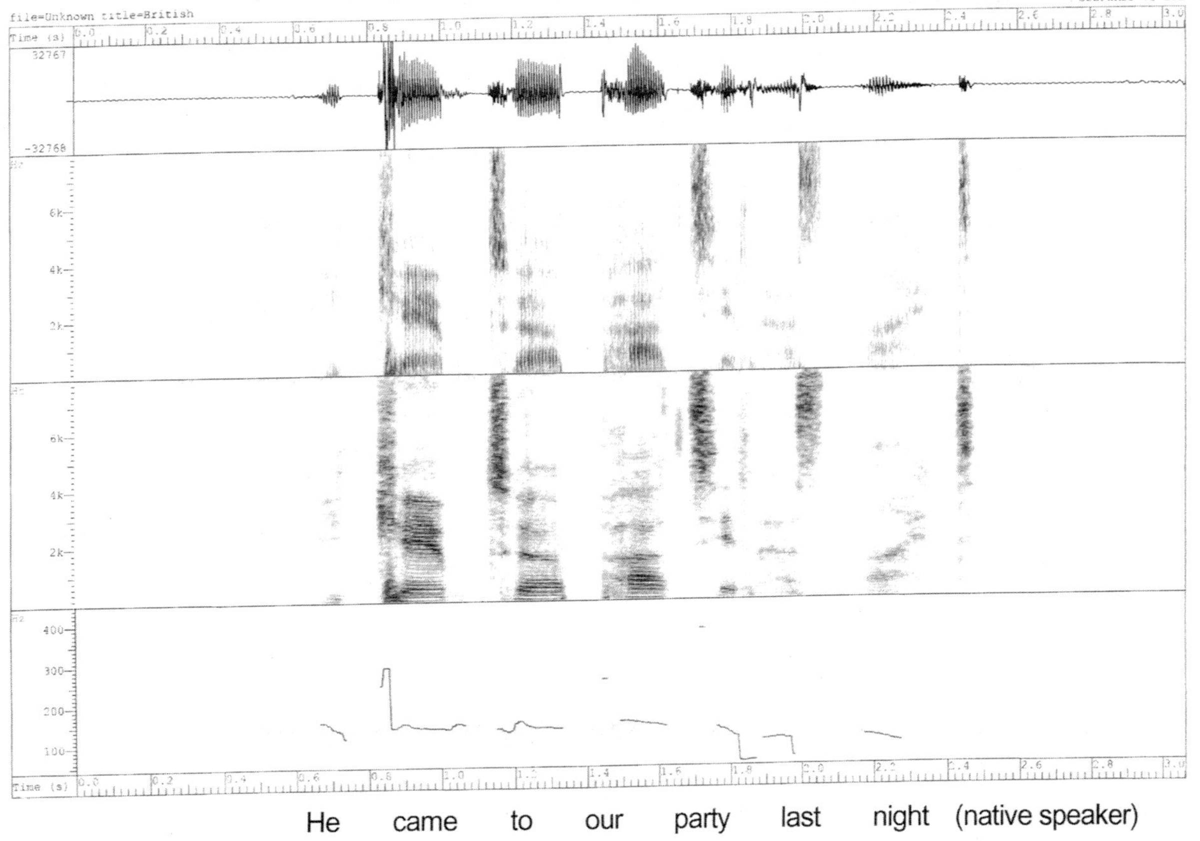
file=Unknown title=British
SFS/WASP Vs 1.2
Time (s)
He came to our party last night (native speaker)

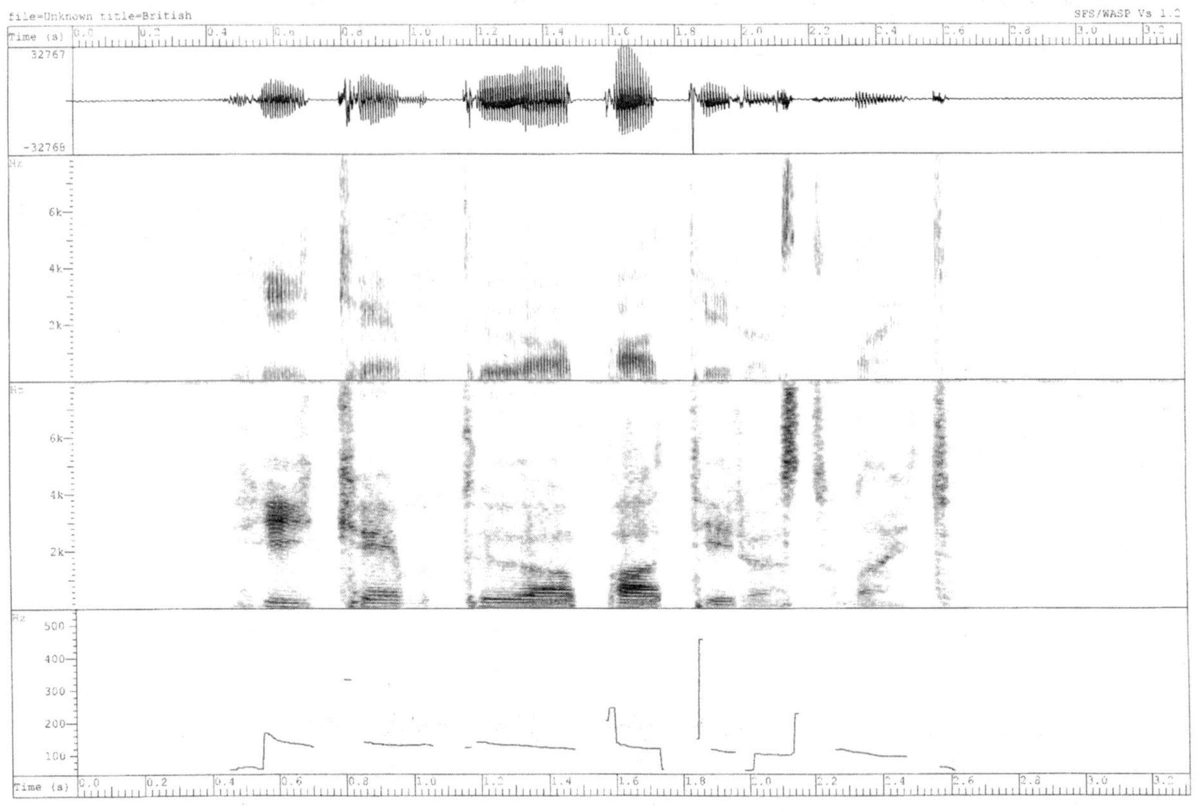
file=Unknown title=British
SFS/WASP Vs 1.2
He came to our party last night (Japanese learner)

Appendix K: Lesson plans (summary)

	Passives	Infinitives	Relative clauses
Introduction (Exposure to the target sentences of the lesson)	Short passage that contains passives. (Pictures used.)	Short passages/stories that contain each type of infinitives.	Short passages that contain each type of relative clauses. (Pictures used.)
Listening (Listening to the text: *New Total English*)	Book 2: Lesson 10 C, D Lesson 11	Book 2: Lesson 3 A (Nominative) Lesson 4 C (Adverbial) Lesson 8 D (Adjectival)	Book 3: Lesson 6 (Subject relatives) Lesson 7 (Object relatives)
Comprehension (Understanding the meaning of the text)	Interpret the text. (Questions & answers)	Interpret the text. (Questions & answers)	Interpret the text. (Questions & answers)
Reading & analysis • Lexical Approach: (chunking, awareness) • Structural Approach: (explain the grammar)	Passive as chunks Passivisation operation as transformation	Infinitive as chunks Infinitive as noticing Infinitivalisation as transformation	Relative clause as chunks Relativisation process as transformation (two-sentence connection)
Task (Language activity)	Pair-work Role-play Picture verification Reading (side-reader)	Pair-work Story-telling & writing (*What I wish to be in the future*)	Pair-work Picture verification Reading (side-reader)

Appendix L: English-to-Japanese translation test and Japanese-to-English translation test for passives

INSTRUCTION: put these English sentences into Japanese.

1. The car is washed by Mr. Jones every Sunday.
2. The picture was put on the wall by Emily.
3. Spot is loved by everyone.
4. The dog was called into the house.
5. Many beautiful pictures were taken by Mr. Miller.
6. Mr. Cohen was sent to Iraq.
7. This tall tower was built before the World War II .
8. This room was cleaned yesterday.
9. The funny picture was painted by Mike.
10. The black dog is called Jackie.

INSTRUCTION: put these Japanese sentences into English.

1. グリーンさんはボブから招待を受けた。
2. 私の祖父は戦争で亡くなった。
3. 長野ではたくさんのりんごが作られている。
4. ジョーンズさんは皆から感謝された。
5. その教科書は次郎の学校でも使われている。
6. その窓はボブに壊された。
7. 彼の車はトラックにぶつけられた。
8. たくさんの熊がその農夫によって捕えられた。
9. そのドアはあまりよく閉まっていなかった。
10. その桜の木は田中氏によって植えられた。

Appendix M: English-to-Japanese translation test and Japanese-to-English translation test for infinitives

INSTRUCTION: put these English sentences into Japanese.

1. Jim started to study math after eleven o'clock.
2. To play baseball is quite fun.
3. Tom wants to go back to America.
4. Bill tried to look into the window.
5. To teach is to learn.
6. Do you have anything to drink?
7. The bird could find a tree to sit on.
8. The man has no house to live in.
9. I have no chance to speak English here.
10. I had enough time to read her long letter.
11. We eat to live, not live to eat.
12. They went to the lake to enjoy fishing.
13. He went to the airport to see Mr. Clinton.
14. I was pleased to talk with her.
15. Ken left school before lunch to help George.

INSTRUCTION: put these Japanese sentences into English.

1. 私はその新しい動物園に行きたい。
2. 列車はゆっくりと走り出した。
3. 英語を話すのは難しい。
4. 私の願いは医者になることです。
5. 健はその箱を開けようとした。
6. 彼らは食べ物を必要としている。
7. 私は今日しなくてはいけないことがたくさんある。
8. 私は何か読むものが欲しい。
9. 健は宿題を一緒にしてくれる人を探している。
10. 彼には話し合える友達がいない。
11. 私の母は掃除をするために二階へ行った。
12. 彼らはキツネを探しに森へ行った。
13. 彼女はその本を見つけに本屋へ行った。
14. 私はその知らせを聞いて驚いた。
15. あなたに会えてとてもうれしい。

Appendix N: Fill-in-the-blanks, English-to-Japanese translation test, and Japanese-to-English translation test for relative clauses

INSTRUCTION: Fill in the blanks with appropriate relative pronouns, and then, put the sentences into Japanese.

1. I know a man __ is a doctor.
2. The dictionary __ my uncle sent to me is very useful.
3. He is the student __ everyone likes.
4. The man __ wrote this book is a famous writer.
5. The book __ you gave me is interesting.
6. I will give you the picture __ is on the desk.
7. The students __ did not do their homework must stay after school.
8. Picasso is a famous artist __ everyone knows.
9. The bird __ can talk like a man is called 'parrot'.
10. Tell me the story __ you told them.
11. Tom has a bicycle __ is better than mine.
12. The doctor __ all of my family members trusted has left our town.
13. I have a friend __ swims very well.
14. The boy __ wrote this letter is Mike Brown.
15. This is the watch __ my grandfather gave me as a present.
16. The vase __ Mr Ito loves is a souvenir from China.
17. Here is a woman __ you know very well.
18. The man __ spoke to you in a loud voice was deaf.
19. This is the man __ wants to see you this evening.
20. The camera __ was made in Japan sells well in America.
21. The man __ I met yesterday will come to my house tonight.
22. I bought a book __ was written by Malcolm X.
23. The tall building __ you see over there is our school.
24. I went to the garden __ you recommended me some days ago.
25. The house __ you can see over there was built in the 15th century.
26. I visited the park __ is famous for its cherry blossoms.
27. The girl __ is singing on the stage is a member of the church chorus society.
28. Do you know the boy __ broke the window?
29. The doll __ has blue eyes reminds me of my childhood.
30. This is the poor bird __ you saw on the television.
31. The driver __ the policeman arrested ran over a young child.

32. I saw the famous picture __ are known to everybody.
33. The scientist __ everybody in the world knows died yesterday.
34. English is the subject __ I like the best.
35. The museum __ stood on the hill was destroyed by the atomic bomb.
36. There was once a king __ has no children.
37. The princess __ people have loved was killed in the traffic accident.
38. That is a woman __ my brother is going to marry.
39. The house __ has a red roof belongs to Paul Banyan.
40. I know the rock singer __ you and your girl friend like.

Centre embedding Subject Human: 4,7,14,18,27; Non-human: 9,20,29,35,39
Object Human: 12,21,31,33,37; Non-human: 2,5,16,23,25
Right branching Subject Human: 1,13,19,28,36; Non-human: 6,11,22,26,32
Object Human: 3,8,17,38,40; Non-human: 10,15,24,30,34

INSTRUCTION: put these Japanese sentences into English.

1. 歌を歌っていた少年が、突然泣いた。
2. 私の友人は、英語が上手に話せる生徒です。
3. 私の好きな歌手が、明日私たちの学校に来る。
4. 父は、この小説を書いた人を良く知っています。
5. 石でできている橋は、とても丈夫です。
6. 彼女が読んでいる本は、昨日おじさんからもらったものです。
7. これは、誰も解くことができなかった難しい問題です。
8. 私は、昨日、君の好きなあの場所へ僕の妹と訪れた。
9. 私たちの先生は、授業中騒ぐ生徒が嫌いだ。
10. 私は、犬が壊した鏡を捨てました。
11. ボブは、僕が紹介した人をとても気に入っているようだ。
12. 私は、父が撮ってくれた写真をなくしてしまった。
13. 私の妹は、赤い目のうさぎが好きです。
14. 私には、学校で英語を教えている友達がいます。
15. あなたが昨日作ったケーキは、とてもおいしかった。
16. 私たちが公園であった男の人を知っていますか。
17. 私のよく知っている少年は、昨日アメリカへ行ってしまいました。
18. ピアノをひいている少年は、サムです。
19. 彼女は、ボブが愛している少女です。
20. トムは、耳の長い犬を飼っています。

21. 昨日私が会った少年は、とても有名です。
22. テーブルの上にあるペンは、あなたのものです。
23. 彼女は、丘の上に立っている家に住んでいます。
24. 私の叔父が立てたその白い家は、今、売りに出ています。
25. 私に話し掛けてきた女性は、カナダ人でした。
26. 大きな桜の木があるその家は、私のおばあさんのものです。
27. 香港で話されている言語は、英語です。
28. 向こうで本を読んでいる少年は、とても親切です。
29. 私の弟が描いた絵が、テレビに出た。
30. ペンギンは、飛ぶことのできない鳥です。
31. 私も、皆が好きなその数学の先生のことを好きだ。
32. 黄色い洋服を着ているその男の人が、私の担任です。
33. 太郎の書いたその詩は、とても美しい。
34. 昨日あなたがキスした男は、私の兄です。
35. 私は、この工場で働いている人をたくさん知っている。
36. 校長は、彼が本棚の後ろから見つけた書類をすぐに焼いた。
37. 直子は、彼が大変愛している娘です。
38. 丘のほうへ向かって走っている馬は、私のものです。
39. 私の隣に座っていた犬が、突然噛みついた。
40. 私の母が話している女の人は、私の叔母です。

Centre embedding Subject Human: 1,18,25,28,32; Non-human: 5,22,26,27,38
Object Human: 3,17,21,34,40; Non-human: 6,15,24,29,33
Right branching Subject Human: 2,4,9,14,35; Non-human: 13,20,23,30,39
Object Human: 11,16,19,31,37; Non-human: 7,8,10,12,36

Index

【著者紹介】

中森 誉之（なかもり たかゆき）

〈学歴〉 横浜国立大学教育学部中学校教員養成課程英語科（学士）、ロンドン大学（UCL）大学院音声学・言語学研究科（言語学修士）、東京学芸大学大学院連合学校教育学研究科（教育学博士）。

〈職歴〉 日本学術振興会特別研究員、横浜国立大学非常勤講師を経て、現在京都大学大学院人間・環境学研究科准教授。

Hituzi Linguistics in English No. 11

Chunking and Instruction
The Place of Sounds, Lexis, and Grammar in English Language Teaching

発行 2009年2月14日 初版1刷
定価 8800円＋税

発行者 松本 功
装丁 向井裕一（glyph）
印刷所 互恵印刷株式会社
製本所 田中製本印刷株式会社
発行所 株式会社 ひつじ書房
〒112-0011 東京都文京区千石2-1-2 大和ビル2F
Tel.03-5319-4916 Fax 03-5319-4917
郵便振替 00120-8-142852
toiawase@hituzi.co.jp http://www.hituzi.co.jp/

ISBN978-4-89476-404-0 C3080